TODAY'S FAMILY:

A Critical Focus

TODAY'S FAMILY:

A Critical Focus

EDITORS:

Phyllis Meiklejohn
Education Consultant

Annette Yeager
Associate Professor, Faculty of Education
University of Toronto

Lenore Kuch
Former Department Head, Family Studies
Thomas A. Stewart Secondary School
Peterborough, Ont.

Maxwell Macmillan Canada

Maxwell Macmillan Canada
1200 Eglinton Ave. East, Suite 200
Don Mills, Ontario
M3C 3N1

Design: Sarah Laffey
Graph Illustrations: Catherine Farley

Photo Credits
Cover: Ellen Schuster/Image Bank Canada
Page xiv: Margaret Kaufhold
Page 26: Canapress/Chris Morris
Page 82: City of Toronto Archives/James #102
Page 152, 238: Nikki Abraham

Canadian Cataloguing in Publication Data

Main entry under title:

Today's family : a critical focus

ISBN 0-02-953999-4

1. Family. I. Meiklejohn, Phyllis
II. Yeager, Annette. III. Kuch, Lenore.

HQ518.T63 1990   306.85   C90-095420-5

   3 4 5 6 94 93

Printed and bound in Canada by John Deyell Company

CONTENTS

UNIT 3: THE EMERGING FAMILY

UNIT 4:   THE ENDURING FAMILY

☐ **Overview Essay,** Emily Nett

☐ **Readings**

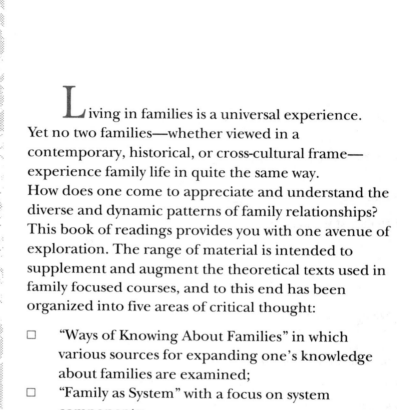

Living in families is a universal experience. Yet no two families—whether viewed in a contemporary, historical, or cross-cultural frame—experience family life in quite the same way.
How does one come to appreciate and understand the diverse and dynamic patterns of family relationships? This book of readings provides you with one avenue of exploration. The range of material is intended to supplement and augment the theoretical texts used in family focused courses, and to this end has been organized into five areas of critical thought:

- "Ways of Knowing About Families" in which various sources for expanding one's knowledge about families are examined;
- "Family as System" with a focus on system components;
- "Family Systems Through Time" with a focus on life cycle concepts;
- "The Emerging Family" with a focus on recognized and anticipated change;
- "The Enduring Family" with a focus on the ongoing nature of family as institution and future images of family life.

Each of the last four units begins with an overview essay that explores the theoretical underpinnings of the readings to follow. The essays have been written specifically for this book by Canadian academics teaching in the Family Studies field at the post-secondary level.

Source material is drawn from a wide spectrum of thought. Theoretical and research perspectives are balanced with demographic profiles, informed opinions, personal experiences, and excerpts from literary works. The selections have been chosen to stimulate critical and reflective thinking, to provide fresh insights into the many aspects of family life, and to furnish the pleasure of recognition of familiar life experience. The diversity of selections is intended to clarify and broaden your perceptions of family and to accurately reflect the variety found in contemporary family life.

Each selection is preceded by a brief introduction that provides the reader with a concept focus. The questions and inquiry suggestions that follow each selection are designed to evoke a diversity of intellectual and emotional responses, to encourage examination of social issues, and to focus class discussion. Interspersed throughout the readings you will find salient quotations, aphorisms, and adages. It is hoped that these will prompt both critical and reflective discussion.

It is the overall objective of the editors that through reading, reflecting, and sharing your thoughts you will develop a lasting framework for interpreting the family and your experience of it.

WAYS OF KNOWING ABOUT FAMILIES

Intimate relationships represent one of the most critical, yet least studied, settings for critical thinking. In relationships we practise critical thinking a great deal, yet we rarely recognize or name it as such. Given that relationships are dynamic entities, distinguished by constant change, shifts in focus, and periods of reframing and renegotiating, critical analysis is often demanded. . . .

. . . how to listen, how to comfort, how to air doubts and criticisms while preserving another's self-respect, how to compromise, negotiate, and communicate as fully and clearly as possible. I have tried to learn how to enter others' frames of reference, so that I can see situations in which my actions play a part from their points of view. I have had to work hard to understand other people's arguments, justifications, and beliefs from within the framework of their own perceptions. All these efforts have involved critical thinking.

S.D. BROOKFIELD, *DEVELOPING CRITICAL THINKERS: CHALLENGING ADULTS TO EXPLORE ALTERNATIVE WAYS OF THINKING AND ACTING*

READINGS
- Demographic Data
- Conceptual Frameworks
- Research
- Literature
- Personal Experiences
- Informed Opinions
- Cross-Cultural Views
- Historical Perspectives
- Future Forecasts

DEMOGRAPHIC DATA

Demographic data provide a particular view of Canadian families. Through federal census data and vital statistics on births, deaths, marriages, and divorces, a vast field of numerical information is made available for the study of families. Statistics Canada serves as the central repository of valuable data that are gleaned from a number of different government departments. This information can be analyzed in order to identify social trends and problems, to guide policy making, and to provide benchmarks that reveal present and future needs for government services.

The following is a graphic depiction of family structure in Canada as determined by the 1986 census. Figures do tell a story!

FIGURES TELL A STORY

Percentage Distribution for Census Family* Structure and Presence of Children, Canada, 1986

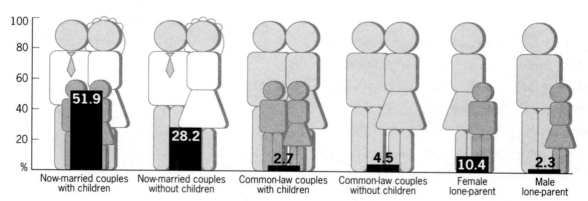

* Husband and wife (with or without children who have never married, regardless of age), or a lone-parent of any marital status, with one or more children who have never married, regardless of age, living in the same dwelling.

From "The Family in Canada: Increasing in Numbers," *Transition*, June 1989, p. 7.

1. What summary statements can you make regarding Canadian family structures as depicted in the graph?

2. Throughout this collection of readings you will encounter different approaches to the question of what constitutes a family. The percentage distribution shown in the graph is based on a particular way of defining "family." How would *you* define family?

3. Identify various non-governmental groups that generate statistics. What are their respective purposes for generating such data?

4. Outline a set of criteria one could use to judge the credibility/reliability of statistics.

5. Suggest guidelines that could help one to acquire the most accurate and up-to-date data on the Canadian family.

6. In a column in *Newsweek* magazine, Robert Samuelson stated:

   > If statistics remind me of the complexity and confusion of everyday life, they're also one of the ways that we attempt to simplify these confusions. Statistics create an aura of certainty and neutrality. They're supposed to convey truth, settle debates and make it easier to control our environment. Up to a point, they do. But they can also be manipulated or misunderstood, and thereby distort reality. Even the absence of statistics is sometimes a deliberate attempt to shape perceptions. . . .

   Provide illustrations of how statistics can convey truth, settle debates, control our environment, and be manipulated or misunderstood.

CONCEPTUAL FRAMEWORKS

A number of conceptual or theoretical frameworks have been developed to provide coherent, comprehensive pictures of marriage and family life. Concepts are identified, and organized into a related whole. Such a framework provides a focus and a language whereby people interested in the family can communicate in efficient and effective ways. Conceptual frameworks are also useful for generating and testing hypotheses in social science research. In the reading that follows, family therapists

Betty Carter and Monica McGoldrick discuss the family life cycle as an important conceptual framework that, nevertheless, has some limitations.

□

We want to emphasize two cautions about a life cycle perspective. A rigid application of psychological ideas to the "normal" life cycle can have a detrimental effect if it promotes anxious self-scrutiny that raises fears that deviating from the norms is pathological. The opposite pitfall, overemphasizing the uniqueness of the "brave new world" faced by each new generation, can create a sense of historical discontinuity by devaluing the role of parenthood and rendering meaningless the relationship between generations. Our aim is to provide a view of the life cycle in terms of the intergenerational connectedness in the family. We believe this to be one of our greatest human resources. We do not mean to oversimplify the complexity of life's transitions or to encourage stereotyping by promoting classifications of "normality" that constrict our view of human life. On the contrary, our hope is that by superimposing the family life cycle framework on the natural phenomenon of lives through time, we can add to the depth with which clinicians view family problems and strengths.

The family life cycle perspective views symptoms and dysfunctions in relation to normal functioning over time and views therapy as helping to reestablish the family's developmental momentum. It frames problems within the course the family has moved along in its past, the tasks it is trying to master, and the future toward which it is moving. It is our view that the family is more than the sum of its parts. The individual life cycle takes place within the family life cycle, which is the primary context of human development. We think this perspective is crucial to understanding the emotional problems that people develop as they move together through life.

It is surprising how little explicit attention therapists have paid to a life cycle framework until recently. Perhaps it is the dramatically changing life cycle patterns in our time that are drawing our attention to this perspective. In any case, it is becoming increasingly difficult to determine what family life cycle patterns are "normal," and this in itself is often a cause of great stress for family members, who have few models for the passages they are going through.

From *The Changing Family Life Cycle: A Framework for Family Therapy,*
Second Edition, by Betty Carter and Monica McGoldrick
Copyright ©1989 by Allyn and Bacon. Reprinted with permission.

> Facts must be correct; theories must be fruitful. A fact if incorrect is useless, it is not a fact. But an incorrect theory may be even more useful than a correct one if it is more fruitful in leading the way to new facts.
>
> HANS SELYE

1. The family life cycle is a developmental framework that views families as passing through predictable stages of expansion and contraction. The stages, while variously labelled, usually include beginning families, families with young children, families with adolescents, families as launching centres, families in the middle years, and families in later life. Summarize

what the authors feel are the strengths and the weaknesses of the family life cycle approach.

2.   The concept of intergenerational connectedness is central to this framework. Why?

3.   Research available material in order to identify some of the other conceptual frameworks used by family sociologists. Do you think any one approach is better than the others? Why?

4.   In what ways does a theory differ from a conceptual framework?

5.   "The family life cycle perspective views symptoms and dysfunctions in relation to normal functioning over time." Do you agree or disagree with the use of the idea of "normality" in the context of the family? Explain why.

RESEARCH

The aim of family-related research is to provide accurate information that can be used to formulate generalizations about particular aspects of marriage and family life. In recent decades, rigorous and systemic social science research focusing on the family has increased in both quantity and quality. Ideally, it is through the use of research findings that objectivity is encouraged, biases, distortions, and value judgements are minimized, and myths and stereotypes are avoided. The following is a synopsis of a classic Canadian study.

□

*T*he Silent Majority (Westley and Epstein, 1969) reports on a large study of college students and their families carried out from 1955 to 1964 at McGill University in Montreal. The aim of the study was to determine how the emotional health of individuals relates to the overall structure and function of their families.

The study was carried out in two phases. The first was a pilot phase in which nine families were intensively studied. The second and final phase was based upon the findings and methods developed during this pilot study. During this second major phase, 97 families were chosen for the study. Only 59 of these 97 families agreed to be studied; however, partial data were available from the 38 refusing families. The second phase of the study concentrated on the families of the 10 healthiest and the 10 most disturbed subjects. There were one to three psychiatric interviews, leading to a psychiatric evaluation, a sociological interview (a 70-page

I am never afraid of what I know.

ANNA SEWELL

questionnaire covering all aspects of personal and family life), TAT protocols, and a psychological evaluation. In addition, for each of the index subjects, a battery of 38 pencil-and-paper tests drawn from the Minnesota Multiphasic Personality Inventory (MMPI), the Vassar Personality Scale, the California Psychological Inventory, and the Guilford-Zimmerman Inventory was administered. The members of the families in the middle group were seen only by the psychologist who gave each of them the TAT and Rorschach tests and by the sociological research assistant who administered the sociological questionnaire. Further details are given in the book.

On reviewing this study, one becomes aware of how rapidly our society has undergone changes in values and mores in the two decades since the completion of this study. These changes have not only affected family life, but have altered the methods of examining and evaluating families in many important areas. The largest value shifts are those arising from the changes that have occurred with regard to women's place in society, especially their role in today's family. These changes have obviously affected both spouse and parent-child relationships. The fact that the majority of women now work outside the home, and the common occurrence of single-parent families, have enormous impact on the family organization.

Work, power, status, roles, and psychodynamics were the aspects of families examined in detail in *The Silent Majority*. We do not have comparable data currently available, but an educated guess would be that the attitudinal and behavioral changes in society since then would significantly change the findings today. Consequently, there is no need to go into detail in these areas; we merely refer the curious to the original findings.

We do feel that two of the basic findings in the original study are still applicable. This notion is based on clinical impressions only, as we have no experimental or empirical information. We hope to rectify this with studies over the coming years. First, the organizational, structural, and transactional pattern variables are more powerful in determining the behavior of family members than are the intra-psychic variables. This statement merely refers to the relative power of the variables and does not mean that intra-psychic factors are unrelated to behavior.

Second, the most important finding of *The Silent Majority* study was that the children's emotional health is closely related to the emotional relationships between their parents. When these relationships are warm and supportive, so that the husband and wife felt loved, admired, and encouraged to act in ways that they themselves admired, the children were happy and healthy. Couples who were emotionally close, met each other's needs, and encouraged positive self-images in each other were good parents. This positive relationship between husband and wife did not depend on their being emotionally healthy themselves as individuals, though obviously this was a great help. In some cases, one or both of the parents were emotionally disturbed, but they still managed to develop a good marital relationship. When this happened, the children were emotionally healthy. It seemed that the good marital relationship had insulated the children and prevented contagion from the individual parental deficiencies.

We continue to be impressed by the importance of such a loving and mutually supportive relationship between the parents. The presence of such strong support,

The family merits study now more than ever, when rapid changes within it stir emotions at once fervent and mixed.
KENNETH WESTHUES

Exceptions prove the rule.
PROVERB

genuine concern, and loving care, and the absence of chronic, persistent, naggingly destructive hostility in the relationships of the parental couple, apparently serves as a foundation that can bear the weight of much strain inside and outside the family group in a manner that protects the ongoing interrelationships and development of the family members. . . .

From *Normal Family Processes* by Froma Walsh
(New York: The Guilford Press, 1985), pp. 130-131.

BIBLIOGRAPHY

W.A. Westley and Nathan B. Epstein, *The Silent Majority* (San Francisco: Jossy Bass, 1969).

1.   Identify the principal findings from this study that may have meaning for today's families. Does your own experience confirm or deny these findings?

2.   In his text *Marriage and the Family: Development and Change*, Stephen Jorgenson makes the following statements about research:

     ☐   Scientific research and the knowledge it generates are based on the laws of probability.
     ☐   Exercise caution in generalizing research findings.
     ☐   The quality of research varies from one study to the next.
     ☐   Statistics do not always tell the whole story.
     ☐   Research studies age right along with us.

     Use these statements as a basis for a class discussion about the use of research in the study of families. Which of these statements seem particularly relevant to the *Silent Majority* study? For example, the fact that this study focuses on college students leaves it open to charges that it is "classist." How might class bias have affected the findings of this study?

3.   Outline the steps in the scientific research method. Research the nature of the various tests referred to in this reading. Describe how the techniques used in the *Silent Majority* study correspond to this method. Survey a number of family-related journals and compile a comprehensive list of research methods and techniques.

4.   In what ways do you think your daily life has been influenced by research findings?

■ LITERATURE

Another way of expanding your view of families is through the field of literature. Writers of fiction, poetry, and drama can provide readers with richly textured tapestries of family life. Through their skillful use of language and narrative technique, writers can inspire you to think and feel in new ways. Reading literary works enables you to experience vicariously the tremendous range of pleasure and pain found in various families.

In his life-affirming novel *Since Daisy Creek*, W.O. Mitchell encourages his readers to experience the special love between a father and his daughter. Colin Dobbs, his wife Sarah, and their daughter Annie all expose strong feelings and attitudes in the dialogue that follows. First Annie speaks to her father about her mother. This is followed by a conversation between Colin and Sarah.

□

> Literature is not only a mirror; it is also a map, a geography of the mind.
>
> MARGARET ATWOOD

She is a dirty fighter! She's a bush-whacker! She's a back-stabber! She's a welsher!"

"All of those, is she?"

"She said I could go out tonight if I cleaned up my room and I did and now she says I can't!"

"She must have a reason why you—"

"She hasn't!"

"Any at all?"

"She always has reasons but her reasons aren't the true reasons!"

"If she thinks they are—"

"Thinking they are doesn't make them real reasons!"

"Now, hold on, Annie—"

"She doesn't trust me!"

"Oh."

"At all! On anything!"

"Do you give her reason to trust—?"

"And you don't either, any more!"

"Are you angry with me, Sarah?"

"No."

"I keep getting signals that you are."

"Oh. Do you? I wonder why?"

"I don't know. That's why I'm asking you."

"Have you any reason to think there's some reason I might be angry with you?"

"No, I haven't."

"So."

"God damn it—why are you? Just let me know!"

"Have you done something I should be angry with you—for?"

"No. Not to my knowledge."

"Then I must have no reason to be angry with you. I must not be angry with you."

"Level with me! For once!"

"All right. The doorbell."

"What about it?"

"You don't ring it like other people do."

"And what is so inflammatory about the way I ring a door—"

"I've told you. I've asked you. Push it. Just once. Not—ding ding ding ding ding ding! Better still, stop losing your key so you won't have to ring it at all!"

"I hadn't realized—"

"Also, this morning—again—you did not put water in the porridge pot after you'd dished out your porridge. I've asked you a hundred times—explained how it hardens to glue if you don't."

"Anything else?"

"Your pants—all your clothes—you just leave them on the floor where you drop them—"

"And everything I eat turns into faeces! Come on, Sarah. Let's just peel these silly things off and get down to the—"

"Annie!"

"What about her?"

"And you! The way you—what you're trying to do with her!"

"What am I trying to do?"

"She's a girl."

"I know that."

"If she were a boy would you want her to play with dolls and tea sets and skipping ropes?"

"I—I don't—just what the hell are you driving at?"

"I am driving at the way you are driving *her* into doing things that are not girl things. You are forcing her—"

"I am not forcing her into anything!"

"Yes, you are! Fishing, camping—"

"Only because she wants to."

"Only because you make sure she wants to! She's a girl and she has the right to be a girl—"

"She has the right to be Annie!"

"She has the right to do girl things and realize herself as a girl and not as a boy!"

"God damn it—she is a little girl and she'll grow up to be a lovely—"

"Not if you have your way, she won't!"

"We'll see."

"When it's too late!"

"I'll watch for it. If her voice changes or she starts to shave."

There is no impression of life, no manner of seeing and feeling it to which the plan of the novelist may not offer a place.

HENRY JAMES

"That's another thing. She's just as sarcastic as you are—as well as foul-mouthed."

"All right, Sarah. All right. Now I'll level with you. I hate your purse!"

"Whaat!"

"Especially in the car, the way you plock it down beside you and practically in my lap! Or ask me to hold it for you! I hate all your * * * purses!"

From *Since Daisy Creek* by W.O. Mitchell, ©1984.
Reprinted by permission of Macmillan of Canada,
A Division of Canada Publishing Corporation.

1. In what ways are you able to identify with any one or all of the Dobbs family?

2. Describe the feelings expressed by each family member. Is any one feeling shared by all? If so, what might it be?

3. Comment on the sex-role stereotyping evident in this family situation.

4. Keeping in mind this literary portrayal of the Dobbs family, examine some of the ways conflict and anger can be dealt with in a family.

5. Explain how a literary view can supply a unique dimension in the study of family.

6. W. O. Mitchell is only one of the many Canadian novelists, short story writers, poets, and playwrights who have written about families. Explore the Canadian literature in your library for an eye-opening range of family portrayals.

PERSONAL EXPERIENCES

Each of us knows what family life is like, since almost everyone grows up in some form of family. Personal experiences provide you with information, attitudes, and feelings about what is normal or typical about life in a family. But are these perceptions a true barometer of what is really "normal" or "typical"? In the selection to follow, well-known Canadian journalist Michele Landsberg reflects on her relationship with her mother. Her recollections span the many ages and stages in the evolution of a mother-daughter relationship.

☐

I t's not surprising that my mother, coming from a home where babies had died, was a strict follower of medical advice in the wholesome upbringing of infants. She listened to the cruel tyrannies of Alan Brown, famous paediatrician of the day, and agonizingly refrained from cuddling us when we cried and from feeding us between the rigid four-hour intervals he decreed. We also had our fresh air, our oatmeal, our two colours of vegetables every night (with their vitamins intact, thanks to her new-fangled pressure cooker), our home-preserved fruits in winter, our brown lisle stockings, our nothing-but-white-cotton-underwear-against-the-skin, our regular bedtimes and regular risings, and our biblical injunctions to scrupulous cleanliness, and in this calm order, we grew. . . .

Our souls were tended to more diffidently than our bodies. Perfect grammar and clear enunciation were almost more important than religion; I was scolded sharply for unconsciously imitating a friend's sing-song inflection, but my mother was silent when we clamoured for a Christmas tree and didn't explain why we couldn't have one. She was shy and reticent in talking about abstract ideas, and believed in shielding children from difficult knowledge.

Perhaps the most important thing we can bring to a study of the family is an open mind and a willingness to accept that our own strongly held ideals of family life represent one truth but not all the truth.

EMILY NETT

We were taught the strictest honesty. When, at age five or six, I was delighted to find a tawdry lapel ornament on the street outside Eaton's, my mother made me stop and think about "the poor soul" who had bought and lost such a pathetically cheap trinket. But when she wanted to articulate her most passionately felt convictions, my mother often had to fall back on platitudes.

She, who so valued her own feminine beauty, was baffled when I became a rebellious teenager, sullenly insisting on jeans, pigtails, and a calculated defiance of ladylike convention. "But even nature adorns herself!" exclaimed my mother, appealing to my poetic intensity. She was mystified when I laughed. She was not much given to introspection, but kept on scrubbing pots, patiently and efficiently, as I paced up and down the kitchen, spouting my half-comprehended gobbets of existentialism and Simone de Beauvoir.

We couldn't agree on anything, but she had the grace to interfere with me as little as possible. When I came back from a year in Israel at eighteen, we were able to be friends, and never quarrelled seriously again.

Being Jewish was problematic in some ways. Though her own Jewishness was never in question, my mother was so determined to put narrow sectarianism behind us that she nearly whisked us straight out of Judaism altogether.

When she was five or six, in London, she was deathly ill with scarlet fever. Waking in the whiteness of a convalescent hospital, she thought she had died and gone to heaven. "Say just one word, *tateleh*," wept my grandfather beside the bed, "say just one word in *mamaloshen* [mother tongue] and I'll give you a shilling." But she had forgotten all her Yiddish, and never spoke it well again.

She grew up in a time when being Jewish could get you shunted around Europe, sent back to point of embarkation, harried from one country to another, even murdered. I felt the first tremors of this when she registered me for kindergarten in 1944. "Religion?" snapped the school secretary. Pause. My mother's hand tightening on mine. "Hebrew," she answered. Hebrew? That was when I learned that it could be dangerous to say "Jewish."

So we were brought up in the watery pieties of Holy Blossom Temple, a ludicrously named Reform congregation, then in the flush of assimilationism, with its all-English service, Christianly throbbing organ, and gentile choir. The rabbi, Abraham Feinberg, once stopped a service to rebuke a man who was wearing a yarmelkeh. He wouldn't go on until the offensively ethnic skull-cap was removed.

After my grandma died, there was little to anchor us to the rhythm of the Jewish year.

> We tend to assume either that our own family experiences are typical or that other families approach some kind of ideal and our own is an exception.
>
> ALISON HAYFORD

I knew, as soon as I knew anything, that my mother was particularly beautiful, and I thought that her perfection was like a doom-laden judgement on me, who could never grow to equal her. She was astonished, later, to hear this from me.

If I envied anything, it should have been her easy competence in practical things, skill that grew from her calm sense of order, the way her violets and tomatoes and lilac cuttings leaped riotously into bloom for her while she benignly ignored them.

At the log cottages my parents would rent in Muskoka when we children were small, my mother would rise before dawn, flick my father's hand-tied flies into a nearby brook, and come back laden. We would wake to the sizzle of brook trout in the pan, and blueberry pies from yesterday's picking, their purple juices welling up through the crust.

Part of my mother's rare charm was her low, musical voice and her tact. She had the mild touch, the feel of just what to say when young colleagues appealed to her for advice or when she was drawn into other people's family storms. She never blurted. She could bite back a retort or hold a secret for twenty years, if she had to; there was plenty of reserve there, whalebone behind the silk.

When I gave my first child her first bath, it was the first baby I had ever held in my arms. I was so slow that her little fingers turned blue and she howled piteously. My mother stood by, arms folded, smiling encouragement. Years later, she confessed that she had yearned to snatch the poor wee thing and wrap her up warmly. But she didn't breathe a word at the time lest I feel inadequate.

Her age was one secret she kept, fiercely, so that her colleagues wouldn't dismiss her as an old lady. She was older than fifty when she nervously dyed away the few gray strands in her hair and went out to apply for her first job, as a receptionist in a new real estate office. Ladies didn't work, but we were broke and trying to pay for our new house in the suburbs. The real estate office coaxed her to become an agent. All through my teens, I realize now, when people asked me if that beautiful woman was my older sister, she was in her fifties and sixties.

She was a hard-working and shrewd real estate agent, but too scrupulous to get rich. But she made enough to support us all. And she would come home late at night from her work to scrub floors, cook—even the stews she made for the dog, flavoured with herbs and garlic, smelled so delicious that she had to label them sternly to prevent our eating them—and even to dig and haul rocks for a garden she had planned. She planted portulaca between the flagstones and transplanted crab apples. She weighed one hundred pounds. I would emerge from an evening's reading to find her out in the summer night, hauling boulders or wrestling a stone bird-bath into place.

We grew, my mother and I, to cherishing each other's real qualities instead of yearning for the ones that weren't there. She gave up on my ever becoming a lady—all those years of taking me to ballet lessons, posing me for photographers with satin bows in my hair, all those years of gentle reproofs when I smoked and swore—and took delight in, of all things, my Jewish home. Many of the old customs I had to learn out of books, and then, "But this is just what Papa used to do!" she would exclaim, coming in before Passover to find me and the children hunting through the darkened house, candles in our hands, for the hidden bits of leavened bread that had to be ritually burnt.

The last Passover we spent together, she and I cooked for three days in my kitchen. We laughed helplessly at our yearly-expanding extravagance. We had chickens to roast, ducklings, brisket, chicken soup with matzah balls light as small clouds, freshly made horseradish she wept over, gefilte fish as puffy and tender as quenelles, prickled with pepper, served elegantly, of course. My mother hurried after me as I rushed the plates to the table, stopping me to decorate each piece of fish just so with a coin of carrot and a sprig of parsley.

An ardent but collapsing acolyte, I marvelled at her style in the kitchen: inexhaustible, whisking away the dirty pots so that in the midst of many concoctions, the kitchen stood in trim order; her tiny form wreathed in fragrant steams and alight with energy and good humour. "My *Yiddishe tochter*," she said to me that year, beaming. It was a deep pride to her that I would consciously carry on the Jewish traditions she had nearly lost by taking them for granted. And I adored her.

From *Women and Children First* by Michele Landsberg, ©1982.
Reprinted by permission of Macmillan of Canada,
A Division of Canada Publishing Corporation.

1. Trace the changes in this mother-daugher relationship as the family life cycle progresses.

2. What aspects of this mother-daughter relationship might likely be found in other such relationships? Explain why.

3. Determine how cultural/religious background can influence perceptions of acceptable family roles and relationships. Provide supporting illustrations from the reading.

4. Identify what appear to be the core values held by Landsberg's mother. How does she endeavour to pass on these values to her family?

5. Suggest how personal experience can cloud an objective view of family life.

6. Explain how personal experience can serve as a basis on which to build a rounded view of satisfying family life.

■ INFORMED OPINIONS

A dictionary tells us that an opinion is a belief or judgement that falls short of absolute conviction, certainty, or confirmed knowledge. In this information age, opinion about family bombards us daily through the media. Everyone can learn from informed opinion, which is the combination of life experience and considered deliberation served up with at least a twinge of emotion. Lorna Marsden is a Liberal Senator and a sociology professor at the University of Toronto. In this column from the *Financial Post* Marsden gives her opinion of the demographic phenomenon of this century: the Baby Boomers—all 7 million of them born in the fifteen years following World War II.

□

Forty candles will glow on almost one million Canadian birthday cakes in 1999 and 2000, illuminating the peak of the baby boom that came in 1959 and 1960.

As the symbolic crisis of their 40th year confronts this huge part of our population, the rest of us will be watching carefully to see how they're taking it. For the feelings they have about aging and the attitudes they hold toward coping with the "other half of life" will be a major influence on what happens to the rest of us.

Ever since they were born, these post-war babies have dominated the concerns of Canadians.

When they left the breast for baby food, profits soared. When they entered the school system, the expansion of classrooms, teachers, and educational theories focused our attention and captured our tax dollars. When they entered the labour market, the competition for good jobs was fierce.

Although those caught in the last recession are still fighting for a place in the economy, the majority of these "boomers" are now poised to take over the most important positions in all parts of our society. Their politics, their preferences, and their lifestyles are the norm. And the rest of us are trying hard to influence their thinking.

All of those who will be in the labour force by the turn of the century are already in school. Whatever skills they are acquiring had better be the right ones for the labour market of the next century. And all those who will be in the pensionable years are already examining their financial plans and security. We must hope the plans are solid.

The demands on the social programs—pensions, unemployment insurance, health care, and education—will receive some elbowing by the new demands from young families over the next decade. . . .

Child care, on a nationally funded basis, will arrive over the next 11 years. But child care of what quality and kind?

Elsewhere in the developed world, systems of care from the cradle to stimulating, after-school programs for adolescents are state-supported. France has had such a system for almost a hundred years.

In Canada, the provinces have developed their own systems, which range in quality from first-rate to pathetic. Nowhere are there enough spaces to meet demand. The federal government has promised national funding outside the Canada Assistance Plan, but has included profit-making child care in the scope of tax-supported subsidies. Making a profit from an active and demanding two-year-old is difficult.

The proposed system will serve mainly the older, well-behaved, urban, middle-class child, while parents with infants and toddlers, children with a disability, or those who live in less densely populated areas, will be largely excluded from this public system. Right now, most Canadians have not focused their attention on these issues of social services, but by 2000, we'll know where we stand. Baby-boom parents will demand it.

The two-income family—now the norm—will become even more prevalent by 2000. Not only will the labour market demand that every adult be a wage-earner, but the fragile nature of marriage means every adult will also want to be sure about his or her pension plan, savings program, and monthly income.

Single parents, who have replaced older Canadians as the country's largest poverty group, will have fought their battles with municipal and provincial governments for housing, training, and job placement. Seniors will have fought their battles for housing, access to jobs, and economic security. For both groups, the issues of dignity, a place in society, and sensitivity to discrimination will be important.

There is the potential for social-class divisions to emerge, creating truly different and competing worlds. There is the successful, high-flying young business and professional person insulated in office towers, captured on television, offering a monied lifestyle and consumer excess. But on the margins live a lot of Canadians who don't appear in the lifestyle advertisements.

On one side is the successful nonconformist—the bright, inventive, self-supporting Canadian who doesn't buy into the neo-right dream of materialism and conformity. Unusually absent from public debates, this group can be found in the many reform movements, charities, overseas service, and sometimes in the universities or small businesses. Many Canadians share the values of this group but few will live out these values.

On the other side is a much larger group shoved out of the system by the

> It is better to know some of the questions than all of the answers.
>
> JAMES THURBER

circumstances of their birth (poverty, unwanted child, or disability) or by their experiences (in school, in the justice system, or the class system).

A third group consists of older Canadians without indexed pensions, who are living precarious lives often dependent on social-assistance programs or the community. Whether all these worlds will converge into a shared vision of Canada or diverge into bitter class struggles, depends mainly on how the large group of baby-boomers see their obligations to those on the margins; how they conceptualize the problems of inequality for their generation.

These younger Canadians are living in a world of new and little-understood pressures. What will Mikhail Gorbachev's reforms mean to the Western Alliance and the economics of East-West and North-South relations? We don't yet know.

What will the pressures of the new world trading patterns mean to Canadian workers and enterprises? We know that there are many adjustment costs to be absorbed in the short term.

Can we meet the challenge of the World Commission on Environment and Development and solve the problem of sustainable development? Canadians, more than most people, are aware that we must if our resource-based economy and fragile ecology are to be kept productive. The intertwined nature of economy and environment confronts us daily.

These new pressures are not yet framed in public debate and when they are, it will be in the hearts and minds of those now in their 20s or 30s that the answers will be focused. Heading for leadership in science, government and business, it will be they who determine our future. . . .

Traditionally, as the Gallup Poll results over the years have shown, Canadian men have been more supportive of women's equality than their American counterparts. Because of the increasing pressure of the labour market and children on Canadian couples, we can expect the values of both women and men to feature in the solutions to contemporary problems.

In the case of the environment that is good news. The "women's culture" of preservation, conservation, and co-operation points to potential solutions in the production of sustainable development. The traditional Canadian recognition of internationalism, peace-keeping, and humanitarianism is good news for developing revived East-West and North-South relations.

Much more difficult will be the pressures on Canadians to produce more goods and services, of better quality, faster and at no higher costs to compete in world markets. Learning how to do that and remain Canadian is the challenge of the decade.

Fortunately, we have a rich and varied culture to draw on, which has sustained us through generations of regional, ethnic, and language disputes and tensions. We have also learned the values of tolerance and negotiation. Let's hope that we have conveyed these traditional values to the new generation, for we are in their hands and, as 2000 rolls in, it will be too late for change.

From Lorna Marsden, "Values of the Baby Boomers Will Set the Tone for Next Century," *Financial Post*, January 2, 1989.

In matters of opinion our adversaries are insane.
MARK TWAIN

1. The baby boom generation, 30-50% larger than what demographers had predicted, has had and will have a tremendous impact on life in Canada. Describe how this reading may have altered your views of today's society.

2. Focus on the main issues raised in this article. Condense these into one paragraph.

3. Select the major areas of life that Lorna Marsden suggests will be affected by the baby boomers in the next decade. Assess the significance this impact could have for you and your family.

4. When reading opinion pieces how do you: judge the credentials of the author; distinguish between verifiable facts and value claims; detect bias; identify assumptions; determine accuracy; judge the adequacy of the thesis or argument presented? Use this reading to practise your skills in making these distinctions.

CROSS CULTURAL VIEWS

With the exception of Native peoples, all Canadians are either immigrants or descendants of immigrants. Immigrants bring with them a cultural heritage that continues to influence the way family life is lived and the manner in which roles and relationships are played out. David Suzuki, a respected environmentalist, was greatly influenced by his Japanese heritage. In the following selection from his autobiography, Suzuki reflects on some of these lasting influences.

☐

I n Japanese society, the birth of twins is not a happy event—it is frowned upon. The first child to appear is considered the younger of the pair. The Japanese believe that out of politeness, the elder steps aside, so to speak, to let the younger out first. So my twin sister, Marcia, having been delivered minutes after me on March 24, 1936, is considered older than me.

Irrespective of my chronological status, as a male I occupied the top rung in the family pecking order as the family filled out with two more daughters. To my father, in typical Japanese fashion, I was the favoured and most important child, the only son. It was a burden my three sisters had to bear all their lives. While dad would go

No one ever looks at the world with pristine eyes. One sees it edited by a definite set of customs and institutions and ways of thinking.

RUTH BENEDICT

fishing and camping with his male chums or me, it would never occur to him to take my mother or sisters.

What is remarkable is that my sisters accepted this hierarchy. They never questioned my right to be so highly regarded, though I had done nothing to deserve it. I never heard them complain that I was getting special favours or ask why I didn't pull my weight. They had to fight to express themselves as individuals and in the process each became a special and tough person in her own way. But those early years of social conditioning still persist. My wife marvels at how my sisters, now mature women, continue to rush around and look after my creature comforts whenever we drop in for a visit. And I too very easily slip into the comfortable familiarity of the old role. That's why, while I struggle to live up to being a feminist, I would never claim to be "liberated." I've lived most of my life with the cultural assumptions of male dominance and they are not exorcised easily.

By the 1930s, over 75 percent of the Japanese in Canada were living within a seventy-five-mile radius of Vancouver, mostly clustered around Powell Street in Vancouver, the fishing village of Steveston, and other areas around lumber mills, canneries and farms. Our family, however, lived in predominantly white Marpole. Being Canadian or Japanese was not a matter I thought about in the five years we lived there; our family was assimilated into that village as Canadians. English was the only language spoken in our home.

We lived in the back of our dry-cleaning shop, next door to our Canadian neighbours, the McGregors. Their youngest son, Ian, was my age and my best friend. One day a new boy who had moved in down the street approached Ian and me. The boy told Ian not to play with me because I was a Jap. At that point I shot back, "But I'm a Canadian, just like you. I speak English, don't I?" He reluctantly agreed. "I eat the same kind of food as you." Hesitant acknowledgement. "My clothes are the same as yours." "Well, I guess you're right," he finally admitted. "You must be a Canadian—but you still *look* like a Jap to me."

There were some traditional Japanese obligations which we observed—family get-togethers, meals and holidays. I remember our family celebrations on Boys' Day in May, a Japanese festival where miniature warrior dolls and costumes and swords would be laid out on a tiered altar. Grandfather had bought a very elaborate set of Japanese dolls for me and another for Marcia to be used for Girls' Day in March. These had been gifts at our birth and dad was relieved that his father had accepted the birth of twins so well. I loved these ornaments and their related festivities because they had such an aura of specialness. I never knew it was a Japanese celebration, any more than English children think Guy Fawkes' Day is an English event, or Québecois kids know St-Jean Baptiste Day is French. They just have fun because that's what festivals are for.

From *Metamorphosis: Stages in a Life* by David Suzuki, pp. 48-51.
Reprinted with the permission of Stoddart Publishing Co. Limited.

Most Canadians belong to an ethnic group, since to do so is simply to have a sense of identity rooted in a common origin . . . whether this common origin is real or imaginary.

BAHN ABU-LABAN

1. Select from the reading examples of cultural beliefs/assumptions about family. Drawing on the ethnic representation in your classroom, generate a list of cultural beliefs/assumptions specific to family life.

2. Explore how family life in Canada has been enriched by varied ethnic groups.

3. Discuss how some cultural beliefs/assumptions may enhance or inhibit the experience of family.

4. Reflect on the significance of the statement from the reading, "You must be a Canadian—but you still *look* like a Jap to me."

5. "In typical Japanese fashion, I was the favoured and most important child, the only son." What other cultures traditionally favour sons over daughters?

6. Compile a list of available sources of information on cross-cultural families in Canada. What types of data do these sources provide? Together, do they present a well-rounded view of family life? Why or why not?

HISTORICAL PERSPECTIVES

It has been said that history repeats itself. Whether this is so or not, the history of the family as a changing institution down through the ages can help you to both understand and appreciate contemporary Canadian family life. This reading is from a lecture at the University of Waterloo Conference on "The Theme of the Family in Canadian Writing." Writers Susan McDaniel and Wendy Mitchinson here examine some marriage patterns in the late nineteenth century.

☐

I t is our view that no understanding of the family can be ahistorical since families have history built into their generational flows. Neither can family images ever be stripped of their fictions, since these form the stuff of family legend and self-image, as well as enhancing our enjoyment of family traditions and common rituals. Fictions and realities blend to form families and to shape how we live in them. The attempt to separate fictions and realities must perhaps be futile. Nonetheless, we should try to examine those fictions from both past and present that masquerade as fact. These fictions are the myths on which ill-conceived family policies and laws can be, and have been, built. Unlike the fictions of photo albums, family legends and literary images, myths on which policies are based can punish people for the failure of their family to conform to someone else's fictionalized image. Myths can have painful consequences.

Given that change is a fundamental part of families, a historical perspective on families seems to us essential . . . families in Canada were and are varied. This is certainly true when you consider the latter decades of the nineteenth century. Just picture in your mind the diversity of families which existed: a fishing family on the coast of Nova Scotia, a family whose income came from the industrial sector of Québec, a prosperous farm family in rural southern Ontario, a family homesteading on the newly opened prairies, or a mining family in the interior of British Columbia. Add to that a variety of cultural traditions stemming from different ethnic origins: English, Scots, Irish, French, Native, Japanese, Chinese, Northern, Central and Eastern European, as well as American. Stir in different religions and different classes, and you can begin to understand why the historical study of the family is fraught with danger and over-simplification. This is especially true when we remember that history is a discipline which concerns itself with change.

This concept of change is sometimes difficult for us to accept when looking at the family. There is in most of us a yearning for stability, for a world which can be controlled, which is simpler than the hectic and ever-changing one with which we are familiar and in which we live. As a result, there is much nostalgia for the past, often for a past which never really existed but which still seems to have a tremendous attraction for us. This is especially true for the latter years of the Victorian era. Our concepts of it are very strong, coming to us through the living legends of grandparents and great-grandparents. We assume a familiarity with it which is as potent as it is mythic. We all know what the Victorian family was like: it was very large, incorporating different generations. A strong father headed it and dominated both his wife and his children with a firm yet loving hand. There was little discussion of role division in this family—a man had his place and certainly a woman knew hers. Morality permeated this family, a bit prudish from the twentieth-century perspective, but the stability it gave the family was worth it.

When the reality of the Victorian family is examined, the above description is true but not true. The family described existed in an ideal form but the day-to-day lives of families then, as always, seldom approached the ideal. This is particularly true with respect to the two themes which we have chosen to examine: marriage and childbearing patterns.

☐ MARRIAGE PATTERNS IN THE LATE NINETEENTH CENTURY

Contrary to what many people assume, Victorians did not marry at an early age. Indeed, one characteristic of the Western family is the advanced age at which people have married. In 1891, the average age of marriage for women was 26 years, with men marrying at a slightly older age (Gee, 1982:315). There were sound reasons for this. In a society with few welfare provisions and little security against disaster, people did not marry until they could afford to set up a home of their own. For many women, marriage represented upward mobility, freedom from the constraints of parents but more usually from the burdens of a low-paying job with no future. For men, marriage was a public acknowledgement that they had achieved enough success in the world to support a wife and children. The kind of independence marriage represented for both sexes did not exist outside it. Before marriage, young people remained within the bosom of their own families or boarded with another family. They certainly did not live alone as many do today. Living alone for unattached youth was frowned upon. Thus family permeated the experience of the young, whether it was their own family or another family with whom they lived.

Relationships within marriage were somewhat different than today. Equality of the two spouses was certainly not something which Victorians felt they had to enshrine in law. As a result, mothers did not always have guardianship rights over their own children unless they were unwed. In that case, the law was generous and gave the woman full rights over her bastard child. Love was considered important between husband and wife, but it was only one of many factors which held a marriage together, and not necessarily the most important one. Economic contribution and the survival of the family unit was significant, as was raising children. Indeed, the image of the large Victorian family comes from the recognition that children were important. Children dominated family life in that spouses had few years when they lived together without children being present. Children came quickly after marriage, and when the last child finally left home, there was little likelihood of both spouses being still alive. In 1871, there were more than twice as many widows as widowers in Canada (Leacy, 1983:A110-153). Clearly, widowhood was a problem then as it is today.

Although the Victorians did not stress the importance of love between spouses to the same extent that we do today, it would be incorrect to believe that the Victorians did not understand passion. They certainly did. As Lucy Maud Montgomery wrote in her diary about a young man she loved:

> I *loved* Herman Leard with a wild, passionate, unreasoning
> love that dominated my entire being and possessed me like a
> flame—a love I could neither quell nor control—a love that in
> its intensity seemed little short of absolute madness (Rubio
> and Waterston, 1985:209-210).

This idea of control was important, for control over the emotions was, Victorians believed, a trait which separated them from the uncivilized. Control of their emotions was not a denial of them, as evidenced by Lucy Maud. But sexuality was a force to be contained, particularly for women. The double standard was certainly alive and well during this period and enshrined in law. For example, the laws against seduction protected only women of chaste character. The emphasis on female chastity, of course, came from the real likelihood of undesired pregnancy which women faced. It was a dilemma more and more women were trying to escape.

In our technological age, we sometimes have a very patronizing attitude toward the past, thinking that it is quaint and wondering how those people survived without the modern conveniences of television, microwaves, and in the realm of sexuality,

Learn from the mistakes of others, you can't live long enough to make them all yourself.

GROUCHO MARX

birth control. Well, as we know, they did survive and they were quite good at surviving, even in the realm of sexual endeavours.

Birth control is not a new discovery. People have long known how to limit the number of children they had. They knew that abstinence worked, as did *coitus interruptus* and vaginal sponges. By the end of the nineteenth century, condoms were available, although they still tended to be associated more with prevention of venereal disease than with contraception. Women passed on age-old remedies for birth control. One consisted of cocoa butter, tannic acid and boric acid (Chapman, 1985:8). The point is that birth control in some form was available. What had not been there previously was the desire to limit the number of children a family had. Children had traditionally been viewed as wealth, as workers, and the more you had the more wealthy you considered yourself. However, this view began to shift by the end of the century. The birth rate began to drop in the early 1870s, and except for the aberration of the post-war baby boom has continued to decline. In an increasingly industrial society, children were no longer the asset they had been on the farm. This is particularly true once the Victorians accepted childhood as a special phase in life; laws were instituted to ensure that children were cared for. For example, child labour laws prevented them from working, and educational laws insisted that they be in school. As a result, children were becoming a financial drain, especially for families who wanted to maintain a modicum of comfort.

Yet birth control was frowned upon. The medical profession led the attack, arguing that birth control went against nature and was consequently unhealthy. They argued that a young country like Canada needed as many people as it could get. Even more upsetting to them was their perception that the wrong type of person was practising birth control. It was fine for the lower orders to limit their numbers, but it was not all right for the middle classes to do so. There was concern expressed about racial suicide. What would the future of Canada be like if the new non-English-speaking immigrants continued to reproduce and the solid dependable Anglo-Saxon stock limited itself? It was a horror they wanted to resist. And resist they did, on behalf of other people, for the irony was that doctors of all groups in Canada had the smallest families.

If doctors were incensed at husbands and wives using birth control, they were apoplectic about abortion. Yet abortion did occur, and not just among single women. Doctors railed against married ladies who besieged them for abortions. They could not convince women that abortion was wrong. Indeed, women continued to believe in the age-old doctrine that a fetus was not alive until quickening, and thus abortion up until that time had no moral connotations to it at all. As well, since it was the women who knew whether or not their families could cope with the expense of another child, they were not particularly fussy about discussions of morality and when life began. For many, priority had to be given to the lives that already were, over those who might be.

From *Family Fictions in Canadian Literature*,
by Susan McDaniel and Wendy Mitchinson
(Waterloo: University of Waterloo Press, 1988), pp. 13-19.

BIBLIOGRAPHY

Chapman, Terry, "Women, Sex and Marriage in Western Canada 1890-1920," *Alberta History* 33 (4):1-12, 1985.

Eichler, Margrit, *Families in Canada Today: Recent Changes and Their Policy Consequences.* Toronto: Gage, 1983.

Gee, Ellen, "Marriage in Nineteenth Century Canada," *Canadian Review of Sociology and Anthropology,* 19:311-25, 1982.

Glossup, Robert, "Renewed Focus on the Changing Family and its Challenges," Keynote Address to the First Annual Unified Family Courts Conference. Hamilton, Ontario, 29 March, 1987.

Leacy, F.H. (Editor), *Historical Statistics of Canada.* Ottawa: Statistics Canada, 1983.

Light, Beth and Joy Parr (Editors), *Canadian Women on the Move* 1867-1920. Toronto: New Hogtown, 1983.

McDaniel, Susan A., "The Changing Canadian Family: Women's Roles and the Impact of Feminism," S. Burt, L. Code and L. Dorney (Editors), *Changing Patterns: Women in Canada.* Toronto: McClelland and Stewart.

Royal Bank Reporter, "The Family: The Way We Were; The Way We Are," Spring: 2-6, 1986.

Rubio, Mary and Elizabeth Waterston (Editors), *The Selected Journals of L.M. Montgomery, Vol. I: 1889-1910.* Toronto: Oxford, 1985.

Wargon, Sylvia, "Canada's Families in the 1980s: Crisis or Challenge?" *Transition,* March: 10-12, 1987.

1. With today's families in mind, comment on these statements from the selection:

   Fictions and realities blend to form families and to shape how we live in them.

   The family described existed in an ideal form but the day-to-day lives of families then, as always, seldom approached the ideal.

2. Select examples from the reading of what are today pressing issues of gender equity. Determine how attitudes have changed since Victorian times.

3. Cite some marked differences between Victorian family life and your family life today.

4. Investigate the types and availability of historical material on families in your area. Locate one historical family document or record and share it with the class.

FUTURE FORECASTS

Change is a constant in today's world—some say that change is the *only* constant. Must the family let change take over and sweep it into the future? Or can the family use change to shape a better future for itself? Informed forecasting can help people foresee and control to some degree the flow and direction of change. Who can predict alternative family futures? What is possible? Probable? Preferable? What follows is one sociologist's prediction for the emergence of three major family types.

□

Sociologists no less than the public seem to have an almost religious faith in the eternal nature of the Western middle-class nuclear family model. When I read that the family is "alive and well"—the implication being that all the true essentials are really unchanged—I know I am really reading a fervent desire, perhaps a prayer. How else can I explain such a statement when I know the actors no longer need or enforce the same division of labor, the same expectancies of permanence, the same authority structure, or the same evaluation of kinship affiliation and obligation. Goodwill and some altruism still exist, of course—but not, for the majority, self-abnegation in the service of family solidarity and intergenerational progress.

I think we are in a new evolutionary stage. Individual self-interest will create three major family types. The single head of household family will proliferate among the poor and economically unstable unless the partnership can provide benefits that single status cannot. Right now, with the combination of government support for children, the ability of a poor woman to exist financially without a husband (indeed, finding it difficult to incorporate a low-earning husband into the household), and not enough incentive for a low-earning man to stay married, the family composition of this class seems destined to be reorganized around women and children.

The "blended family" (a misnomer if ever there was one) is the model for the middle class. This class is increasingly composed of two earners, both of whom earn decent salaries, but neither of whom alone can earn enough to provide the desired lifestyle. Thus there is a strong incentive to marry and remarry if the match proves unsatisfactory. There are high financial costs for leaving, so divorce will remain undesirable but still unavoidable for some, given the search for self-fulfillment and/or "a good life." Because marriage is beneficial to both parties, families from previous relationships will be combined, which exacts a high cost. Recent research indicates that the high divorce rates of remarriage are at least partly attributable to the pressures of combining families. Thus divorce in this class will still be high, pushing some people into remarriage and some into single head of household status.

The third type of family will be the executive family, with high enough income so that the woman can decide not to work, or, if they are a dual-career couple, they will have even more money and discretionary income to contribute to home and

Seen with new eyes, our lives can be transformed from accidents into adventures. We can transcend the old conditioning, the dirt-poor expectations. We have new ways to be born and symbolic ways to die, different ways to be rich, communities to support us in our myriad journeys, new ways to be human and to discover what we are to each other.

MARILYN FERGUSON

family. Economic self-interest will be enhanced by either mutual contribution or such high income that the non-earner, anxious to maximize class position, will try to make the other partner feel benefited enough to remain in the marriage. Divorce should be common here too, however, as the level of independence of the individuals in this group is so high that reassessment of the value of one's circumstances, from time to time, is inevitable.

All of these scenarios have this in common: Both individuals are doing the best they can—for themselves first, for their children a far second, and for extended ties, family and peers, least of all. This is not to say there is an absence of generosity or love. This is not the case now, nor do I expect it to be the case in the future. It is *relative* emphasis that is important here, and the point is that the individual will not only come first, he or she will have a social structure that will allow individual agendas to be accomplished.

> The future is not predetermined. It is at least partly subject to our influence, and our interest must therefore focus on the preferable futures as well as those that are possible and probable.
> ALVIN TOFFLER

From "Family: Changed Institution," by Pepper Schwartz,
Journal of Family Issues, Vol. 8, #4, December 1987, pp. 457-458.

1. In order to predict the future, Schwartz uses the method of trend extrapolation. This method is based on the assumption that a present trend will continue in the future, much as you would extend a line on a graph. Investigate other methods for predicting future scenarios. In what ways can various types of bias colour a prediction?

2. This prediction focuses more on family form than on family function. Comment on this.

3. What evidence of the three family types described here can you already observe in the families that you know? Discuss whether or not you agree with Pepper Schwartz that it is primarily "individual self-interest" that will direct the course of the family.

4. Identify current cultural, social, technological, and economic forces that would need to be considered when forecasting future family scenarios.

5. Investigate the variety of future forecasting techniques. Using one of these, picture your family life ten years from now, then in the year 2025.

THE FAMILY AS SYSTEM

... the daily life of families is like a spider's web. Every thread has an essential relationship to every other thread. A disturbance in one part creates a ripple effect in another part. The family web is anchored by the mainstay threads of housing, food, clothing, and nurturance. These are bound by a network of communications, labour, love, income, customs and the like to achieve physical and mental health of the family.

SHARON NICKOLS,
INTERNATIONAL FEDERATION FOR HOME ECONOMICS CONFERENCE

It was a family that did not pull together, but whose efforts were either feeble and uncoordinated, or disparate, so that an adversary could often pull them over the line in a mental tug of war. She thought how Helen's desperate passions, so out of control, coupled with Ted's gelatinous ineffectiveness and Paul's sullen indifference, produced a tangled web, and the two little girls struggling like tiny flies to escape the sticky filaments. She had not liked looking below the surface of the Clay marriage.

RUTH GALBRAITH, *A CONVENIENT DEATH*

OVERVIEW ESSAY
by Marshall Fine, Ed.D.
Associate Professor
Department of Family Studies
University of Guelph

READINGS

THE FAMILY AS SYSTEM

by Marshall Fine

Today in the 1990s we face increasing evidence that our planet is heading toward ecological disaster. More and more people are becoming aware that our actions are having crucial effects on the environment. We are an integral part of the earth's ecological system, and as such, we affect natural processes just as we are affected by them.

But what does the world's ecology have to do with Family Systems Theory? This theory, like the study of ecology, reminds us that we are inseparable from our surroundings (Bateson, 1979). Just as each of us is part of an ecological system, so too is each of us a member of a family. This should incite us to think carefully about how we treat each other, and our planet.

☐ FAMILY SYSTEMS THEORY

Family Systems Theory (FST) has its roots in a number of fields of study. Two of the most important of these are General Systems Theory (Bertalanffy, 1968) and Cybernetics (Ashby, 1961; Weiner, 1954). General Systems Theory arose out of the biological sciences. It focuses on the interdependence of all the components of a biological system. Cybernetics, on the other hand, is the study of control and communication in machines and human beings. Cybernetics focuses on the mechanisms that keep a system in a dynamically balanced state. Almost simultaneously, the contributions of cybernetics enhanced the systems concept, as did systems to cybernetics. The systems and cybernetics explanatory union soon found its way into the social sciences, and FST was born.

A system can be defined as "an entity with component parts or units that co-vary, with each unit constrained by or dependent on the state of other units" (Goldenberg and Goldenberg, 1980, p. 29). For two or more component parts to "co-vary" they have to move together, with the movement of one stimulating the movement of the other. All the parts making up a system are interconnected, and the action of any one part affects all the other parts of the system. It seems like such a simple and obvious idea. We apply it readily to machines, like a car engine, where we are able to see the parts and how they work together. Yet human systems do not behave in the same predictable and observable fashion as machines.

Our daily lives, down to the smallest detail, are influenced by so many different systems that it is difficult to know exactly how we "work" and what stimulates our behaviour.

The ecological model helps us to understand the functioning of that system closest to our hearts: our families. The actions of each member of a family affect and are affected by every other member. But we don't often think of a family as a system unto itself. Instead we view family relations through what is sometimes known as the "billiard ball" model of human behaviour (Watzlawick, 1984). Ball A hits ball B and causes the latter to move. B, meanwhile, does nothing to A. This one-way, or linear, way of thinking can result in misunderstandings that can in turn have harmful consequences.

It is hoped that FST, as described in the following pages, will provoke you to question some of your own linear ways of thinking. This theory can also help you to understand and cope with the changes and tensions that are inevitable in today's families.

Family Systems Theory can best be understood if the basic characteristics of the theory are delineated separately.

Wholeness

Wholeness can be explained using two principles. The first is that a system cannot be understood when broken into its component parts. In other words, behaviour cannot be understood in a vacuum, or when separated from its context. For example, you might criticize a schoolmate for being withdrawn and unfriendly. If you knew, however, that this person was sexually or physically abused, it would place his or her behaviour in a more meaningful context. Now, rather than being labeled as unfriendly, s/he may be viewed as experiencing a great deal of pain and as having an understandable apprehension about relationships. More detailed readings would suggest that the schoolmate's "unfriendliness" is even more complex than implied here. I have not mentioned that the "observer" (one who is viewing the "unfriendly" peer) is "adding" his or her own perceptions. In other words, the peer has no "unfriendly" genes in his or her body. "Unfriendliness" may be rather a point of view of the observer, not of the observed.

The second principle of wholeness is that a change in one part of the system will stimulate changes in other parts. For example, all family members will be affected if one parent (traditionally the mother) goes back to work outside the home after full-time in-home work. Many women who work full-time outside the home also work practically full-time inside the home. Children who were used to that parent's presence may feel that they are not receiving the "required" attention—no one is home after school to greet them, suppers are late, and so on. Their dissatisfaction may take the form of misbehaviour, which puts pressure on both parents. The more the spouses have to deal with the children, the less time they have alone together. Both spouses may become irritated. The spouse who had always worked outside the home (usually the husband) may come to resent the inconveniences of more child care and household duties. His resentment will be felt by the wife, who may in turn resent the husband's lack of support. The added tension between the parents may affect the children, who consequently misbehave more, and so further increase the pressure on the parents. This circular, interdependent process, initially stimulated by one change, may spiral and escalate into a chaotic and distressed family situation.

Hierarchy

Every system is composed of subsystems. For example, every individual is composed of countless subsystems, (i.e., cells, organs, etc.) that make up the biological being. In turn, every person/system is a subsystem within the system defined as family. This progression to larger systems is hierarchical in that the larger the system, the more complex it is and the more subsystems it encompasses.

Family theorists have delineated a number of subsystems within the family. These subsystems pertain to apparently "universal" distinctions within families (Minuchin, 1974). The most noted "universal" subsystems are the parental, sibling, and marital subsystems. The parents are the directors or "architects" of the family system (Satir, 1967). They are responsible, in large part, for the socialization of children. The sibling subsystem has less responsibility to direct or set the structure of the family. Children experiment with peer and sibling relationships, support and discover from one another, and learn to negotiate and cooperate (Minuchin, 1974). The marital subsystem can act to meet the spouses' needs for love, companionship, and economic survival. In addition to these three conceptual subsystems, Minuchin (1974) states that other subsystems can be formed according to generation, sex, interest, and function.

All systems are encompassed within larger systems. Therefore, they are simultaneously systems and subsystems, depending on one's level of analysis. The family system is itself a subsystem. It is, for example, a subsystem of the neighbourhood, which is in turn a subsystem of the city, which is in turn a subsystem of the province. As systems become larger they are considered to be suprasystems. The cosmos may be considered the ultimate suprasystem, since it encompasses the universe—everything as we know it. All of these subsystems and suprasystems are related systemically; they are interdependent.

This hierarchical ordering of systems is crucial in allowing us to recognize how larger systems influence any given situation. These systems include gender, class, culture, race, ethnicity, religion, politics, and education. To return to the above example, it would be unfair and quite mistaken to "blame" the schoolmate's behaviour solely on his or her family. (More specifically, child sexual abuse is typically perpetrated by the father or a male family-related member.) The family may be dealing with external stress from the larger society. For example, they may be struggling with the pressure and lack of opportunity associated with poverty, with prejudice, excessive job demands, lack of education, and so on. These factors may tax a family's coping strategies, making it difficult to deal effectively both with itself and society (McCubbin & Figley, 1983). Such social and economic factors should definitely not be used to justify sexual abuse or to absolve a man of the responsibility for his actions. However, it would also be a mistake to overlook the effects of the difficult circumstances that many people endure.

Another factor regarding hierarchy is that there is a relationship between the size of the system, the time it takes for a system to change, and the force of the impact required to induce change (Broderick & Smith, 1979). The larger the system/institution, the more impact and time needed for learning and change to take place (Henderson, 1987). Change in large systems involves many subsystems.

Boundaries

Every human system is bounded by, or differentiated from, another system by the nature of the relationship between them (Steinglass, 1978). A boundary in human systems is described in terms of its permeability with respect to the output and input of information, and/or flexibility of roles. For example, the type of roles and information that a parent has access to defines the difference (boundary) between a parent and a child. *Rigid* systems have relatively "impenetrable" boundaries (maximum difference and little flexibility). This allows for little information exchange or role flexibility. *Diffuse* systems allow far too much information exchange or role flexibility (minimum difference and excessive flexibility).

In a rigid family system, parents are parents and children are children. Parents might have difficulty being playful with their children. Or, they might have difficulty responding to the changing autonomy needs of their maturing children. Children might be discouraged from experimenting with their evolving adulthood, such as comforting or nurturing their parents, or becoming age-appropriate members of the family decision-making team.

Diffuse boundaries present another concern. Children may be expected to care for the needs of their parents. A parent might share too much adult information with the children (e.g., intimate problems with the spouse). Outsiders viewing the family might be confused as to who is responsible for what. Children experiencing this type of relationship with their parents might feel confused about having to assume "parent-like" roles prematurely.

The ideal family structure, according to Minuchin (1974), involves the maintenance of *clear* boundaries. Clear boundaries allow for the interchange of roles and information while maintaining a solid structure. Individuals know their roles and where they fit. Parents set the structure, but are also able to act on their children's changing needs. Children are allowed to comfort their parents at times, but are not expected to become full-time parents. As the children grow older, they begin to assume more power in family decision making.

Rules

Every human system develops a set of unique rules that define the nature and operation of the system. Rules can be overt or covert. The former describes rules that are openly understood or verbalized. Keeping to curfews may be an overt family rule. Not smoking in school may be an overt school rule.

Covert (hidden) rules are not obvious, and are unspoken. The family may have a covert rule that anger is not acceptable. No one may say this directly, but displays of anger may be met with negative consequences. This may lead family members to deny angry feelings.

While family members may experience conflict with such overt rules as curfew times, these rule conflicts can be at least handled in the open. Covert rules create more complex dilemmas. Family members are not to talk about such "hidden" rules. Discussion of rules might cause great personal anxiety, or fear of family disruption. It is difficult to solve a problem if one cannot talk about it.

Finally, each family system can be distinguished from every other family system by its unique set of rules. Similarly, on a larger scale, it is the idiosyncratic rules within cultural groups that may be the primary characteristics differentiating one culture from another.

Control

Every system tends to operate within certain defined parameters. Cybernetic theory explains how these parameters are controlled. Essentially, every system can be viewed as tending toward and maintaining a dynamic steady state. This state is referred to as homeostasis. If homeostasis is not achieved the system experiences chaos, which may lead to system disintegration. Paradoxically, the experience of chaos in human systems often leads to some form of homeostasis. For example, the inability of a married couple to compromise and work together as a team could eventually lead to the disintegration of their marriage (divorce). However, the divorce will eventually lead to some form of homeostasis for each person as they settle into their own separate lives.

Homeostasis in human systems is maintained cybernetically by positive and negative feedback loops. Negative feedback is a concept used to explain manoeuvres that control against deviation from the system's homeostasis. It is *not* a "negative" value judgement about behaviour. Negative feedback is often manifested through the family status quo. For example, a family may establish a rule stipulating that dating is not to begin before the age of fifteen. The twelve-year-old son or daughter who rebels and attempts to date will be challenging one of the rules contributing to the family's homeostasis. The threat to the status quo "stimulates" family members to give messages (negative feedback) to the son or daughter preventing him or her from getting involved with sexual relationships before s/he is emotionally mature enough to handle them.

A family system cannot maintain homeostasis using negative feedback alone. In order to keep pace with the changing demands of society and needs of family members, families need to change—to allow movement away from the status quo. Positive feedback is the term used to describe the change mechanism. For example, as the adolescent begins to grow and individuate, family members will encourage the young adult to develop his or her own unique set of relationship rules. These rules may indeed vary from their own set of rules—their own status quo.

It is very important to understand that both stability and change are required for homeostasis. One state cannot exist without the other. In a changing world, stability is maintained only by making changes.

Although positive and negative feedback are simple control features within a system, they are not self-governing. At what point do these mechanisms turn on and off? The off-on apex is referred to as the calibration point. Think, for example, of a room thermostat. Every time the temperature falls too far below a preset point, the furnace is triggered to turn on. When the temperature rises too many degrees above the calibration point, it is turned off. A family system can be seen to operate in a similar, though obviously much more humanly complex manner.

As noted above, all families set rules. These rules have built-in "predetermined" levels which can vary. The "predetermined" level operates as the "temperature setting," or calibration point, within the family. Once the rule has been violated past a certain point, the family's "furnace" is turned on, and the rule is more strictly enforced. When everyone is operating more in accordance with the rules the family can relax (the "furnace" can be turned off) until once again someone varies too far from the calibration point. For example, many families develop rules, overt or covert, about the amount of general noise that can be tolerated within the household. The level is often different for every family. Children often make noise in the course of play and they may become increasingly noisy until the parents or other siblings have had enough (and are past their calibration/tolerance point for noise). The children are told to calm down and the noise de-escalates below the calibration point. As most parents know, this pattern may be repeated endlessly.

Causality

One specific concept called into question by Family Systems Theory is linear causality. Consider the following scenario—one that is not uncommon in the office of a marital therapist. The wife states that her husband nags too much. The husband retorts that he would not nag so much if she would not withdraw from him. The wife then states that she would not withdraw from him if he did not nag so much, and so on.

It is possible to see that the nagging behaviour does not simply have a unilateral effect on the wife. She reacts to the nagging by withdrawing, which in turn affects the husband, who nags more, which triggers the wife to withdraw further, and so on. Researchers in the parent-child area are also beginning to report this reciprocal pattern. Studies which traditionally investigated the effects of the parent's behaviour on the child now appreciate that the child also contributes to the way the parent behaves (Mash and Johnson, 1983; Stollak, Messe, Michaels, Buldain, Collins, and Paritee, 1982). For example, we often suggest that babies have "temperaments." Think about how you might relate to a baby who had colic, cried a lot, and couldn't be pacified. Now think about how you might relate differently to a baby who was very quiet, calm, and smiled a lot. Chances are that over time you would see yourself as behaving differently toward the two babies. So the babies might be contributing something to how you relate to them. But in "real" life there is a much more difficult question. Does the baby's temperament affect how you relate to the baby or does how you relate to the baby affect the baby's temperament? It is difficult, if not impossible, to determine who started what, when—they seem reciprocal. Family systems theorists prefer to identify such ongoing reciprocal relationship patterns as circular. While there are clear limitations to circular thinking (discussed below), the concept does help explain that behaviour does not occur in a vacuum.

☐ FAMILY SYSTEMS THEORY: SOME ISSUES

Theories can be great assets in helping to understand the world, as long as it is understood that theories do not represent "reality." Theories are like maps: they can never exactly correspond to the actual territory. FST, like any theory or map, has its explanatory weaknesses, a few of which are here worthy of note.

Feminist thinkers, particularly in the family therapy field, can be credited with exposing some of the main weaknesses of FST. Chief among these is the dynamic between power and gender (Goldner, 1988; Hare-Mustin, 1989; Taggart, 1985; Walsh and Scheinkman, 1989). FST tends to view people as equal participants in human relationships. For example, the above scenario of the husband and wife in therapy suggests that both partners are equally involved in the maintenance of their circular pattern. Feminist theorists suggest that this type of circular scenario obscures the fact that traditionally men have been granted more power within society and family. Therefore the interpretation of the interaction between a husband and wife needs to acknowledge and account for the possibility of this power imbalance. If the power imbalance is ignored, women will continue to be treated unfairly.

This same argument is important in the understanding of child sexual abuse. A child is not a contributor to sexual abuse. The adult (typically a man) has the power and *forces* a child to participate—the relationship is not reciprocal.

Another criticism of FST is that its focus on the system has been at the expense of the individual's inner experience (Nichols, 1987). In other words, many family systems therapists tended to be concerned about the dynamics of relationships among family members, rather than what these individuals might be thinking and feeling within themselves. The person's inner experience was overlooked because of the emphasis on the family as a group. Lately, however, some theorists are building rather complex theories that place the individual as observer very much within the systems framework (Maturana and Varela, 1980).

☐ CONCLUSION

It is hoped that the basic concepts of FST will help you to question traditional, linear ways of thinking about the nature of relationships. For regardless of what form a family may take, we all crucially affect and are affected by our family members.

These, our most intimate relationships, are in turn affected by the many external forces that shape our lives. For each of us is a player in the hierarchy of ever-larger, overlapping systems. More and more people, for example, are increasingly concerned about the fate of our planet and what we do to maintain it. What we "put in," and how we treat our systems, will affect us all.

It is vital that we be aware of the roles we play both within our family system and in the larger systems of society. Only in this way may we come to appreciate the responsibility each of us has toward others.

BIBLIOGRAPHY

Ashby, W. Ross, *An Introduction to Cybernetics*. London: Chapman & Hall, 1961.

Bateson, Gregory, *Mind and Nature: A Necessary Unity*. New York: Bantam Books, 1961.

Bertalanffy, L. von, *General Systems Theory*. New York: George Braziller, 1961.

Broderick, C. & Smith, J., "The general systems approach to the family," Wesley R. Burr, Reubin Hill, F. Ivan Nye, and Ira L. Reiss (Eds.), *Contemporary Theories about the Family, Volume II*, pp. 112-129. New York: The Free Press, 1979.

Goldner, V., "Generation and Gender: Normative and Covert Hierarchies," *Family Process*, 27, 17-31, 1988.

Hare-Mustin, R. T., "The problem of gender in family therapy theory," M. McGoldrick, C. M. Anderson, F. Walsh (Eds.), *Women in Families: A Framework for Family Therapy*. New York: W. W. Norton & Company, 1989.

Henderson, H. "A guide to riding the tiger of change: The Three Zones of Transition," W. I. Thompson (Ed.), *GAIA: A Way of Knowing: Political Implications of the New Biology*. New York: Lindisfarne Press, 1987.

Mash, E. J. & Johnson, C., "Parental perceptions of child behaviour problems, parenting self-esteem, and mother's reported stress in younger and older hyperactive and normal children," *Genetic Psychology Monographs*, 107, 3-60, 1983.

Maturana, H. R. & Varela, F. J., *Autopoiesis and Cognition: The Realization of the Living*. Boston: Reidel, 1983.

McCubbin, H. I. & Figley, C. R. (Eds.), *Stress and the Family. Volume 1: Coping with Normative Transitions*. New York: Brunner/Mazel, 1983.

Minuchin, S., *Families and Family Therapy*. Cambridge, Mass.: Harvard University Press, 1974.

Nichols, M. P., *The Self in the System: Expanding the Limits of Family Therapy*. New York: Brunner/Mazel, 1987.

Satir, V., *Conjoint Family Therapy*. Palo Alto, Calif.: Science & Behaviour Books, 1967.

Steinglass, P., "The Conceptualization of Marriage from a System Theory Perspective," T. J. Paolino & B. S. McCrady (Eds.), *Marriage and Marital Therapy*. New York: Brunner/Mazel, 298-365, 1984.

Stollak, G. E., Messe, L. A., Michael, G. Y., Buldain, R., Collins, R. T., & Paritee, F., "Parental inter-personal perceptual style, child adjustment, and parent-child interactions," *Journal of Abnormal Child Psychology*, 10, 61-76, 1982.

Taggart, M., "The feminist critique in epistemological perspective: Questions of context in family therapy," *Journal of Marital and Family Therapy*, 11, 113-126, 1985.

Walsh, F., Scheinkman, M., "(Fe)male: The Hidden Gender Dimension in Models of Family Therapy," M. McGoldrick, C. M. Anderson, F. Walsh (Eds.), *Women in Families: A Framework for Family Therapy*. New York: W. W. Norton & Company, 1989.

Watzlawick, P., "Self-fulfilling Prophecies," P. Watzlawick (Ed.), *The Invented Reality: How Do We Know What We Believe We Know?* New York: W. W. Norton & Co, 1984.

Wiener, N., *The Human Use of Human Beings: Cybernetics and Society*. New York: Doubleday Anchor, 1954.

ONE FAMILY SYSTEM

In his book *Two Hugs for Survival: Strategies for Effective Parenting*, psychologist Harold Minden introduces us to Jamie and his family. This is a family in trouble. Minden asks his readers some interesting questions, such as "Is this family really so unusual?" and "Do they really differ from millions of families or are the casualties just heavier?" What do you think?

On one of my consultations at the hospital, I met an old school friend I hadn't seen for over twenty years. He was waiting for the elevator but whenever it opened he would back away from it and not go in. He looked very distraught. As I approached him to say hello, it occurred to me why he was in the hospital—it was his son who had been admitted for an overdose of drugs and was in a very serious condition. We sat and talked for over an hour. He was overcome with grief and guilt. He felt his stupidity and rigidity were the cause of his son's condition. "If only I could turn the clock back. If only I had another chance. I love that kid so much. We never understood Jamie. He was always the butt for everything that went wrong at home. Where did we go wrong?"

That night I talked with Jamie's mother, or rather, I listened. She had so much to say that had been bottled up for so long.

"Well, Jamie has forced us to stop playing our charade. Our life has been such a masquerade. To friends and outsiders we have been a model family. Our family problems were always well hidden or lied about. We all need help."

And through her tears she began to tell her story. . . .

"I sat in the waiting room of the psychiatric ward and sobbed. My body, my head, my heart—everything hurt so badly. John sat hunched trying to muffle what he always had considered unmanly—crying. What we had just seen couldn't have happened to us. Our son, Jamie, whom we both loved, was lying in this hospital with a brain that has been severely damaged by an overdose of drugs. We were told that the prognosis for full recovery was questionable. We saw this pathetic, thin little figure lying in the intensive care unit with tubes and wires and incoherent babbles.

"I thought back seventeen years to the time we brought our first baby home from the hospital. What excitement! We had great plans and great expectations. He

> Happy families are all alike; every unhappy family is unhappy in its own way.
>
> LEO TOLSTOY, from ANNA KARENINA

was going to be an excellent athlete, the valedictorian. He would go into engineering and then join his father's company. He was going to be a big success! We also secretly hoped that Jamie would help resolve the differences we were having in our marriage, which seemed to be a constant series of quarrels, skirmishes, battles, and peace treaties.

"Jamie was irritable and hyperactive from the very first month. He cried continuously and kept us up all night. John often moved down to the recreation room with 'I have to go to work tomorrow and I need my sleep.' For him, parenthood was motherhood—that's how it was in his parents' home. He would make me feel guilty if I asked him to hold Jamie or change him during the night in between feedings. There were nights when I was so sick and tired I could fall asleep standing up.

"Jamie didn't heal our marriage and I think we began to blame him and use him as a scapegoat for escalating our battles to a full-scale war. Our pediatrician said he would grow out of the hyperactivity, irritability, and mixed-up sleeping cycles. When Jamie finally went off to school, his teachers complained about his constant fidgeting, inattention, lying, and rudeness. We took him everywhere—to a psychiatrist, an allergist, a nutritionist, a pediatric neurologist. He was finally put on a heavy dose of Ritalin. While Jamie was being treated with an amphetamine my doctor prescribed Valium for my anxiety and nervous condition. John coped with his miseries with alcohol and silence.

"My in-laws fuelled the fires by comparing Jamie to their 'golden boy.' Their innuendos were a constant indictment of me for spoiling and indulging Jamie.

"We had another child, a little girl, Patricia, and she was almost everything Jamie wasn't. She was good at school, never got into any difficulties, matured and developed according to all of Dr. Spock's guidelines, but she always seemed distant and detached from the family. She was her own support system; never appeared to need encouragement, direction, or even a cuddle. She would disappear whenever there were family quarrels and we were so busy attacking and defending that I guess we welcomed her non-involvement—there were enough antagonists. She was our 'star boarder.' She kept everything neat, tidy, but separate—her things, her thoughts, her emotions, her friends, and her school life. My in-laws kept comparing Patricia to their son and were convinced that Patricia had inherited John's independence, diligence, neatness, control, and high need for personal privacy. When I think of Pat growing up, it was like ships passing in the night. We knew she was there but we didn't see her and our radar equipment showed no distress signals. Our radar was faulty.

"By the time Jamie turned sixteen he had a record, a bad record—at school and at home. The agenda of our whole life now seemed centred around this 'bad kid.' I seemed to have become a secondary adversary since the action was now between father and son. Jamie's long hair, patched jeans, and failures at school irritated and embarrassed his father. The battles became more and more intense, and when Jamie was caught smoking marijuana he was verbally and physically beaten and warned that if he was caught smoking again he would be kicked out of the house. That night, I think both Jamie and I cried ourselves to sleep.

"One month later, John kept his promise. He caught Jamie smoking grass in the

Your family is what you've got. . . . It's your limits and your possibilities. Sometimes you'll get so far away from it you'll think you're outside its influence forever, then before you figure out what's happening, it will be right beside you, pulling the strings. Some people get crushed by their families. Others are saved by them.

PETER COLLIER

laundry room. He grabbed him, hit him, threw him out, and told him he never wanted to see him again. John and I had our biggest quarrel that night and it ended up with John packing an overnight bag, grabbing a bottle, and leaving the house. My life seemed to be a complete disaster. I thought about divorce, suicide, or just running away. John and I got back together for a temporary truce, but it was a house where the three of us, John, Pat, and I, lived with only the minimum of communication. We each carried out our household responsibilities, but it was an empty, silent house.

"One year later we received an urgent call from the local hospital. 'Your son has been admitted to our psychiatric ward. Could you come right down?'

"When we arrived, before we were allowed to see Jamie, the attending physician wanted to talk to us. 'Your son has had a bad time and for a while we didn't think he would make it. He took enough LSD to kill him. There may be some brain damage. How much improvement there will be over time is anyone's guess. He babbles, he rocks, he cries. He's been this way for two weeks. What he needs now is a combination of our medical treatment and your love and affection. This is not the time to sit in judgement on what he has done. Just hold him and hug him. Be with him totally and if you know how to pray—pray for him.'

"Our war is over and like all wars there are no winners. Where did we go wrong?"

From *Two Hugs for Survival: Strategies for Effective Parenting*
by Harold A. Minden, pp. 14-16. Used by permission of the
Canadian Publishers, McClelland and Stewart, Toronto.

1.   Drawing on the case of Jamie, provide illustrations for each of the basic characteristics of systems theory.

2.   Describe the ways a crisis in any family system either brings its members closer together or drives them apart.

3.   In this reading you are given a picture of family life over a span of several years. Compare insights gained from an evolving, dynamic picture of a family to those possible from a static, one-moment-in-time snapshot.

4.   Outline some of the "sculpturing" techniques that are used in family therapy (cf. *Peoplemaking*, a book by Virginia Satir). Using one such approach, position members of Jamie's family to simulate the pattern of relationships in the family system prior to the crisis. Reposition family members several times to represent possible changes in the family system following Jamie's drug overdose.

5.   Symbolic Interaction is a theory that focuses on how people interact and how they communicate during these interactions. With this reading in mind, use authoritative sources to explore the Symbolic Interaction Theory.

HEALTHY FAMILY SYSTEMS

What images come to mind when you think of a healthy family system? Perhaps some of the most realistic images are provided by therapists who help troubled families discover their strengths. Michael P. Nichols, one such therapist, presents a blueprint for healthy families in his exciting book *The Power of the Family*. His work has led him to the conclusion that healthy family systems share three characteristics. He describes these below. The second selection focuses on the childhood recollections of Eva Saulis, now in her sixties. Saulis is a Native woman living on the Tobique reserve in New Brunswick. She describes a unique family system in a particular time and place. How does this family system of some fifty years ago show evidence of the timelessness of Nichols' blueprint?

☐

CLEAR BOUNDARIES

Strong families manage to balance closeness and separateness, and to satisfy individual and group needs, resulting in personal freedom as well as belonging and togetherness. Family members understand that the whole system must function for the individuals to prosper.

Strong families have *clear boundaries*. Like the membranes of living cells, their boundaries have enough strength and integrity to permit a highly involved interaction within, yet are permeable enough to permit an exchange of energy and information with the outside world. Members of healthy families are actively involved in the world beyond the family, relate to it with optimism and enthusiasm, and from their encounters outside bring varied interests and excitement back to the family.

Recently I spoke to a man whose wife was thinking about going back to work after six months of maternity leave. Naturally he was concerned about the balancing of household responsibilities that her return to work would necessitate. Still, he had no doubt that her working was best for all of them. . . .

Healthy families also have clear boundaries between members. They understand and respect that each of them is somewhat different. Dad likes Chinese food, Mom likes salads and seafood. Johnny likes swimming and ice skating, Suzie likes ice skating but prefers hiking. They do not attempt to establish a facade of pseudo-mutuality that says they must all like the same things. Yet they manage to work things out. Negotiation consists of accepting differences and working toward shared goals. In such a differentiated family group, individual choice is expected, family members speak up, and even the youngest children are respected as autonomous individuals with sovereign rights and responsibilities.

HIERARCHICAL ORGANIZATION

In healthy families there is a clear hierarchy of power, with leadership in the hands of the parents, who form a united coalition. There are clear generational divisions: parents have more power than children, and older children have more responsibilities and privileges than younger ones. Though many decisions are shared freely, there is no question as to who is parent and who is child. Successful parents rule with good-humoured effectiveness. They do not overcontrol their children, but neither do they feel obligated to disclaim their adult power. Only a weak executive subsystem establishes restrictive control; an excessive need to control occurs mostly when those in charge are ineffective. Children are less overtly powerful than their parents, but their contributions influence decisions, and their power grows as the children grow toward adulthood.

Respect for individual boundaries encourages intimacy. Members of healthy families have the opportunity to openly share honest thoughts and feelings, experiencing each other as different but sympathetic. A child may be willing to talk over a problem with her father if the family is flexible enough to allow special time for the two of them, and if the father is willing to listen without taking over. If a woman knows that her husband respects her autonomy over her career, it will be easier for her to share her doubts and conflicts. Some of the worst marital conflicts arise where there is a blurred distinction between separate turfs. This may be unavoidable on issues that affect both partners equally, like whether to have another baby or what city to live in. But many arguments arise simply from a failure to respect each other's prerogatives. . . .

To some, the idea that families function best when they have a hierarchical structure and that there should be a clear boundary separating parents and children suggests that parents should be detached and aloof from their children. This distorted conclusion is particularly likely to be drawn by those people to whom the idea of boundaries is foreign and repugnant. Not liking the idea of separateness, they mock it: "Oh, you mean the parents should be like Marine drill sergeants, and that children should be seen and not heard? Well, sor-ree, Doc, *we* just aren't like that."

It is true that a clear boundary between parents and children makes room for a private relationship between spouses, excluding the children from certain adult activities—making important family decisions, lovemaking, adult conversations. But what really separates the generations is not distance but modes of relatedness. Effective parents relate to their children from an unquestioned (and unself-doubting) position of authority. They are older, wiser, and stronger; they know it, and the children know it. At times, effective parents play at being equals with the children—tussling perhaps, or playing make-believe—but they are not equals. They know it and the children know it. They do not argue with their children ("I don't wanna . . ." "Yes, you do." "No I don't!"), and they don't burden the children unnecessarily with their own problems.

Moreover, this appropriate mode of relatedness changes as the children mature. Infants need nurturance and little else. Some people lecture to their babies, but it's only practice—practice for future sermonizing and future deafness. Small children need nurturance too, but also discipline and control. When parents say in

One of the oldest human needs is having someone to wonder where you are when you don't come home at night.

MARGARET MEAD

despair, "I can't control anything!" I usually ask them if their children run in front of cars. The point is, of course, that all parents teach their children to obey those rules they consider essential. Most parents could profit from making fewer—far fewer—rules. But there should be one superordinate rule: *The parents are in charge.* Too much discipline, control really, is as bad as too little. An excellent guideline is to let children learn for themselves the consequences of their own behavior. Some things, like running in front of cars, are too dangerous, and some things, like cruel treatment of pets, don't have consequences immediate enough for children to grasp. But an awful lot of what we nag children about, such as wearing sweaters on cold days, taking care not to break their toys, and eating supper, have consequences that the children themselves, if left alone, will learn from. Overuse dilutes authority.

FLEXIBILITY

In healthy families social roles are clear yet flexible. Boundaries and alignments must be readjusted to accommodate to changes in the life cycle of the family. . . . A new couple must strengthen the boundary separating them from their parents in order to protect the autonomy of the new union. With the advent of children, a boundary must be drawn that allows the children access to both parents while excluding them from spouse functions. Some couples who do well as a twosome are never able to make a satisfactory adjustment to a group of three or four. And the familiar example of two people who live happily together for years but suddenly break up after they marry can be understood as a failure to tolerate the stronger boundary that marriage vows imply.

Raising children requires nurturance, control, and guidance. What makes being a parent so damned difficult is not only the complexity of the task, but also the fact that the parenting process differs depending on the children's age. When they are young, children need little more than nurturance. Later, control and guidance become more important. The growing child's developmental needs tax the parents' capacity for flexibility. As children grow, their developmental needs for both autonomy and guidance impose pressures on the parental subsystem, which must be modified to meet them. One aspect of this modification is to strengthen the boundary between parents and children, which permits the children greater access to friends and school and other social institutions.

Our parents were very strict. During Lent we had to stop eating candy, cake. Boy, we really looked forward to Easter. Really appreciated our food! (laughs). We didn't really mind, though I wouldn't do it now. We celebrated Easter, but in our family we celebrated New Year's more than Easter, even more than Christmas. It was a French tradition. They'd prepare days for that, have a banquet and a gathering. Mass would be at ten o'clock in the morning and after church relatives would all get together, greet each other with "Happy New Year!" Then they'd have a big feast—well, it wasn't that fancy—but everything: corn soup, pot pie, meat pies, big roasts and potatoes, all kinds of pastry. No drinking. They'd just get together and really celebrate. Later on my parents bought a piano and people would sing, others would play cards. My uncle, William Laporte, played the fiddle.

The old times were good for my mother; good for us too, really. Sometimes when Louis, Raymond, Peter and I get together, we talk about times when we were growing up. Louis said, "After I got married and had children I realized that our parents had to do what they done—be strict. Teach us responsibility; how to take care of ourselves and our families." Because when the boys were old enough our father used to take them to the woods and teach them how to cut wood; also how to plant gardens; how to make baskets; even how to cook, wash clothes and knit. Everything. When they were told to do something, they did it.

There must have been Indian celebration days and stories, of course, but the priests were so against anything traditional, I think they tried to break all those traditions. When people say, "The missionaries christianized the Indians," that means they tried to take their language, their traditions, their legends, everything. I heard a lot of jokes about that too. For example, "When the missionaries came they told us to bow our heads and pray. When we looked up, our land was gone." They were stealing our land while our heads were bowed! (laughs)

Some *practical* things we kept, though. Like we had midwives until the hospital was built here. Before that, ladies had their babies at home. The hospital was built in 1924, about the same time as they built the church—after the old church had burned. The doctor used to come here by canoe—the people would go after him. Same thing with the priest. Until the early 1900s there was no priest here; he used to come in four times a year for baptisms, marriages. If somebody died, they'd have to go after the priest by wagon or canoe, then take him back again.

When we were real young we didn't have that much freedom like children do now. We were just kept right at home; we had a big yard all fenced in and that is where we stayed. The only time we were let out, they let us go to church, to school. We didn't go into other people's yards, especially evenings.

I had nine brothers in all; I was the only girl. We had one horse, one cow, chickens, pigs. Where I'm living now, my family cultivated all that in garden. So that provided food for us all winter. Each one of us had our chores; my parents put it down on a sheet near the door. I didn't have to go out and work in the garden or anything, I helped my mother wash clothes by a washboard, scrub the wood floors twice a week, bring in water, heat the water.

So much has changed on the reserve now. In my time there was fishing and then hunting in the fall time. My mother used to tell me about her parents and I guess they had harder times then. The men used to go in the woods in the fall time and hunt all winter. They'd come home Christmas time. That was her father's generation. The women stayed home and took care of the family, made fancy baskets.

In the spring—they'd call it *sobekwatook* ("going to the coast")—they'd go by canoe down to Saint John. They'd take their furs and baskets and sell them because that was where the traders were, I guess. Some of them even settled in Saint Andrews (by-the-Sea). I was talking to this elderly lady in Eastport, Maine. She was from here originally. She was telling me this same story. She said, "I was seven years old when we left Tobique." She said, "I remember coming to St. Andrews, but I can't remember how we got to Pleasant Point (Eastport)." She remembered these old people from here, even my grandmother.

So our people used to grow their own food, go trapping, go hunting and fishing. My father used to salt that salmon in crocks. They didn't have no fridges or freezers then; they had like a closet outside where they'd hang the meat up in the fall time. Some of it they smoked, some of it they dried. By my time they no longer dried meat, but my grandmother used to dry berries—blueberries, *looweemeenals* (chokecherries), loganberries. That was from before people had canning. The women made all their own clothing too; knit the socks, mittens, made moccasins, snowshoes. My mother was very practical, very resourceful. She done all of that besides cooked for all of us, washed clothes, kept house and then made moccasins and snowshoes in the evenings.

The whole family would move over across (to Maine) in the fall time for potato picking. My father would take a job and then he'd hire some pickers and take the whole family over there for the season. We'd all pick and my mother cooked for the whole crew. We had good accommodation—a house. We used to pick for this farmer in Limestone for many years. When my mother had twins, that's the first time we had a cow. That farmer gave us a milk cow to bring back here.

Families helped their own family, their elders. They didn't have no old age homes. My grandmother had her own place until she was too feeble to look after herself; then she moved in with us till she died. It wasn't very long. In those days the elderly were real active, strong, healthy. My grandmother died in her sleep, and she smoked all her life. She smoked a pipe; my mother did too.

My mother did Indian medicine, and we spoke only Indian until we went to school. That's when we lost our language because we weren't allowed to speak Indian on the school grounds. It was hard for us when we were little. My parents spoke Indian and French at home. We could hardly understand anything at school and that's why it took us a long time to learn. Once I spoke to the nuns who used to teach us here. I went to visit them at their "home base" in Saint John. We talked about the old days and the nun said it wasn't their idea; it was the rules laid down, the policy that we weren't supposed to talk Indian. She said, "We had nothing to do with it ourselves. We were just doing what we were told." I said, "I don't think it was right because that's how we lost our language." I guess they intended that for us.

From *Enough is Enough: Aboriginal Women Speak Out* as told to Janet Silman
(Toronto: The Women's Press, 1987), pp. 32-35.

The family only represents one aspect, however important an aspect, of a human being's functions and activities. . . . A life is beautiful and ideal or the reverse, only when we have taken into our consideration the social as well as the family relationship.
HAVELOCK ELLIS

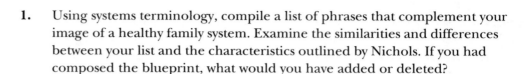

1. Using systems terminology, compile a list of phrases that complement your image of a healthy family system. Examine the similarities and differences between your list and the characteristics outlined by Nichols. If you had composed the blueprint, what would you have added or deleted?

2. Nichols discusses hierarchy of power only as it functions between generations. Inevitably, however, and to greater or lesser degrees of inequality, power relations exist between couples. Cite examples of some important gender-related power struggles that arise in today's families. Are any of these reflected in Nichols' reading?

3. Cite examples of boundary and hierarchy changes at each stage of the family life cycle. At which stages do you think the family is most flexible and least flexible in its ability to negotiate the changes? Support your conjectures.

4. From Eva Saulis's account of her family life cite illustrations of clear boundaries, hierarchical organization, and flexibility.

5. Refer to the system characteristics outlined in Fine's essay. With these characteristics in mind, examine how the Saulis family functioned.

6. Compare the parenting process in today's urban families with that of the Native family described in the reading. How and why are they different/ similar?

7. "So much has changed on the reserve now." Using a variety of resources, investigate the impact of societal change on the lives of Native Canadian families today.

■ FAMILY RULES

Every family has rules, and each family's are different. Family systems work because of these rules which, ideally, impose regularity and not regulation. You are about to meet the Cruikshanks, a family with West Indian roots that has its own unique set of rules. The following excerpt is from the award-winning Canadian novel *Harriet's Daughter* by Marlene Nourbese Philip. The focus is on teenage Margaret and her relationship with her mother and father (Tina and Cuthbert), her older sister Jo-Ann, and her brother, fondly known as "Rib Roast."

I could hear my mother calling me: I knew why, to go to church, but I pretended not to hear. Finally she came to my room and told me it was time to get up and go to church.

"I'm grounded, remember. I'm not supposed to leave the house."

"You still have to go to church," was all she said. I could hear my stupid sister laughing in her room. I was still wearing my clothes from the day before. I looked around my room and wondered whether Harriet would have had a room like this. My mother was dying to get her hands on it and make it over "like Jo-Ann's," all pink and white. I kept telling her I liked it the way it was. Pukey was Jo-Ann's word for my room. Whenever she said this to me, I agreed with her: "That's right Jo-Ann, pukey—just like you." That always got her.

I showered, changed, and put on my new jeans and my "DON'T BOTHER ME I CAN'T COPE" T-shirt. When I went down for breakfast my mother asked me where I thought I was going.

"To church, where else? You said I had to go."

"Like that?"

"Like what? These are clean clothes."

"Yes, but I'm not dead yet, and no one's going to say that Tina Cruickshank don't know how to look after her children, or dress them properly, so go up and change *and* put on a dress. Have a little respect for the house of the Lord."

I was really tempted to say I thought I lived in the house of the Lord; instead, I put up a fight about wearing a dress.

"Aw Mum, you know I hate wearing dresses. I don't want to wear a dress."

She was like rock itself: "Go and put on a dress."

My mother thinks that when she dies, all hell is going to break loose. I don't know how else to explain her most favourite saying after "You're too rude and faysty." If my hair doesn't look quite the way *she* wants it to look, "I'm not dead yet," if my sneakers aren't clean enough, "I'm not dead yet," if she thinks I look untidy, "I'm not dead yet." I don't know what she thinks is going to happen when she dies; that I'll stop bathing and wearing clean clothes? Become a bum?

Anyway I got through the boring old service, wearing a hated dress. I managed to sit as far away from my sister as I could. Of course Rib Roast never goes unless he wants to, and of course my mother never makes him go. She and my father go sometimes; very, very sometimes—like once a year, at Christmas or Easter. That's what I mean about adults not being fair—but *every* Sunday, unless I have a real good excuse, I have got to find myself in church, listening to this boring old man talk about the Holy Ghost. I would sneak off and go somewhere else, but slobbo Jo-Ann is always there; she sings in the youth choir and just "loves the church." Yuck! Her boyfriend sings in the choir too, I'm sure that's why she loves it so much.

I don't like to go on like this about my problems, especially those I can't change, but I remember this weekend. Apart from being grounded, it was also the weekend when HE threatened once again to send me to Barbados. And we all know what I am supposed to get there: GWID—Good West Indian Discipline.

Any fool can make a rule.
HENRY DAVID THOREAU

We were having Sunday supper; the chicken tasted great and my father was eating and not talking. Praise be. I got the wishbone and Jo-Ann wanted to break it with me, so I agreed. I won the wish and she started bugging me to tell her what I wished for, although she knows that to tell means bad luck. I had wished for Zulma to go back home to her gran and I really didn't want to talk about it. She wouldn't give up, just kept bugging me to tell her and finally I did.

"I wished for something for you, Jo-Ann."

"For me? Oh that's great, Margaret, I've been dying for a dress I saw at Le Chateau last week." She was being all sweet and Jo-Annish. "Tell me, oh tell me Margaret."

"I wished for you to gain fifty pounds," I laughed.

Her face crumpled up, like when you crush a paper cup, and I felt like a real jerk. I really hadn't meant to hurt her and I was sorry I had said it, she just kept bugging me so much. She looked like she was going to cry.

"Oh I'm sorry Jo-Ann, forget it. I was just teasing. I didn't really wish that."

To change the subject and get her mind off the fifty pounds she saw rushing on her like a ten-ton truck, I asked my mum if she would help me with my project on Rastas and reggae music. I really should have known better, for before she could answer—she probably would have said no—HE butted in.

"Did I hear you say you were doing a project on Rastas and reggae music?"

"Yes Dad." I knew what was coming. I should have kept my big mouth shut, but it was too late. He went on and on about how Rastas were criminal, and how they gave decent, hard-working Coloured People—I wanted to say like Mr. Cuthbert Cruickshank, hip, hip hurrah!—a bad name; how they smoked dope, and how their music was primitive. I turned to Mum. "Say something," I said, "you know that's not true, you're from Jamaica."

"Be quiet when I'm talking," he said.

"But what you're saying is not true. I've read about them, they're really quite religious. They believe Haile Selassie was their God!"

"I said be quiet. I don't care who their God is or where he is, he's not my God. I don't know what they think they are teaching at that school, but the Principal's going to hear from me."

"But there's nothing wrong with Rastas and reggae music. Have you ever listened to it?" My sister and brother didn't even come to my rescue, and both of them listened to reggae music. "Jonathon," I said, "tell Dad how much you like Peter Tosh." Liking Peter Tosh meant, in my books, that there was still hope for Rib Roast. "Go on tell him, he's not going to kill you, you know." My brother didn't say a word, the yellow-bellied coward. Peter Tosh, Bob Marley, none of those people had had any effect on him. He just sat there looking down at his plate.

I turned to Jo-Ann. "Jo, you borrowed all Ti-cush's reggae albums from me, didn't you? You think it's great music don't you?" She just rolled her eyes, maybe she was still angry with me about her fifty pounds. I hoped it all fell on her and crushed her—swine. Nobody helped, not even my mother who comes from Jamaica and knows differently.

"Tina, do you see what I mean? Do you see now what I have been telling you . . . ?"

Laws too gentle are seldom obeyed; too severe seldom executed.

BENJAMIN FRANKLIN

"Never mind Dad, I'm not going to do the project. I don't want you going to the school—you're just going to embarrass me."

"Embarrass you! Is that what you think of our interest in what you're learning? You children don't realise how important it is for Coloured People . . . "

"Here we go again—how important is for Coloured People—underlined three times in red . . ." I clapped my hand over my mouth to shut myself up. I couldn't believe I had actually said what I had just said—but I had—I had said those words. My father was looking at me with his mouth open, then he shut it suddenly, as if he hadn't known he had had it open. I heard his teeth click as he closed his mouth and his eyes got sort of poppy—his face got darker and darker. *Everyone* was dead, dead quiet. I mean nobody, but nobody ever interrupts my father when he's talking—let alone to be rude like I had been.

Then he started again: "All right, all right young woman" (young woman is worse than young lady), "you are making it clearer and clearer to me that I have to take certain measures with you." I looked at him. I knew what was coming. "Tina we're going to write to my mother . . . "

"Cuthbert, go easy on her . . . " I couldn't believe my ears—my mother was actually saying something to defend me. "You know how faysty she is . . ."

"She's too rude Tina, too rude. You're not doing your job properly. That's why I don't want you working . . . "

"Cuthbert . . . " was all my mother said, but her tone was real heavy.

The way my father huffed and puffed, I swear I could see puffs of smoke coming out of his ears. Then he said, "I'm warning her, Tina, if there is one more incident like this, she's going to my mother when school's out. Do you hear that young lady?" (I had moved back up to young lady.)

I was feeling real bad, it's so awful to have that sort of threat hanging over you. I mean it's bad enough that you don't get along with your family, but to be always worried about being sent away . . .

My mum must have felt sorry for me—she let me off the dishes that night. I went up to my room and lay across my bed for a while and cried. Zulma was coming over to spend the night but I couldn't even get excited about that. When she came, I told her what had happened.

"Maybe I'll run away with you Zulma."

"Where we going to go though?"

"I don't know. I wish Harriet Tubman was around. She would help, she would know what to do, I know she would."

Zulma was in the top bunk, I was below. She always liked to sleep there when she slept over; it made her feel like she was in her favourite mango tree back home. We had been talking like this for a while, then I said to her, "Hey Zulma, would you call me Harriet? I would really like you to . . . Zulma? Zulma?"

There was no answer, Zulma had gone to sleep. I rolled over and repeated the name to myself: "Harriet, Harriet, Harriet . . ." until I fell asleep.

From *Harriet's Daughter* by Marlene Nourbese Philip
(Oxford: Heinemann Publishers Ltd., 1988).

1. Identify some of the rules that govern norms and expectations in the Cruikshank family. Which of these rules sound familiar to you?

2. Experience has shown that family behaviour is different when overt and covert rules are broken. Find examples of the difference in this reading. How do the patterns differ in your family?

3. Generate a list of rules found in the cross-section of families represented in your classroom. Classify these as either overt or covert rules. Draw some conclusions about your findings.

4. Family therapist Virginia Satir states that rules are actually a vital, dynamic, and extremely influential force in family life. Examine the list of rules you compiled in question 3 with this idea in mind. Do you agree with Satir? Explain.

5. The kind and nature of family rules can change as children mature. How and why is this so?

6. Determine the ways in which family rules may be influenced by ethnic, religious, and cultural background.

7. Consulting authoritative sources, explore the effects of family rules on gender socialization and, in turn, the effects of gender socialization on family rules.

TRIANGLES AND COALITIONS

Your understanding of how a system works can be enhanced through an analysis of the composition and nature of family triangles and coalitions. Murray Bowen, a prominent figure in the history of family therapy, claims that the triangle is the smallest unit of a relationship pattern. The following excerpt describes the power and functioning of triangles and coalitions.

□

When Sue was young, she often saw her parents arguing. Her dad got red-faced and shouted at her mother. Her mother cried and gave in to him. Sue felt sorry for mother and angry at dad. After dad stormed out of the room, Sue tried to comfort her mother.

As Sue got older, her mother told her about other incidents of father's mistreatments. In her teens, Sue began to fight back with dad in a way mother never would. She was especially incensed whenever dad attacked her brothers or sisters. Those fights would then take a back seat to the fight between dad and Sue. Eventually, in her last years at home, Sue began to see that mother's inability to speak up for herself was part of the problem. She then got angry at mother and called her a wimp whenever she didn't stand up for herself. Mother would cry and dad would tell Sue to stop being mean to her mother. Then Sue and her dad would be fighting again.

Sue and her family were caught up in a common relationship game called triangles. . . .

. . . Basically, a triangle is any three-way relationship. In each corner there can be an individual or a group of people. The basic family triangle is father, mother, child. A basic social triangle might be criminal, victim, police. The classic triangle everyone knows of, and probably thinks of when they hear the word, is husband, wife, mistress. One corner of a triangle can also be a thing, or an activity, or an issue. . . .

The triangle is the main dynamic in T.V. soap operas. All the drama and frustration of these shows is created by people not saying things directly to each other. The characters give their information, or pass on gossip, to a third party, rather than to the person directly involved. Watch the soaps in this perspective and you will see how easy it is for people to make a mess of their lives, and how accurately these shows reflect this aspect of our own lives.

Triangles have both positive and negative functions. People in relationships have optimal levels of closeness and distance. Anxiety arises when there is either too much closeness or too much distance. If there are a lot of people around, the anxiety can be diluted. This means there is more potential stability available in large families. When one person gets too anxious, he or she can go to someone else in the family for a while until things cool down and then come back to the original relationship. For example, when a parent and child got into unmanageable conflict in our grandparents' generation, the child would often be sent to live with an uncle or aunt in the neighbouring community. Each party had a chance to think things through, get some new ideas from others and then, perhaps, renew the relationship on different terms. Most families today are too scattered geographically and emotionally to do this.

Today's nuclear family is like a pressure cooker; there are very few places, other than a therapist's office, where family members can go to learn how to deal with anxiety. And because so many people believe that they ought to be able to handle it themselves, the pressure keeps growing until the family explodes. More people, and more triangles, in the family could ease this tension.

However, in most families, triangles increase rather than reduce the problems. Triangles occur because it is usually difficult for any two people in a relationship to focus just on themselves and maintain a one-to-one relationship. The less differentiated they are, the less they are able to do this.

> When a couple turns into a triangle, an interesting tension begins and is never resolved. The three of you can never be together and be at rest, it seems. One person is always forced to orbit.
>
> MARNI JACKSON

In a one-to-one relationship, the tension usually grows. People handle this tension by triangling in a third person or issue and talk about that. They can continue in the relationship that way for hours, days, weeks, and years. Some couples get along fine as long as they talk about their kids, or their friends, or their work, but they have trouble focusing on themselves in the relationship. . . .

In any group of three people there will tend to be two who are close (inside) and one who is distant (outside). It is difficult to maintain equal closeness between all three at the same time. The closeness can rotate so that any one person can be on the outside while the other two are close, or the close two and distant third might be permanently fixed. The usual pattern is that the close two form a coalition against the outside person and overlook their differences with each other. In its milder forms, this pattern of interaction is called gossip. . . .

Closeness works just fine when two people are in agreement, but when their differences emerge, they tend to distance and/or create power struggles. It is at this time that one of them will be tempted to triangle in someone or something else. One common example of this is when husband and wife are arguing; at some point in the argument one of them triangles in one or more of the kids and says, "and Johnny agrees with me. He thinks you're wrong too!" The implication is "if we two think you are wrong then you must be wrong and you had better change and be the way we want you to be." Triangles have two different states: calm and tense. In the calm state, the triangle consists of two close people who are getting along well and a distant person who would like to be in closer.

In this triangle, the outside person may try to entice one of the close partners to enter a new coalition and leave the other partner. One example is a teenager who feels on the outside of her parents' united front and develops a strategy for playing one off against the other so that one of the parents ends up agreeing with her and fighting her cause with the other parent.

In the tense triangle, the two close people may become anxious over the closeness and potential loss of self and begin a fight. In this case, the outside person usually wants to stay distant and avoid the other two, if possible, while one of the two close members tries to establish a coalition with the outside person. For example, while the parents are fighting, dad may try to triangle in a teenage child to be on his side against mom. The teenager may then try to distance herself from the argument and say, "Leave me out of this. This is between the two of you." On the other hand, if the teenager wants more closeness with dad, she may agree with dad about mom and imply that she and dad are alike and mom is wrong. In this case, her need to be closer to dad (and perhaps to "get" mom) overrides her need to distance from these two arguing parents. . . .

. . . Coalitions between two points of a triangle serve two functions: to reduce anxiety and to control the third point of the triangle. Coalitions provide both additional support and additional strength to a person who is feeling anxious and weak. Coalitions are a normal experience in families. The new-born baby is triangled into coalitions before it even has any awareness of itself. But as self-awareness develops, the baby learns how to play the coalition game.

Coalitions help those who feel weak deal with those whom they see as stronger.

Those who feel less sure of themselves see their salvation (i.e., their chances of getting their way) in the support of others. Coalitions are an attempt to help us deal with our poor self-esteem and increase our influence. . . .

In coalitions, the inside person is good and attractive and the outside person is bad and unattractive. When we make coalitions, we tend to distort reality. This demonstrates that the real intent of coalitions is to shore up one's sense of self and to get "good things" from others.

Therefore, coalitions become disillusioning, and we end up feeling weaker, or taken advantage of. . . .

. . . In fact, it is not always an advantage to be seen as the strongest person in a family, because others will be provoked into forming coalitions against you. . . .

Secret coalitions also develop in families. They are quite difficult to deal with simply because they are not openly acknowledged, so cannot be challenged. They can be quite destructive.

Another common coalition is between parents and "the good child" against "the bad child." The bad child will always be in the outside position. The good child is in coalition with the parents, because he or she overtly does what they want or emulates their values, and thus is seen (as is the case in coalitions) as almost all good. And the bad child, is, of course, seen as almost all bad. Frequently, in therapy, the good child, now grown up, will say that he or she did nearly all the same things as the bad sibling but never got caught and that the parents seemed to think he or she could do no wrong. This is often the situation when one child is being scape-goated (i.e., when one child is blamed for being the source of all the family's problems).

In scapegoating, family members covertly agree that "we are all okay but this other person sure has problems. If we can't get him or her to straighten out, we will have to reject him or her." Scapegoating is a way to deal with the anxiety one feels about one's own sense of self and about being in close relationships. If the focus can be on one who appears to be abnormal, the other family members do not have to look at their own failings.

From Family Ties That Bind by Ronald W. Richardson,
published by Self-Counsel Press, 1987.
Reproduced by permission of the publisher.

1. Identify the strengths and limitations of triangles and coalitions in a family system.

2. Illustrate the triangles in a real or fictional family system. Identify those triangles that are calm, tense, and most powerful. Indicate the coalitions in each triangle.

3. "The power of triangles lies in their ability to stabilize relationships and to

freeze relationship problems in place." Provide examples of these phenomena using these family situations:

☐   a set of parents and a child;
☐   sets of in-laws and husband/wife.

4.   Triangulation is but one relationship pattern. Survey relevant sources to determine other common patterns.

5.   In what ways does a knowledge about patterns of relationships help you understand how your family system works?

CIRCULAR CAUSALITY AND CONFLICT

A systems perspective avoids the "who's to blame," or lineal causality way of thinking that so often dooms families to endless eruptions. In this excerpt from Constance Beresford Howe's novel *The Marriage Bed* we meet Anne as she recalls a conflict with her husband, Ross. Anne has just given Ross a kitten—a surprise birthday gift that provokes an unexpected response. Does the sequence of events and the pattern of the couple's exchanges illustrate lineal or circular causality?

☐

I began to feel affronted in a personal kind of way. The kitten jumped off my knee and went over to sniff at Ross's shoes. He paid no attention to it, and my blood began to simmer. Nothing could be more insulting than the dignified coldness Ross had inherited from all those successful ancestors of his. "Well, is that all you have to say?" I demanded.

His glasses came around the edge of the newspaper. "Anne, there is nothing to say. Wherever that cat came from, it's going back. I've got enough on my plate as it is. One more thing to be responsible for I do *not* need."

"Are you implying I'm a dead weight? You know damn well Professor Stein's promised to take me back at the lab as soon as Hugh's weaned. I think you're being unnecessarily bloody, anyhow, about a birthday present—when it was the nicest thing I could find to give you."

"I am not going to fight with you, Anne. Only that cat goes back."

"What you mean is, you don't give a shit what I think or how I feel, right?"

The hand gripping the paper shook; then he threw it to the carpet, startling the kitten into a sideways leap.

"What I mean is," he shouted, "I'm fed up with you tanking over me as if I didn't exist. When do I ever get to vote around here? About *anything?* The mood takes you to paint the kitchen purple or adopt a dog, and I'm supposed to tag along, Mr. Yes Dear. Well, I'm not going to do it any more. I warn you, I'm fed up. Dangerously fed up."

The violence of this attack shook me, and to my own disgust I heard a querulous little voice say, "I thought you liked cats."

"For Christ's sake, what's that got to do with it! You're a woman supposed to have brains, but you can be so *dumb—*"

"It's not dumb to wonder why anybody would get into such a fizz just because his wife gives him a birthday present."

He took a deep breath and tried to get hold of himself. "This present of yours— if you insist on bringing it down to cases—it's going to do nothing for me but run up vet's bills, eat the plants, and wreck the furniture your father's probably still paying for. Now, I don't know about you, but if Max and Billie came here for dinner and found the chairs in rags, I would personally be embarrassed. It's bad enough to be under an obligation like that in the first place, or have you forgotten that another man's had to furnish my house?"

"So that's it. Why didn't you say all this in the first place, then? I'd have been glad to live with Goodwill cast-offs if I'd known you felt that way. But I thought you were big enough to be grateful to Max, not sour and jealous. After all, you accept those cheques your mother keeps on leaving around the house cheerfully, don't you?"

"Will you just leave my mother the hell out of this! Among the other things I'm fed up with is you making a face like sucking lemons every time she comes here, or is even mentioned. You seem to take it as a personal insult every time she does something nice for us."

"Yes, because she does it for you, not me. She makes it so clear she's sorry for you, handcuffed to me, you poor victim!" . . .

"Don't yell like that," he said, assembling the newspaper fussily.

"I'll yell all I like! You just don't want to admit you're married to your bloody mother, that's all!"

"You can sit here and scream at the walls if you like. I'm going up—I'll sleep in the study. And that animal goes back tomorrow, is that clear?"

"Tomorrow's Saturday, they'll be up at their ski place."

"Monday, then."

And he continued mounting the stairs, back very stiff, the newspaper grasped like a sword in his dexter talon. The kitten watched him go, head on one side, and then began to sharpen its claws on the sofa. Upstairs Hugh woke and began to squall for his ten o'clock feed. Angrily rubbing tears off my face, I went up to him.

It was bad luck that the next day was Saturday, because that meant we had no chance to get away from each other and pretend nothing had happened. It was the

When I was young, I set out to change the world. When I grew a little older, I perceived that this was too ambitious so I set out to change my state. This, too, I realized as I grew older was too ambitious, so I set out to change my town. When I realized I could not even do this, I tried to change my family. Now as an old man, I know that I should have started by changing myself. If I had started with myself, maybe then I would have succeeded in changing my family, the town or even the state . . . and who knows, maybe even the world!

WORDS OF A CHASSIDIC RABBI ON HIS DEATHBED

first time we'd ever needed that kind of space. Until now, our fights had been short and sharp but, as it were, reversible. This time it was different. I woke up feeling sore all over, as if I'd been beaten. As for Ross, he spoke to me only when absolutely necessary, and with a cold politeness that was worse than abuse. He hung out the baby-wash, he amused Martha while I did another feed, all with a kind of glaze of reserve over him. He appeared not to notice the existence of the kitten, except once to pluck it off the kitchen counter where it was playing with an eggshell.

The day seemed to drag on forever. He went up to the study and worked for part of the morning, but lunchtime was another cold and silent encounter. In a tacit peace overture, I made creamed salmon on toast, a dish he liked, with chopped mushrooms, celery, and green onions in it, and cleared the kitchen table so we could sit down and eat, instead of leaning against the counter or wandering around the house with bowls. But Ross only threw a dismissive glance at the lunch and said briefly, "I'm not hungry."

Many vivid answers to that sprang to mind, but I swallowed them all, because it was clear too much had been said already, on both sides. Instead I scrubbed the kitchen floor with particular ferocity, wondering as I did so how much housewifely cleanliness came from the same bitter source.

Sunday was a duplicate of Saturday, and I began to feel a muffled sort of panic beating under my skin. How long could this kind of thing go on? Surely it could only mean that there was nothing left between us, unless you counted this bitter mutual resentment. The hours crawled past. I caught myself sitting down in snatches or leaning against things for support like someone very old. The perpetual demands of the two babies struck me for the first time as monstrous. Outrageous. Colossal. I mouthed these and other words from time to time. By way of response, no doubt, to the atmosphere generally, Martha was impossibly cranky and demanding. She pattered from room to room whining or pulling at things, until in desperation I dressed her for a walk. While I was getting on my own coat, the phone rang.

"Hi, Anne. Is Ross there?"

"Hullo, Randy. Yes, just hold on. Ross—for you."

My voice sounded as leaden as I felt, but when Ross lifted the upstairs extension and spoke, he sounded perfectly normal. As I shepherded Martha out, I heard him, chatty and cheerful, and I thought bitterly, "It's only me he hates."

Tediously the hours drained away. When I got back, Ross was downstairs reading, with a wailing, hungry Hugh in his arm. He handed the baby over silently and went on reading. I sat down and began to feed him. Martha stumped out to the kitchen and began to open cupboard doors, her favourite game. One after another she opened them and clapped them shut. The silence of the house was stretched so tight that little normal sounds like a dripping tap or a creaking floorboard cracked like pistol shots.

From *The Marriage Bed* by Constance Beresford Howe, copyright ©1981.
Reprinted by permission of Macmillan of Canada,
a Division of Canada Publishing Corporation.

> Conflict is as normal a part of family life as is harmony.
>
> ELAINE SOLWAY

1. Differentiate between lineal and circular causality. Why is circular causality a systems characteristic whereas lineal causality is not?

2. Using examples from the reading, explain why this couple's conflict is circular. Is there a common thread running through their mutual attacks? Do you see any evidence of lineal causality in the relationship? If you were this couple's marriage counsellor, what advice would you give them?

3. Probe and evaluate the assumptions underlying each of the following statements:

   ☐ Conflict is inevitable and necessary for the development of family relationships;
   ☐ Changing oneself will force others to change;
   ☐ Systems thinking is a remedy for "mother-blaming."

4. Many people in close relationships fear conflict and seek ways to avoid it. What is the rationale for our fear of conflict? What techniques do we use to avoid it? What may be some positive outcomes of conflict?

5. Books on the subject of conflict management are widely available. Most of them contain models or descriptions of conflict styles. Locate one such model or description. Identify the style(s) you tend to use. Assess the effectiveness of your style(s).

6. Using authoritative texts and/or journals, locate studies that examine the relationship between conflict and family life cycle stages. Abstract (summarize in a paragraph) a number of these studies.

7. Write a summary statement that clarifies the link between circular causality and conflict resolution.

INDEPENDENCE AND INTERDEPENDENCE

More than sixty years ago, Kahlil Gibran in his book *The Prophet* gave beautiful expression to the delicate balance between independence and

interdependence. In the second selection, freelance columnist
Eve McBride discusses how healthy family systems strive to achieve that
balance today.

☐

T hen Almitra spoke again and said, "And what of Marriage, master?"
And he answered saying:
"You were born together, and together you shall be forevermore.
You shall be together when the white wings of death scatter your days.
Aye, you shall be together even in the silent memory of God.
But let there be space in your togetherness,
And let the winds of the heavens dance between you.
Love one another, but make not a bond of love
Let it rather be a moving sea between the shores of your souls.
Fill each other's cup but drink not from one cup
Give one another of your bread but eat not from the same loaf.
Sing and dance together and be joyous, but let each one of you be alone,
Even as the strings of a lute are alone though they quiver with the same music.
Give your hearts, but not into each other's keeping.
For only the hand of Life can contain your hearts.
And stand together yet not too near together:
For the pillars of the temple stand apart,
And the oak tree and the cypress grow not in each other's shadow."

From *The Prophet* by Kahlil Gibran
(New York: Alfred A. Knopf, Inc., 1955), pp. 16-17.

☐

A t 3:30 p.m., on this day 17 years ago, with yards of organza crushed
under my knees and a froth of silk tulle around my head, I knelt beside my new
husband and admired the shiny gold band that now touched the pawnshop engagement ring I'd worn for a year. Later, after we'd signed the register, I recall that same
new husband gripping my elbow to hold me back, and hissing, "Slow down!"
because he thought I was moving too fast to the traditional Mendelssohn wedding
recessional. I hadn't the least idea what I was rushing so impatiently to.

Four children and many rocky paths and stubbed toes later, we are still
together, though June 1968 feels like a long time ago: another era, in fact. It was the
same month Robert Kennedy was shot and Pierre Elliott Trudeau's passionate goals
for this country got him elected prime minister. We were too young to get married; I
was 22, my husband 24, both us fresh from school. I had wanted to get married the
year before—Confederation year—as all my friends were doing. I went to four weddings in the summer of '67. But my husband refused to be married while he was still
in law school so I had to be content just to be engaged. It never occurred to us to live

together. People didn't do that in those days, but I remember the day after the wedding, on the train to Vancouver where we were going to live, we talked over the previous day and said to each other, "Why did we bother?"

I don't know if that ceremony in the white marble chapel and all its attendant ritual has played a part in the longevity of our marriage. The other evening as I broke romaine leaves into a big wooden salad bowl that had been a wedding present, I thought how few gifts had survived the 17 years. The mohair blankets have and the silver trays but the French porcelain casserole and the Royal Worcester soufflé dishes broke long ago and the toaster and iron have been replaced many times. And I have a cupboard full of fancy teacups I never use. My beautiful, expensive wedding dress, which I wore for a total of five hours, has lain folded with the veil at the bottom of a trunk all these years.

I spend a lot of time thinking about marriage—my own and the institution and where it's going. I have single friends in their 30s who'd love to be married and other friends who are separated after long marriages and delighted to be free. It occurs to me constantly that whoever put " 'til death do us part" in the marriage vows way back when never imagined it would mean 40 or 50 years of togetherness—40 or 50 years of shaving hairs in the sink (his), ice-cold hands and feet in the bed (mine) and arguing whether the egg in the Caesar salad should be whipped into the dressing or just broken onto the leaves. (I say in the dressing.)

> It is our responsibilities, not ourselves, that we should take seriously.
> PETER USTINOV

Even after 17 years of what I think has been, despite some rough times, a pretty terrific one, I still don't know a thing about marriage. The rules keep changing, or rather we keep changing them as we get older. Our relationship now is nothing like the one that emerged from that Gothic chapel so many years ago. I do know I think it's much easier not to stay married. I know when you look at that person in your bed, who has been there for centuries, and you're both in one of those gloomy valleys you frequently fall into the longer you've been married, and you think, "What are you *still* doing here?"—given what you have to give to climb out of that dark time— the hours of talking and immeasurable layers of compromising, it feels then as if it would be much more pleasant to run.

Why have my husband or I, though we've contemplated it on several occasions, never run? Our four children? Not likely. Whenever we've talked of splitting, it's always, "*You* get the kids!" It's not for each other's money, fame or power. It could be for our good looks, but probably not after this many years. And it's not because I'm a good housekeeper or he's a fine handyman.

Once I stuck a grapefruit seed just under the soil of an avocado plant. It grew up alongside the avocado until they were both struggling for space in the small pot. I decided to re-pot them separately but when I tried to pull apart the roots, they were so entangled, it was obvious I'd do damage to both plants if I tried. So I replanted them together in a bigger container. And they thrived. When, a couple of years later, they seemed in trouble again, I simply gave them more space. And they just kept on growing. And growing.

And that's just what the grapefruit tree I live with and I are doing.

From "Rules for a Fine Marriage Simply a Matter of Space," by Eve McBride,
Toronto Star, June 1, 1985.

1. Compare your interpretation of Gibran's phrase "space in your togetherness" with those of others in your class. Account for the diversity of interpretations.

2. Select a system characteristic that you feel is suggested by "space in your togetherness." Compare your selection with those of others.

3. Using authoritative sources, develop a set of guidelines for effective negotiation. Use these guidelines to assist the following families in negotiating "space in their togetherness":

   ☐ Dual-income couple with young children;
   ☐ Dual-career couple, no children, workplaces 300 miles apart;
   ☐ Couple with teenagers and a live-in elderly parent.

4. React to Eve McBride's statements:

   > Even after 17 years . . . I still don't know a thing about marriage.
   >
   > I do know I think it's much easier not to stay married.

FAMILY COMMUNICATION NETWORKS

"Message paths indicate much about family relationships." So claim Kathleen Galvin and Bernard Brommel in their book *Family Communication: Cohesion and Change*. The following selection from this book describes four types of message paths, or communication networks, found in family systems. Which ones have you seen operating within your own family system?

☐

To become aware of networks, observe the usual flow of verbal exchanges between members of a family. Who talks to whom about what? This processing of communication may be horizontal or vertical and take one of several forms: a chain, Y, wheel, or all-channel. Message paths indicate much about family relationships.

"There are four girls in our family, and we have a very set pattern for requesting things from our mother or father. Gina tells Angela, who tells Celeste; Celeste tells me, and I talk to Mom. Usually, things stop there, because she makes most of the decisions.

If it is something really important, she will discuss it with Dad and tell me their decision. Then I relay the message down the line."

The previous example demonstrates the *chain network*. It has a hierarchy built into it in that messages proceed up through the links or down from an authority source. Quite often, a father or mother controls the chain network and passes out orders to children. For example, in male-dominated families, the father may control the flow of messages on vital family issues. As in all of these networks, there are times when the chain has definite advantages. All busy families tend to rely on a chain network when certain members cannot spend much time together.

Sometimes, chains keep certain family members separated. If Annemarie always avoids dealing with her stepfather by communicating all her desires or concerns through her mother, she will remain very distant from him. People may obey the rules about who you cannot talk to directly about a subject by using a chain network. In this type of network, there can be a two-way exchange of information between all except the end members, who have only one member with whom to communicate.

> Human beings only grow and change, gain satisfactions and learn, in interaction with others. Communication is vital to the development of a self. It is the essence of existence.
> **GISELA KONOPKA**

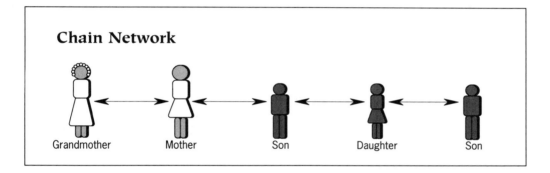

Chain Network

Grandmother — Mother — Son — Daughter — Son

In the *Y network*, messages are channeled through one person to one or more other family members. In blended families with a new stepparent, the biological parent may consciously or unconsciously set up a Y network separating the stepparent from the children. For example, such families may have a rule that only the biological parent can discipline the children.

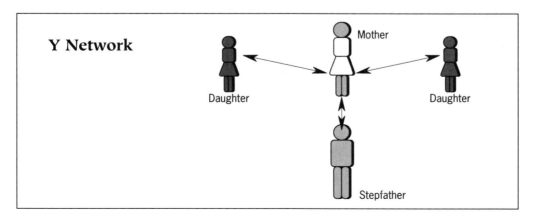

Y Network

Daughter — Mother — Daughter — Stepfather

The *wheel network* depends upon one family member to channel all messages to other members. It can be quite autocratic if the control figure in the network operates that way. He or she can filter and adapt messages positively or negatively or enforce the rule about how things are said as they pass through the network. He or she can balance tensions in the family system effectively or ineffectively. The central individual's function may result in dominance or exhaustion. Since only one person communicates with all the others, this person becomes critical to the ongoing family functioning. When the communication load is heavy and concentrated, as it can be when all family members want to get off to work or school, the talents and patience of the family member in the wheel network can be severely taxed. In some families, the central member of the wheel network can be quite nurturing and effective in holding a family together.

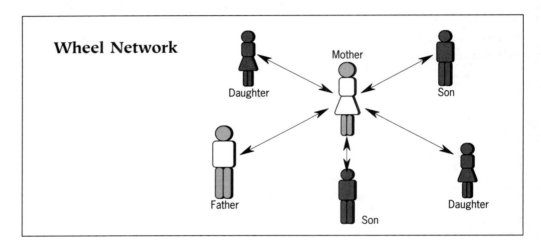

"My mother was the hub of the wheel in our family. When we were children, we expected her to settle our problems with other family members. She always knew what everyone was doing and how they felt. When we left home, each of us always let Mom know what we were doing and continued to use her for a sounding board. We felt almost compelled to write or telephone once a week. Mom digested the family news and told my brothers and sisters what each of us was doing. For several years after her death, we children had little contact except occasionally with our father. Now, seven years later, we have formed a new subsystem in which four of us stay in contact with each other. One sister, Mary Alice, is the new hub."

Messages in the chain, Y, and wheel networks are filtered and so can become distorted as they pass from one person to another. A family member can selectively change parts of a message he or she dislikes. This may help to defuse some family conflicts, but misinformation could escalate others.

The *all-channel network* provides two-way exchange between or among all family members. Communication flows in all directions, and effective decisions can be made because all members have an equal chance to discuss family issues and respond to them. This network provides for the maximum use of feedback. All interaction can be direct and transactional. No family member serves as a "go-between," and each participates freely in the process of sharing information or deciding issues. Yet, if the rules say that certain subjects should not be raised, access will have little effect. Although this network allows equal participation, it can be the most disorganized and chaotic, since messages flow in all directions. Each family member may compete for "air time" to ventilate his or her views.

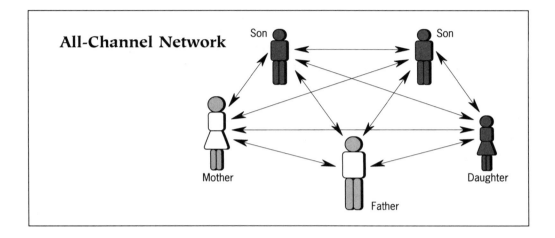

Network Variations. Other networks are possible in families, including combinations under certain circumstances. The ends of the chain may link forming a circle; chains may lead toward the central figure in the wheel. Most families use a variety of networks as they progress through daily life. Special issues arise that may cause a family to change the usual network patterns and adopt new ones to solve the issue. In daily life for example, a family may operate essentially in the chain and wheel networks, but when vacations are planned, the network used is all-channel.

The definition of networks includes the possibility that significant others outside the immediate family may have an influence upon the communication patterns within it if the boundaries are permeable. A *significant other* is a person who has an intimate relationship with one or more of the family members. This may be a grandparent, aunt or uncle, close family friend, lover, or fiancé of one of the children. In some cultures, godparents or old family friends are included in the network. The family member who has ties to a significant other outside the family may very well make decisions within the network that were determined by this relationship. When children leave home and form their own family networks, a parent may remain a significant other and influence the operation of the new network. Problems with in-laws arise often because the networks are intertwined and boundaries are not established.

Family networks tend to change over time. As children grow up and increasingly take over the direction of their own lives, adaptive families often move from the chain or wheel network to the all-channel. The wheel and chain networks facilitate order and discipline but may no longer be needed when children become autonomous and capable of directing their own decision making. Parents may signal their recognition of these changes by permitting more issues to be discussed via an all-

Communication is the magic wand that can transform an average relationship into a wondrous and grand marriage.

HARVEY L. RUBEN

channel network. The loss of a member can send the system into chaos. When a key member dies or leaves, entire systems may fragment. After a divorce, family members must establish new networks, often involving additional members, in order to maintain certain types of contact. . . .

Because each family functions within the larger ecosystem, it must involve itself with a wide variety of social system networks, both informal and formal. For many families, the informal networks created by the community or friends provide support and comfort in crises. For example, families experiencing divorce or remarriage report a high need for community and friend support. Such informal networks also provide valuable information and feedback to a family. In addition, family members become involved in formal networks created by educational, religious, and health institutions. Members must exchange information with representatives of these institutions in order to survive in our interdependent society.

Thus, networks serve a very important function within families. They determine who talks to whom, who is included or excluded, who gets full or partial information, and who controls certain information. Yet, the rules for what, how, and to whom to communicate exist within each style of network.

From *Family Communication: Cohesion and Change,* 2/e
by Kathleen M. Galvin and Bernard J. Brommell.
Copyright ©1986, 1982 by Scott, Foresman and Company, pp. 57-62.
Reprinted by permission.

1. List the advantages and the disadvantages of each family communication network described by the authors.

2. Refer to the characteristics of healthy family systems outlined in a previous reading. Discuss how each characteristic influences the four types of communication networks.

3. "Networks and rules have mutual influence—rules may dictate the use of certain networks; networks create certain rule patterns" (Galvin and Brommel). Illustrate this mutual influence in a family situation.

4. Using a real or fictional family, describe the changes that may occur in communication networks at different life cycle stages or at the time of a family crisis.

5. What may be some probable effects of gender inequality on family communication networks?

POWER IN THE FAMILY

Power struggle, power differential, power base, power inequality, balance of power. These and other terms elicit strong emotional reactions when relationships are discussed. Consider the emotions surrounding the relationship described in this excerpt from *The Tree of Life* by Fredelle Maynard. The second selection, from *Reconstructing the Canadian Family: Feminist Perspectives* by Nancy Mandell and Ann Duffy, examines power inequalities in family relationships. Is it true that "power dynamics may be so deeply buried that the participants themselves are unaware of them"?

I remained in my marriage for a quarter of a century, until 1973. By then . . . I had an established career as educational consultant and writer. The course of Max's life—emotionally, physically, professionally—was down. Depressed and desperate, he was drowning in drink; I assumed, as I had for years, the martyr stance, a woman struggling to keep a self-destructive man from ruin.

The first challenge to this flattering view of my own role came when, after my marriage ended, I consulted a therapist. I needed help in dealing with my bitterness and rage. I hoped for a deeper understanding of what had gone wrong. Certainly I expected sympathy. The therapist listened to my indictment of Max: his drunkenness, his irresponsibility, his grandiose pretensions, his childlike egocentricity. "You stayed 25 years?" he said at last. "Well. You must have been getting something out of it."

Of course, the therapist was right. No woman puts up with such treatment unless, beneath the obvious cost, there's a payoff. I used to tell myself that I stayed because I loved Max. Because I wanted the children to have two parents. Because I hadn't the money to pick up and go. Beneath all such real considerations, the more profound reality, the ultimate payoff, was power. I controlled the money. The children were mine. I chose the house and everything in it. Always, I enjoyed the position of moral superiority that comes from living with an alcoholic. Max drank, ignored obligations, wasted our small substance. Frugal, temperate, conscientious and cautious, I was—it became a family joke—*always right*.

Of course, this sort of power is illusory. Though I may have imagined myself in charge, Max effectively controlled me by his dependence. While he performed on the high wire, I acted as safety net. I covered up his delinquencies, catered to his moods, accepted restrictions on my own life so that I might be available for his. Power? I carried a big stick and danced to his tune.

From *The Tree of Life* by Fredelle Maynard, pp. 169-170.
Copyright © Fredelle Maynard, 1988.
Reprinted by permission of Penguin Books Canada Limited.

Power in family relations may be expressed in a subtle and indirect manner. Without arguments or disputes, simply by acting out their prescribed roles, husbands and wives may create and sustain a family reality in which the men are more likely than the women to "get their way," to have their needs and desires respected, and to be personally benefited. Power inequality between men and women is embedded in the normative structures of family life.

For generations, agents of socialization have urged women to accommodate and comply. Canadian women's magazines have long cautioned their readers to be glad, whenever necessary, "to give more than your share" (Killoran 1984, 419). Conversely, many men have been socialized to expect such compliance and accommodation. Luxton finds in her study of Flin Flon housewives that being a "good wife" often means "doing things his way" (1980, 50). The wife's part in the marriage is to be cautious and not to upset the balance of the relationship by pushing beyond "what their men will tolerate" (Rubin 1979, 152). Good wives do not need to be controlled by their husbands; they are controlled by a lifetime of appropriate gender socialization. Without overt struggle, the wife's subordination is written into the marriage script.

As a result, the power dynamics may be so deeply buried that the participants themselves are unaware of them. Lillian Rubin interviewed one such couple. The wife became unintentionally pregnant and wanted an abortion. The husband informed his wife that it was her decision, adding, however, that if she had an abortion he would never agree to another child. The wife decided to have the baby: "It was a hard choice, but it was mine" (Rubin 1976, 98). Neither partner acknowledged that the husband had defined the situation in such a way that the wife could not make any other decision.

This undercurrent of indirect power in family relations may also be found in patterns of communication. Spousal inequality is acted out, for example, in the conversational styles of men and women. Research indicates that women do most of the conversational work in a marriage—trying to get conversations going by asking questions and expressing interest when their male partners speak. Men, in contrast, do much less conversational work and exercise more control over their conversations—by offering minimal responses ("uh-huh") and more frequently establishing "successful" topics. Gender-based conversational norms set the stage for inequality. When they are not otherwise needed, women are expected to sit and "be a good listener." When there are silences or when the conversation slows down, women's role is to talk a lot (Fishman 1982, 179).

In short, power colours family life not only in terms of who makes decisions and who uses force, but also in terms of the basic parameters of family interaction. Research into both these direct and indirect expressions of power suggests that, in general, it is men who continue to wield power in the family. Research also indicates, however, that within this general pattern there are many shades and subtleties.

Power relations between husbands and wives vary considerably depending on the cultural context, historical and economic factors, region, social class and life-

> One of the outstanding features of this age is the number of intelligent women who do not marry. I have talked to hundreds of these fine, alert and very capable women in business, the professions, and the arts, and their reason was the same as mine: THE PERSON could not be subjected.
>
> AGNES MACPHAIL

stage. For example, the normative structure of the family varies significantly from one culture to another. In societies with patriarchal norms (such as India and parts of Africa) the husband is expected to dominate, regardless of the wife's resources in terms of education and income. In modified patriarchal societies (such as Japan, Greece, Turkey, and Yugoslavia) husbands, particularly well-educated men who have been more exposed to the new egalitarian norms, accept a more equal division of family power (Rodman, 1972). There is recent research which indicates that cross-cultural variations in customs of descent and residence also affect power relations in the family. In matrilineal/matrilocal societies, women tend to have more domestic power. Presumably her kin network and continued residence amongst kin members provides the woman with a valuable support system in the event of family dispute. Woman in patrilocal/patrilineal societies have significantly less power (Warner, Lee, and Lee 1986).

> Power means not having to raise your voice.
> GEORGE WILL

Women in patriarchal societies are not, however, always passive and power-less participants in family life (Ramu 1988). Although women's strategies and actions may differ from men's, and men may ultimately dominate social and family life, women do not necessarily simply acquiesce. Anthropologist Sharon Tiffany (1979), for example, cites the case of a woman in Papua, New Guinea, who opposed her husband's decision to take a second wife. Through the use of quarreling, public humiliation and threats, the wife succeeded in forcing her husband to change his mind. At one point she climbed on top of the family hut and through a hole in the thatch roof urinated on her husband, the second wife, and assembled guests. Tiffany suggests that women in many cultures successfully mobilize their own expressions of power, "manipulation, bluff, influence, gossip, possession, illness, threats of ritual pollution, witchcraft, sorcery, or, suicide" (434). Family power dynamics in patriarchal as well as egalitarian families may be more complex and subtle than generally assumed.

Power relations also vary depending upon historical and economic factors. Certain historical events, such as war, dramatically alter family life. Men go off to war, wives become titular head of the family and, often, wives and daughters acquire a more prominent role in the labour force (Pierson 1986). Even in the absence of crisis, there are considerable historical variations in family life.

Various accounts suggest that the "frontier family" that typified early Canadian history was relatively egalitarian. As Eichler (1981) points out, this type of family was characterized by symmetrical dependency. Husband and wife were mutually dependent for survival, status and riches. While a wife would have been hard-pressed to survive without her husband's co-operation and contributions, this was equally true of the husband. In contrast, in the contemporary breadwinner-house-wife family, there is asymmetrical dependency. While the wife depends on the husband for food, shelter and clothing, the husband can, if necessary, purchase replacements for his wife's services. Since she needs him more than he needs her, he probably has more power in family relations.

There are, in addition, significant regional differences in the family power dynamics. Farm wives in Saskatchewan, Ontario, and Prince Edward Island are likely to be more over-worked and isolated than their urban counterparts (Nett 1979,

69-70; Cebotarev, Blacklock, and McIsaac 1986). Similarly, Anglophones hold more egalitarian views of marriage than Francophones, and Francophones are more egalitarian in their views of the wife's role (right to employment, household responsibilities) than Anglophones (Hobart 1973).

Cutting through these regional and cultural variations, there are important social class differences in family power relations. Some research suggests that husband-dominance tends to be more prevalent in upper-class and lower-class families while middle-class families tend to be somewhat more egalitarian (Brinkerhoff and Lupri 1983, 207; Ostrander 1980, 37; Seeley, Sim, and Loosley 1956, 140). The mechanics of family power may also differ from class to class. While the upper-class husband simply transposes his public status and prestige to the family setting, the working-class husband may insist on power in the family because he lacks it in the public domain. For the middle-class professional, a (publicly) egalitarian marriage may be part of the respectable front he is required to maintain in his work and in his community (Rubin 1976; Smith 1973). Further, the meaning of certain powers may differ depending on the class context. Women tend to manage the money in working-class families while men manage the money in professional middle-class families. However, in the typical working-class family there are few real decisions to be made since the money is already allotted to monthly expenses and there is little left over to manage. In contrast, in the (reportedly) more egalitarian middle-class home, money management is often an important task that generally belongs to the husband (Rubin 1976: 106-112).

Power dynamics in the family also vary over time. Despite the massive movement of women into the paid labour force, the birth of children still signals the withdrawal of many women into the home. Two years after having given birth, on average 40% of previously employed women have not returned to paid employment (Waite, Haggstrom, and Kanouse 1985, 270). This period of increased economic and social dependency results in a relative loss in marital power (Gillespie 1971). Some 60% to 70% of mothers experience emotional problems after birth. According to Harriet Rosenberg's (1987) interviews with mothers in Toronto, Vancouver and New York, this is a particularly stressful time for women because high demands on them are coupled with low levels of control over the family situation. Giving up waged work generally results in economic dependence and social isolation. Staying in the job often means overwork and guilt.

This pattern is often reversed when the husband retires or becomes jobless. The resource on which his public and familial status rested is diminished, and with it his power in the family (Brinkerhoff and Lupri 1983, 208). Similarly, as her husband ages or becomes disabled, the wife may become the more powerful member of the couple (Gee and Kimball 1987, 89).

Lastly, the surrounding economic context directly affects family relations. The Nova Scotia fishing community studied by Pat Connelly and Martha MacDonald (1986) underwent important economic changes—war, depression, prosperity—in the past 100 years. With these shifts came changes in family life. When men were unemployed or employed far away from home (fishing, the military), wives might enjoy greater domestic autonomy along with heavier family responsibilities. When

> We're half in and half out of a new time, where we are shifting away from a male ideology, based on dominance and aggression, to female values with more of an emphasis on communication and cooperation.
>
> SHERE HITE

paid work for women became available in the local economy, women could enjoy some measure of economic independence. More generally, changes in the national and world economy—the increased demand for women workers, the availability of consumer goods—help to establish the basic parameters of contemporary family relations.

Power relations in the family are, in short, more complex, varied, subtle and changing than appreciated by either 1960s feminists or Parsonian functionalists. The contemporary family does not fit neatly into either a male-dominated or egalitarian model. In general, it is men who have more 'say' in the family, who perform fewer undesirable or onerous chores, and who set the tone for family interaction. However, this male domination is conditioned by cultural, historical, class, life-cycle, and socio-economic factors. These complexities must be examined if power in the family is to be fully understood. In particular, as Engels pointed out long ago, the connection between family power relations and the surrounding social and economic conditions must be fully explored. The private troubles of family life are often rooted in public issues—unemployment, lack of child care, popularization of violence, and erosion of the community. The costs of family inequality to the individual are, frequently, also costs to the society at large.

From *Reconstructing The Canadian Family: Feminist Perspectives*
by Nancy Mandell and Ann Duffy
(Toronto: Butterworths, 1988), pp. 124-128.

BIBLIOGRAPHY

Brinkerhoff, Merlin B., and Eugen Lupri, "Conjugal Power and Family Relationships: Some Theoretical and Methodological Issues," *The Canadian Family*, edited by K. Ishwaram, 202-219. Toronto: Gage Publishing Ltd., 1983.

Cebotarev, N., W.M. Blacklock, and L. McIsaac, "Farm Women's Work Patterns," *Atlantis* 11 (Spring): 1-22, 1986.

Connelly, Patricia and Martha MacDonald, "Women's Work: Domestic and Wage Labour in a Nova Scotia Community," *The Politics of Diversity: Feminism, Marxism and Nationalism*, edited by Roberta Hamilton and Michele Barrett, 35-80. Montreal: Book Center Inc., 1986.

Eichler, Margrit, "Women as Personal Dependents," *Women in Canada*, edited by Marylee Stephenson, 36-55. Toronto: New Press, 1973.

Eichler, Margrit, "Power, Dependency, Love and the Sexual Division of Labour," *Women's Studies International Quarterly* 4 (No. 2): 201-219, 1981.

Fishman, Pamela, "Interaction: The Work Woman Do," *Women and Work,* edited by Rachel Kahn-Hut, Arlene Kaplan Daniels and Richard Colvard, 170-180. New York: Oxford University Press, 1982.

Gee, Ellen and Meredith M. Kimball, *Women and Aging.* Toronto: Butterworths, 1987.

Gillespie, Dair, "Who Has the Power? The Marital Struggle," *Journal of Marriage and the Family* 33 (August): 445-588, 1971.

Hobart, Charles W., "Egalitarianism after Marriage," *Women in Canada*, edited by Marylee Stephenson, 138-156. Toronto: New Press, 1973.

Killoran, M. Maureen, "The Management of Tension: A Case Study of Chatelaine Magazine 1939-80," *Journal of Comparative Family Studies* 15 (Autumn): 407-426, 1984.

Nett, Emily, "Marriage and the Family: Organization and Interaction," *Courtship, Marriage and the Family in Canada*, edited by G.N. Ramu, 59-77. Toronto: Macmillan Company Ltd., 1979.

Ostrander, Susan A., "Upper Class Women: The Feminine Side of Privilege," *Qualitative Sociology* 3 (Spring): 23-44, 1980.

Pierson, Ruth Roach, "Women's Emancipation and the Recruitment of Women into the War Effort," *The Politics of Diversity*, edited by Roberta Hamilton and Michele Barrett, 101-135. Montreal: Book Centre Inc., 1986.

Ramu, G.N., "Marital Roles and Power: Perceptions and Reality in the Urban Setting," *Journal of Comparative Family Studies* 19 (Summer): 207-227, 1988.

Rodman, Hyman, "Marital Power and the Theory of Resources in Cultural Context," *Journal of Comparative Family Studies* 3 (Spring): 50-69, 1972.

Rosenberg, Harriet, "Motherwork, Stress, and Depression: The Costs of Privatized Social Reproduction," *Feminism and Political Economy: Women's Work, Women's Struggles*, edited by Heather Jon Maroney and Meg Luxton, 181-196. Toronto: Methuen, 1987.

Rubin, Lillian, *World of Pain: Life in the Working-Class Family*. New York: Basic Books, Inc., 1976.

Rubin, Lillian, *Women of a Certain Age: The Midlife Search for Self*. New York: Harper Colophon books, 1979.

Seeley, John R., R. Alexander Sim, and E.W. Loosley, *Crestwood Heights: A Study of the Culture of Suburban Life*. Toronto: University of Toronto Press, 1956.

Smith, Dorothy, "Women, the Family and Corporate Capitalism," *Women in Canada*, edited by Marylee Stephenson, 2-35. Toronto: New Press, 1973.

Tiffany, Sharon W., "Women, Power, and the Anthropology of Politics: A Review," *International Journal of Women's Studies* 2 (No. 5): 430-442, 1979.

Waite, Linda J., Gus W. Haggstrom, and David E. Kanouse, "Changes in the Employment Activities of New Parents," *American Sociological Review* 50 (April): 263-272, 1985.

Warner, Rebecca L., Gary R. Lee, and Janet Lee, "Social Organization, Spousal Resources, and Marital Power: A Cross-Cultural Study," *Journal of Marriage and the Family* 48 (February): 121-128, 1986.

1. Like many of us, Fredelle Maynard thought power was a personal characteristic. The sudden realization that "I carried a big stick and danced to his tune" gave power an entirely different dimension—that of the system. Locate or create a systems definition for the term power.

2. Provide evidence from the selections to support or refute the idea that no one can control another unless the other permits it.

3. Describe the parallels between covert rules and indirect power.

4. Spousal power relations vary with cultural context, historical factors, economic factors, region, social class, and life stage. Select examples from the reading by Mandell and Duffy to illustrate these variations.

5. Develop a series of guidelines to promote power equality between the genders for childless couples, parents of young children, and parents of teenagers.

6. The second reading concludes with the statement, "The costs of family inequality to the individual are, frequently, also costs to the society at large." What do you think those costs might be?

FAMILY DECISION-MAKING

Corporate consultant John D. Arnold claims that "the decision-making process begins with the perception of a gap. Something is wrong and needs to be corrected, something is threatening and needs to be prevented, something is inviting and needs to be accepted, something is needed and needs to be provided." Making a decision narrows or closes the gap, and the result is change. George Blondin closed the gap when he gave up the Dene way of life for his children.

☐

When I got sick, the doctor thought I had kidney trouble and decided he would have to send me "out" to Edmonton. I was sad to leave my wife and four small children, and I grew more worried when the doctor at Camsell Hospital in Edmonton told me I had tuberculosis. I would have to stay there for at least two years, he said.

After I had spent nine months in hospital, they let me go home. I had to take it easy for at least a year. After six months, I was strong enough to hunt and fish, and by fall, I could go trapping. But I couldn't cut wood, because I couldn't lift heavy things.

Then my wife got tuberculosis, and she had to go to Camsell Hospital as well. They had found a better treatment by that time. When Indian Affairs came to visit us, I asked if there were any boarding schools I could send my children to. I sent the two girls to Fort Providence.

I decided I couldn't live the old kind of life any more, moving around the country in cold weather. I'd already lost my oldest boy. I needed to live near a doctor, and I thought maybe I could live the same way as the white people did. I decided to go to Yellowknife, even though it was far away. Changing my way of life wouldn't be easy, but I had to do it for my children.

When I told my father what I wanted to do, he flew into a rage. "That's all the teaching your grandfather and I gave you? You're going to throw it aside and live the other way?" I said that Dene would have to change their way of life sooner or later, because the world around them was changing all the time. By then, the federal government had set up schools, and that was the real start of the change. If parents were travelling in the bush, how would their children get properly educated?

My father was stubborn, and I couldn't convince him with that kind of talk. But I was stubborn too. . . . I told him, "My mother had fifteen children and fourteen of them died in the bush. I don't want that to happen to my children. I will go somewhere where I can have them near me, with a hospital also nearby, and get a job for maybe twenty years. Later I can go back to the bush."

My father didn't say anything for a long time. Finally, he asked, "Where are you going?" I told him the closest big town was Yellowknife, 480 kilometres away, and that was where I would go.

My wife came back from Edmonton in the fall. In the spring, I sold everything I could and gave the rest to my dad. I shipped most our stuff to Yellowknife on the barge, and we took a plane.

It was hard, being new in a town that size. I had to get a job right away. I got one in a sawmill on the Slave River and worked there until Christmas. Then I went back to Yellowknife. That year, there were lots of claims being staked around Pine Point. My dad came in from Great Bear Lake by dog team, and a mining company asked us to stake for them. We worked as a team for a month and a half and made a lot of money.

When it got warm, I got a contract to cut 750 cords of wood at a new development north of Yellowknife called Ray Rock mine. I got people to cut wood for me and made good money on the job. In the spring of 1956, I got a job at Giant Yellowknife gold mine and worked for straight wages—for someone else—for the first time.

In the early days, some small companies had bribed native people with low wages and whiskey, so that they could use their dog teams to stake claims and move camp cheaply. When Yellowknife got larger, these people didn't need Dene anymore, and they didn't want anything to do with them.

In the summer, Dene were hired by the commercial fishing outfits to fish for them in their own canoes. But Dene living in town generally couldn't get jobs, and it was hard to get welfare. Some Dene moved to the bush in the fall, came back for Christmas, and then went on their spring hunt as they had always done. But they found it hard, because there were so many new things to spend money on: taxis, buses, shows, cafés, alcohol.

Changing my way of life was just as hard for me as it was for other Dene. When I had lived at Great Bear Lake, life was simple. My elders had taught me to share; cash money hadn't meant much to me. In Yellowknife, I didn't know the value of money and didn't know how to save. There were so many new things I had to buy. I worked for $1.49 an hour, and I had to pay for our power, phone, rent, oil, and groceries.

I lived in the slum area. I shared things, so there were many Dene coming to the house and I had to feed them. I guess I couldn't change. I learned too late that you cannot live two different ways of life at the same time.

That's why all my children live only one way, the non-Dene way. I made sure that all my kids went to school every day. I never taught them to hunt or to work the Dene way. Once you get into working for wages, it's routine and you do the same thing day after day.

One's philosophy is not best expressed in words, it is expressed in the choices one makes . . . in the long run, we shape our lives and we shape ourselves. The process never ends until we die. And the choices we make are ultimately our responsibility.

ELEANOR ROOSEVELT

I'd been working for the mine for fourteen years when my wife got sick with cancer of the blood. After four years in and out of hospital, Julie died. After I lost her, I couldn't work in the mine any more. My children were adults, able to look after themselves, so I decided to go back to Franklin to hunt and trap, like I used to do.

Some Dene say the earth is our body. Others say the land is like a big warehouse. In the old days, they thought things would never change. But the change that came was so strong that it changed the Dene way of life. It was change that went its own way without any control.

The government started the change in order to help people. But the problems have gotten bigger and bigger. Education has meant that children don't listen to their parents. Dene don't hunt and trap very well any more. They live in communities, so they need jobs to make money. But there aren't many jobs.

The government isn't to be blamed for everything that changed people's lives. All kinds of things worked together to change the Dene. But the government started the change.

> What is not possible is not to choose, but I ought to know that if I do not choose, I am still choosing.
>
> JEAN-PAUL SARTRE

From *When the World Was New: Stories of the Sahtu Dene* by George Blondin. Published by Outcrop the Northern Publishers, Yellowknife NWT, 1990.

1. Families do not make decisions in a vacuum. Discuss how outside systems altered the life course of the Blondin family.

2. What are the differences between family decision-making and decision-making in a small group setting? Account for the differences.

3. What do you consider to be the most important decision your family has ever made? How was it made? How were you involved in the process? In what ways was each family member involved? Why? Speculate on the most important decisions you will likely make in your lifetime. Anticipate the many factors that could be involved. What roles do you imagine your family might play in the process?

4. Select one of the decisions identified above. Prepare a discussion paper on how that decision affected or could affect each family system characteristic discussed in Fine's essay.

5. While many factors affect family decision-making, consider the following five: coalitions and alliances within the family, resources of individual family members, gender roles, outside influences, and past successes or failures in decision-making. Select illustrations of each of these factors from the reading. How do these factors affect all families in their decision-making?

FUNCTIONS AND ROLES

Every society expects family systems to carry out prescribed functions. In the first selection, Froma Walsh outlines five areas of necessary family functions, and the related aspects of role allocation and responsibility. Following this are a series of excerpts from Charlene Gannagé's book *Double Day Double Bind*. The women interviewed here are all too familiar with the exhausting work of fulfilling domestic roles while holding down a paying job.

☐

"Family roles" are defined as the repetitive patterns of behavior by which family members fulfill family functions. There are some functions that all families have to deal with repeatedly in order to maintain an effective and healthy system. We identify five such necessary family functions, and they are the basis for necessary family roles. Each of these areas subsumes a number of tasks and functions.

1. Provision of resources. This area includes those tasks and functions associated with providing money, food, clothing, and shelter.

2. Nurturance and support. This involves the provision of comfort, warmth, reassurance, and support for family members.

3. Adult sexual gratification. Both husbands and wives must personally find satisfaction within the sexual relationship and also feel that they can satisfy their partners sexually. Affective issues are therefore prominent. A reasonable level of sexual activity is generally required. It has been our experience that in some instances, however, both partners may express satisfaction with little or no activity.

4. Personal development. This includes those tasks and functions necessary to support family members in developing skills for personal achievement. Included are tasks relating to the physical, emotional, educational, and social development of the children, and those relating to the career, avocational, and social development of the adults.

5. Maintenance and management of the family system. This area includes a variety of functions:
   a. Decision-making functions include leadership, major decision making, and the question of final decisions when there is no agreement. In general, these functions should reside at the parental level. . . .
   b. Boundary and membership functions include functions and tasks concerned with extended families, friends, neighbors, the taking in of boarders, family size, and dealings with external institutions and agencies.

c. Behavior control functions include disciplining of children and the maintenance of standards and rules for the adult family members.

d. Household finance functions include the tasks of dealing with monthly bills, banking, income tax, and household money handling.

e. Health-related functions include making appointments, identifying appropriate health problems, and maintaining compliance with health prescriptions.

We consider two additional aspects of role functioning: "role allocation" and "role accountability."

1. Role allocation is concerned with the family's pattern in assigning roles and it includes a number of issues. Does the person assigned a task or function have the power and skill necessary to carry it out? Is the assignment done clearly and explicitly? Can reassignment take place easily? Are tasks distributed and allocated to the satisfaction of family members?

2. Role accountability looks at the procedures in the family for making sure that functions are fulfilled. This includes the presence of a sense of responsibility in family members and the existence of monitoring and corrective mechanisms.

At the healthy end of this dimension, all necessary family functions are fulfilled. Allocation is reasonable and does not overburden one or more members. Accountability is clear.

From *Normal Family Processes* by Froma Walsh
(New York: The Guilford Press, 1985), pp. 118, 124.

> Even the most egalitarian marriages aren't 50/50; they're 2/98 this week, and 98/2 next week or next year. . . . For ultimately, 50/50 is a matter of spirit, flexibility and give and take—whether in dishwashing, decision-making, child tending or any other activity of love.
>
> CAROL TAVRIS

□

THERESA GREEN: Of course, it was harder. I mean you weren't just sitting home and taking care of your children and planning your meals. You were going out to work and taking care of the children and tending to meals. Everything. I think a woman has two jobs always. A job outside and a job at home . . . I was tired. You knew these things had to be done and you took it into your [stride]. . . .

GRACE CAMPISI: I used to do the same in Italy. The lady stay home, clean the house and make everything so good at home. When the husband come, he got everything so ready to eat, he eat. Maybe he dress nice and go some place. And the lady stay [home] to clean, to look at the kids. That's it . . . I can't say anything because this is my style . . . my style, anyway [she laughs] I cannot say [to him] you wash the dishes. No . . . He doesn't know [how to] cook, he never cook. . . .

SHEILA GLABER: Sometimes I was angry. But man are not [supposed to do housework], especially European man. Canadian are more modern, they help out their wives, I think . . . But he used to help me. Sure he used to go down fix things on the machine. Like on Sunday—fix for me . . . sew up things. He used to do the driving. He was a good man. And like dishes, some men they dry the dishes. I didn't want him to dry. I didn't want him around—the kitchen is too small. And cleaning I used to do mostly myself . . . weekends. I got up Sunday morning. Laundry, I did Friday night once in two weeks. . . .

GRACE CAMPISI: I spend my weekend a little bit to clean, to wash, to press everything, to clean the backyard, the front, everything. Somebody tell me "You want to come to the cottage this weekend?" I say "No." She say "Why?" I say, "Because I am so busy [at] home. I want to make everything so clean [at] home. Saturday, my daughter, she come. She got a small baby. She leave at my house on Saturday. She's a hairdresser. She work Saturday, so I do everything when the baby come home she make me so busy. I cook . . . sometime she bring the baby Friday night . . . Come the night, I am so tired—my legs—I can't work anymore because I work all the day. Sunday the same. I want to provide everything because Monday, start again to go to work. I don't want to leave everything. I want to fix everything. I kill myself sometimes. Maybe when I die, I relax. When I die, I finish everything. . . .

RUTH DOMANSKI: I used to take off a couple of hours to do shopping. So I bring home the shopping. Washing was done on Sunday. Saturday I worked only ten hours, Sundays I worked twelve hours. (The rest of the week was sixteen hours.) In those hours I did everything. Put the menu on. Bought the food. I did the washing, the children did the ironing. And the cleaning . . . all at night . . . .

All on two days of the week, Saturdays and Sundays. That's why I say I give up my own life—my social life . . . And like I said, my daughter helped me a lot. Everyday work she did after school. She came home, she saw dinner is prepared. Dinner—we had weiners and beans, and hamburgers and potatoes . . . I'll always prepared for the night before and I leave a note what's for supper. She used to come home and do it.

> Many couples . . . would accept any division of household chores . . . if they could just restore their relationship.
>
> PHILIP BLUMSTEIN

THERESA GREEN: I think it's just the usual when any mother works. You get up and you have your breakfast together. And you're rushing out to work and the children go to school. And you come back and you're cooking supper and tidying up and maybe preparing something for the following night . . . Doing your laundry at night. With family you have to do it. It's not like being on my own and working and I can wash when I feel like it. You have to have a routine. . . .

DONNA JUKUBENAITE: I wake up six o'clock. Formula I always make in the evening and put in bottles in the fridge. And when I wake up six o'clock, wash myself and make coffee . . . for husband . . . Then baby wakes up. Wash him with wet cloth. Change him. Put everything in a carriage and take to my girlfriend's house . . . and [her] mother looks after the two babies. I make formula. I give everything, food, diapers, everything what [she] needs 'til I . . . pick up my baby and I come home. Make supper . . . my husband helps lots in the kitchen. He loves cooking . . . And I feed the baby after that we play little bit with the baby. . . . Prepare him for bed. After that wash diapers. Ironing. I put him seven o'clock or six o'clock in bed. He wakes up eleven o'clock. I give him last feeding and he sleeps 'til next morning.

From *Double Day Double Bind: Women Garment Workers* by Charlene Gannagé
(Toronto: The Women's Press, 1986), pp. 53-58.

1. Compare the family functions described by Walsh with those from other sources. What similarities and differences do you find? Account for the differences.

2. Analyze the vignettes for indications of conscious role allocation and accountability. In what ways have cultural and socio-economic factors affected the maintenance and management roles in these family systems?

3. Comment on ideal versus real role allocations in families.

4. Analyze a case study or interview a family where the mother has recently re-entered the labour force on a full-time basis. Focus your analysis or interview on role allocation, role reassignment, role accountability, role conflict, and role sharing. Summarize your findings and share them with others in your class.

5. React to the following statements:

    > Recent research indicates that housework is a major area of discord in families, often creating problems more difficult to resolve than issues relating to money, sex, or relatives.

    > The potential for conflict between domestic responsibilities and full-time employment is often so great that many women are forced to choose between holding a job and having a family.

FAMILY SUPPORT SYSTEMS

The 1980s saw a dramatic development in our understanding and creation of family support programs. Dr. Edward Zigler, professor of psychology at Yale University, termed the '80s "the decade of family support." Robert Glossop and James Anglin, authors of the following essay, call for an appreciation of and commitment to helping relationships that are truly supportive of the family system.

W hile the search for a fixed and universally applicable definition of the family has remained constant, such a definition has itself always proven elusive.

Today, one can no longer speak without hesitation, if at all, of the family. On the contrary, it is now customary for researchers, service providers, teachers, and other professionals to declare their interest in families. The plural designation serves to acknowledge and respect the patently evident diversity of the contemporary family forms.

☐ FAMILIES IN CONTEXT

Along with the acknowledgement of the diversity of family forms there has developed a sensitivity to the entire range of institutional and societal forces that facilitate, impede, and variously influence the capacities of family members to manage the complex facets of their family lives and to assume their associated material, educational, legal, and psychological responsibilities. Interest in the topic of the family per se has been displaced by the current interest in "family in context" as both researchers and practitioners pursue the promises of a "social ecological" or "contextual" frame of reference (Bouchard, 1980; Bouchard and Mongeau, 1982; Bronfenbrenner, 1979; Friesen, 1983; Garbarino, 1982; Keniston, 1977).

With attention now directed towards family's "total social situation and the environmental context of their lives" (Jordan, 1972, p. 45), emphasis is given to the functional relationships that exist between families and other societal institutions and systems—educational, economic, technological, political, cultural, and the like.

It is what families do, more than what they look like, that provides a basis with which to acknowledge that single-parent families, blended families, dual-wage-earning families, single-earner families, extended families, and what have you are all variations on a common familial theme. There may be a relationship, at any particular point in time, between one kind of family structure and the way in which its members will or can fulfill their familial functions. Yet, the relationship between form and function is largely contingent upon diverse factors of social organization that lie well beyond the characteristics of any specific family and which are relative to time, place, and circumstances.

Consider, for example, how today's expressed concern over the plight of lone-parent families would lead one to believe that never before had we as a society had to cope with the "problems" associated with the high incidence of lone parenthood. Lone parenting is by no means new to our society and, in fact, the current proportion of lone-parent families compared to two-parent familes falls well short of the percentages of the 1930s and '40s (Statistics Canada, 1984). In the past, lone-parents and their children remained largely invisible, supported by the families of origin to which they most frequently returned after the loss of a mate through death—in war, at childbirth, or from natural causes. Today, on the other hand, it is more common for the lone parent (who is more likely to be separated or divorced than widowed) to seek to preserve independence from parents and in-laws by relying upon the provisions of the state which are only begrudgingly sustained by the taxpayer. It is not, therefore, simply the form or structure of family that determines the living circumstances of its members or a family's capacity to fulfill its principal responsibilities; it is, rather, a broader range of factors including historically and culturally relative attitudes and practices as embodied in social and economic institutions.

Until quite recently, we had allowed ourselves to believe that the "modern" family had evolved into a specialized unit of emotional and psychological commitment, a societal institution no longer devoted to its earlier historical functions of economic production, education, health care, and welfare. But, today, the idea of family has been rediscovered and families are heralded as potential agents of health promotion; providers of care for the aged, sick, and disabled; as the principal loci of attitudinal and behavioural change; and as the first source of economic and financial security for their members.

It is not merely coincidental that the functional significance of family is being rediscovered at a time when industrial economies throughout the developed world and the welfare states that support such economies have been experiencing serious contraction. It is in these circumstances that we are invited to turn our attention, once again, to the intimate relationships people establish within their families and to see these relationships as not only emotionally, psychologically, and individually significant, but as socially, economically, and culturally significant.

Regardless of form, families share common needs and seek to fulfill common aspirations and societal expectations. There are multiple and complexly interwoven dimensions of family living that include: economic needs and obligations; emotional commitments and expectations; distributions of power and property; customary practices regarding residence; legal rights and responsibilities; rules pertaining to effective expression, sexuality, and procreation; and expectations with regard to cross-generational responsibilities for socialization and personality development as well as material and social support.

Although these dimensions of family living are common to families at different times and in different places, one must not, as Eichler (1981), reminds us, assume that these legal, procreative, socialization, sexual, residential, and economic functions of family are necessarily fulfilled congruently, concomitantly or only within the boundaries of family interaction. For instance, recent decades of social and family change involving high rates of divorce and remarriage make it impossible to safely assume that the adults who take on primary financial and legal responsibilities for a child would also necessarily assume responsibility for the emotional, social, linguistic or cognitive development of that child. Emotional sustenance and psychological support may be provided to one another by an adult and a child who do not live together. The socialization of children is now frequently a responsibility of adults who are biologically and even socially unrelated to their charges. Upon seeing a family enjoying an afternoon in a park, one cannot know (as perhaps we once did) that: the children are biologically related to one another; whether or not they live together and, if so, for how many days a week; whether or not the adults are married, used to be married, are living together or are simply friends. Just as many of our . . . assumptions about family life can no longer be taken for granted, so too must we assess critically the nature of the policies, services, and systems of support . . . which according to Pitman (1980), remain, in essence, moulded by a vision of family life more in tune with the Victorian era than the present age.

The family is not disintegrating. It's the systems that do or don't support it that are disintegrating . . . the family is working overtime to survive.

WHITE HOUSE
CONFERENCE ON
THE FAMILY

☐   FAMILY SUPPORTS

Too often, in the fields of education and social service delivery, we find ourselves struggling with the unintended consequences of a static, unitary or "monolithic" (Eichler, 1981) image of the family. Such an image may seem to serve well the needs of professionals, policy-makers, and bureaucrats for policies and programs that can be applied on a wide scale with apparently predictable and generalizable outcomes. Yet, even these objectives cannot be met by programs that fail to take account of the diversity of family structures and the diversity of family circumstances (Rappaport, Rappaport & Strelitz, 1977; Scanzoni, 1983; Sussman, 1971).

It is now well recognized that families have always been and continue to be the most powerful and pervasive source of their own support (Howell, 1975; Garbarino, 1982). It is still primarily families who do the work of: feeding, cleaning, and clothing children; teaching by example and by listening and talking; nurturance and providing materially, emotionally, and spiritually for one another. Families do not, however, carry out this time-consuming, expensive, complex, and often exhausting work by themselves. Furthermore, one must also acknowledge the recent studies of helping and social support networks indicating that members of one's own immediate or extended family are not always sources of support, but rather, can indeed be sources of considerable stress (Gottlieb, 1981). Frequently, parents turn to friends or self-help groups of various kinds (Froland, Pancoast, Chapman and Kimboko, 1981; Katz and Bender, 1976). Although families are still helping families, the sources and modes of support are evolving to accommodate changes brought about by a mobile population, rapidly shifting values, technological innovation, economic change, and social trends (Karal, 1985) that lessen the availability and/or suitability of cross-generational support within families.

A comprehensive consideration of helping services for families will need to consider the broad range of informal (non-professional) supports as well as formal (professional) supports. We have attempted to encapsulate the full spectrum of helping relationships in [the diagram below].

Spectrum of informal and formal support

Informal			Formal		
Families	**Friends & Acquaintances**	**Self-help Groups & Organizations**	**Semi-formal Helpers**	**Family Support Programs**	**Professional Helping Services**
immediate & extended-family members	friends neighbours workmates letter carriers hairdressers bartenders, etc.	group members	teachers clergy physicians lawyers, etc.		volunteers paraprofessionals counsellors social workers child care workers psychiatrists, etc.

In all advanced economies, the so-called Welfare State that has evolved as compensation for the erosion of informal family- and community-based sources of material and social support is now threatened by severe restraint. The isolation and geographic mobility of the nuclear family which has exacerbated our dependence upon the welfare, social support, health and educational services provided by the state has reached critical proportions. The crisis in caring and the rediscovery of family and community support is taking place in a context of social, economic, technological, political, and cultural changes that have been assessed by many to be as profound as those changes that ushered in the era of industrialization.

In the midst of these changes, we face the prospects of a realignment of our responsibilities and identities as workers and as parents. As the Government of Quebec (1984) has recently stated: "In the final analysis, we must strive toward a major objective: that of according as much importance to the role of persons as parents as we do to them as workers" (p. 64).

If, indeed, the future calls upon us to integrate better our working lives and our family lives, it is not only the individual who will search for meaning in new ways and new directions. Equally, those who lend support in this process—through their research, service, and teaching—will have to acknowledge the extent to which the current systems of formal support embody the assumptions of an age gone by. . . .

. . . We would suggest that simply more research will never be enough. What appears to be called for is a different form of research and inquiry than that which has been traditionally utilized in the field. Any attempt to study, or to change or to enhance people's social supports or networks must enlist their active participation (Cochran and Henderson, 1985; Cochran and Woolever, 1983). The rigid distinction between research and intervention is no longer helpful. The researcher/intervenor and other participants become fused in a process of interaction and the findings/outcomes will reflect this interaction.

The recent resurgence of interest in "action research" (Carr and Kemmis, 1983), "qualitative knowing" (Campbell, 1974), and "naturalistic inquiry" (Lincoln and Guba, 1985) indicates a growing appreciation for an approach which suggests to us that the future well-being of families will entail the creation of new patterns of societal organization based upon collectively constructed and shared understandings and actions.

From "Families and Family Support: A Reappreciation,"
by Robert Glossop and James P. Anglin,
Canadian Home Economics Journal, Vol. 36(1) Winter, pp. 4-7, 1986.

BIBLIOGRAPHY

Bouchard, C. *Perspectives écologiques de la relation parent(s)-enfant(s): des compétences parentales aux compétences environne-mentales.* Laboratoire de recherche en écologie humaine et sociale, Université du Québec à Montréal, 1980.

Bouchard, J.M., and Mongeau, J.C., *Rapport de recherche pour L'année 1979-80.* Université du Québec à Montréal, 1982.

Bronfenbrenner, U., *The Ecology of Human Development: Experiments by Nature and Design.* Cambridge, Mass.: Harvard University Press, 1979.

Campbell, D.T., "Qualitative knowing in action research," paper presented as the Kurt Lewin Memorial Address to the American Psychological Association, Northwestern University, Evanston, Illinois, September 1974.

Carr, W., & Kemmis, S., *Becoming Critical: Knowing through Action Research.* Deakin University: Deakin University Press, 1983.

Cochran, M., & Woolever, F., "Beyond the Deficit Model: The empowerment of parents with information and informal supports," I.E. Siegel & L.M. Loasa (Eds.), *Changing Families*, pp. 225-245. New York: Plenum Press, 1983.

Cochran, M., & Henderson, C.R. Jr., "Family matters: Evaluation of the parental empowerment program" (Contact No. 400-76-0150; Final Report to the National Institute of Education). Ithaca, N.Y.: The Comparative Ecology of Human Development Project, Cornell University, 1985.

Eichler, M., "The Inadequacy of the Monolithic Model of the Family," *Canadian Journal of Sociology*, 6 (3), 367-388, 1981.

Friesen, J., "An Ecological Systems Approach to Family Counselling," *Canadian Counsellor*, 17 (3), 98-104, 1983.

Froland, C., Pancoast, D.L., Chapman, N.J., & Kimboko, P.J., *Helping Networks and Human Services.* Beverly Hills, Calif.: Sage, 1981.

Garbarino, J. *Children and Families in the Social Environment.* New York: Aldine, 1982.

Gottlieb, B.H., *Social Networks and Social Support.* Beverly Hills, Calif: Sage, 1981.

Government of Quebec, "For Quebec families: A working paper on family policy."

Quebec City: Ministry of Social Affairs, 1984.

Howell, M.C., *Helping Ourselves: Families and the Human Network.* Boston: Beacon Press, 1975.

Jordan, W. *The Social Worker in Family Situations.* London: Routledge & Kegan, 1972.

Karal, P., "Transforming Relationships: Implications for Family Studies Teachers," *Canadian Home Economics Journal*, 35 (2), 66-68, 1975.

Katz, A.H., & Bender, E.I., *The Strength in Us: Self-help Groups in the Modern World.* New York: New Viewpoints, 1976.

Keniston, K., *All Our Children: The American Family Under Pressure.* New York: Harcourt, Brace, Jovanovich, 1977.

Lincoln, Y.S., & Guba, E.G, *Naturalistic Inquiry.* Beverly Hills, Calif.: Sage, 1985.

Pitman, W., "The cause of our crisis: Institutions cannot keep pace with change," *Institutions in Crisis*, pp. 161-173, 48th Geneva Park Conference of the Couchiching Institute of Public Affairs. Toronto: Yorkminster Publishing, 1980.

Rapoport, R., Rapoport, R.N., & Strelitz, Z., *Fathers, Mothers & Society: Perspectives on Parenting.* New York: Vintage Books, 1977.

Scanzoni, J., *Shaping Tomorrow's Family: Theory and Policy for the 21st Century.* Beverly Hills, Calif.: Sage, 1983.

Statistics Canada, *Canada's Lone-Parent Families.* (Cat. No. 99-933) Table 1. Ottawa: Supply and Services, 1984.

Sussman, M.B., *Themes for the 1970s*, K. Ishwaran (Ed.), *The Canadian Family: A Book of Readings*, pp. 517-527. Toronto: Holt, Rinehart and Winston, 1971.

1.   Write your own definition of the term family. Compare your definition with those of others in the class. Compose one eclectic definition that has class consensus.

2.   Using authoritative sources, locate a variety of definitions of family put forth

over a 25-year time span. Does a common thread run through them? If so, what is it? Can you discern the theoretical perspective underlying each one? What unique features are included in a systems definition of family? Explain how a definition of family has social, political, ethical, and legal implications.

3. Generate a list of the institutional and societal forces that influence the capacity of family members to manage their lives. Specify how these forces can influence, impede, and facilitate successful family functioning.

4. Defend the following statement by providing supportive evidence.

    It is convenient but ineffective to implement family support programs based on a monolithic image of family.

5. Provide evidence from objective sources to reinforce the "crisis in caring" phenomenon of the 1980s.

6. A large company has formed a committee to revise its policy manual. The committee is composed of the company president, a union employee, a non-union staff member, the manager of human relations, and a plant supervisor. The company president has publicly announced that future policies will reflect the following recommendations outlined by James Anglin in the December, 1989 issue of *Transition:* a strong commitment to family empowerment; an appreciation of the diversity of family forms; a belief in the power of personal and social support programs; a fundamental respect for the importance of the parental role.

    Divide the class into groups representative of the committee make-up. Formulate some policies that reflect the company's commitment to families.

FAMILY SYSTEMS THROUGH TIME

UNIT 2

■

OVERVIEW ESSAY

by Rheta Rosen, Ph.D.
Professor, School of Nutrition,
   Consumer and Family Studies
Ryerson Polytechnical Institute

The imagery of seasons takes many forms . . . . First, there is the idea of a *process* or *journey* from a starting point . . . to a termination point. . . . To speak of a general, human life cycle is to propose that the journey from birth to old age follows an underlying, universal pattern on which there are endless cultural and individual variations. . . . But as long as the journey continues, it follows the basic sequence. . . .

Second, there is the idea of *seasons:* a series of periods or stages within the life cycle. The process is not a simple, continuous, unchanging flow. There are qualitatively different seasons, each having its own distinctive character. . . . Change goes on within each, and a transition is required for the shift from one season to the next.

DANIEL LEVINSON, *THE SEASONS OF A MAN'S LIFE*

FAMILY SYSTEMS THROUGH TIME

by Rheta Rosen

The family, as a system and as we experience it, is not a static entity. Just as individuals are born, grow, develop into mature adults, age, and eventually die, families also develop and change over time. Families form, expand, contract, and come to an end. They change in their structure, function, and interaction as both the family members and the larger society progress through time. Though the parents of a particular family may die, that family lives on through the successive generations. These generations in turn will be influenced by the generations that have come before.

The scientific study of family involves a range of theoretical and conceptual frameworks from social, behavioural, and physical sciences. Together, these frameworks are used to explain and analyze family behaviour and interaction. Only in the field of sociology has a framework been developed specifically for the study of family. The "family development" framework introduces the concept of family change over time. This essay will describe the development of this framework, its use, some of its limitations and contemporary modifications, and finally, some of its major concepts.

☐ FAMILY DEVELOPMENT

The family development framework was first articulated by Evelyn Duvall and Reuben Hill in 1948. It was an attempt to overcome the limitations of the existing frameworks, which tended to examine families at one point in time (Hill and Hanson, 1964). This new framework introduced the concept of the "family life cycle." It identifies specific stages common to all families, and suggests that families going through the same stages face similar issues in completing the tasks relevant to that stage. These issues differ from those at previous stages, and require that families alter or learn new interaction patterns to deal with particular stages as they develop. There are also similarities in the nature of the roles played by family members at the same stages of the family life cycle (Aldous, 1978).

The terms "Family Life Course," "Family Career" (Aldous, 1978), and "Family Life Spiral" (Combrink-Graham, 1985) are also used to designate family stages. The definitions of each of these frameworks vary, but they all embrace the idea that there are identifiable stages common to all families as they progress through time. Knowledge and insight into the common experience of these stages contributes in a very positive way to the understanding of families and family interaction.

The family development framework incorporates both a macroanalytic (broad societal) and a microanalytic (relationship-based) view of the family. At the macro level it recognizes that family as an institution reacts to and is affected by changes in the larger social system. At the microlevel it focuses on changes and commonalities in the interaction among family members at particular stages of the family life cycle. A significant example of the intersection of the two levels of analysis is the employment patterns of women. Changes in both the economic and the political institutions in today's society have contributed to the large number of women working outside the home. This has had considerable impact on the interpersonal dynamics of family interaction at various stages of the life cycle.

Development of the Framework

The research of family development theorists has focused to a considerable extent on identifying the stages that all families experience. These stages have differed depending on the criteria used to determine them. For example, Duvall's earliest articulation of family life cycle stages was based on age and level of schooling of the oldest child, as well as the employment status of the husband. (The wife's employment status was not considered, since the assumption in the 1950s was that she would not be employed outside the home. This would not be the case if the model were developed in the 1980s.) An original four-stage model (Duvall and Hill, 1948) was expanded to eight stages (Duvall, 1977; Duvall and Miller, 1985). Until very recently, the eight-stage model has been the one most recognized by scholars, practitioners, and researchers in family studies (Nock, 1979; Aldous, 1978; Norton, 1983; Eichler, 1988). The stages of this model are: married couples (without children); childbearing families (oldest child birth to 30 months); families with preschool children (oldest child 2 1/2 to 6 years); families with school children (oldest child 6-13); families with teenagers (oldest child 13-20 years); families as launching centres (first child gone to last child leaving home); middle-aged parents (empty nest to retirement of the husband); and aging family members (retirement of the husband to death of both spouses) (Duvall and Miller, 1985).

Critical of the use of only the oldest child as a criterion for designating stages, Hill (1964) developed a nine-stage model related to the ages of the youngest child, and Rogers (1964) identified a 24-stage model including the ages of both the oldest and the youngest child.

Demographers, interested in identifying average ages of significant family events for national populations, have also developed the concept of the family life cycle stage. For example, an eminent demographer in the United States has focused on the ages of women at critical transition points in their lives as a criterion for identifying family life stages, such as age at marriage, separation, divorce, widowhood, labour force participation, etc. which are relevant transitions for contemporary women (Glick, 1955; 1977; 1989).

Social and behavioural scientists, family life educators, and family counsellors have all found the life cycle concept to be a valuable tool. It helps them to organize knowledge about families, report and understand research, and identify, anticipate, and teach about changes in family interaction over time.

The examples above illustrate a general acceptance of the concept of family life cycle as a valuable descriptive and analytic tool (Nock, 1979) in research and study of the family. Yet there has not been any conclusive research identifying any one set of criteria for marking the stages as any more valuable than the next (Norton, 1983). The important thing is that all the models identify transitions from one life cycle stage to the next. In addition, all models recognize that as families change across time, members are added and others depart. All families go through a process of "expansion, contraction, and realignment of relationship systems to support the entry, exit and development of family members in a functional way" (Duvall, 1989).

Criticisms and Limitations of the Model

By the mid-seventies, models of the family life cycle based on primary marriages and the nuclear family from formation to dissolution (like Duvall's model) began to be viewed as normative rather than scientifically and empirically verifiable (Nock, 1979; Norton, 1980; Spanier and Glick, 1980; Glick, 1989). In other words, families who went through the defined stages in the model were assumed to be "normal" families. Families who did not conform to the stages were "deviant."

This was an inappropriate assumption, and quite unrealistic. Over the past three decades, significant social changes have taken place in Canada and other western societies. There has been a rapid increase in both non-traditional family structures and the complexities of family life cycle types (Eichler, 1988; Glick, 1989). In the seventies and eighties, there was an increase in the following: cohabitation both prior to marriage and as a permanent lifestyle; the number of adults delaying marriage; lesbian and gay relationships; single-parent families; separation and divorce; and remarriage and reconstituted families. More young adults were choosing not to marry and many who married were choosing not to have children (Statistics Canada, 1989; Eichler, 1987).

More Relevant Models

In view of the changes noted above and the realities of contemporary family life, new models of the family life cycle are being developed. Demographers have created models that include both first and second marriages as well as the never marrieds (Norton, 1983; Sweet and Bumpass, 1988). Reuben Hill has recently developed a complex model of family life stages. It compares the process of family formation and dissolution for a wide range of non-traditional family forms. Hill also identifies the changes in the roles of family members and the stresses that are likely to occur at significant transition stages (Hill, 1986; Mattessich and Hill, 1987; Glick, 1989).

Carter and McGoldrick (1988) are family therapists who have suggested that clinicians working with "real families in the real world" need to be aware of the variations in the family life cycle as well as religious and cultural differences among families. They caution therapists working with families about the detrimental effects of rigidly applying a "normal" life cycle framework to any one particular family. Their own model is a comprehensive one. It has value as an educational, analytical, and therapeutic tool, and merits further description here.

The Carter and McGoldrick model examines the interconnectedness of the family and the larger social system. They recognize that "many problems are caused when changes at the social level lag behind changes at the family level, and therefore fail to validate and support the changes" (Carter and McGoldrick, 1988). The family is viewed not only as moving through time, but also as a system across three and four generations. This model recognizes that the generations in a family are interdependent and that the transitions experienced by one generation have an impact on the successive generations. For example, changes in the abilities of grandparents to maintain their independence often occur at the same time as their adult children may be experiencing the departure of the last child from their home. The interconnectedness of the stresses experienced by the transitions of both these generations needs to be acknowledged and understood.

For Carter and McGoldrick the life cycle stages begin with single adults leaving home. Not unlike the other models, it then proceeds with: the joining of families through marriage (recognizing, however, that many young adults may live together for varying lengths of time with no formal commitment); families with young children (recognizing that today many mothers at this stage are employed either full or part time in the work force and that this affects family dynamics); the family with adolescents (a stage at which one or both parents may be experiencing some kind of mid-life transition of their own); launching children and moving on (new dimensions have emerged at this stage in view of the fact that families are having fewer children, children may leave the home later but return several times before they are finally launched, parents are living longer and may have twenty years alone together before the death of one spouse—a very new phenomenon with far-reaching implications); and, finally, families in later life (a late twentieth-century phenomenon where three and even four generations may be very interconnected and interdependent with one another).

While these family life cycle stages appear to be similar to the original Duvall and Hill model, the incorporation of contemporary realities creates a model that is less subject to the recent criticism of the more traditional family development models. Practitioners using this model would need to be sensitive, as well, to the variations of the family life cycle experienced in the increasingly prevalent phenomena of separation, divorce, and remarriage.

MAJOR CONCEPTS

The one central concept of family development is the developmental task. Others have emerged as the framework has developed over time. The following are brief explanations of some of these concepts.

The Developmental Task

An individual developmental task is one that arises at or about a certain period in the life of an individual. Successful achievement of the task leads to happiness and success with later tasks, while failure leads to unhappiness in the individual, disapproval by society, and difficulty with later tasks (Duvall, 1977). Family development theorists have borrowed this concept of individual developmental task and created the idea of a family developmental task (Aldous, 1978; 1989).

For families to be successful units, they need at each stage of their development to satisfy: 1) the biological requirements of the family members (feeding, protecting and providing an environment for the members to develop and mature physically); 2) cultural or societal expectations; and 3) the personal aspirations and values of the individual family members. In reality, individual and family developmental tasks are intricately interrelated. If the family is accomplishing its developmental tasks in a successful manner at the appropriate life cycle stage, the opportunity for individual developmental task accomplishment is also enhanced.

First- and Second-Order Change

Both Terkelson (1980) and Combrink-Graham (1985) elaborate on the relationship between individual and family developmental tasks. They distinguish between first- and second-order change in families. First-order change relates to the development of family members as individuals within the family system as each makes transitions in his or her life. Second-order change is the family's adaptation to the individual's changes, leading to alterations in the interaction as well as in the structure of the family (Combrink-Graham, 1985).

As an example, we can consider a rural family where the eldest daughter, Hillary, commutes by bus each day to a town 40 miles away to attend high school. She is a serious student, who is shy and uncomfortable about participating in any extracurricular activities. But Hillary's Phys. Ed. teacher asks her to train with the senior swim team, with practices three days a week after classes. Hillary is about to refuse—there's the commuting problem, as well as her responsibility for certain chores around the farm each day. However, a close friend suggests that she could live at her house for the rest of the term. Hillary's parents recognize that her involvement with the swim team would give her more self-confidence, yet there are adjustments they would have to make in their family organization and interaction to accommodate Hillary's move out of the house, even though it is temporary.

A successful resolution of this situation would mean that the first-order change in Hillary's needs and development will be met by appropriate second-order family changes.

Critical Transitions

The critical transitions hypothesis (Rappaport 1963) describes how families progress from one stage to the next. First, there is interaction, then disorganization, and finally reorganization. Drawing from the family stress literature (Hill and Hanson, 1964), Rappaport notes that a family operates at a given level of interaction until a particular transition (either individual or family) is experienced. This transition causes stress and a level of disorganization. Duvall (1989) points out that a crisis is not necessarily a misfortune. A family can adjust to a crisis and reorganize, either at the same level of organization as it experienced before the stress of the transition, or at a lower or higher level.

The resources of individuals and families, the interpretation of the event, as well as the mastery of previous life stage events, will all determine how well an individual or family can reorganize following the stress of a life cycle transition. Scanzoni and Szinovacz (1980) point out that crises, stress, or conflict are not in themselves destructive to family interaction. Rather it is the inability to resolve the conflict or deal with the stress that may be dysfunctional.

Multi-Generational Perspective

Like Carter and McGoldrick, Combrink-Graham (1985) suggests that individual and family transitions are experienced in a multi-generational context, and that they can be reciprocal and enhancing rather than linear and stressful. For example, the retirement of grandparents may enhance rather than place stress on their adult children, who might stand to benefit by the additional time grandparents may have for babysitting. Combrink-Graham prefers the term "family life spiral" to family life cycle since it reflects how the developmental tasks of each generation in the family affects the others. She also suggests that there are periods in the multi-generational family's development when there are strong forces holding families together (which she describes as "centripetal" forces) and stages when there are forces promoting individuality and separateness ("centrifugal" forces). It is important to understand that moving back and forth from one state to another is a normal adaptation for families as their members move through time experiencing significant life transitions.

Roles, Role Clusters, and Role Sequences

Through research and observation of families, and equipped with the family development framework, sociologists have been able to describe the specific roles and behavioural patterns that correspond with each stage of the family life cycle. The role of father, for example, is identifiable at any particular stage. Certain behaviours can be described as appropriate to that role, such as sharing caretaking responsibilities with the mother of a new infant. Obviously the expectation of these role behaviours has changed significantly over time. This may create some interpersonal issues for some young fathers that need to be negotiated. Failure to negotiate these changes in a functional way can lead to increased stress in a marital relationship.

A role cluster refers to the total complement of roles and expected behaviours relating to a particular position during any one stage of the life cycle (Aldous, 1978). The role of "wife-mother," for example, may include the role of teacher, affection giver, disciplinarian, and breadwinner. Viewed over time, the role cluster of "wife-mother" can be described as a changing role sequence as new dimensions are added and others subtracted. For example, the woman's role of disciplinarian with respect to her children may be changed over the years to that of friend and companion.

The concepts of roles, role clusters, and role sequences are central to the family development framework. Researchers and practitioners have been able to identify specific behaviours that can help family members develop realistic expectations of their individual and family developmental tasks across family life cycle stages.

☐ CONCLUSION

The concept of family life cycle stages has made an important contribution to the study and understanding of family as a system moving through time. The earlier articulations of the family development framework have been criticized for their normative perspective, as they did not allow for the range of non-traditional family forms. The more recent models, however, recognize the societal and demographic changes in our contemporary society. Current research within this framework is beginning to integrate the realities of family life, and is creating models that include the wide varieties of family forms and changing family functions.

From a practical point of view, awareness of family life cycle stages and the developmental tasks accompanying these stages can be helpful to young men and women in the family formation stage. They may be better able to anticipate changes in future stages and the potential stresses in their individual and family life cycles. Understanding that relationships in families change across time can contribute to more realistic expectations and, it is to be hoped, more nurturing and satisfying family interactions.

■ BIBLIOGRAPHY

Aldous, J., *Family Careers: Developmental Change in Families*. New York: John Wiley and Sons, 1978.

Aldous, J., "Two Perspectives on Family Change: Family Development and Life Analysis." Unpublished paper presented at the annual meeting of the National Council of Family Relations annual meeting, November, 1989.

Combrink-Graham, L., "A Developmental Model for Family Systems," *Family Process*, 24: 139-150, 1985.

Duvall, E., *Marriage and Family Development*. Philadelphia: J. P. Lippincott, 1977.

Duvall, E. M., and B. C. Miller, *Marriage and Family Development*, 6th ed. New York: Harper and Row, 1985.

Eichler, M., *Families in Canada: Recent Changes and their Policy Implications*, 2nd ed. Toronto: Gage Educational Publishing Co., 1988.

Glick, P. C., "The Life Cycle of the Family," *Marriage and Family Living*, 17: 3-9, 1955.

Glick, P. C., "Updating the Life Cycle of the Family," *Journal of Marriage and the Family*, 39: 5-13, 1977.

Glick, P. C., "The Family Life Cycle and Social Change," *Family Relations*, 38: 123-129, 1989.

Hill, R., "Life Cycle Stages for Types of Single-Parent Families: Of Family Development Theory," *Family Relations*, 35: 19-29, 1986.

Hill, R., and D. A. Hanson, "The Identification of Conceptual Frameworks Utilized in the Family Study," *Marriage and Family Living*, 22: 299-311, 1964.

Mattessich, P., and R. L. Hill, "Life Cycle and Family Development," B. Sussman and S. K. Steinmeyz (eds.), *Handbook of Marriage and the Family*. New York: Plenum Press, 1987.

McGoldrick, M., and E. A. Carter, "The Family Life Cycle," F. Walsh, ed., *Normal Family Processes*. New York: The Guilford Press, 1982, 167-195.

Nock, S. L., "The Family Life Cycle: Empirical or Conceptual Tool," *Journal of Marriage and the Family*, 41: 15-26, 1979.

Norton, A. J., "The Family Life Cycle: 1980," *Journal of Marriage and the Family*, 45 (2): 63-69, 1983.

Nye, F. I., and F. M. Berardo, *Emerging Conceptual Frameworks in Family Analysis.* New York: Macmillan, 1966.

Rappaport, R., "Normal Crises, Family Structure, and Mental Health," *Family Process*, 2: 68-80, 1963.

Rogers, R. H., "Toward a Theory of Family Development," *Journal of Marriage and the Family*, 262-270, 1964.

Scanzoni, J., and M. Szinovacz, *Family Decision Making: A Developmental Sex Role Model.* Beverly Hills: Sage Publications, 1980.

Spanier, G. B., and P. Glick, "The Life Cycle of American Families: An Expanded Analysis," *Journal of Family History*, Spring: 97-111, 1980.

Statistics Canada, *The Family in Canada: Selected Highlights.* Ministry of Supply and Services, Catalogue: 89-509, 1989.

Sweet, J. A., and L. L. Bumpass, *American Families and Households.* New York: Russel Sage Foundation, 1988.

Terkelson, K. G., "Towards a Theory of the Family Life Cycle," E. Carter and M. McGoldrick (eds.), *The Family Life Cycle.* New York: Garden Press, 1980.

FAMILY LIFE SPIRAL

One conceptual framework or developmental model for examining
the family system over time is that of the Family Life Spiral. It offers a clear
view of the ongoing nature of the family system wherein, traditionally,
a couple gets married, children are born, raised, become adults, and part
to form new families. The cycle begins again and the chain is continued.
This conceptual framework is based on a major hypothesis: some life
experiences require intimate family relationships and strong
interdependence, while other life situations stress the independence
and individuality of family members.

□

The family life cycle is not a linear event; it does not begin with a stage, nor
does it end with the deaths of members of a particular generation. In fact, because
death can happen at any stage in the family life cycle, it is not a life cycle event but
a life change event. That is, death is an event that occurs within the context of the life
cycle and may profoundly affect its evolution.

To conceptualize a family system's life cycle, we can superimpose the developmental tasks of each generation in the family upon one another. For example,
Erickson's stage of "generativity" in adults will be the most appropriate stage for
childbearing and for the rearing of young children. Similarly, the reconsideration of
status, occupation, and marital state, called by Levinson the "forties crisis," may
coincide with the adolescence of the children in the family. It is possible, in either
instance, to think of one generation's developmental issues as "caused" by the
other's. For example, the generativity of adults causes the production of children;
and the adolescence of children causes the turmoil of their parents in their forties.
Another perspective emerges when we look at the reciprocity between these generational events to see, for example, how the presence of young children enhances or
complements the generativity of their parents and how the turmoil of the forties crisis
resonates with the adolescence of the children. A further level of reciprocal complexity results from including the grandparents. Stacking these generational events on
top of one another yields a *family life spiral.* The family life spiral is a representation
of the cycles of individuals in the family in relationship to the cycles of individuals in
other generations. The individual life cycles may be conceptualized as the threads

There is no cure for
birth and death save
to enjoy the interval.
GEORGE SANTAYANA

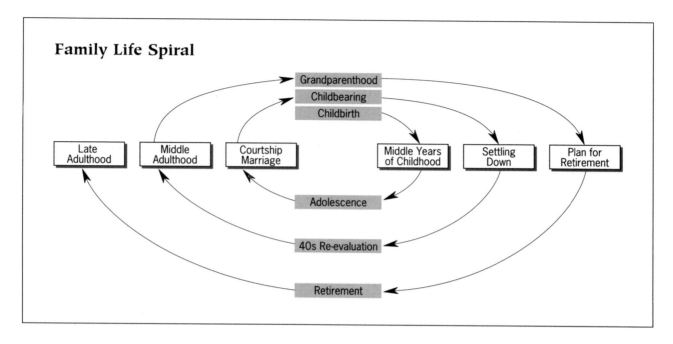

Family Life Spiral

from which the family context is woven. What we see, however, is that changes in the individual threads are reflected in the appearance or shape of the family context. From this notion, we can get an idea about changes in family contexts during different eras of family life.

Note that the spiral [above] is compact at the top and spread out at the bottom to illustrate that the family system's density changes in these periods. The system appears to oscillate between periods of family closeness, periods of natural and nonpathological enmeshment, and periods of family distance. The close periods will be called "centripetal," to indicate the predominance of forces in the family system that hold the family together. The distant, or disengaged, periods will be called "centrifugal," to describe the predominance of forces that pull the family system apart and pull the family members out. Neither "centripetal" nor "centrifugal" defines a pathological condition but only describes the shape of the family.

Some of these forces can be identified in the wider social context of the family, and other forces can be identified within the family. The ties of loyalty that bind family members together, for example, are sometimes stronger than ties to persons outside the family. What appears to happen through the family life spiral, however, is that these forces shift, or more precisely, they oscillate as the family system evolves. Although the spiral concept is simplified and ideal, it begins to demonstrate some natural developmental relationships in the family system.

[The diagram on p. 94] presents the notion of family shape as oscillating or moving back and forth from periods with strong centripetal forces to ones with stronger centrifugal forces. At each coming together, or centripetal period, the generations change and move to another part of the chain. When a child is born, the spouses, who were until then children of their own parents, become parents themselves, and their own parents become grandparents. Between the centrifugal periods

> The family, not the individual, is the real molecule of society, the key link in the social chain of being.
> ROBERT NISBET

It is only at the end that we know where we have been; and only by ending that we can once again begin.
LAUREL RICHARDSON

in the family's life and the centripetal come periods of exploration of individual identity and sexual intimacy that may lead to marriage and childbearing. A parallel exploration process occurs in the older generation with reevaluation of the marriage. From the centripetal periods of childbirth and child-rearing to the centrifugal periods represented in adolescence, the family develops repertoires to differentiate and disengage. The grandparent generation is concerned with retirement and preparation for death or life alone after the death of a spouse. Of course, the contribution of family systems thinking is that differentiation always occurs in relation to the family. No one ever differentiates apart from the family.

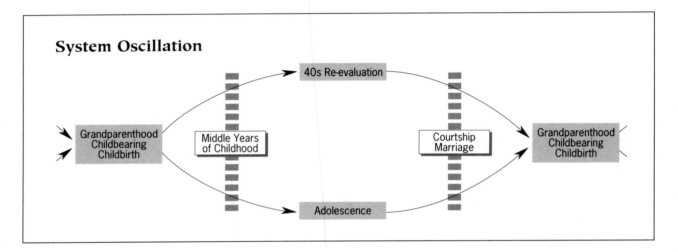

The family will undergo three oscillations during an individual's average expectable lifetime: the birth and adolescence of the child, the birth and adolescence of the child's children, and then the birth and adolescence of the child's grandchildren. Repeating the experiences at each level of the spiral may provide the individual with opportunities for reworking personal issues, as described by Therese Benedek. Viewed from the perspective of the family as a system, these oscillations provide a practicing ground for experiencing intimacy and self-actualization and for reexperiencing these at different levels of maturity and through different tasks as the individual develops in the family.

From "A Developmental Model for Family Systems,"
by L. Combrink-Graham, *Family Process*, Vol. 24, June 1985.
Reprinted by permission of Family Process, Inc.
All texts and charts by Lee Combrink-Graham, M.D.

■ BIBLIOGRAPHY

Benedik, T. "The Psychology of Parenthood," E.J. Antony and T. Benedik (eds.), *Parenthood: Its Psychology and Psychopathology*. Boston: Little, Brown, 1970.

Erickson, E., *Childhood and Society*. New York: Norton, 1963.
Levinson, D.J., et al., *The Seasons of a Man's Life*. New York: Alfred Knopf, 1978.

1.   As a conceptual framework the Family Life Spiral must be adaptable to variations in family form. Outline a family system that does not fit the model as presented. Compare this family system with that of someone else. Discuss how both centripetal and centrifugal stages can vary with any particular family system.

2.   How might centripetal and centrifugal periods be influenced by a family's socio-economic level? By a family's ethnic origin?

3.   Identify how changes in larger social systems could affect generational events in the Family Life Spiral.

4.   Comment on the view of death expressed in the first paragraph of this reading.

5.   The author suggests that families that have not fared well in the centripetal periods will be at great risk during the centrifugal periods. Explain the possible reasons for this.

6.   "No one ever differentiates apart from the family." Search the social science literature to broaden your concept of differentiation of self.

7.   In their book *Postponed Parenthood*, Schlesinger and Giblon predict that the trend to postponed parenthood "will increase as we move toward the 21st century." How might the birth of a first child at the age of 40 affect the family life spiral?

MASTERING TRANSITIONS

Life is full of changes. Some you are glad to make; some are hard to take. Others are forced on you. In her landmark book entitled *Passages*, Gail Sheehy stated that if you don't change, you don't grow—and if you don't grow you're not really living! Read on to learn how to "take the mystery out of change."

☐

A local television reporter recently asked me about the mid-life crisis. "It's an artifact of the media," I said. "Crisis, transition and change occur all through life."

The interviewer was shocked and crestfallen. I had wrecked a story. But I hope I paved the way for a better understanding of the adult years.

Based on my research and that of many others, I have come to believe that there is no single predictable, universal adult experience—there are many, and they frequently involve transitions. From childhood through adulthood, people are continually at the beginning, in the midst of and resolving transitions—some expected, others not. We initiate some but are forced to weather others. At times, we feel comfortable in our roles, at other times uncertain about what is ahead. Although we all experience transitions, our lives are so different that one person may go from crisis to crisis while another may experience relatively few strains. These differences depend on many factors, but one of the least telling is chronological age.

I believe it is less important to know that a person is, say, 50 years old than to know that the person is a newlywed, the parent of adolescent children, recently divorced or about to retire. People facing retirement encounter many of the same problems whether they leave their jobs at 50, 60 or 70. Newlyweds of any age are engaged in similar tasks of bonding, discovery and negotiation. In short, transitions are more important than chronological age in understanding and evaluating a person's behavior. And because the adult years are so variable, we cannot assume that particular transitions will necessarily occur at specific ages.

The transitions in our lives are those events—or nonevents—that alter our roles, relationships, routines and assumptions. They include:

- ☐ *Anticipated transitions:* the major life events we usually expect to be a part of adult life, such as marrying, becoming a parent, starting a first job or retiring.

- ☐ *Unanticipated transitions:* the often-disruptive events that occur unexpectedly, such as major surgery, a serious car accident, a surprise promotion or a factory closing.

- ☐ *Nonevent transitions:* the expected events that fail to occur, such as not getting married, not having a baby or living longer than expected.

Transitions such as the birth of a first child or taking early retirement appear to have little in common, but both change a person's life. It's not the transition per se that is critical, but how much it alters one's roles, relationships, routines and assumptions, and how able one feels to cope with the situation. Psychologist Richard Lazarus finds that we cannot understand the impact of a transition unless we look at the way the individual appraised the transition and his or her resources for dealing with it.

Transitions take time, and people's reactions to them change—for better or worse—while they are under way. At first, people think of nothing but being a new graduate, a new widow, a new parent or newly jilted. Then they begin to separate from the past and move toward the new role, for a while teetering between the two. A year, sometimes two years or even more pass before moving from one transition to another. While some transitions may be over and forgotten, others never seem to end. In a study looking at men whose jobs were eliminated, I found that once men

Life is what happens
when you're making
other plans.
BETTY TALMADGE

obtained new jobs they felt the transition was completed, while the men unable to replace what they had lost felt stuck in the midst of the transition.

Clearly, people differ in how they cope with what seems to be the same transition, and often cope well in one transition but feel ineffective in the next. How, then, do we handle this journey, live through it and learn from it?

To help answer these questions I have developed a systematic way to predict, measure and modify people's reactions to change. By examining the features common to all transitions, however dissimilar they appear, some of the mystery can be taken out of change.

Studies of change—whether job loss, geographical moves, returning to school, caring for aging parents or retiring—have shown that people in transition have both strengths and weaknesses. I have clustered these potential resources or deficits into four major categories, the four S's: situation, self, supports and strategies. By looking at the balance of people's resources and deficits in each of these categories, it is possible to predict how they will cope.

> Today well lived, makes every day a dream of happiness and every tomorrow a vision of hope.
> HINDU SAYING

- ☐ *Situation:* Does the person see the transition as positive, negative, expected, unexpected, desired or dreaded? Did the transition come at the worst or best possible time? Is it "on time" or "off time?" Is it surrounded by other stresses? Is it voluntary or imposed? Is this the transition's beginning, middle or nearly the end? Is this a personal transition or a reaction to someone else's?

- ☐ *Self:* There are many ways to gauge a person's inner self or strengths for coping with the situation. What is the person's previous experience in making a similar transition? Does the person believe there are options? Is the person basically optimistic and able to deal with ambiguity? If so, he or she will bring to the transition the greatest resource of all: a strong sense of self.

- ☐ *Supports:* External supports and options include both financial assets and potential emotional support from family, close friends and co-workers. Dealing with transitions successfully requires that those close to us offer more support than sabotage. Unfortunately, this is not always the case.

- ☐ *Strategies:* Understanding the nature of transitions can help us find ways to cope with them. Sociologist Leonard Pearlin points out that there is no "magic bullet" coping strategy. Rather, the creative coper uses a number of strategies, including those that change the situation or the meaning of the situation, as well as those that help the person to manage stress.

By taking readings on the state of the four S's, we can target the problem area, then ease the pain of change by modifying that area. Consider, for example, the case of Mary, a middle-aged graduate student whose recent life is a study in transitions. Before she had a chance to grieve the deaths of both her parents, her aged in-laws decided it was time to move to a nursing home. Because her husband, the breadwinner, couldn't afford to take leave, she commuted regularly out of town to help his parents plan their move. At the same time, her daughter, unable to afford her own apartment, moved back home, and Mary's son and daughter-in-law had a baby just as he lost his job. To an outsider, Mary's situation was obviously overloaded with transitions. Yet she was so unaware of the additive impact of these changes on her life that she could not understand why it was so hard to complete her graduate degree!

> Unless you start from where you are, you will never arrive.
> JAPANESE PROVERB

Merely evaluating the four S's made Mary realize that she had three strengths: support, self and strategies. Her personal strengths included her maturity and resourcefulness, and she had the support of a collaborative, loving relationship with her husband, as well as a sympathetic church group. She added prayer to her many coping strategies to help herself get through these difficult times, and developed new supports by seeking professional counselling. Just realizing the many resources she had helped Mary deal with a very stressful time in her life.

We know transitions are inevitable and recurrent, but their specific form, timing, and intensity cannot always be anticipated or controlled. We can, however, control how these changes will affect us. By systematically sizing up transitions and our own resources for dealing with them, we can learn how to build on our strengths, cut our losses—and even grow in the process. With a lifetime of practice, some people even get good at it.

From "Taking the Mystery Out of Change," by Nancy K. Schlossberg,
Psychology Today, May 1987, pp. 74-75.
Reprinted with permission from Psychology Today magazine.
Copyright ©1987 (PT Partners, L.P.).

1. Using a life cycle model, chronicle the transitions that could be anticipated for a particular family at each stage. Select any two of these transitions. How could roles, relationships, routines, and assumptions change? Point out the similarities and differences between the two selected transitions.

2. Focus on someone you know who has dealt successfully with an anticipated transition. Using the categories outlined in the essay (situation, self, supports, and strategies) try to determine what resources this individual had to assist in coping with the transition. If possible, interview the person. Compare the resources identified by him or her with your list. Any surprises?

3. Explore how transitions tend to cluster in a family.

4. Nancy Schlossberg states in the reading that the event/transition itself is more important than the age at which it occurs. But social psychologist Bernice Neugarten points out that life cycle events are much more likely to be traumatic if they occur "off time" than in the expected life course. Which viewpoint seems more valid to you? Defend your choice.

5. Review a number of current periodicals and note how many articles focus on life cycle transitions. Share your findings with the class.

6. Consult a dictionary or thesaurus for synonyms for "change." How do these synonyms enable you to view change differently?

7. Using stress ratings of life events (such as the Holmes-Rahe Scale or the McCubbin-Patterson family inventory of Life Events and Changes), draw some inferences about the relationship of stress to life cycle changes.

GETTING TOGETHER: SEARCHING FOR A MATE

Each society has legal and customary stipulations that to some degree regulate marital choice. One's family of origin also exerts many influences on the process of choosing whom one marries. Individual preference is certainly a major determinant in picking a partner—but exactly what qualities do we look for? The following is an overview of a global study that focused on mating preferences across cultures.

☐

No one disputes that the bull differs in disposition from the cow, the wild boar from the sow, the stallion from the mare . . . Woman seems to differ from man in mental disposition.

CHARLES DARWIN, 1871

But does woman differ from man merely because of the norms of particular cultures? Or is each sex predisposed to views and values that are embedded by generations of natural selection? In every time and territory, combatants in the battle of the sexes have wrangled about the issues—and the main question on both sides has been: What qualities do men and women *really* want in a prospective mate?

Ever since Darwin's exploration of evolution, scientists have speculated that the differing attitudes of each sex do not depend on nationality, but no one has ever tested the supposition. Now, in the first broad study to examine human mating preferences across cultures, psychology professor David Buss of the University of Michigan reports that women of every nationality share some nearly universal preferences in the mates they desire. And, though their preferences are different, so do men.

The study, which appears in the current issue of *Behavioral and Brain Sciences*, a leading psychology journal, involved 10,000 people in 33 countries on six continents. Each subject was asked about the relative importance of 31 traits in the marital partner. All of those attributes were phrased in sex-neutral terms—for example, good looking, rather than handsome or beautiful. The results confirmed the study's two main hypotheses: 1) despite geographic and cultural differences, males everywhere value attractiveness and youth in mates more than women do; 2) females are more likely than males to seek mates who are older and are thought to be good providers. Says Buss: "Literally every sample found these sex-linked differences, whether it was among the Zulus, the Brazilians or the Indonesians."

The reason for such universality, Buss posits, is reproduction: "These are adaptations to the problems that males and females have to solve to reproduce and survive." A woman will usually look for a prosperous man because he is better able to support a family, whereas a man will look for a woman whose age and appearance signal fertility. These preferences have been passed down over time, Buss notes, because "individuals lacking favored characteristics tend to become no one's ancestors."

Ingrained as such attitudes are, they can be affected by cultural influences. Buss found, for example, that there are significant cultural differences in the value placed on chastity from country to country. In France and Britain each sex tends to place low value on premarital chastity. At the other end of the spectrum, Chinese males and females put strong emphasis on it. Liu Daling, director of the Shanghai Sexology Research Center, agrees with Buss's findings. "The old preoccupation with chastity has profound roots in the traditional culture," he says. "In the eyes of most Chinese men, a girl who loses her virginity is dirty and impure."

Despite the variations, men in many countries are more concerned than women that their partners be virgins when they wed. The evolutionary reason? "If the female mate is not chaste," says Buss, "then the male could risk investing in offspring that are not his own." Canadian psychologist Martin Daly, a professor at McMaster University in Hamilton, Ont., suggests that these concerns are even more widespread than the statistics indicate. "I would expect chastity to be extremely highly valued by men everywhere, although sometimes they might deny for social reasons that they care."

Conducting a five-year study that spanned the globe proved a daunting task. Buss, who oversaw 50 scientists, recalls that in South Africa gathering data was "a frightening experience" because of the political turmoil and the wariness of prospective respondents. In Nigeria, where polygamy is sometimes practiced, questions had to be added to reflect the possibility of multiple future wives. The researcher in Sweden found it necessary to modify the queries to reflect the fact that many couples there live together but are not married. In all, the global group was extremely diverse, the largest ever surveyed on the subject. "This study is a landmark because of its breadth," says Anthropology Professor Don Symons of the University of California at Santa Barbara. "There has never been anything remotely like this before."

> When a man and woman see each other, they oughta come together . . . wham! Like a couple of taxis on Broadway. Not to be analyzing each other like two specimens in a bottle. Once it was see somebody, get excited, get married. Now it's read a lot of books, fence with a lot of four syllable words, psychoanalyze each other till you can't tell the difference between a petting party and a civil service exam.
>
> THELMA RITTER in the movie REAR WINDOW

While many scientists are applauding Buss's work, others, including some feminists, speculate that cultural conditioning plays a greater role than the study suggests. Psychology Professor Linnda Caporael, who teaches at Rensselaer Polytechnic Institute in Troy, New York, dismisses the findings: "Why do women want to marry men who have money? Because women don't have their own money, as a result of the many obstacles in their way." Caporael questions the value of the findings in Western societies. "Does this mean that we [women] are going to get jobs, and then have a stirring within us that is going to drag us back to look for a man with more money? I doubt it." Buss disagrees. "The evidence shows that highly successful women do not want to marry the gas-station attendant," he says. "They still want to mate with a male who makes as much money as or more money than they do."

Buss notes that his findings do "not imply that what exists should exist." New cultural values of greater sexual equality could bring changes. Nor do his findings imply that men and women are always unalike. The study found that certain traits are equally important to both sexes—and can be the most crucial determinants in mating decisions. In all 33 countries, men and women say that "kindness-understanding" and "intelligence" are more important than any other characteristics. Buss suggests that these preferences are so strong because they provide a significant clue to the quality of a mate's future skills as a parent. Other scientists point to these similarities as evidence that men and women are psychologically more alike than different in areas that do not directly involve reproduction.

> Love comes after marriage.
> **INUIT PROVERB**

In a study filled with statistics about mating preferences, one subject is notably absent: romance. Does the research explain why a man and a woman are sometimes drawn to each other after a single glance? Not really, explains psychologist Daly. "This doesn't say a heck of a lot about who's likely to fall in love with whom." There are still some mysteries, it seems, that even science dares not calibrate.

From "Secrets of the Mating Game," by Andrea Sachs,
Time Magazine, May 1, 1989, pp. 74-75.
Copyright 1989 The Time Inc. Magazine Company. Reprinted by permission.

1. In what ways can an overview of a study provide a useful picture? A limited view? Select what you consider to be the most interesting findings of this study. Pinpoint the major obstacles encountered while conducting such a global study. Determine how these obstacles could affect the findings.

2. This reading provides a good example of how the same statistics can inspire quite different interpretations. Explain the issues that are central to this gender debate. What is your own position? Discuss with the class.

3. Draw up a list of qualities you feel are essential in a prospective mate. Compare your list with someone of the same sex, and someone of the opposite sex. What conclusions can you reach?

4. Using authoritative texts, examine the wide range of theories relating to mate selection. Summarize each of the theories.

5. Interview an engaged or newly married couple about the process of mate selection they went through. Identify the major factors that attracted one to the other. Compare your findings with those of the Buss study. Were any theories of mate selection evidenced by the couple?

6. Sociologists suggest that young people internalize certain values, attitudes, and expectations towards marriage. This has been termed "anticipatory socialization." Mass media is one such socializing influence. Suggest others and describe their particular effects.

7. Dating and courtship patterns change over time. Today there are many alternatives to standard dating practices, one example being the "Companions Wanted" ads. List a number of other alternatives to traditional dating, and describe the societal factors that have contributed to their emergence. What effect have AIDS and other sexually transmitted diseases had on dating practices?

ARRANGED MARRIAGES

In many non-Western societies, parents, other kin, or matchmaking intermediaries assist in the choice of marriage partners. This is done because greater emphasis is placed on the orderly continuance of family culture within the kinship system than on the feelings of the couple. So strong is the need to preserve distinct social and cultural attributes that some immigrant groups in Canada continue to practise the custom of arranged marriage. Such is the case in the Sharma and Shreedhar families.

The girl has never seen her fiancé. She waits in the living room, picks at the spangles on her sweater, sends off her little brother (the karate champion) to investigate. She has bought a dozen roses for the visitor. It is Valentine's Day, 1987.

In the car, steering toward the rendezvous, the boy had been nervous. He is a serious young man, studious, intent. He is tense about meeting his future bride, but not frightened. He talks things over with his parents in the front seat. "What will she look like? How do I act?" He tells himself, "Don't do anything stupid."

The girl is with a couple of her friends. Again she dispatches her brother with specific instructions: "Does he have a mustache?" She has long held visions of her ideal mate: lush, feathery hair, musky cologne, a tuxedo, a diamond earring, a vision from a Stitches store. Or, alternatively, a spiky, sexy Corey Hart of Punjabi extraction, come to fetch her to a life of prosperity and affection, on Valentine's Day in Burlington, Canada. But she has made one law: no mustaches.

The boy is in a grey jacket, a burgundy sweater, slim, his mustache neatly trimmed. He is 23, sells life insurance, plays a little squash, holds his degree in economics. He has made a couple of false starts—correspondence from the parents of an eligible daughter, photographs of three or four candidates—but never has he come this far, to the house of a fiancée he has never seen.

The two families, who know each other because the boy's father was a classmate of the girl's maternal uncle, sit with each other and make small talk. The boy is impressed; the girl's little brother holds more than 100 trophies for his prowess in the martial arts. The boy senses discipline, good upbringing.

The girl, in the living room, gasps, "Oh, God. The time has come." Now they send off the suitor to meet Sunita Sharma, who has known since childhood that this moment would arrive.

Nilesh Shreedhar, who is known as Neil, tells her about his work, his education, his hobbies. He has his own dreams of a woman full of caring—"a total person," a good wife in the Indian sense of the English word "homely"—and he has waited for her to be chosen for him. Sunita, 20, holding the roses, manages four words exactly, "Sheridan College Retail Management." In her heart, she thinks, "Yes."

The Shreedhars—Neil's father is an accountant—drive back to Richmond Hill. Sunita tells her parents, "You have found a good boy." She returns to the friends and cousins, talks for hours, tells them she wants to spike Neil's hair, dress him trendily, walk through the malls with him, hold his hand.

There is a week of nervous waiting, and then the Shreedhars call again to confirm the engagement. It is agreed. The engagement is made official in late March. The boy and girl date a few times, go skating, plan their life. Neil's mustache comes off. They are married on July 25.

"One should marry a woman whose virginity is intact," reads an ancient Hindu volume called the *Yajnavalkya Smriti,* "endowed with auspicious marks, not previously wed to another, dear to one's heart, younger than oneself, not diseased, possessing a brother . . . from a great lineage of Brahmins learned in the Vedas, but not from one afflicted by hereditary disease, however wealthy it may be."

We are sitting in the food court of Fairview Mall in Don Mills and, all other requirements apparently satisfied, Neil is perusing Sunita for auspicious marks. It is 16 months after their wedding. Neil, ever the serious one, is recalling the night he met his fiancée and he says, "She wasn't an opportunity I wanted to let by."

Sunita, who reminds me of the skater Elizabeth Manley—perky, buoyant, a joy—is reminiscing. She describes what she hoped her parents would find for her, "a romantic, caring, loving, understanding husband, and a total party animal."

Neil Shreedhar doesn't resemble any party other than Conservative. He reiterates how, from that first meeting, Sunita "fit the bill." He says, "After university, marriage was the logical next step." At York, he shrugs, he was "almost a book-worm." He reminds me of me.

Like his bride, he had never dated. He says, "My friends knew I wasn't gay, so it was a non-issue. It was a question of priorities. My studies always came first. I knew love was something my parents were going to take care of."

" 'It is commonly a weak man who marries for love,' " I tell him. "Do you know who wrote that?"

"Who?" Neil asks.

"Dr. Johnson."

"Oh," he says, "you mean like Masters and Johnson?"

Sunita manages the Cotton Ginny store on the ground floor of the mall. She watches the passing parade, munches a taco and then says, "I don't mean to be prejudiced, but I did want to marry an Indian. Like, Burlington was really prejudiced compared to Toronto. In Burlington, you won't see a black guy with a white girl. Here, you see *everything*."

She waxes serious. "Of course I thought about love," she says. "In high school, I did have a crush on a couple of guys, but there was nothing I could do. Right from when I was a little girl, my mother always told me I'd be having an arranged marriage. Guys would ask me out and stuff, and I'd tell them, 'If I start a relationship with you, I'll have to end it.' "

"What did the guys think?"

"They thought it was pretty stupid."

The Sharmas came to Canada from India via England when Sunita was three years old. "I was born," she points out, "in Middlesex, but not in the middle of sex." Her father, Krishan, works in Burlington at a company called El-Chem. Krishan Sharma was strict about certain traditional things; back in India, he had not seen the face of his own bride until her veil was lifted during the wedding ceremony. An arranged marriage is a blind date that never ends.

When she was a teenager, Sunita would be taken to Hindu weddings some-where in the Golden Horseshoe and marvel at the fact that often either the bride or the groom had just flown in from the subcontinent.

She would ask her Dad, "You mean he just came in from India and he doesn't even *know* her?" So Krishan Sharma, known as K. at the factory, gave in and agreed that his daughter could get to know her man before they were ritually joined.

"There's no meat market, no shopping around," Neil says. "Our parents have influence. They point us in the right direction. Then we're on our own."

"Respect for your parents is the biggest thing," Sunita interposes, "and respect for tradition. . . ."

"Life is hectic," Neil says, "but we try to fit Hindu traditions into our life-style."

"Yeah, I wear saris and dots on my forehead," says Sunita. "The whole bit."

"What about suttee?" I ask her. Among the more odious Indian traditions is the belief that a widow is a creature without value; the *Yajnavalkya Smriti* holds little hope for her. Suttee is the ritual suicide of a bereaved wife on her husband's funeral pyre.

"Kill myself?" Sunita yelps. "Kill myself? He's in life insurance. Do you know how much money he'd leave me? You think I'm gonna kill myself?" . . .

. . . A few weeks after Neil and Sunita Shreedhar tell me the story of their courtship, I meet Aruna Nagpal. Educated, refined, coolly beautiful, she is one of six daughters of a wealthy Hindu. In 1966, back in the Punjab, her parents produced for her a husband, as the Sharmas in Burlington have done for Sunita.

She remembers every instant of the process. She says, "You're conditioned. 'This is the guy—my parents have decided.' I mean, you're 19, he's 24, and you've never been *near* another guy. It was extraordinary—my father drove us someplace the day we met and *left* us there. The boy hugged me, he kissed me—but no sleeping together.

"I had never even *touched* a boy. Dance? Forget it. You've been suppressed so long. You *have* to fall in love, if it is love, whatever it is. You've saved it so long, it just explodes out of you. You have nothing to compare it with. It's top-quality love."

The groom had been found through a matrimonial advertisement. He and Aruna married within 12 days of meeting.

The marriage failed. In Canada, the husband began sleeping around, not coming home, leaving his wife and daughters alone. Aruna got fed up, sought a divorce. "We had completely different attitudes toward life, our morality was so different, but how could we know that when we got married?" she asks. She remarried a few years later, after "a very Western courtship," to a professor at Bishop's University in Quebec—"very charming, very jolly"—and revels in his acceptance of her equality. Her second husband is a Sikh.

Aruna Nagpal is a judge of the Canadian Court of Citizenship. She has seen a lot of courtships come and go. She says that the matrimonial ads contain "a lot of fraud." A friend of hers with a PhD and a good government job advertised for a mate and wound up with "so many liars. Guys who said they weren't divorced but were. Guys who said they had no kids but did."

Many Indo-Canadians have asked Aruna to arrange a match for their children. Sometimes she has acceded, but she has tired of the business. "All Indians are obsessed with looks," she says. "Really ordinary men want and expect beautiful girls. What about the ordinary girl? Well, a lot of men in India want to come here. The easiest way is to get married. The plain, average girl here winds up with a six-foot physician. Sometimes it works out fine. Sometimes the man comes in with the 100 per cent intention of saying goodbye."

There are happier instances. In 1973, one of Aruna's sisters, a gynecologist in India, married a cardiologist, an inter-caste match of a different sort. Both were rich, both were prominent; both insisted on not seeing the other until the moment of union. "I flew over from here," Aruna says. "I said to my sister, 'How could you, an educated woman, do this?' She said, 'I want the suspense.' Now they're the most happy couple I know."

In 1983, a University of Calgary study surveyed 67 Indo-Canadian parents on the subject of dating and marriage. Only seven said teenagers of opposite gender should meet without supervision. Fifty-one said that marriage should be arranged by the parents with the consent of the children involved. Fifty-two said teenage

> Each family's interaction creates the context for individual family members' own unique solutions to universal problems and its cultural context provides the broad outlines for that defined as normal.
> **JOHN SCHWARTZMAN**

girls should not be allowed to date before marriage. Forty-five said the same about boys. Thirteen said that children should find their own partners, guided by their own two hearts.

Last fall, the Canadian Council of Hindus, convening at Thornhill, selected dating and marriage as the most complex issues facing the Indian community. "In most cases," the conference's final report stated, "parents follow an extreme policy of either hands off or total regimentation and neither succeeds." The council recommended that sex should follow "only after the attraction has materialized in love and there is a long-term commitment on the part of both." It encouraged inter-regional and inter-denominational marriages, within the Hindu fold. Caste, it declared, must no longer be a bar.

The council was chaired by Dr. Budhendra Doobay, who leads the Sunday worship service at the Vishnu Mandir temple on Yonge Street, north of Highway 7. Dr. Doobay alternately chants, meditates and sermonizes from a platform on which stand seven statues of assorted deities. A rather stern-sounding man, Dr. Doobay is intoning on the worth of experience. "The kid argues with the parent and he says, 'I learned in school.' And the parent says, 'But I have lived. I learned in *life*.' "

I am sitting in the lobby with Ashok Chhabra, who is a Brahmchari, sort of a Hindu monk. Ashok is 20 years in Canada, a pharmacology graduate, and unmarried. Whenever he goes home to India, his parents have two or three girls lined up, but he says, Thanks but no thanks. "In two or three generations, this temple will have a For Sale sign on it," the Brahmchari predicts. "Last summer, I was at a Hindu camp for kids in Pennsylvania. We gave the kids a questionnaire about what they liked and didn't like about Hindu culture. Most of the kids wrote, 'I hate Indian music. I hate Indian songs. I hate Indian food.' "

Ashok tells me that the custom of arranged marriages in India began with the invasion by the Islamic Moguls. The Muslims were polygamous but would not take a Hindu girl who was already married or betrothed. To protect their girls from usurpation by invaders, Hindus began to arrange matches for their toddlers.

The custom was not unique to India. In his book *Who Will Marry Whom?* psychologist Bernard Murstein notes that love was not accepted as a reason for marriage in Europe until the middle of the 19th century. "In medieval and later Europe, its place was outside marriage," he writes.

Wrapped in robes at the Vishnu Mandir, Ashok elaborates. "The British gentry didn't marry the chambermaids," he says. "It's the same here with millionaires. Love is something that is developed after marriage, not before. If you start with love and then you get married, problems develop and you fall out of love."

Dr. Doobay, when the service concludes, grants me an audience in his office. He says, "Understand one thing. The greatest gift a man can give is his daughter, the gift of *kanya daan*. Marriage is not a boy-and-girl business. It's a family business."

I call Sunita at work at Cotton Ginny in Fairview Mall. It is Valentine's Day, two years to the day that she dispatched her brother to see if Neil had a mustache.

"I was leaving for work this morning and Neil was sick in bed," she says. And I asked him, 'Got anything to say?' "

"He said, 'Have a good day at work.' "

"So I asked him, 'Got anything else to say?' "

"He said, 'Oh yeah, I love you.' "

"So I said, 'Nee-ull. Isn't there anything *else?*' "

"And you know what? He couldn't think of anything. Ooooooh, MEN!"

From "Scenes from an Arranged Marriage," by Allen Abel,
The Globe and Mail, Toronto Magazine, June 1989, pp. 32-35, 63, 70.

1. Arranged marriages are often made with a view to preserving family solidarity, social standing, and financial security. What seem to be the main concerns in the Sharma-Shreedhar union?

2. React to the following statements from the reading:

    > The greatest gift a man can give is his daughter, the gift of *kanya daan.*

    > You've been suppressed so long. You have to fall in love, if it is love, whatever it is. You've saved it so long, it just explodes out of you. You have nothing to compare it with. It's top-quality love.

    > Our parents have influence. They point us in the right direction. Then we're on our own.

3. Factors such as love, compatibility, and personal need fulfilment are central to most marriages in Western societies. How can these factors be accommodated in arranged marriages?

4. In what ways could the transition to married couple be made more difficult by an arranged marriage? What family or individual developmental tasks may be facilitated by this custom?

5. Search the literature to compile a list of the wide range of factors that have a significant bearing on relationships in marriage.

COHABITATION

Cohabitation is an increasingly common phenomenon in North America. Sociologist Bernard Farber refers to the "institutionalization of cohabitation," seeing it as a prelude to marriage, as a post-marital or intermarital lifestyle, or as an alternative to official marriage.
The following selection by Craig McKie examines marriage-like unions across Canada.

M arriage-like relationships, which have a wide variety of names including common-law unions, cohabitation arrangements, and consensual unions, form the basis of family life for a significant number of Canadians. While this type of domestic arrangement has always been a clear alternative to marriage, documentation of its prevalence was not available until the 1980s. This was the case in spite of the fact that most provinces made explicit provisions for these marriage-like unions in family law in the 1970s. The 1981 Census of Canada broke new ground in this area by counting these relationships for the first time. In addition, the monthly Labour Force Survey carried out by Statistics Canada in February 1984 contained a supplementary questionnaire (the Family History Survey) directed to 14,000 respondents which asked for a detailed account of previous and present marital arrangements. This included marriage-like relationships which involved "living together as husband and wife without being legally married." While the passage of the three years between 1981 and 1984 is insufficient to indicate trends, the two sources taken together illuminate this type of relationship as it existed in the early part of the present decade.

In 1981, there were over 350,000 marriage-like unions in Canada, representing 6% of all husband-wife families; and persons reporting themselves as being a partner in a marriage-like union made up 9% of the unmarried population 15 and over that year.

The overall total of marriage-like unions, however, reflects only then-current unions and does not indicate whether a respondent had ever lived in such an arrangement. As such, current unions may understate the significance of the phenomenon since living in a marriage-like relationship does not appear to be a permanent situation for a large proportion of those involved in these partnerships. Many couples subsequently marry; or else they separate without ever marrying, or the unions are dissolved because of the death of one of the partners.

Data from the Family History Survey of 1984 indicated that 16.5% of adult Canadians between the ages of 18 and 65 had at one time or another lived in a marriage-like union. Different age groups, however, form such unions at varying rates. For example, almost 22% of Canadians born between 1960 and 1964 (who were between 20 and 24 years of age at the time of the survey) had been a partner

Each new generation smiles with amusement at the courtship patterns of the preceding generation and each new generation of parents looks with some consternation on the innovations introduced by its children. In this way intergenerational change calls attention to itself so that our interests are focused on the differences.

RICHARD UDRY

in a marriage-like union. In comparison, fewer than one percent of those born prior to 1940 had been involved in such a relationship when they were in their early twenties.

That living in a marriage-like union is a phenomenon largely characteristic of the young is reinforced by data from the 1981 Census. For example, over half (51%) of all persons living in these unions in 1981 were in their twenties, and over 70% were under the age of 35. At the same time, persons living in a marriage-like union as a percentage of the population in all types of unions for particular age groups was highest among younger age groups. In 1981, 49% of all Canadians aged 15-19 living in any union, 23% of those aged 20-24 and 11% of those 25-29 years, were involved in a common-law arrangement. In contrast this figure was 2% or less among those aged 45 and over.

Marriage-like unions are, for the most part, a one-time phenomenon in life. Fewer than 2% of adult Canadians had ever been in two or more such relationships, strongly suggesting that such unions are not entered into either frivolously or repeatedly. In fact, they are often a prelude to marriage; for example, 8% of all Canadian men and 7% of women who had ever married reportedly did so with a common-law partner. This percentage is even higher among younger persons—26% of ever-married men aged 18-29 and 22% of ever-married women in the same age group married their common-law partner.

In addition to providing an estimate of the number of present marriage-like unions, the Family History Survey provided some information on unions which had ended prior to the survey. First unions ended either in marriage (63%), separation (35%), or the death of one of the partners (2%). The fact that almost two-thirds of these first unions resulted in marriage reinforces the notion that the typical first marriage-like union may be a pre-marriage relationship.

Impediments to marriage, such as an existing undissolved marriage or age barriers, may be a formative factor in the creation of some marriage-like unions. If one or other of the partners had previously been married and was waiting for a divorce, such a relationship could bridge the gap until marriage was legally possible. In fact, first unions which led to marriage were the shortest in duration of all types of marriage-like unions. Those that resulted in marriage lasted on average 2.3 years, in contrast to 9.4 years for first unions which ended on the death of a partner, and 3.0 years for first unions which ended in separation. First unions which were ongoing at the time of the survey had lasted an average of 4.3 years.

As is the case with marriage, men tend to be on average about 2 years older than women when they enter their first marriage-like union. The average age of men entering their first marriage-like union was 26.4 years compared with 24.7 years for women.

Census data from 1981 showed that marriage-like relationships were unevenly distributed across the country. Those living in a cohabitation arrangement without marriage made up just over 11% of all unmarried persons 15 years of age and older in British Columbia and Alberta, the provinces with the highest proportions. The figure for Quebec was also close to 11%. The provinces with the lowest proportions were Newfoundland (with 3.4%) and Prince Edward Island (4.5%). In the remaining

Many thousands of people cohabit without benefit of marriage in homes where there are children by their partner's [former] marriage. Though they may look and act like parents, there is no name for this species. In real terms they are unparents or unwed stepparents.

ELIZABETH MEHREN

provinces, the proportion of the unmarried population 15 and over living in marriage-like relationships fell in the 6-7% range.

Living together as husband and wife without being married is now an established feature of Canadian domestic life. Although it is still far from the norm, the experience of younger Canadians as recorded in the Family History Survey strongly suggests that unmarried couples living together will be more prominent as time goes by.

From Statistics Canada, *Canadian Social Trends,* Autumn 1986, pp. 39-41.
Reproduced with the permission of the Minister of Supply and
Services Canada, 1990.

BIBLIOGRAPHY

T. K. Burch, "Family History Survey: Preliminary Findings." Statistics Canada, Catalogue 99-955.

Pierre Turcotte, "Les Unions libres au Canada: quelques mesures et comparaisons." Unpublished paper, Housing, Family and Social Statistics Division, Statistics Canada, 1985.

1. Summarize in point form the significant facts brought out in this overview of cohabitation in Canada.

2. When the focus is on statistical analysis, as it is in this selection, the reader gets no sense of the different meanings, motivations, or intentions partners bring to a cohabitation relationship. In a small group, explore the wide range of reasons why couples may cohabit.

3. Demographer Paul Glick states that

   > Rarely does social change occur with such rapidity. Indeed there have been few developments relating to marriage and family life which have been as dramatic as the rapid rise in unmarried cohabitation.

   Determine some of the reasons why cohabitation has become more widespread and more generally accepted.

4. List what you consider to be the pros and cons of cohabitation.

5. Research findings on cohabitation can help us understand how it can serve as a general preparation for marriage, what its effect on subsequent marriage may be, and what contribution this stage may have to happiness in marriage. To date, research studies provide us with different and sometimes quite contradictory and inconclusive findings. Explore the journals for recent research findings.

6. What features may distinguish living together from being married?

MARRIAGE CONTRACTS

Marriage is an economic partnership as well as a legal, social, and emotional commitment. Yet, until only recently, marriage contracts have been illegal in every province except Quebec. Today, as a result of changing provincial laws governing the division of marital property, a marriage contract is considered a necessity by a growing number of couples. For without a contract there can be a heavy price to pay for not living "happily ever after."

$\square$

When Sandy J. Morris got married two months ago, she didn't dream of doing it without first having signed a marriage contract with her husband.

As a family lawyer who specializes in drawing up contracts to protect the property and interest of other newlyweds, she knows how important a contract can be in the unfortunate event of marriage breakdown.

As a young professional, she wants to protect her assets and her financial independence.

She's not unique. Metro lawyers are reporting a flood of requests for marital contracts—previously the preserve of the wealthy upper crust—from couples from all walks of life.

"It's definitely becoming something that more and more couples are thinking about," said Morris, an associate with the Toronto firm Torkin, Manes, Cohen & Arbus.

Morris says she has written some 30 contracts for couples contemplating wedded bliss this summer alone.

They fall into three distinct categories, she says, with people contemplating second marriages being by far the largest group.

"I do a lot of those. Some people won't get married for the second time without one. They've been married before and they've gone through the trauma of litigation on separation. Once burned, twice shy," she said.

Then, there are the semi-young professionals who, having delayed marriage until their mid-30s or later, are starting to build their own assets—for example, a condo, car or boat, vacation property.

And there are the young brides and grooms, says Morris, "who come in saying, 'My father wants me to get a marriage contract.' " In those cases, the contract may cover what will happen to shares in the family business in the event of marital breakdown.

"It should become a way of life," says family law specialist J. Kelvin Ford, a Mississauga lawyer.

Ford, who also handles divorces and separation agreements, says Ontario's new Family Law Act has made marriage contracts a necessity.

The Act, proclaimed in 1986, dictates that all assets acquired during marriage must be split equally between spouses when they divorce.

That means that all assets brought into a marriage must have a value put on them, so that amount can be deducted from the value of the assets acquired during the marriage. The resulting figure represents net family property.

In the event of divorce, the partner who holds the greater amount of family property must make a payment (or other type of settlement) to the poorer spouse.

Under the law, business partnerships, pensions, stocks, bonds, savings accounts—which used to be considered the property of the spouse in whose name they were registered—are now considered community property (if acquired during marriage).

"A contract can save the parties a great deal of aggravation, time and headaches," says Ford.

He points out that attempting to put a price on a television set or a car 10 years down the road, when receipts have been destroyed and marriage partners are not in a cooperative mood, can be a nightmare.

And if you and your spouse-to-be believe it's fairer to share acquired assets any other way than 50-50, writing down those intentions and signing on the dotted line is the only way to ensure that happens.

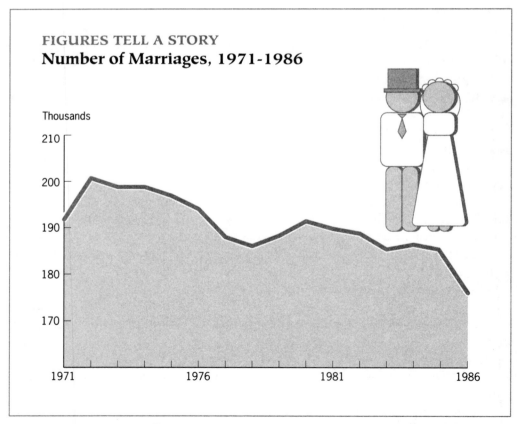

FIGURES TELL A STORY
Number of Marriages, 1971-1986

From Statistics Canada, Catalogue 84-205, Marriages and Divorces: Vital Statistics

Ford stresses that anything not specifically covered in the agreement is subject to the Act.

"What the government has done is to impose upon all marital couples a regime which they may not want to follow," says Ford, "and a contract is the way to opt out of that."

"We encourage people to have them the same way we encourage people to have a will."

Morris finds that the demand for contracts is cyclical, with a rush from mid-April to August to coincide with the busiest wedding season.

She doesn't understand why some of her clients leave such an important negotiation for so late.

"Sometimes they come to you just a few weeks before the wedding, and then it goes right down to the wire," she says, recalling an occasion on which one of the firm's lawyers actually had to take the contract to the church to be signed just before the ceremony.

One of the reasons dewy-eyed couples may put off the task is the perception that getting down to the nitty-gritty of who gets the stereo and who keeps the car is the first introduction of the serpent into paradise.

"It's not a romantic thing. It's stressful," concedes Morris, with a rueful smile.

During the negotiations on her own contract, she found out what it's like for someone sitting on the other side of the desk.

"It's very difficult. It's difficult to talk about the flowers and the type of print on the invitations, and also say to your partner, 'Now you give up X, Y, and Z, and be happy about it.' "

Morris says she now understands why the standard question her clients ask is: "Am I being fair?"

"You want to be a nice person, but you also need to be tough and protect yourself," she says.

Sometimes the negotiations can get pretty heated.

Twice this summer, says Morris, clients who couldn't agree on what to put in the contract decided not to get married at all.

"In one case, after some pretty intense sessions, I got a telephone call saying not to bother any more with the contract—the wedding was off. I felt horrendous," says Morris.

The second case was worse: Two days before the ceremony, the bride-to-be put her foot down and ordered her fiancé to sign, or there would be no wedding. He didn't, and there wasn't.

In that case, it was the bride who made contract demands on the groom. But usually it's the other way around.

"Generally, it's the person with the assets who asks for the contract, and in more cases than not, it's the man who has the assets," says Toronto lawyer Linda Silver Dranoff.

She stresses the need for both parties to the contract to have independent legal advice—which is required to make the contract valid, and is good common sense.

Marriage contracts may not be for everyone. They require a hard-nosed approach to matters of the heart, a zone of vulnerability most of us prefer to keep hidden away from the economic realities of life. But historically, marriage has been recognized as an economic partnership. Success on that basis alone was considered enough. Love was just the icing on the cake. Now, the icing is all we care about. At the end of the day, the real value in marriage contracts may be their ability to preserve the romance, not destroy it.

PATRICIA CHISHOLM

UNIT 2 114

Dranoff says a younger woman marrying a wealthy older man may be pressured by him to sign away future rights to property or other assets.

"It happens all the time and they don't recognize the implications until later," she says.

Marriage contracts override the provisions of the Family Law Act, with some major exceptions.

The contract cannot deal with custody of children (although parties can include in the contract what religion to raise the children, for example).

The contract can't dictate possession of the matrimonial home. This is in order to avoid hardship cases in which one spouse might use the contract to kick the other spouse out during divorce proceedings.

Contracts may include clauses outlining who is entitled to the greater share of the property when it's sold, depending on who has put the biggest investment into the property. But lawyers are cautious about whether those clauses would hold up in court.

"There is some dispute about what the Act says you can do with the matrimonial home," says Ford. He says most lawyers feel that the matrimonial home is intended to be split equally, whether there is a contract or not. . . .

(Couples who want specific advice on how the Act or a contract would affect division of the matrimonial home should contact their lawyers.)

Just about anything else is up for negotiation, according to B.C. lawyer Heather Fayers, author of *If You Love Me—Put It In Writing* (Self-Counsel Press Ltd.).

The "all-Canadian marriage contract kit" is designed to help couples hash it out before they go to their lawyers for final drafting of the legal agreement.

"It used to be that no person who wasn't wealthy would even think about a contract, but now the perception of the public has really changed," says Fayers.

She wrote the book in 1979, after the famous "palimony" case between Lee Marvin and Michelle Triola rocked the California courts.

"Some people spend $7,000 on dresses and flowers, but won't sit in a lawyer's office for half an hour to work out a contract," says Fayers, who calls marital contracts "unromantic, but good insurance."

She adds, "If you are one of the unfortunate statistics and you've taken this step, your costs to separate will be less."

The kit is a how-to manual that includes sample contracts outlining the possessions each partner brings to the marriage and agreements of maintenance of the house or support while one spouse goes to school.

It also includes a section dictating who will walk the dog and who will put up the storm windows.

"Oh, that's just for fun; that's an ice-breaker," laughs Fayers, who does admit that some of her clients come in with the mistaken idea that they can dictate how many times they'll have sex in a week.

"You can't put that in a contract," she says.

From "The New Marriage Vow—Get It In Writing," by Lindsay Scotton,
Toronto Star, August, 1989, Life Section, pp. 1, 3.
Reprinted with permission—The Toronto Star Syndicate.

1. When writing a marriage contract couples have to articulate, negotiate, and agree on specific rights and obligations. With the three categories cited in the selection in mind, identify some of the issues and expectations that would need to be considered for each.

2. The reading suggests that both parties should seek independent legal advice in drawing up a marriage contract. Explain why.

3. Investigate the Family Law Act in your province. Summarize its most important aspects.

4. Many couples work out personal marriage contracts that would be more aptly termed "relationship agreements." These contracts include the areas of marital goals, decision-making, financial matters, division of labour, relations with in-laws, etc. If you were drawing up such an agreement, what areas would you include? List some of the basic questions couples would need to ask each other. How does this type of agreement vary from the type of marriage contract described in the reading?

GETTING MARRIED IN A DIFFERENT ERA

Weddings are rites of passage in which all family members are caught up in transitions to a new stage of life. In the selection to follow you will read about a wedding and the early months of a marriage—events that took place some one hundred years ago in Ontario's Long Point Settlement in Norfolk county. As you read, think of the marked contrast between this account and the experience of today's newlyweds.

☐

L ove goes where it is sent" was a philosophical old saying in our good old grandmothers' days, and one that they religiously believed in; and so Sarah Corliss fell in love with Job Slaght. It was in the days of bows and arrows, and Cupid, no doubt, was a better marksman at that time than he is nowadays. In those days Cupid was looked upon as a veritable tyrant. His darts were shot off arbitrarily without the least preconsideration as to matters of adaptability, marriage endowments, "compatibility of temper" or worldly prospects; and the invincible little missiles always "went where they were sent." Job Slaght was not "all wool" according to the standard of inspection adopted by Mr. Corliss, and so, when Sarah fell in love with him, the paternal head of the Corliss log-house raised a strong and vigorous objection. He told her she would lower the dignity of the house of Corliss if she married Job Slaght, and that if she persisted in her unwise course, he would be compelled to put down his cow-hide boot squarely and firmly, and nip the whole business in the bud. Was the bud nipped? Sarah Corliss is within a few months of her 91st milestone in the journey of life, and as she can tell the story as well today as she could seventy years ago, we will let her tell it herself:

"I never openly and wilfully disobeyed my father but once in my life, and that was when I got married. Father didn't like Job and he didn't want me to marry him. But you see I'd promised Job, and I had to either disobey father or break my word and honor with the man I loved and wanted to marry. Put any girl in a place like that, and if she is conscious of having a heart—and she would be if it wasn't calloused all over with the evil effects of a vain, trifling, idle life—she would be guided by its pulsations and the dictations of her own conscience rather than the cold business-like advice of a father, however kind and affectionate he might be. Job and I had to run away to get married. He hired a man to take us down to Squire Bowlby's in the night in his lumber wagon. Nowadays the girls go away in a covered buggy, or in the cars, when they cut up a caper of this kind. Well, the Squire married us, and on our way back we met father, who passed us without sayin' a word. When he got down to Waterford the tavern-keeper told him that we were lawfully married, and that the only thing he could do about it was to go home, make the best of it and get up a nice little "infare." Father didn't give us the "infare" or get over it till he saw that Job and I were gettin' along all right. We stayed at a neighbor's that night, and the next day we took possession of our home. My, what a place it was! Job's mother had been dead about eight years, and the old man had let everything go to rack an' ruin. The land had been cropped by the neighbors in any way to suit themselves, and even the fences had been carried off. Job was handy with tools, and he had been away from home workin' for himself. In the old log-house there were three old rickety, broken-down chairs, and an old square table. Well, the first thing Job did was to buy six cups and saucers, six plates, six knives and forks and a teapot. A bedstead was made by fitting small poles into auger-holes bored into the logs. These poles were about six feet long, and were small enough to have a good spring. The lower ends of these spring poles lay on a cross piece, one end of which was inserted in an auger-hole in the wall and the other supported by an upright. Job got a feather bed and some bedding from a man who owed him for work done, and being a carpenter he soon got things in a livable shape. In the barn there was a quantity of flax which had been grown before everything had gone to rack, and as soon as we got things righted up a bit in the house, Job went out to work and I pitched into that flax. Job broke it for me and then I took the shives, hetcheled it, takin' out the tow, which was carded and spun on the big wheel like wool, and which furnished the fillin' in weavin' the coarser cloth used for towelling, tickin', bagging, etc. The flax

If love is the answer, could you rephrase the question?
LILY TOMLIN

Marriage is like twirling a baton, turning handsprings, or eating with chopsticks. It looks so easy till you try it out.
HELEN ROWLAND

was spun on the little wheel. We were married in October, and during the winter I made up forty-three yards of cloth out of that flax, and this gave us a supply of table cloths, towels, sheets, tickin', bags, etc; and while I was thus engaged, Job worked around for wheat and pork, and, when not employed in this way, improved the time in makin' me a wash-tub, a little churn and two or three pails. In the spring Job bought a cow, and the busy work of life began. God in His mercy smiled on our efforts, and we prospered; but my, my! how quickly it has all passed away. It seems only night before last that I climbed into that lumber wagon and bumped along over the corduroy by the side of Job, on our way to Squire Bowlby's, and yet many years have come and gone since Job's life work was ended, while I am passed ninety. Yes, tell the story to the young, and if it will inspire them with renewed courage in fighting the battles of life, or lead them to a keener realization of the rapid flight of time, you will be doing a good work."

From *Pioneer Sketches of Long Point Settlement* by E. A. Owen
(Toronto: William Briggs, 1898), pp. 366-369.

1. Love is often considered to be the primary prerequisite for marriage. Comment on the view of love in the reading, and compare it to that expressed in the Arranged Marriages section of this book. Compare these ideas with your own.

2. An "infare" is a feast or a reception for a newly married couple. Trace the changing nature of the wedding ceremony and celebration in the past hundred years.

3. Investigate how the following variables could influence a couple's wedding: ethnicity, religion, socio-economic level, age of the couple, first or subsequent marriage for one or both.

4. Recent market research indicates that weddings in Canada constitute big business. *Report on Business Magazine* in June 1987 estimated that nation-wide an annual $2 billion is spent on all aspects of couples "tying the knot." Do a cost analysis for an average wedding in your community.

5. In the transition to married couple new role patterns inevitably evolve. Examine the roles that Job and Sarah assumed. Determine the wide range of marital roles and responsibilities that today's couples need to work out.

6. "God in His mercy smiled on our efforts, and we prospered." Do you think Sarah and Job could be considered a dual-earner couple? Could the same be said for today's farm couples? Explain your answer.

7. Interview several newly married couples to confirm or reject the following statement: "Early marriage is more a time of role-making than of role-taking."

CROSS-CULTURAL MARRIAGES

Each culture outlines for its members accepted rules of behaviour and recognized ways of doing things. Every culture's rules and ways are somewhat different. So when two people from different cultures marry one another, they face an additional and significant layer of adjustment. Clark Blaise and Bharati Mukherjee have lived many years together in a cross-cultural union. Blaise nonetheless remarks that "cross-cultural marriage, no matter how comfortable, how practised, is an unnatural act."

Just a generation ago, most people married within their culture. They knew precisely who they were and where they came from. My parents, however, broke with tradition. My mother was Anglo-Saxon, Protestant, Prairies. My father was French, Catholic, Quebec. No one in the memory of either family had ever violated the codes of their respective culture or married outside it. Yet, sexual attraction overcame cultural suspicion, and they took their marriage to North Dakota and then to Florida. In its time (1937) and place (Montreal), it was called "intermarriage." The cultures never crossed: my mother never learned a word of intelligible French; my father remained a conventional "Latin" husband.

In 1963 in Iowa City, Iowa, sexual attraction again worked its magic, and I married Bharati Mukherjee, a fellow graduate student in the Writers' Workshop. She was a Bengali Brahmin from Calcutta. Ours was the first recorded exogenous marriage in her family since the Aryan invasion of 1500 B.C. We took the marriage to Montreal, then Toronto. Our older boy was born in Iowa City, but our younger son, born in Montreal, is an official "French Hindu" in the ethno-religious classification of that city. For him, any marriage will be cross-cultural.

Now, 23 years later, I can't think of a single marriage among my closest friends that does not cross serious religious, linguistic, racial or national divisions. To be half-Jewish these days is to join a throng. To be half-Indian, like our two sons, is barely more distinctive.

The purpose of conventional marriage is to solidify traditions, pass on shared values and unite individuals with one another and with the dominant culture. The special demand of cross-cultural marriage is the need of both parties to absorb the other's culture. Such marriages are fragile organisms; little sustains them beyond the implicit bargain and mutual fascination.

At the time of our marriage, I was totally ignorant of India and hostile to its caste-ridden social vision. More than a shell of that complacency remains, despite dedicated efforts. The effort on both our parts has been considerable; I'd even call it a low-grade art form.

To be happily married two people must like each other, which means accepting each other as they are and knowing in what ways to leave each other alone.

NORA JOHNSON

Bharati and I have made a more complicated world—complex, rich and painful—in our marriage than we might have known outside it. There's no going back to our denied and dismembered roots. We have created our own little world of restless resettlement.

"Cross-culturalism" in marriage isn't really possible. Cultures don't really cross; they don't mix; they can't be preserved except as folklore. In marriage, meltdown of separate integers must occur; some third thing must emerge. To wit: I can never be Indian but I can overcome my aloofness in the midst of all that is bizarre and frightening in India. Bharati can never be Western, but she can loosen her deep unalloyed attachment to India. When that happens, I become open to the incongruous warmth and comedy of India, and she feels her passions stirring in an apparently sterile and impersonal North America.

I'm no stranger to the complacent imperialism of cross-culturalism. In the winter of the first year of our marriage, I brought my pregnant wife to the ancestral farm near Winnipeg. She was dressed to meet her husband's family in her traditional wedding sari. Outside, it was 30F below. We toured the pig house. My mother and grandmother showed off the equipment. Bharati was beautiful, we were tolerant, so why was she crying? She held a squirming piglet. How could we know that no woman in her family had ever held a pig?

Ten years later, I was the "second groom" at a traditional Hindu wedding, mumbling my Sanskrit, my face made up in sandalwood paste. It was only a distant cousin's marriage, yet it was also *my* marriage in the culture I had somehow joined. That year, Bharati and I were writing *Days and Nights in Calcutta*. It was the beginning of the meltdown.

Cross-cultural marriage, no matter how comfortable, how practised, is an unnatural act. As such, it is vulnerable to external reality. What if I'd fallen in love with a Palestinian? A Haitian or Filipino? Being married to an Indian was bad enough in mid-70s Toronto; then, a wave of "Paki-bashing" swept these shores, transforming a pair of securely based Canadian academics into mid-life refugees, who are still trying to recover a modicum of professional stability. For all our mutual adjustment to each other, how does a white Canadian husband react to high schoolers' taunting of his wife, to the refusal of shopkeepers to serve her, to her detention in hotels on suspicion of soliciting? "I'm sorry," explained the house detective, after pulling her off the elevator to our floor. "She was well dressed, attractive . . . er . . . Paki."

There is an old Canadian proverb which says a fool and his heritage are soon parted.

JUDITH ROBINSON

It's in the external unexpected threat that the cross-cultural marriage faces its harshest challenge. Bharati and I can become mutually acceptable to the norms of each other's culture, yet still be destroyed by events that barely rate a mention in the evening paper. The special insights we have spent a lifetime gathering and the perspectives on ourselves and on society that our marriage uniquely affords us can be dismissed in a destabilizing instant. Society still takes revenge against those who challenge its authority.

From "Cross-Cultural Marriages" by Clark Blaise,
Chatelaine, August, 1986, p. 44.

1. Comment on the general tone of this reading. In your own words express the essence of it.

2. Blaise suggests there are both perils and pleasures inherent in a cross-cultural marriage. Select some illustrations of both from the reading. Determine through class discussion what others may be.

3. "Society still takes revenge against those who challenge its authority." Cite situations relating to today's families that reinforce this statement.

4. Use the following statements from the reading as triggers for class discussion.

   I'm no stranger to the complacent imperialism of cross-culturalism.

   Cultures don't really cross; they don't mix; they can't be preserved except as folklore.

■ BEING PREGNANT

Having a baby is considered one of the most significant of our human experiences, for one is party not only to the continuity of a particular family, but to the ongoing nature of the entire human family itself. Preparing for the arrival of a new baby in the 90s can involve a dizzying array of choices, from prenatal classes and how-to books to amniocentesis, ultrasound, in utero fetal stimulation, and a range of birthing options. Then with every birth comes significant changes in status: sons and daughters become parents, parents become grandparents. For many reasons this life cycle stage is both an exciting and stressful one, as Angela Neumann Clubb so ironically describes.

□

Oh pregnancy—oh holy state
Although I did procrastinate
and waited until 28
To find myself a willing mate
With whom I could collaborate
Someone who I could liberate

Or should I say, domesticate
I qualify; make no mistake
I do not mean subordinate

In retrospect, I must relate
I still cannot appreciate
Nor did I ever radiate
A *glow* whilst in the pregnant state

Perhaps because I overate
Gained forty pounds of excess weight
Was prone to sleep and vegetate
Completely disproportionate
I had to circumnavigate
Myself through all the subway gates

What really did infuriate
Was friends who would pontificate
And otherwise exaggerate
Their own childbirths to illustrate
Until my heart would palpitate

And God forbid, I should berate
My mother who is very "straight"
And still feels we should segregate

All husbands on delivery dates
Not meaning to discriminate
She claims men are too delicate

At last, the long-awaited date
My labour pains began at eight
With little time left to debate
My doctor would evaluate
If I'd begun to dilate

Baby began to agitate
Contractions did accelerate
I wish I'd had a surrogate!

With no choice now to speculate
I had to breathe and concentrate
I barely could articulate
For fear I'd hyperventilate

Imagine then, how jubilate
I felt, when I first held my Kate

From *Love in the Blended Family* by Angela Neumann Clubb
(Toronto: Family Books, NC Press Limited, 1988), Postscript.

Women's dominant role in the reproduction of the species is the source of both their power and their powerlessness.
RONA ACHILLES

1. Abstract from the poem some of the new trends in pregnancy and childbirth.

2. Make a historical and/or cross-cultural trace of some of the myths related to pregnancy.

3. Generate a list of reasons why people have children. In a recent population study, six general reasons for having children were cited: biological, cultural, political, economic, familial, and personal. The personal reasons included extension of self, status, power, parental experience, competence, and pleasure. Do your reasons fit into this classification?

4. During pregnancy there are both complementary and conflicting individual developmental tasks for the expectant couple. Provide illustrations of these. How might these tasks vary with a single mother? For parent(s) of an adopted child?

5. What do you consider to be the main developmental tasks for the expectant family? How might these tasks vary with a single mother; a subsequent child? Identify the role changes that might occur with the birth of the baby.

6. Survey your community for the resources to facilitate this life cycle stage.

7. The increasing incidence of infertility in women has led to such practices as contract (or "surrogate") motherhood and in vitro fertilization ("test tube babies"). Research the emotional and political issues relating to reproductive technologies.

8. Using current data estimate the cost of raising a child from birth to age eighteen.

TRANSITION TO PARENTHOOD

The parents of a newborn embark on a prolonged commitment to their child that is in many ways less negotiable than the commitment to marriage. A new baby is a most demanding creature, and one can't put a baby "on hold." Research indicates that most couples have some difficulty making the switch from the husband-wife dyad to the mother-father-baby triad. Rita Smith describes how she actually went through a mourning process as she made the transition. When Alan Pence's first-born arrived he became a full-time housefather, a radical shift that brought some surprising results.

☐

Mothers and babies, contrary to popular belief, are not necessarily born at the same time. One of the least-discussed aspects of new motherhood is that while it may be the beginning of the ultimate relationship, it is still an ending: the end of life as you knew it. The old you—single, self-centred, oblivious—dies a slow and agonizing death, and in her place will stand a Mother.

As in mourning any loss, I went through the predictable stages at the birth of my first child (and the end of my old life): denial, anger, bargaining, depression and acceptance. But it wasn't until years later that I could recognize them for what they were.

First came denial: "This baby won't change my life. I won't be outdone by someone who's had eight hours of sleep; I can handle this." This attitude resulted in my planning a six-course gourmet dinner for eight the day of David's first diphtheria-polio-tetanus shot (no one told me he'd react like *that*).

Determined not to be one of those soft-touch mothers who runs every time the baby whimpers, I once spent a memorable evening listening to four hours of wailing, wondering how high a person's blood pressure had to get before she suffered a disabling stroke. Why had I been selected to give birth to the only baby in history who functioned totally without sleep? There had to be a better way.

Eventually, I gave up denying that my life had changed at all and began to resent bitterly the ways in which it had changed. This, of course, was anger. I had convinced myself that David cried for one reason only: to aggravate me. I woke up angry at childless people who were still asleep. I went to sleep angry at people who weren't tired. I hated my husband for being cheerful and energetic when I was miserable and exhausted. I hated him for being thin and wearing handsome suits to an exciting job, when I was fat and wearing track suits to rinse diapers. I just hated.

I did pull myself together long enough to try bargaining. I bargained with myself, with God and with the baby. "If I can just get this one hour of sleep, I won't lie down again till bedtime." "Please make him stop crying this one time and I'll be cheerful as anything next time he wakes up." "David, just let me eat one meal in peace and I'll walk you till I drop, okay?"

God and babies, as it turns out, do not make bargains. The realization that this was one deal I couldn't negotiate my way out of plunged me into a depression that lasted weeks. Life consisted of sleeping, looking after David as best I could and eating chocolate. None of my friends understood what I was going through. How could they?

They were living it up at fitness clubs, talking to people without cereal on their chins, while I was trapped with a tiny tyrant I loved desperately, frantically searching to find some way we could live with each other.

The end came one day when, after a bubble bath, stroller walk, his favourite

Child rearing is baffling, hence our addiction to expert advice.
BRUNO BETTLEHEIM

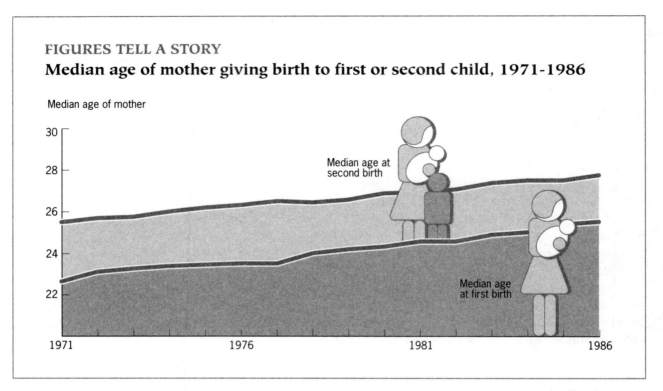

FIGURES TELL A STORY
Median age of mother giving birth to first or second child, 1971-1986

Median age of mother

Median age at second birth

Median age at first birth

From Statistics Canada, Catalogue 84-205, Births and Deaths: Vital Statistics

lunch, a bottle, cuddle, and a song, I put David to bed and collapsed into bed myself. Before I'd even dozed off he was up and howling, not to be outlasted.

Exasperated to the point of tears (and no doubt the picture of maturity), I stormed into his room and actually shouted at an 8-month-old: "Why do we always have to do what *you* want to do? Why can't we ever do what *I* want to do?"

Suddenly, in a crystalline instant of perfect insight, I understood. What I wanted counted for nothing with the baby: he was, after all, a baby. It was as simple as that. All the months spent pleading, cajoling, fuming, assuming that my feelings counted for anything were an extended exercise in resistible reality. Reality dictated that this baby's needs came before mine; that I would adapt my life to his and not vice versa. *That's what a mother does. . . .*

That moment was, in fact, the real birth. Life improved immeasurably once I accepted the fact the old life and the old me were gone for good. The work was still there, but the tension was gone. Wet diapers and crying babies were no longer personal affronts but simply diapers to change and babies to cuddle. And magically, as I resigned myself to being permanently on call, David started sleeping through the night.

By the time our second son was born, there was no question about who was calling the shots. He was. His mother wouldn't have it any other way.

From "The Birth of a Mother Comes Later" by Rita Smith,
Toronto Star, March 25, 1988.

☐

Fatherhood began with 5:30 a.m. contractions. By 2:30 p.m. we were in the labour room. And at 11:30 that night we were quickly wheeled into delivery. The months, weeks and days of slow, steady development compressed into anxious moments. Head now out, one last push/pull and the long, cream-covered, blue-tinged body lay moving slightly on the nearby table.

In intensive care I watched as they cleaned the mouth, the nose, and drained more fluid from the lungs, then laid her in the incubator. Blood and cream-covered face peering through the heavy plastic: nose forced flat, she moved with the rhythms Myriam had felt those last months. The rhythms that seemed to stop whenever I reached to feel.

That night was worry and wonder, acceptance, rejection and fear. Would she survive, this little flesh and breathing creature, when that initial leap, the first passage, had been so difficult? I felt myself ready to do anything to ensure her survival, while at the same time I feared the great change she had already introduced into our lives. My acquaintance with her was only hours old, not months. Her coming was not a slow growing, a transition, but an abrupt and traumatic entrance. Fatherhood was not a gentle becoming, but a rush of anxiety in a bright delivery room. Both mother and daughter required rest and care from their physical ordeal. My battle was mental and emotional, and it had just begun.

Her schedule became ours. Days were measured in feedings, not sunrises. Alert periods were short and led into feedings that once more lulled her back into sleep. There were feelings of impotence at not being able to stem her tears, and sudden joy at a special moment shared. . . . Slipping through the many cloaks and species of fatherhood in my acceptance of this one that entered my life, not through an evolving understanding and appreciation, but through social and biological dictates beyond my control. . . .

Myriam's two months of home-leave passed quickly and the fuller responsibilities of housefathering prepared to settle on me. By this time my development and Leah's had begun to converge. I was now beyond the impulses of infanticide or adulation as the pragmatics of our daily living together took centre stage. Chief among the duties were the shuttle service to and from breast feeding and the co-operative timing of naps with the research and writing I had hoped to maintain as a housefather. Fortunately, a certain regularity of both feeding and napping had evolved by the beginning of the third month. That, coupled with two work-closure days the first week of our experiment, allowed for the successful completion of work-week one. Because Leah did not imbibe of anything other than breast milk, our timing was essential. The morning feeding was sometimes preceded by a mollifying drive to work, while the after-work feeding I anxiously awaited with floor pacing and back patting.

The first few weeks of our housefathering experiment passed quickly as we adjusted to the mechanics of the novel situation. I had never spent much time around the house and none with a baby, but the lunch-time drive and long nap

The process of bearing and raising children is profoundly creative.
MEG LUXTON

periods lent a certain structure to the day and it seemed that our decision the summer before had been calculated wisely.

The previous summer Myriam had been finishing her degree in a new professional area. The hint of increased hours at home while those newly developed skills slipped away did not rest easily with her. On the other hand I was feeling worn, torn, and exhausted after pursuing academic studies and working full-time for a couple of years. The opportunity to concentrate on research alone seemed idyllic, while my training and experiences as a child-care worker and pre-school teacher seemed a natural preparation for housefathering. We all looked forward to our "natural" accommodation.

The regimen of daily child-care for two- to four-year-olds, which had served as the basis for my professional work in early childhood education, had been performed in the context of wage employment in the company of 10 to 12 other staff. Child contact included adult contact—staff meetings, team planning, team teaching—and a sense of shared mission. As a housefather the daily mission was mine alone. Neither my research interests nor my care-taking required or lent themselves to outside contact. When Leah slept, I studied; when she was awake, I was with her.

Neither activity produced a pay cheque at the end of the month; neither provided a sociable coffee break, nor lunch with others in a shared situation. The early weeks of novelty gave way to routine, and the personal opportunity to drift into isolation—post-partum depression descended. . . .

. . . It is now eight months since Leah's entry into the world "out there" jolted me into fatherhood. My nights are now restless for my own re-entry into that world. The isolation, loneliness and contempt our society holds for non-wage earners forces me to choose between my two legitimate duties of caring for my child or continuing my career. In eight months Leah has passed from total dependency and an observer role to a measure of independent, initiatory behaviour. She has begun to act on her environment. It seems we must have passed each other in transit on my slide from confident actor to incapable recipient.

Eight months is such a short time in the life of an individual, but it is time enough to learn, to change, to view the world in a very different way. Leah and I have both learned a great deal from our "experiment," and we have provided each other with some incomparable moments. But the price of those tangible rewards is dear in a society that values wages over work, and products over people.

I fear the migration of mothers to the workplace will not be balanced by a countering flow of fathers to the home. The liberation of women to new roles and new identities has far outpaced the transformation of men to new roles. The battle for sexual equality is being waged solely on the traditional male turf, and that struggle over the role of breadwinner threatens to deplete the home, and the children within it, of parents. The ability to care for and to nurture children is not sex specific—nor is the need to feel valued and esteemed. Until we consider the development of people on a social par with manufacturing things, homes will be the arid wasteland that feeds the growing pool of wage-earners.

From "Confessions of a Housefather" by Alan R. Pence, *Transition*, December 1984, pp. 4-8.

Look Maggie, don't worry about how you bring up your children. Whatever you do will turn out to be wrong. Not only whether you go to work or not. Everything else. If you are permissive, you'll find out you were secretly hostile. If you're strict, you had a hang-up about sex. Do things with them and you stifle them. Don't and you neglect them. You can't win. So do what you want to do. At least you will wind up pleasing one person . . . yourself.

VIOLET WEINGARTEN, from A WOMAN OF FEELING

1. In what ways does Rita Smith reflect a traditional view of parenting? A realistic view? Comment on the fact that there is no mention of the fathering role.

2. Compare and contrast the parenting experiences of Rita Smith and Alan Pence. What observations can you make?

3. A recent study stated the following hypothesis: "The incorporation of the child into the family system is a complex, multifaceted process occurring during the early months of the child's life. The essence of this process involves the child's becoming an active participant in the family's enduring patterns of activity and effective change." Pinpoint ways in which these two parents attempted to do this. Suggest additional ways.

4. Conduct a journal search for studies on adjustment in the transition to parenthood.

5. Canadian sociologist Robert Whitehurst strongly suggests that families will need help from like-interest support groups in the decade ahead. Specify how a support group of young parents might ease the transition to the parental role. Identify other family transitions that could benefit from support groups.

6. Investigate the extensive literature on parent-child bonding.

7. Reflect on the following statements:

> Parenting in its more fundamental and necessary dimensions requires more sacrifice, cooperation over competitive values and conservation of invested energy to produce an ongoing chain of life.
>
> —J. O. Bradt

> The evidence speaks all too clearly to the fact that children are diminishing as a national priority. While it may not be a deliberate shifting of values, it is nonetheless influential in impact upon our lives and the development of our country. Despite personal sacrifices, the lack of sleep and the pain, adults require children in their lives. Without children we have no commitment to the future. We become a society without heart. It is simply too high a price to pay for temporary comfort.
>
> —Robert Couchman

8. Research the current level of federal funding of daycare. To what degree does this funding fall short of needs? What are the specific demands of daycare advocates?

ON SOCIALIZING CHILDREN

Families in all societies share a significant function: the nurturant socialization of children. Socialization through parent-child interaction should help children reach their full potential. What follows is a list of what might be considered guidelines for socialization. These are taken from an essay by Virginia Satir, who was an author, researcher, family therapist, and teacher who profoundly influenced how families view themselves and how others view families. Although written twenty years ago, there is a freshness in these ideas that makes them still valid for today's families. (References to the female gender have been added by the editors of this book.)

☐

a. The emphasis in child-rearing would be on helping the child find out, crystal-clearly, how s/he looked and sounded, how to tune in on how s/he felt and thought, how to find out how s/he experienced others and affected them, instead of only the admonishment to be good and find out how to please others.

b. From the moment of birth s/he would be treated as a person with the capacity to hear, to see, to feel, to sense, and to think, different from the adult only in body development and, initially, in putting his/her sensory and thought experiences into words.

c. S/he would have a predictable place in time and space.

d. S/he would have real and openly welcomed opportunities to feel his/her power and his/her uniqueness, his/her sexuality, and his/her competence as soon as his/her resources permitted it.

e. S/he would be surrounded by people who openly and clearly enjoyed each other and him/her, who were straight and real with one another and with him/her, thus giving him/her a model for his/her own delight in interacting with people. Thus, the joy in relationships might overcome the grimly responsible outlook "becoming an adult" often has for a child.

f. "Yes" and "no" would be clear, reliable, appropriate, and implemented.

g. Realness would be valued over approval when there had to be a choice.

h. At every point in time, regardless of age or label, s/he would always be treated as a whole person and never regarded as too young to be a person.

i. Every child's feelings would be regarded with dignity and respect, listened to and understood; those around him/her would do the same with each other. There would be a basic difference between his/her awareness and expression of his/her feelings and thoughts, and the action s/he took in relation to them.

j. Every child's actions would be considered separately from his/her expressions, instead of linking expressions of feeling with an automatic specific act. S/he would be taught that actions had to be subject to time, place, situation, other persons, and purpose, rather than being given a stereotyped "should" that applies universally.

k. Difference from others would be seen clearly as an opportunity for learning, holding an important key to interest in living and real contact with others, instead of being seen primarily as something to be tolerated, or destroyed, or avoided.

l. Every child would have continuing experience that human life is to be revered, his/hers and that of all others.

m. Every child would openly receive continuing knowledge of how s/he and all his/her parts work—his/her body, mind, and senses. S/he would receive encouragement for expressing, clarifying, and experimenting with his/her thoughts, feelings, words, actions, and body, in all its parts.

n. S/he would look forward to each new step in growth as an opportunity for discovery, encompassing pain, pleasure, knowledge, and adventure. Each phase of growth has special learnings that could be particularly planned for; evidence showing that a new growth step had been achieved would be openly and obviously validated. . . . Mistakes are an inevitable part of risk-taking, which is an essential part of growth, and needs to be so understood.

o. S/he could see males and females as different, yet interesting and essential to each other, free to be separate instead of being implicit enemies or feeding on each other.

p. S/he could get training in male-female relations, could prepare openly for mating and parenting in turn, which would be explained as desirable, and demonstrated as such.

> The parent's life is the child's copybook.
>
> **PROVERB**

From Virginia Satir, "Marriage as a Human-Actualizing Contract,"
in *The Family in Search of A Future*, Herbert A. Otto, ed., ©1970, pp. 60-61.
Reprinted by permission of Prentice Hall, Inc., Englewood Cliffs, New Jersey.

1. Through small group discussion, determine which of the guidelines seem most applicable for all stages of childhood. Which for a pre-schooler? A grade-school child? An adolescent?

2. Explain how ethnic, racial, socio-economic, or religious differences could alter the interpretation of these guidelines.

3. There have been a number of comprehensive theories developed to explain the socialization process. Investigate these theories, and summarize your findings in chart form.

4. Certain theories suggest that socialization is a life-long process. Agree or disagree, supporting your stance.

5. Identify unusual socializing agents that may be introduced into families that include a physically disabled child, a gifted child, or a terminally ill child.

6. It is well known that truly nurturant socialization—characterized by close, continuous instructional and affectional interaction between parent and child—takes a great deal of time. What major social trends affecting family life make nurturant socialization difficult?

7. The evolution of feminist ideology in the past two decades has encouraged families to look at sex-role socialization quite differently. (One of the best texts on non-sexist child-rearing is Letty Cottin Pogrebin's book *Growing Up Free: Raising Your Child in the 80s.*) What are your beliefs concerning gender socialization?

■ ADOLESCENCE

The following excerpt from Anne Tyler's novel *Morgan's Passing* offers you a glimpse of the Gower family through the eyes of Morgan, husband and father of five girls ranging in age from ten to seventeen years. You may recognize the common push-pull situation that exists in families with teenagers—an emerging generation that somehow always manages to puzzle and frustrate the one that precedes it! The second reading is an excerpt from the book *No Kidding: Inside the World of Teenage Girls* by Myrna Kostash. Through personal interviews Kostash has compiled a riveting collection of case histories of Canadian adolescent girls. As you'll read, not all families survive adolescence intact.

□

His daughters had begun to seep downstairs. They were quarrelling in the hall and dropping books, and their transistor radios seemed to be playing several different songs at once. A deep, rocky drumbeat thudded beneath electric guitars.

"*Peter Jacobs, at 44,*" Morgan read. "Forty-four! What kind of age is that to die?"

"Girls!" Bonny called. "Your eggs are getting cold."

"I hate it when they won't say what did a man in," Morgan told her. Even 'a lengthy illness'—I mean, a lengthy illness would be better than nothing. But all they have here is 'passed on unexpectedly.' " He hunched forward to let someone sidle behind him. "Forty-four years old! Of course it was unexpected. You think it was a heart attack? Or what?"

"Morgan, I wish you wouldn't put such stock in obituaries," Bonny said.

She had to raise her voice; the girls had taken over the kitchen by now. All of them were talking at once about history quizzes, boys and more boys, motorcycles, basketball games, who had borrowed whose record album. . . .

The twins were mixing their health-food drink in the blender. The French book flew out of nowhere and hit Liz in the small of the back. "I can't go on living here any more," Liz said. "I don't get a moment's peace. Everybody picks on me. I'm leaving." But all she did was pour herself a cup of coffee and sit down next to Morgan. "For heaven's sake," she said to Bonny, "what's that he got on his head?"

"Feel free to address me directly," Morgan told her. "I have the answer, as it happens. Don't be shy."

"Does he have to wear those hats of his? Even in the house he wears them. Does he have to look so peculiar?"

This was his thirteen-year-old. Once he might have been offended, but he was used to it by now. Along about age eleven or twelve, it seemed they totally changed. He had loved them when they were little. They had started out so small and plain, chubby and curly and even-tempered, toddling devotedly after Morgan, and then all at once they went on crash diets, grew thin and irritable, and shot up taller than their mother. They ironed their hair till it hung like veils. They traded their dresses for faded jeans and skimpy little T-shirts. And their taste in boyfriends was atrocious. Just atrocious. He couldn't believe some of the creatures they brought home with them. On top of all that, they stopped thinking Morgan was so wonderful. They claimed he was an embarrassment. Couldn't he shave his beard off? Cut his hair? Act his age? Dress like other fathers? Why did he smoke those unfiltered cigarettes and pluck tobacco shreds from his tongue? Did he realize that he hummed incessantly underneath his breath, even at the dinner table, even now while they were asking him these questions?

He tried to stop humming. He briefly switched to a pipe, but the mouthpiece cracked in two when he bit it. And once he got a shorter haircut than usual and trimmed his beard so it was square and hugged the shape of his jaw. It looked artificial, they told him. It looked like a *wooden* beard, they said.

He felt he was riding something choppy and violent, fighting to keep his balance, smiling beatifically and trying not to blink.

"See that? He's barefoot," Liz said.

"Hush and pour that coffee back," Bonny told her. "You know you're not allowed to drink coffee yet."

The youngest, Kate, came in with a stack of school books. She was not quite eleven and still had Bonny's full-cheeked, cheery face. As she passed behind Morgan's chair, she plucked his hat off, kissed the back of his head, and replaced the hat.

"Sugar-pie," Morgan said.

Maybe they ought to have another baby.

> Adolescence is like a roller coaster ride: the highs are incredible, the lows are gut-wrenching and the times when you coast somewhere in between make up the biggest part of the ride.
>
> NANCY KOLODNY

The daughter, who has decided to move out, calls the break-up with her parents "torrid." Her grievances are deeply felt if ambivalent. How can she fail to admire parents who have their own successful computer-programming business in Ottawa, to which they devote sixteen hours of every day and from which they extract a living that supports life in a big house on The Driveway, two cars, fur coats? On her own now in Toronto, living hazardously on student welfare, she sometimes accepts money from them: "I got traded in for computers somewhere around the age of twelve, so I don't feel guilty taking their cash now."

The break-up was a drama of mutually inflicted pain—"I love my parents intensely but we also hate each other very intensely"—and if it occasioned torrents of tears and lengthy, acrimonious argument, it was also, she perceives, accepted with a certain relief. The household, reduced to adults and pets, could reassemble itself in tranquillity and maybe even with some admiration for the spunky daughter who had "stood up" to them in order to pursue her own project. That the parents themselves disapproved of this project, the daughter acknowledges: "What do you mean you want to write poems, act in plays, sculpt?" She imitates their harsh, censorious voices. "What kind of practicality is that?" The fact is, while chasing after these ambitions, she wreaked havoc on the household, stumbling in the door at five in the morning, sleeping until noon, getting up only to wash and dress and go out again, to join God knows whose company. This was, of course, her way of saying, "I want to do and learn and create, to *breathe*, and I can't do it here among your goddamn computers and Italian furniture." But they could only see her as irresponsible, disorderly, and gratuitously bad-mannered. She is convinced that they are convinced that she is a "terrible human being."

Yet they all wept when she left and she wishes, yes she wishes, there could have been "some other way" to go.

Behind them, many adolescents see a Golden Age when the family was close and its members were amiable and solicitous of one another, when the child was unequivocally taken care of and the parents had no higher purpose than to nurture their young, and each other. Then, suddenly, parents have become unreasonably demanding, hectoring, peremptory. They're nosy, bossy, and unpredictable. How is one to live with such people?

"I didn't get in until midnight and my dad was waiting up for me and he goes, 'Where the hell were you?' And I go, 'I went to a movie.' And he goes, 'I didn't know that.' I *had* told him. So I got into massive crap about that. Then he said my room was a mess and my clothes have to be put away just so and he went through my drawers, *really* messing them up, and he's giving me shit and I agree to everything, just to get it over with."

In their survey of Canadian teenagers, Bibby and Posterski write that "only 65% of teenagers report that the family is 'very important' to them." Yet 90 per cent say that they "highly value" friendship and love, a statistic that leads to the conclusion that large numbers of teenagers must be looking for intimacy and affection in some relationship other than with their families. Why are their families "unavailable"?

In a word, they are living under extraordinary stress. Hundreds of thousands of adults are unemployed, unemployable, or marginally employed and live with their children in poverty. As various regions of the country move in and out of boom-and-bust cycles, whole communities flourish and then wither, and families uproot themselves and move on. Children are raised in apartment complexes or suburban tracts where their parents cast about in vain for a sense of neighbourhood. Parents quarrel, become drunk and violent, and divorce. Single mothers, confined to female job ghettoes, pay disproportionate amounts of money for child care and struggle at home with housekeeping, regret, and loneliness. Meanwhile, divorced fathers may or may not pay support, may or may not have the time on Saturday to take the kids to the zoo. Like barometers of the domestic climate, children register their distress in the face of such difficulties. They run away, attempt suicide, become bulimic and anorectic; some doctors report that they even exhibit symptoms of stress-related diseases: headaches, stomach aches, high blood pressure, and high blood-cholesterol levels.

> You can take my word for it, when it comes to trade relations almost everyone would like to.
>
> **HENRY KISSINGER**

For all its obvious inadequacies, the family remains the institution where the most fundamental issues of relationship are negotiated: trust and loyalty, power and independence. A young ego can be constructed or destroyed here. Whatever the ostensible reason for conflict (curfew, allowance, dating rules), what is at stake is the teenager's struggle for the right (as acted out in relationships with others) to dispose of his or her own being. Small wonder, then, that the family, in all its various constitutions, can be the site of the most intensely felt exchanges.

From No Kidding: Inside the World of Teenage Girls *by Myrna Kostash.*
Used by permission of the Canadian Publishers
McClelland and Stewart, Toronto.

1. Identify some of the conflicting emotions expressed by the members of the Gower family. In what ways are these emotions typical of this life cycle stage?

2. The stage of adolescence can be fraught with conflict between the generations, since both parents and children are involved in major life cycle transitions. Using psycho-social changes and physical-hormonal changes as a framework, determine what these transitions are. Discuss some of the possible challenges.

3. In what ways is the adolescent experience the same for males and females? In what ways quite different? Explain the reasons for the differences.

4. List what you consider to be the most common areas of conflict between parents and teenagers. In small groups, using these lists and other pertinent resources as catalysts, compile a 10-point plan for coping constructively with conflict. Discuss the factors that can cause problems in the implementation of such a plan. Share the plan with your family. Report back to the group with the responses you get.

5.   Comment on Kostash's explanation for why families are sometimes "unavailable" to teenagers when they most need them.

6.   React to the following statements:

> The major predicament facing adolescents in our society is that virtually no opportunity exists to do anything (legal) which really makes a difference.
> —John Mitchell, *The Adolescent Predicament*

> Adults make it tough to be a teenager. They either actively resist their movement into adulthood or simply are unable to cope with it. They commonly want to play by the irrelevant rules of childhood.
> —Reginald Bibby, *The Emerging Generation*

7.   Conduct an in-depth examination of one of the far-reaching problems that can beset today's youth. The range of problems could include teenage pregnancy, drug addiction or alcoholism, teenage runaways, emotional, sexual, or physical abuse.

8.   Refer to the reading "Today's Youth—Tomorrow's Families" in The Enduring Family section. Critically evaluate some of the findings in light of your own adolescent experience.

FLEDGLING ADULTS AND THE NOT-SO-EMPTY NEST

In the recent past it was assumed that at a particular age and stage young adults would leave home and parents would experience, for better or worse, "the empty nest" syndrome. This is not happening in many families today, for a variety of reasons. Read on to learn some of these reasons and some of the family repercussions, as described by Monica Boyd and Edward T. Pryor.

☐

Recent decades have brought unanticipated turns in family composition and living arrangements among both the young and old. More elderly Canadians are living alone, while, until recently, the young have been leaving their parents' homes at increasingly early ages. In Canada, this latter tendency emerged as a growing trend for young adults to establish their own households, thus emptying the parental nest. Between 1971 and 1981, the percentages of unmarried adults who lived at home declined.

However, recent evidence from the Canadian Census has shown a reversal of this trend between 1981 and 1986. The percentage of unmarried young adults who were living with parents rose over the period 1981-1986.

The shift is particularly noteworthy for unmarried people aged 20-29 in respect to the choices they made between living as unattached individuals (that is, alone or with non-relatives) or living in a family household. As of 1986, six out of ten of these women aged 20-24 were living with one or both parents. Seven out of ten men aged 20-24 were still living with parents. Even by their late twenties, over four out of ten unattached or unmarried men and three out of ten women were living at home.

The increasing percentages of young adults in their twenties who are living at home have contributed to an aging of the entire population of children aged 15-34 living at home. In 1971, slightly more than one-quarter of the young women who lived at home and one-third of the young men were aged 20-29. By 1986, nearly 40% of the unmarried women and nearly half of the unmarried men living with parents were aged 20-29. Not only is a higher percentage of the unattached or unmarried young adult population living at home, but they are also more likely to be older than young adults living at home in previous decades.

> The primary purpose of raising a child is to help that child get out of your life and into a life of its own.
>
> JOHN ROSEMOND

The reasons for interest in adult children living with parents are manifold, but two aspects are obvious: (1) recent trends in the living arrangements of young adults go against the grain of the previous long-term momentum of the young to make an early departure from their parents' homes, and (2) the underlying question of explaining such a reversal and its consequences for the understanding of contemporary family life.

In part, the reversal of the previous pattern has been masked by other changes in household formation patterns of Canadians such as living alone, the increase in forms of cohabitation not based on a marriage, and increases in family breakdown.

While each has contributed to a proliferation of residential types and patterns, which taken together have tended to reduce average household size, delayed leaving of the family household and subsequent returns to it have apparently emerged as a countervailing tendency, possibly reflecting changes in marriage patterns and the economic conditions facing young adults today.

FACTORS IN LEAVING OR STAYING IN PARENTAL HOMES

Census data provide the overall pattern with respect to delayed marriage. The percentage of Canadians who had been married by a given age declined between 1976 and 1986, indicating a delay in the timing of marriages. Delayed marriage leaves the other residential options of (1) leaving the parental household for other independent living arrangements either alone or with others or (2) remaining in or returning to the parental home during the years that in previous decades might have been spent in a separate household in the married state.

It appears that an increasing number of unmarried young adults have chosen the second option. They remain in their parents' homes at a time in the family life cycle when parents might once have expected to be freed of direct parental responsibilities. The nest may still be emptying, but the process now extends over a longer transitional period.

Many other factors contribute to a decision to leave a parent's home and to establish a new household. Factors associated with the choice between living at home and establishing a separate household are: sex of the adult children, membership in particular ethnic groups, education level attained, labour force participation, and individual income. Some factors are enabling (e.g., high employment income makes household formation feasible, as does higher educational attainment, which often translates into desirable employment), while other factors are retarding (full-time enrolment in higher education).

Compared with people in their twenties living unattached, unmarried persons in their twenties who were living at home in 1981 were more likely to live in a rural area, to have French as the home language, to have lower levels of educational attainment, to be attending school, to be unemployed or not in the labour force, and to have lower incomes. In 1981, nearly one-quarter of the young unmarried men in rural areas were residing with parents, compared with slightly over 11% of unattached men aged 20-29. For young unmarried women living at home, nearly 30% were in settings in which French was the home language, compared with slightly more than 20% of the unattached population. Over one-third of unmarried people living with parents were attending school, in contrast to the lower school attendance of young adults living alone or with non-relatives. One-quarter of the unmarried-living-at-home population was unemployed or not in the labour force, compared with fewer than 15% of unattached individuals in their twenties. Consistent with the patterns of school attendance and employment, over one-third of the unmarried men and nearly 50% of the unmarried women living with parents had incomes of less than $5,000 in 1980. Approximately two out of ten unattached young women and men had incomes below $5,000.

☐ THE CLUTTERED NEST

When all factors are considered together, there was an increased tendency in the mid-1980s for young adults in their twenties who were not currently married to live continuously in their parents' homes or to return to them. The increase occurred largely between 1981 and 1986, a period that encompassed a severe economic recession and increased time spent in pursuing higher education. The percentage of people in the age group 18-24 enrolled full-time in post-secondary education rose gradually from 19.8% in 1976-77 to 24.5% in 1985-86.

Using 1981 Census data, co-residency with parents rather than living as unattached individuals is seen to be related to low educational attainment, having French as a home language, being unemployed or not in the labour force, and with having a low income. School attendance was also an important factor. Some young adults may be effectively trapped in their parents' homes because of the high costs of establishing a separate household, particularly in large urban areas where the costs of accommodation are conspicuously higher than average.

> Fond as we are of our loved ones, there comes at times during their absence an unexplained peace.
>
> ANNE SHAW

What the effects on family life of delayed leaving, willing or unwilling, may ultimately prove to be are unknown. These findings do raise the possibility that contemporary young adults, unlike their predecessors in the late 1970s, will spend more time in a home life over which they exert less than full control, possibly in the process adopting their parents' behaviour patterns more thoroughly. Whether as a by-product of pursuing higher education, or because of the relatively low salaries available to the young in the late 1980s, many seem destined to remain in their parents' homes considerably longer than was previously expected. This possibility could indicate a fundamental alteration in the living arrangement patterns of young Canadians relative to previous generations.

But the permanence of this trend is questionable. Continued improvement in economic conditions, were it to be passed on to young adults, might again reverse the growing tendency to stay in one's parents' home; or alternatively, higher levels of enrolment in post-secondary education for longer programs of study could reinforce the existing trend by keeping children at home for even longer periods of time.

From Statistics Canada, *Canadian Social Trends,* Summer, 1989.
Reproduced with the permission of the Minister of Supply
and Services Canada, 1990.

1. Summarize the main factors contributing to the "cluttered nest" syndrome. Outline the key concerns and/or repercussions arising out of this syndrome.

2. To expand your view further, examine the journals and current periodicals for articles dealing with the "not-so-empty nest" and "fledgling adults." Then, sharing insights in a small group, address the following questions: What are the possible effects on overall family functioning when young adults live at home for prolonged periods? What are the implications of an extension of childhood and/or prolonged parenting on the individuals within a family? How may the developmental tasks of young adults be made more difficult by remaining in the parental home for an extended period?

3. Form an interview team. One person is to interview someone 20 to 34 years of age who is still living in the parental home. The other is to interview someone in the same age group who is established as a single outside the parental home. Questions should focus on the possible conflicts, pleasures, and challenges inherent in each lifestyle choice. Present your shared findings to the class.

4. Triangles and coalitions can occur in "cluttered nest" families. Describe some of the possible short- and long-term effects of such situations.

5. For another view of the changing face of the "empty nest" stage refer to "The Sandwich Generation" reading found in The Emerging Family section of this book.

MID-LIFE CONCERNS

The mid-life period of the family life cycle seems to be one where the focus shifts markedly to the development of the individual within the family. Many boundary changes take place. The family can shift, contract, and/or expand. Children leave home to pursue individual goals and aspirations or to begin families of their own. Adults often experience transition trauma, sometimes called the mid-life authenticity crisis or the middle-aged crazies. The following are Harold Minden's recollections of this period of his life. In his newly chosen life direction, Minden authored the text *Two Hugs for Survival*, from which the first reading in The Family as System section was taken.

What happened to former Toronto businessman Harold Minden when he was 38 was unsettling. He began to ask himself soul-searching questions: "What do I really want?" and "Where do I go from here?"

The globe-trotting president of three companies had achieved success and the trappings that went with it. Happily married with three daughters, he had what he describes as "a very nice life."

Yet he wanted something more.

Minden realized he wasn't getting any younger and this might be his last chance to change directions. Like many men and women entering their middle years, he felt compelled to re-evaluate his life and risk a change.

"At the same time that I was feeling very elated about my accomplishments, I really sensed that there were other needs that were not being satisfied," says Minden. So he launched a second career in his 40s.

He resigned from his powerful, high-paying job and went back to school full-time to get his Ph.D. in psychology. Today, more than 20 years later, he's chairman of York University's Counselling and Development Centre.

Minden is certain he made the right decision. "You go down from that mountain that you've climbed, and you start another climb. It can be somewhat bludgeoning, knowing the hurdles you have to confront when you go back and start all over again . . . but I would make that choice again."

Many people at mid-life—particularly from age 35 to 55—think about changing careers or jobs, or feel their marriages are under siege.

It can be a period of great emotional turmoil, typically lasting anywhere from six months to two years. Both men and women experience it. They question the status quo, and debate the risk of moving on to something else that will give new meaning to their lives.

Men often start behaving strangely, doing things they never thought they'd do, according to Nancy Mayer, author of *The Male Mid-Life Crisis*.

Mature self-esteem in adulthood is not a global capacity to feel good about oneself regardless of what transpires, but an ability to arrive at a realistic evaluation of the self after considering one's strengths, weaknesses and life circumstances.

P. A. COWAN

"Newly critical of themselves, their families, and their whole mode of living, men in their 40s often entertain dreams of dropping everything—or dropping out.

"And there are those who do more than dream. While some simply switch women, others change their goals, their careers and sometimes their entire way of life."

Men are more likely to have mid-life crises than women, experts say. The theory is that men don't talk enough about themselves or their fears of aging to develop a better attitude toward it. Still, women also face certain pressures in their 30s that can cause mid-life crisis, social scientists say.

For childless women, the middle years can trigger a sense of panic that they'll never be mothers. For homemakers, it may be a return to work when the last child enters school that throws their sense of balance off-kilter.

Mid-life is the end of one stage and the beginning of another, Minden says. Some people pass through it gracefully; others opt for radical changes.

During the transition, some people become depressed or withdrawn. They may turn to alcohol or drugs. They have trouble sleeping or develop sexual problems. Panic attacks, feelings of insecurity and loss of self-esteem are common.

To survive the upheaval, say the experts, people must come to terms with aging and the fact that—despite accomplishments—they're not going to realize all of their dreams. It can be a hard pill to swallow.

"Suddenly, you reach an age where you realize time is running out," Minden says. "So many goals and expectations that you had just seem beyond reach. That ends up causing frustration that can extend to marriage and family."

Minden was lucky. His wife and children fully supported his decision to change his career, though it meant less income.

"My wife had a lot of hesitation and trepidation about what this would do, because we had a lot of freedom. But she was tremendously excited for me as well. So were my daughters," recalls Minden, who spent a couple of years pondering his career change before making his decision.

His friends and colleagues envied his courage. "A number of them said: 'Boy, I wish I could do what you're doing.' "

Switching careers seems pretty straightforward compared to the logistics of switching partners, which is what many mid-life men and women do.

Sometimes it's predictable. Partners outgrow each other or grow in different directions, and the choice made at 20 may not be valid or rewarding at 40.

Sometimes it's laughable. Picture the stereotypical older married man who suddenly acquires a sporty car, a new hairstyle and a girlfriend half his age.

But sometimes, the marriage could have been saved with a new approach.

Lillian Messinger, a social worker at Toronto's Clarke Institute of Psychiatry, says many mid-life marriage break-ups "seem to be tied in with people wanting a change." There may not necessarily be anything wrong with the marriage, but one of the partners feels discontented.

More women are re-examining their marriages than ever before as they become more interested in work and activities outside the home, she notes. There is growing evidence to suggest that a sexual reversal takes place during mid-life: men move

The Middle: when I remember bygone days, I think how evening follows morn; so many I have loved were not yet dead, so many I love were not yet born.

OGDEN NASH

toward sensuality and tenderness, and women often become more autonomous, aggressive and cerebral, Mayer says.

Mid-life also prompts many women to stare into a mirror. They see a few gray hairs and wrinkles and begin to panic that they've lost their sex appeal, says psychologist Blossom Wigdor, director of the gerontology program at the University of Toronto.

"Women who have focused on their physical attractiveness as the centre of their identity may feel that this is a crisis for them."

But, contrary to myth, menopause—when 45- to 50-year-old women stop having monthly periods and can no longer get pregnant—does not lead to a mid-life crisis. "Very few people see this as a lack of sexual desirability," Wigdor says.

To cope with mid-life crisis, people have to be able to identify it, Minden says. The person suffering restlessness needs to know what's bugging him before he can begin to solve the problem.

"I think most people can identify the stresses in their life by themselves but, if they can't, then I think they should go to a trusted friend or a professional; somebody who will try to understand where the problem is and what your options might be in resolving it."

Crises are not always bad, Minden points out. They can energize and motivate, and be part of finally growing up. "When someone says: 'My God, I'm already 40 and there are a lot of things I want to do. I'm not going to panic. I'm going to sit down and draw up a 10-year program, and I'm going to do something.' Well, that's terrific."

From "Mid-Life Crisis" by Virginia Corner, The Toronto Star, May 27, 1986.
Reprinted with permission—The Toronto Star Syndicate.

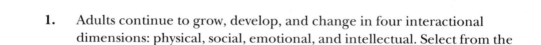

1. Adults continue to grow, develop, and change in four interactional dimensions: physical, social, emotional, and intellectual. Select from the reading illustrations of each of these dimensions.

2. With the reading in mind, suggest how the mid-life transitions could be similar and/or different for: women; men; the unemployed person; the single parent; the never married.

3. The empty-nest stage can now be as long as the child-rearing period. The quality of family life possible in this stage has altered dramatically in the past three decades, owing to demographic, societal, economic, and health changes. Provide specific examples of each of these changes.

4. Compare the sentiments expressed in this article with those expressed in two other readings: "Mastering Transitions" and "New Meanings of Age." How do the various arguments put forth complement or contradict each other? Based on these views, establish your own beliefs regarding age and transition.

5. When does a person shift from mid-life to middle-age to old age? In what ways is any answer to this question subjective? Related to social policy? Government regulated? Be specific in your responses.

6. Retirement usually occurs at the end of middle age, around 65 years of age. It is thought to be a major turning point, influencing family life in many dimensions. Up to the present time, the majority of people who experienced this transition were men. This is now changing. Use current Canadian statistics to predict the ratio of men to women retirees in the year 2020.

BEING OLD: AN AGE AND AN ATTITUDE

The experiences of old age vary tremendously with the individual. Today's elderly are social pioneers, for never before have so many lived for so long. The following reminiscences of Lettie and Emmie—who are 80 and 86 years of age, respectively—might surprise you. For these women are what Leah Cohen, author of *Small Expectations: Society's Betrayal of Older Women,* calls "magnificent survivors."

LETTIE: I'm poor today because I never had a decent job. My husband left me with three small children right in the middle of the Depression. I had no mother to help with the kids, no car, and after the first year, I never received a penny from my ex-husband.

It is possible to do anything if you really have to. I sewed all our clothes and I took in boarders. It was a real struggle, especially while the children were small. At one point I tried to sell beauty products, but without a car and without any capital, I never made very much money. The thing I did best was raise my babies to be strong and healthy people. I remember feeding the four of us on a dollar a day.

Of course, I often thought it would be nice to remarry, but no one wanted a woman with three little children. There never really was a chance. In my day, a single woman was not a happy guest. You tended to become somewhat isolated.

I think my life really became much better from age fifty on. That's when I was most beautiful. I finally didn't have the heavy burden of my children wrapped around my throat. And I started to earn a decent salary for the first time. I moved to a new city and took up private nursing. I've been doing it for thirty years now, and I suspect I will for many years to come. My health is excellent and I take long walks for exercise.

> We grow neither better nor worse as we grow old, but more like ourselves.
>
> MARY LAMBERTON BECKER

My philosophy is to make the best of things. I get up every morning feeling good, looking forward to the day. I don't allow myself to brood or indulge in self-pity. I try never to leave my apartment without a smile on my face.

I work at looking good—I have to. If people knew that I was eighty, they wouldn't trust me to care for their children. It's a foolish, prejudicial attitude. Everyone is different. I have friends who are sixty and look a hundred. I make a point of moving quickly and I work at keeping slender. Maybe dyeing my hair at my age is a bit ridiculous, but people are terribly impressed with appearances.

My doctor has told me that I will probably live to be a hundred. He can't find anything wrong with me and keeps telling me that I am a medical wonder. I think part of the reason I am so healthy is that I read all the time and don't pollute my mind with television. I go to the symphony and to the theatre when I can, but the public library is my greatest entertainment. Every week I take out three or four books on all kinds of subjects. And once a year I take a trip to a country I have never seen. At my age, I have to go on organized tours, partly for safety and partly for financial reasons. But I would love to wander on my own, especially in the Orient, which fascinates me. My other greatest hope is to die while I am taking one of my daily walks.

The only thing really lacking in my life, aside from money, is a good man. I don't think of myself as elderly and most of my friends, male and female, are much younger than I am. I can't stand to be in a place with old, sick people. Everyone my age has given up. It's not their physical disabilities that disturb me—sickness is part of life—it's the fact that they're sitting back and taking it from people. I'm a fighter and I refuse to let anyone treat me like a little old lady. Just let them try.

To be honest, I don't know where I could meet a man I would find attractive. He would have to be at least ten years younger than I am—otherwise, how could I hope to have any fun with him? Men my own age are just too old for me. I do volunteer work in a nursing home and I find the place awfully depressing. I read, sew, and write letters for people much younger than myself. The home is such a waste of women. A lot of them are sick and need help, but I think they would be a lot happier living in their own homes.

I am very confident that I can continue as I am. I do all my own cooking and cleaning. This apartment is just filled with old things that I have collected over a lifetime. They are my old friends and give continuity to my life. The older you get, the more important it is to have a secure and familiar base.

It's too bad I was born when I was. The women's movement has made great changes that would have affected my life significantly. Better jobs, for one thing, are open to women like myself. And young women today are definitely more free than women of my generation were.

But I can't complain. I was born with a good mind and a strong constitution. I'm active and I seem to attract interesting people, who become part of my life. It's a two-way street: I find friendships, particularly with younger women, very stimulating, but I know they find me stimulating, too. At my age, though, life shouldn't have to be such a financial struggle. I like to think that it will get better for other generations.

When the time comes nearer, and even when the day is at hand, people usually prefer old age to death. And yet at a distance it is death that we see with a clearer eye. It forms part of what is immediately possible for us; at every period of our lives its threat is there; there are times when we come very close to it and often it terrifies us. Whereas no one ever becomes old in a single instant . . . until the moment is upon us old age is something that only affects other people.
SIMONE DE BEAUVOIR

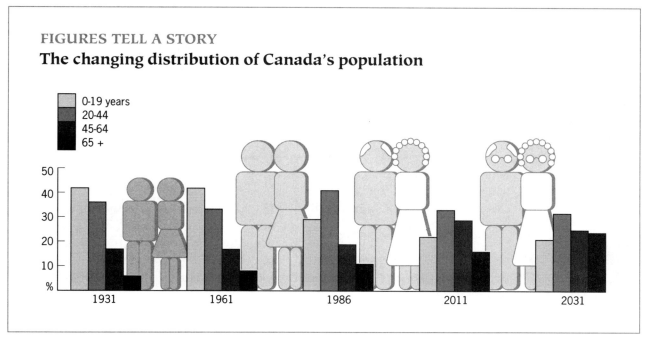

FIGURES TELL A STORY
The changing distribution of Canada's population

Legend:
- 0-19 years
- 20-44
- 45-64
- 65 +

From Statistics Canada, except figures for 2011 and 2031, which are projections
prepared by The Royal Bank Reporter

. . . *At eighty-one, Emmie broke her hip while in the hospital recovering from a cataract operation. Three years later, after being shunted from one institution to another, she packed her few belongings, found a cab, and returned to the home she had lived in before her operation.*

EMMIE: What I hated most about the nursing home was the lack of privacy, the lack of dignity. A typical day at the home would begin with breakfast on a tray. It was brought by very nice young women who unfortunately could not speak English. Perhaps this is petty, but it is enormously lonely to begin the day in silence. I would have my breakfast and then I would start waiting, waiting for someone to bring me water for a sponge bath. Often I waited until eleven o'clock. The staff couldn't help it; I understand that. They were so few and we were so many. But things were so bad that I wore the same nightdress for up to three weeks.

It was almost impossible to keep yourself clean. There was one nursing assistant for seventy-five patients between midnight and seven in the morning. Three or four people wet themselves every night and this poor woman would dash about trying to change all the bedding. It was a bit much for one woman alone.

What I realized very quickly was that the home is a place where people go to die. Everyone around you is old. Aside from the staff, you rarely see a young person. It's all very depressing. All day long people watch TV or sit and stare into space.

Even eating became an awful ritual. The first time I was able to go to the dining room, I was horrified. People were shovelling in their food, eating in total silence. I

We are not permitted to be depressed anymore, nor are we allowed to age. Already people are beginning to wonder where have all the old people gone? They've gone underground because we live in a time when we must go through life like a miracle fabric: drip dry and wrinkle free.

ERMA BOMBECK

asked a nurse why no one talked. She asked me why I didn't take the initiative and start talking to one of the other residents. So I started. I turned to the woman next to me and asked what I thought was an inoffensive question, "Have you any grandchildren?" "Forty-one," she hissed. I thought she misunderstood me, so I repeated, "Have you any grandchildren?" She almost shouted, "Yes, forty-one grandchildren and eleven children and not one of them has a bed for me." I was so upset by her anger and bitterness that I never went back to the dining room.

I realized that unless I escaped I would go mad. And so I approached the head nurse and asked her what I had to do to qualify to leave the home. She told me that I must demonstrate that I could care for myself on my own—wash, dress, make a simple meal, and so on. Well, I was able to do all those things and more. I pointed this out to her and demonstrated. When I had done what was required, I said, "Now can I go home?"

She just looked at me with a wooden stare. She would not commit herself to a yes or a no. Afterwards I found out that she had a load of paperwork because I walked out. I suspect that her paperwork meant a great deal more to her than my potential freedom.

That was two years ago. Today, age eight-six, Emmie leads a full and satisfying life. She works part-time at the library, exercises at the local Y to keep fit, follows a special diet for diabetes, and she is involved in an amazing number of local activities, from conferences on rape to volunteer work at nursing homes.

Not so many years back I could paint my own home. Now I need help and I have found it. I have a visiting homemaker who comes several times a week to mop my floors, water my plants, wash the dishes and clothes—the tasks that I no longer have the strength to do. I guess my house could be more spiffy, but I'm comfortable with my books and magazines.

I am luckier than most—I have my own home. Older women cannot afford the frightful rents they must pay. If it wasn't for my husband's pension, I would be in the same position. Mind you, when my husband died I was only entitled to half the benefits and a veteran's pension that only amounted to a couple of thousand dollars. I was very insulted. After all, they had this money all those years and they had the nerve to dole it out in dribs and drabs.

Still, even with my own home and two pensions, I live very modestly. I can't travel often and I don't have many clothes. But imagine women who live on government pensions—they must struggle terribly. It's no wonder they end up in nursing homes. It's society's way of getting rid of us, tucking us away. I may not have much longer, but I am determined to live here in my own home, in my own way. Nothing short of force could induce me to go back to the nursing home.

From *Small Expectations: Society's Betrayal of Older Women*
by Leah Cohen, 1985. Used by permission of the Canadian Publishers,
McClelland and Stewart, Toronto.

1. From Lettie's reminiscences abstract some sound guidelines for successful aging.

2. Select a number of statements that capture this woman's philosophy of life. Pinpoint the values that are part of this philosophy.

3. Comment on the seeming lack of a familial network in the lives of Lettie and Emmie. What have they done to compensate for this?

4. Record your reaction to Emmie's nursing home experience.
   Cite what Emmie considered to be the main drawbacks to this kind of life. Could the conditions she describes be common to many nursing homes? Why?

5. Investigate the range of housing options for the elderly in your community.

6. Many factors influence the quality of life in this final life cycle stage. These include state of health, economic status, housing needs, family ties, intergenerational and intragenerational connections, social policies, and community support systems. Using these factors as a guide make a study of the state of the aging and aged in Canada today.

7. Compile a list of references to old age expressed in colloquialisms such as "over the hill" and "the golden years." Abstract from these sayings our society's attitude towards the elderly. How does this compare with other cultures' attitudes?

FAMILY CRISES

Crises occur at some time in all families and necessitate adjustments in the usual pattern of living. Sometimes the crisis is short-lived and sometimes it becomes a continuing feature in the life of the family. Success in coping with a crisis revolves around how the crisis is perceived by the family, what inner resources individual family members possess, and what support systems can be called into play. Rick Hansen became world renowned during his heroic "man in motion" wheelchair odyssey around the world. Hansen had become a paraplegic at the age of sixteen as a result of a car accident. In his autobiography he shares the aftermath of the trauma.

So that was the Rick Hansen who came home to Williams Lake in a wheelchair: a sixteen-year-old who'd never developed a really strong family bond, never really gotten to know his parents, never learned to communicate with them or with his brother and sisters, never learned to show the love he had for them; a kid who'd gone his own way, a doer and a leader who'd lived for his independence and freedom to roam.

And now I was helpless and needed everyone.

I'd had a taste of it at Christmas. I'd been flown in from G. F. Strong, bundled up in what amounted to a cart and carried on and off the plane because I wasn't good enough yet on the braces. The humiliation of it just burned at me.

Now I was back to stay, or so everyone thought. Me, I wasn't sure. In my mind, I'd phased myself out of the house and was on my own before the accident. The house was there and was handy, a place to eat and sleep, but I'd always been out as much as possible. Some of that still applied once I was home, but it was a two-edged sword. The house was still handy, there were still good reasons for staying, but I could never be independent because it was so inaccessible. I couldn't pop in and out and go my own way. In a sense I was a prisoner.

My family rallied around. Dad had the basement renovated to give me my own room and bath. Mom and Dad had their own problems, but there was no doubt who was the first priority. I was still being tough on them, but they never pushed me, never tried to overprotect me.

A lot of people have asked me whether the family stress over my accident was a factor in my parents' separation. Actually, it worked the other way around. For a while I think it kept them together through their concern for me. But the stress might have been the final blow, particularly for my mother, who'd had more than most of us ever encounter.

First there was Dad's accident. Then Brad severely burned one leg when firecrackers exploded in his pocket and [he] tobogganed head-on into an oncoming car, breaking the bones around both eyes; he required surgery and was lucky to escape with his eyesight. And a year before my accident, Grandpa Gibson died in a horrible farm accident. He was wearing a wool work shirt buttoned at the neck. The sleeve caught in the combine, and as it twisted into the machinery his shirt literally strangled him. Grandma Elsie found him when she brought his afternoon tea. His hat was on the ground, the combine still running. She climbed aboard and found him lying in the bin.

People can take only so much pressure, particularly when the family life is deteriorating and the support systems aren't there. It was especially tough for Mom because she'd tried to stop me from taking the fishing trip. Grandpa Gibson had travelled that road shortly before he died and had told her, "Don't let the boys drive to Bella Coola." And of course we did, and she was riddled with guilt because she thought he'd had some sort of premonition and she hadn't somehow kept me at home, as if she could have.

My parents hung in there for a couple more years. I was settled into university when they separated and ultimately divorced. For me there was no sorrow, only the hope that they'd both find happiness, and a sense of relief that something that should have ended a long time ago was finally over.

Of all the things I remember about my parents, through good times and bad, I remember this most: when I needed them, they were always there. I loved them then, I love them now, and I always will.

From *Rick Hansen: Man in Motion* by Rick Hansen and Jim Taylor
(Douglas & McIntyre, 1987). Reprinted by permission of the publisher.

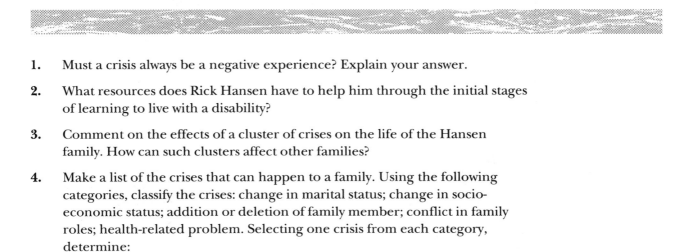

1. Must a crisis always be a negative experience? Explain your answer.

2. What resources does Rick Hansen have to help him through the initial stages of learning to live with a disability?

3. Comment on the effects of a cluster of crises on the life of the Hansen family. How can such clusters affect other families?

4. Make a list of the crises that can happen to a family. Using the following categories, classify the crises: change in marital status; change in socio-economic status; addition or deletion of family member; conflict in family roles; health-related problem. Selecting one crisis from each category, determine:

   ☐ how your family would perceive this crisis;
   ☐ what inner resources they could draw upon;
   ☐ what external support systems would be available;
   ☐ what changes could occur as a result of the crisis.

5. Death is an inevitable crisis situation in any family. However, the dimensions of this crisis differ depending on whether it is a natural occurrence at the end of a long life or whether it is a sudden or untimely death. Conduct a literature search on death and dying.

6. Explore your own attitudes towards and beliefs about death.

INTERGENERATIONAL CONNECTIONS

How many families do you know who have three or even four generations interacting with one another on a fairly regular basis? The relationship between grandparents and children can often be a special one: older people can enjoy their grandchildren without the direct responsibility for their upbringing, and through their grandparents and great-grandparents younger generations are afforded living memories of an earlier time. Joyce Maynard invites you to look at four generations in her family and feel the joys and frustrations of these generational bonds.

M y mother called last week to tell me that my grandmother is dying. She has refused an operation that would postpone, but not prevent, her death from pancreatic cancer. She can't eat, she has been hemorrhaging, and she has severe jaundice. "I always prided myself on being different," she told my mother. "Now I *am* different. I'm yellow."

My mother, telling me this news, began to cry. So I became the mother for a moment, reminding her, reasonably, that my grandmother is eighty-seven, she's had a full life, she has all her faculties, and no one who knows her could wish that she live long enough to lose them. Lately my mother has been finding notes in my grandmother's drawers at the nursing home, reminding her, "Joyce's husband's name is Steve. Their daughter is Audrey." In the last few years she hadn't had the strength to cook or garden, and she's begun to say she's had enough of living.

My grandmother was born in Russia, in 1892—the oldest daughter in a large prosperous Jewish family. But the prosperity didn't last. She tells stories of the pogroms and the Cossacks who raped her when she was twelve. Soon after that, her family emigrated to Canada, where she met my grandfather.

Their children were the centre of their life. The story I loved best, as a child, was of my grandfather opening every box of Cracker Jack in the general store he ran, in search of the particular tin toy my mother coveted. Though they never had much money, my grandmother saw to it that her daughter had elocution lessons and piano lessons, and assured her that she would go to college.

But while she was at college, my mother met my father, who was blue-eyed and blond-haired and not Jewish. When my father sent love letters to my mother, my grandmother would open and hide them, and when my mother told her parents she was going to marry this man, my grandmother said if that happened, it would kill her.

> Every eye brings its own contribution.
> **VIRGINIA WOOLF**

Not likely, of course. My grandmother is a woman who used to crack Brazil nuts open with her teeth, a woman who once lifted a car off the ground, when there was an accident and it had to be removed. She has been representing her death as imminent ever since I've known her—twenty-five years—and has discussed, at length, the distribution of her possessions and her lamb coat. Every time we said goodbye, after our annual visit to Winnipeg, she'd weep and say she'd never see us again. But in the meantime, while every other relative of her generation, and a good many of the younger ones, has died (nursed usually by her), she has kept making knishes, shopping for bargains, tending the healthiest plants I've ever seen.

After my grandfather died, my grandmother lived, more than ever, through her children. When she came to visit, I would hide my diary. She couldn't understand any desire for privacy. She couldn't bear it if my mother left the house without her.

This possessiveness is what made my mother furious (and then guilt-ridden that she felt that way, when of course she owed so much to her mother). So I harbored the resentment that my mother—the dutiful daughter—would not allow herself. I—who had always performed specially well for my grandmother, danced and sung for her, presented her with kisses and good report cards—stopped writing to her, ceased to visit.

But when I heard that she was dying, I realized I wanted to go to Winnipeg to see her one more time. Mostly to make my mother happy, I told myself (certain patterns being hard to break). But also, I was offering up one more particularly fine accomplishment: my own dark-eyed, dark-skinned, dark-haired daughter, whom my grandmother had never met.

Audrey and I have stopped over for a night in Toronto, where my mother lives. Tomorrow she will go to a safe-deposit box at the bank and take out the receipt for my grandmother's burial plot. Then she will fly back to Winnipeg, where, for the first time in anybody's memory, there was waist-high snow on April Fool's Day. But tonight she is feeding me, as she always does when I come, and I am eating more than I do anywhere else. I admire the wedding china (once my grandmother's) that my mother has set on the table. She says (the way Grandma used to say to her, of the lamb coat), "Some day it will be yours."

I put on my daughter's best dress for our visit to Winnipeg, the way the best dresses were always put on me, and I filled my pockets with animal crackers, in case Audrey started to cry. I scrubbed her face mercilessly. On the elevator going up to her room, I realized how much I was sweating.

Grandma was lying flat with an IV tube in her arm and her eyes shut, but she opened them when I leaned over to kiss her. "It's Fredelle's daughter Joyce," I yelled, because she doesn't hear well anymore, but I could see that no explanation was necessary. "You came," she said. "You brought the baby."

Audrey is just one, but she has seen enough of the world to know that people in beds are not meant to be still and yellow, and she looked frightened. I had never wanted, more, for her to smile.

Then Grandma waved at her—the same kind of slow, fingerflexing wave a baby makes—and Audrey waved back. I spread her toys out on my grandmother's bed and sat her down. There she stayed, most of the afternoon, playing and

To form a link in the humble chain of being, encircling heirs to ancestors is to walk within a circle of magic as primitive as humans knew in caves.
MICHAEL NOVAK

In the presence of grandparents and grandchildren the past and the future merge in the present.
MARGARET MEAD

humming and sipping on her bottle, taking a nap at one point, leaning against my grandmother's leg. When I cranked her Snoopy guitar, Audrey stood up on the bed and danced. Grandma wouldn't talk much anymore, though every once in a while she would say how sorry she was that she wasn't having a better day. "I'm not always like this," she said.

Mostly she just watched Audrey. Sometimes Audrey would get off the bed, inspect the get-well cards, totter down the hall. "Where is she?" Grandma kept asking. "Who's looking after her?" I had the feeling, even then, that if I'd said, "Audrey's lighting matches," Grandma would have shot up to rescue her.

We were flying home that night, and I had dreaded telling her, remembering all those other tearful partings. But in the end, I was the one who cried. She had said she was ready to die. But as I leaned over to stroke her forehead, what she said was, "I wish I had your hair" and "I wish I was well."

On the plane flying home, with Audrey in my arms, I thought about mothers and daughters, and the four generations of the family that I know most intimately. Every one of those mothers loves and needs her daughter more than her daughter will love or need her some day, and we are, each of us, the only person on earth who is quite so consumingly interested in our child.

Sometimes I kiss and hug Audrey so much she starts crying—which is, in effect, what my grandmother was doing to my mother, all her life. And what makes my mother grieve right now, I think, is not simply that her mother will die in a day or two, but that, once her mother dies, there will never again be someone to love her in quite such an unreserved, unquestioning way. No one else who believes that, fifty years ago, she could have put Shirley Temple out of a job, no one else who remembers that moment of her birth. She will only be a mother, then, not a daughter anymore.

From "Four Generations" by Joyce Maynard, *New York Times*, 1985.

> In early childhood our mother explained to us the richness in life depended on a blend of past, present and future, that our sources of strength came from that which has gone before and our dreams were flights into the future, a time yet to come. She taught us to look gently over our shoulder.
>
> JANE WATSON HOPPING

1. Express in your own words the overall tone of this selection.

2. Describe the bonds that seem to link the four generations of the Maynard family.

3. It has been said that a four-generation family is an emotional minefield, as each generation is simultaneously involved in critical transition points in the life cycle. With the selection in mind, outline what you see as the distinctive role cluster for members of each generation. Analyze how relationships change as one moves up in this generational ladder.

4. Reflect on the following statement: "Every one of those mothers loves and needs her daughter more than her daughter will love or need her some day, and we are, each of us, the only person on earth who is quite so consumingly interested in our child."

5. As Joyce Maynard observes in the relationship between her mother, grandmother, and herself, possessiveness on the part of a parent can result in feelings of resentment and guilt in children. What social and psychological factors may have contributed to her grandmother's need to "live through her children"? Do you think her grandmother would have had the same relationship with her children if she were bringing them up today? Why or why not?

6. Take any family of your acquaintance and examine it for generational interaction. In what ways does this interaction enhance the life of this family? Are there stresses and strains involved in the interaction? If so, identify them, using a systems perspective.

THE EMERGING FAMILY

[Families have] weathered combinations of step, foster, single, adoptive, surrogate, frozen embryo, and sperm bank.
They've multiplied, divided, extended and banded into communes. They've been assaulted by technology, battered by sexual revolutions, and confused by role reversals. But they are still here . . . playing to a full house.

ERMA BOMBECK, *FAMILY: THE TIES THAT BIND . . . AND GAG!*

☐

. . . The extended family is in our lives again. This should make all the people happy who were complaining back in the sixties and seventies that the reason family life was so hard, especially on mothers, was that the nuclear family had replaced the extended family. . . .

We owe the return of the extended family, albeit in a slightly altered form, to an innovation called joint custody. . . . Your basic extended family today includes your ex-husband or -wife, your ex's new mate, your new mate, possibly your new mate's ex, and any new mate that your new mate's ex has acquired. . . . This return of the extended family reminds me of the favorite saying of my friend's extremely pessimistic mother: Be careful what you wish for, you might get it.

DELIA EPHRON, *FUNNY SAUCE*

■

OVERVIEW ESSAY
by Claude Guldner, Director
Marriage and Family Therapy Program
Department of Family Studies
University of Guelph

■

READINGS

THE EMERGING FAMILY

by Claude Guldner

Families, our oldest and most enduring social institution, survive in spite of a host of internal and external pressures. Further, families are alive and well in this last decade of the twentieth century despite widely published reports that they have served their course and should be put to rest. In fact, it is becoming apparent (emerging) that families are strong and resourceful today because of their ability to change their composition, functions, and relationship structures through the many passages of family experience.

The first forty years of this century produced, for the most part, a homogeneous family type. This today is referred to as the "traditional" family format; however, if one followed families down through history one would find that families have had a range of formations and only in this century have we viewed the father, mother, and children grouping as "traditional." This label distinguishes the nuclear family from the wide variety of family groupings that have evolved over the last half of this century. As we move into the last decade of this century, slightly less than half of all Canadian families meet this "traditional" model. We live rather in a time of heterogeneity in family formation, as is evident in the articles that make up this section of the book.

This complexity of family formation confronts us with the dilemma of developing an adequate and comprehensive definition of just what is "family." Textbooks written as late as the 1970s frequently claimed that children were a necessary ingredient for the use of the term family. This would exclude the voluntary childless couple or a brother, sister and cousin who might choose to live together, or the person living alone who has a primary support system. Current definitions move us away from the model of family that Eichler (1988) calls "monolithic," that is, seeing all families as essentially the same in composition, structure and function, to a "multidimensional" model. Eichler has focused upon dimensions of family interactions that may or may not be experienced by various families, rather than functions seen as necessary to the experience of *all* families.

The multidimensional model involves several dimensions of familial interaction. Eichler discusses six of these dimensions: procreative, socialization, sexual, residential, economic, and emotional. It is not necessary for all of these dimensions to be present, or present at the same intensity, in order to inform a definition of the family. A brief examination of divorce and remarriage will illustrate the point. Many people view divorce as the "breakdown" of *the* family. Family systems thinking has enabled us to recognize that it is not the end of the family but only its reorganization. The family ends one subsystem, the husband and wife dyad, but requires reorganization of the parental subsystem, father and mother, even though these individuals reside in different households. They both have responsibilities for socialization of children and both will usually desire to maintain close emotional bonds with children. The husband and wife subsystem will no longer maintain a sexual relationship, yet they will generally maintain an economic one.

Families have moved from having primarily an economic and procreative emphasis to units having emotional and social support functions. This change has taken place for several reasons. First, most men and women in society today have the capability and desire to function in a work context. Hence they are more financially independent than in the past. Further, many forms of family today either do not lend themselves to having children or those involved may choose not to have children. Even where children are part of the family, over half are provided some other form of child care in order to free the parents to pursue their own work interests. The development of companionable, sharing, and affectional bonds within a context of trust and some measure of continuity become important in our increasingly impersonal world.

These emerging functions of the family necessitate that we move from an essentialist definition of family, meaning the procreation and socialization of children as essential family functions, to a constructivist perspective. The core ideas in the theory of constructivism is that we participate in the construction of our realities and that our views change with our experience. Constructivist thinking enables us to create families of choice. For example, four Catholic nuns living in a home in the downtown core of a city view themselves as "family." All four have extended families of their own, other sisters in their order, and various work systems. These feed into but do not replicate the kind of support, commitment, affection, and "rules" or patterns of consistent interaction that occur day in and day out in their household and that bind them together to "feel" like family. Another example is the couple who wait until their mid-thirties to marry, and focus on the development of their separate careers rather than on having children. Through choice they have constructed their form of family. A single woman lives alone and yet has a small network consisting of two women and a man with whom she interacts upon a regular basis. This "feels" like her family and indeed, it is. Through the consistent interactions and patterns of behaviour that have developed over time she has constructed a family of choice.

Psychologist George Kelley, often considered the founder of constructivism, once said, "There is nothing so obvious that its appearance is not altered when it is seen in a different light . . . Whatever exists can be construed" (Kelley, 1969).

Families exist in many reconstructions. We need to view families in a different light, one that recognizes the strength, resources, and viability of each of the many options in family living. Systems theory has enabled us to recognize that at one level all families are alike. They all have structures (regulated patterns through which people relate to one another); functions (the steps families take to fulfil their purposes); and operations (the specific activities a family undertakes in its process of fulfilling functions). It is through these that every family develops its own idiosyncratic patterns of interaction.

The key to studying families is to look at how they carry out their functions in relation to their particular structures. This provides the criteria by which to measure the degree to which a family, no matter what its composition, is functional or dysfunctional (Aponte and VanDeusen, 1981).

There are a number of structural issues to consider in attempting to understand the quality of family functioning. We shall briefly examine eight of these. *Boundaries* have to do with who is inside/outside the family unit and who participates in the formation of the rules (conscious and unconscious) of the family system. *Power* has to do with the ability to influence the outcome of transactions in the system. *Alignments* are divided into alliances (individuals coming together out of common interests), and coalitions (individuals forming together against another). There is a constant interplay among these three structural components in any family system as it attempts to carry out its functions such as socialization, emotional fulfilment, economic security, etc.

Our society has a tendency to look at functional and dysfunctional in terms of family composition but, as mentioned above, a divorced family is not necessarily dysfunctional as a result of "losing" one member. A nuclear family may be highly dysfunctional if it has rigid boundaries that do not change as children develop; if the power resides in an older sibling rather than a parental unit; or if the kids always side with mother against father. A single-parent family with clear and flexible boundaries, permitting the movement of the non-custodial parent into the lives of the children on a regular basis, with parental power still shared by both custodial and non-custodial parents, and no coalitions blocking access to information from any family member, is a highly functioning family system.

Accompanying the changing nature of the family is the multiplication of *roles* required of each family member. In "traditional" family forms each member had limited and very specific roles. Father was the income provider and final authority in the family. Mother was the nurturant homemaker and steady presence for her children. Children had specific roles related to gender-stereotyped task functions. Today, however, family lifestyles require "role cycling" (Pearson, 1989). Family members must be flexible enough to take on a wide variety of quite diverse roles in order to carry out the functions of family needs and wants. Today, a single parent (usually a woman) is income provider, homemaker, and home caretaker. She may also be responsible for an older parent, or for maintaining community responsibilities while engaging in a peer support network. This multiplicity of roles requires the ability for rapid adaptation and flexibility. We are recognizing that when opportunity avails itself, both men and women are capable of role cycling to meet all family needs. In many households with both adult men and women (husbands and wives or co-habitants), one may find the man in the role of primary caretaking parent and homemaker, with the woman as the essential income producer. Circumstances and personal choice come together increasingly in families to produce a different lifestyle from what has been known "traditionally."

In addition to boundaries, power, alignments, and roles, there are four other key structural issues that influence contemporary families. The first of these is *communication*. Family therapists have always had an interest in communication, since this is what enables the family to carry out the functions of daily living. What is changing is the quality of communication interchanges. Families of the past tended to have a typical format wherein children told mother, who in turn informed father, who then made the decisions.

Moreover, in the past, patterns of communication were more or less "closed." The information (communication) coming into and going out of the family was highly screened by the parents. In today's society, information flows so freely that most parents find it difficult to regulate. Instead, families today attempt to make meaning of the information and how it influences the values and quality of life for family members. Their patterns of communication are thus more "open." Similarly, family members are increasingly concerned with exchanges that are more reflective of personal experience and feeling. Today couples spend more time sharing their "inner" experience. When individuals are unable to function at this level, it is often viewed as a problem for the relationship. Most individuals, no matter what the type of relationship they are in, want it to be meaningful and this generally implies a quality of personal depth communication.

Another structural area is that of *negotiation*. No matter what form a family unit may take—single parent, blended, dual career, etc.—members must become aware that each individual is unique. Whenever there is difference, individuals will by necessity have to negotiate. In relationships, we can never have just what we want without consideration of other members. Families will thus experience conflict as a natural part of their ongoing interaction. Functional families will be able to solve problems, make decisions, and negotiate conflict.

Whatever form a family may take, it is generally maintained and valued because it meets *affective needs*, that is, emotions and feelings. A strong sense of caring will ideally permeate the interactions and encounters of family members. Understanding and accepting the feelings of all members increases family cohesion as well as the ability to adapt to change.

A final component necessary for adequate family functioning is the development of a positive *self-concept* within each member. One's self-concept may be viewed from three perspectives. The first is how one sees him/herself. Our own self-image is a creation of the interplay between the feedback received from others and how it fits with our own self-appraisal. The second component relates to one's feelings about oneself, generally referred to as self-esteem. The final element is self-worth, or the value one places upon oneself. Put simply, our self-concept enables us to say, "I'm OK, I'm lovable, I'm valued."

When one examines the range of family formations and lifestyles that exist in our society today, it becomes very important to make the shift from thinking about family in terms of *who* composes the unit to *how* the members of that unit construct their patterns of interactive relationships. We gain understanding of these patterned behaviours through observing boundaries, power, alignments, roles, communication, negotiations, affective exchanges, and level of self-concept. The manner in which these structural issues evolve within families will enable us to determine how well the family carries out its functions and daily operations.

Every family unit constructs meanings regarding itself that gradually take the form of mythologies. A myth is an attempt to make sense of experience. Belief systems and mythologies create contexts for how we observe reality. If we take something out of context it generally becomes meaningless. It is thus important for you, as reader of this volume, to be cognizant of your personal family context as you explore various emergent family models. This awareness will enable you to be more alert to your own biases regarding families. At the same time, understanding your own family mythology may enhance your understanding of other family forms.

One of the basic tenets of systems theory is that the information of importance is the information of relationship. A first step in understanding a family unit is to be able to observe its relationship patterns from a non-judgemental perspective. A second systems tenet is that the information necessary for change is the information of difference. When family system members are able to make distinctions that highlight difference, they increase their information input, which in turn increases their options, or choices. For example, when a parent states that the whole family enjoys going to the cottage for the summer, this statement implies that all family members feel equal about this activity. If we were to ask each family member to rank in order who most enjoys going to the cottage, who next, and down to who least enjoys going to the cottage, we would discover that not all family members feel equal about spending the summer at the cottage. New information has been added to the system and the family sees each member more uniquely. This all adds to system complexity or movement and growth.

The reader is urged to study the following articles with an eye for making distinctions among single-parent families, either mother-headed or father-headed; blended families; dual-career couples with children; couples childless by choice; and all the other emergent family forms. The reader should also be aware of differences both in gender and in generations (Goldner, 1988). All families are either composed of different genders or have been influenced by gender differences evolving out of our sociocultural history. The experiences of men and women in families are significantly different. As a result, each of us brings gender-based meanings to structural issues of boundaries, power, and alignments.

Age differences are most obvious, of course, in three- and four-generational families. They are also dramatic in those blended families where the older children of one parent and the younger children of the other live together in one household. Age differences, like those of gender, affect the patterning of boundaries, power, and alignments. Because gender and age differences are universal they must be viewed as providing a frame within which one may examine all eight of the structural issues affecting families.

Everything observed is observed from a tradition (Varela, 1979). Many readers of this volume will be familiar with one or more of these emerging family forms, for you have had direct personal experience with that type of family. Despite one's personal experiences, and despite the reality that nearly half of the individuals in Canada live in a "non-traditional" family, it is difficult for us not to "observe from a tradition." It takes time to integrate changes into the matrix of society, even when those changes are increasingly the "norm." This is your opportunity to put on new lenses as you read about various forms of emerging families, observing distinctions rather than dysfunctions.

BIBLIOGRAPHY

Aponte, H. J. and VanDeusen, J. M. "Structural Family Therapy," *Handbook of Family Therapy*, A. S. Gurman & D. P. Kniskern, eds. New York: Brunner/ Mazel, 1981.

Eichler, Margrit, *Families in Canada Today*, 2nd Ed. Toronto: Gage Educational Publishing Co., 1988.

Goldner, Virginia, "Generation and Gender: Normative and Covert Hierarchies," *Family Process*, Vol. 27, No. 1, 1988.

Kelley, G. A. *Clinical Psychology and Personality: The Selected Papers of George Kelley*, B. Maher (Ed). New York: John Wiley & Sons, 1969.

Pearson, Judy C., *Communication in the Family: Seeking Satisfaction in Changing Times.* New York: Harper & Row, 1989.

Varela, F. J., *Principles of Biological Autonomy.* New York: Elsevier-North Holland, 1979.

NEW MEANINGS OF AGE

A 70-year-old divorcée? A 37-year-old grandfather? A 48-year-old
student? A 19-year-old business executive? An 81-year-old jogger? Indeed!
Such are the conflicting images and blurred boundaries of contemporary
life. World renowned scholars on aging, the authors of this selection note:
"Whether you are young, old or in between, acting your age can mean
many more things than it once did."

□

In our society, as in most others, age is a major dimension of social organization. Our school system, to name one example, is carefully arranged around the
students' ages, and the behavior of all students is clearly differentiated from the
behavior of adult teachers. Similarly, to a greater or lesser extent, families, corporations, even whole communities are organized by age.

Age also plays an important part in how people relate to one another across the
whole range of everyday experience. When a young man sits down in an airplane
and glances at the person in the next seat, the first thing to cross his mind is likely to
be "That's an old man," or "That's a young man like me," and he automatically
adjusts his behavior accordingly—his language, manners and conversation.

Age is also a major touchstone by which individuals organize and interpret
their own lives. Both children and adults continually ask of themselves, "How well
am I doing for my age?"

From all three perspectives, our changing society has brought with it changes in
the social meanings of age: blurred boundaries between the periods of life, new
definitions of age groups, new patterns in the timing of major life events and new
inconsistencies in what is considered age-appropriate behavior.

In all societies, lifetime is divided into socially relevant periods, age distinctions become systematized and rights and responsibilities are distributed according
to social age. Even the simplest societies define at least three periods: childhood,
adulthood and old age. In more complex societies, a greater number of life periods
are differentiated, and transition points are differently timed in different areas of life.
In modern America people are considered adults in the political system when they
reach 18 and are given the right to vote; but they are not adults in the family system
until they marry and take on the responsibilities of parenthood. Or people may be

adult in the family system, but if they are still in school, they are not yet adult in the economic system.

Historians have described how life periods became demarcated in Western societies over the past few centuries. Only with industrialization and the appearance of a middle class and formally organized schools did childhood become a clearly definable period of life. Adolescence took on its present meaning in the late 19th century and became widespread in the 20th, as the period of formal education lengthened and the transition to adulthood was increasingly delayed. A stage called youth took on its modern meaning only a few decades ago, as growing numbers of young people, after leaving school and before marrying or making occupational choices, opted for a period of time to explore various life roles.

It was only a few decades ago, too, that middle age became identified, largely a reflection of the historically changing rhythm of events in the family cycle. With fewer children per family, and with births spaced closer together, middle age became defined as the time when children grow up and leave the parents' home. In turn, as the concept of retirement took hold, old age came to be regarded as the time following retirement from the labour force. It was usually perceived as a distinct period marked by the right to lead a life of leisure, declining physical and intellectual vigour, social disengagement and, often, isolation and desolation.

Life periods were closely associated with chronological age, even though age lines were seldom sharply drawn.

But the distinctions between life periods are blurring in today's society. The most dramatic evidence, perhaps, is the appearance of the so-called "young-old." It is a recent historical phenomenon that a very large group of retirees and their spouses are healthy and vigorous, relatively well-off financially, well-integrated into the lives of their families and communities and politically active. The term "young-old" is becoming part of everyday parlance, and it refers not to a particular age but to health and social characteristics. A young-old person may be 55 or 85. The term represents the social reality that the line between middle age and old age is no longer clear. What was once considered old age now characterizes only that minority of older persons who have been called the "old-old," that particularly vulnerable group who often are in need of special support and special care.

When, then, does old age now begin? The usual view has been that it starts at 65, when most people retire. But in the United States today the majority begin to take their Social Security retirement benefits at 62 or 63; and at ages 55 to 64, fewer than three of every four men are in the labour force. At the same time, with continued good health, some people are staying at work, full-time or part-time, into their 80s. So age 65 and retirement are no longer clear dividers between middle age and old age.

Alternatively, old age is often said to begin when poor health creates a major limitation on the activities of everyday life. Yet in a 1981 survey, half of all people 75 to 84 reported no such health limitations. Even in the very oldest group, those older than 85, more than a third reported no limitations due to health, and another one-third reported minor limitations; only one in three said they were unable to carry out any of their everyday activities. So health status is also becoming a poor age marker.

It is not only in the second half of life that the blurring of life periods can be

People do not really age by living a number of years. I am convinced that we grow old only by deserting our ideals. We are, in fact, as old as our doubts and despairs, but we are as young as our faith and our hope. . . .
GEORGES VANIER

seen. Adults of all ages are experiencing changes in the traditional rhythm and timing of events of the life cycle. More men and women marry, divorce, remarry and divorce again up through their 70s. More stay single. More women have their first child before they are 15, and more do so after 35. The result is that people are becoming grandparents for the first time at ages ranging from 35 to 75. More women, but also increasing numbers of men, raise children in two-parent, then one-parent, then two-parent households. More women, but also increasing numbers of men, exit and reenter school, enter and reenter the work force and undertake second and third careers up through their 70s. It therefore becomes difficult to distinguish the young, the middle-aged and the young-old—either in terms of major life events or the ages at which those events occur.

The line between adolescence and adulthood is also being obscured. The traditional transitions into adulthood and the social competencies they implied—full-time jobs, marriage and parenthood—are disappearing as markers of social age. For some men and women, the entry into a job or profession is being delayed to age 30 as education is prolonged. For others, entry into the work force occurs at 16 or 17. Not only are there more teenage pregnancies but also more teenage women who are mothering their children. All this adds up to what has been aptly called "the fluid life cycle."

This is not to deny that our society still recognizes differences between adolescents, young people and old people, and that people still relate to each other accordingly. Yet we are less sure today where to place the punctuation marks in the life line and just what those punctuation marks should be. All across adulthood, age has become a poor predictor of the timing of life events, just as it is a poor predictor of health, work status, family status, interests, preoccupations and needs. We have conflicting images rather than stereotypes of age: the 70-year-old in a wheelchair, but also the 70-year-old on the tennis court; the 18-year-old who is married and supporting a family, but also the 18-year-old college student who brings his laundry home to his mother each week.

Difference among individuals, multiple images of age groups and inconsistencies in age norms were surely present in earlier periods of our history, but as our society has become more complex, the irregularities have become increasingly a part of the social reality.

These trends are reflected in public perceptions, too. Although systematic research is sparse, there are a few studies that show a diminishing public consensus about the periods of life and their markers. In the early 1960s, for instance, a group of middle-class, middle-aged people were asked about the "best" ages for life transitions (such as completing school, marrying, retiring) and the ages they associated with such phrases as "a young man," "an old woman" and "when a man (or woman) has the most responsibilities." When the same questions were asked of a similar group of people two decades later, the earlier consensus on every item of the questionnaire had disappeared. In the first study, nearly 90 percent had replied that the best age for a woman to marry was between 19 and 24; in the repeat study, only 40 percent gave this answer. In the first study, "a young man" was said to be a man between 18 and 22; in the repeat study, "a young man" was anywhere from 18 to 40.

These findings are based on a very small study, but they illustrate how public views are changing.

In some respects, the line between childhood and adulthood is also fading. It is a frequent comment that childhood as we once knew it is disappearing. Increasingly children and adults have the same preferences in styles of dress, forms of language, games and television shows. Children know more about once-taboo topics such as sex, drugs, alcoholism, suicide and nuclear war. There is more adult-like sexual behavior among children, and more adult-like crime. At the same time, with the pressures for achievement rising, we have witnessed the advent of "the hurried child" and "the harried child."

We have also become accustomed to the descriptions of today's adults as narcissistic, self-interested and self-indulgent. Yuppies are described in the mass media as the pace-setters. While they work hard to get ahead, they are portrayed as more materialistic even than the "me" generation that preceded them, interested primarily in making money and in buying the "right" cars, the "best" housing and the most expensive gourmet foods. Overall, today's adults have fewer lasting marriages, fewer lasting commitments to work or community roles, more uncontrolled expressions of emotion, a greater sense of powerlessness—in short, more childlike behavior.

This picture may be somewhat overdrawn. Both children and adults are continually exhorted to "act your age," and they seldom misunderstand what that means. Yet the expectations of appropriate behavior for children and adults are certainly less differentiated than they once were. We are less sure of what intellectual and social competencies to expect of children—not only because some children are teaching their teachers how to use computers, but also because so many children are streetwise by age 8 and so many others, in the wake of divorce, are the confidantes of their parents by age 12.

Some observers attribute the blurring of childhood and adulthood primarily to the effects of television, which illuminates the total culture and reveals the secrets that adults have traditionally withheld from children. But it is not only television. A report in *The New York Times* underlines the fact that children are being socialized in new ways today by parents, schools, churches and peer groups as well. The Girl Scouts of the U.S.A., according to the *Times* article, had decided finally to admit 5-year-olds. The national executive director was quoted as saying, "The decision to admit five-year-olds reflects the change in the American labor market. Women are working for part or all of their adult lives now. The possibilities are limitless but you need to prepare. So we think six is not too early to learn about career opportunities, and we also think that girls need to learn about making decisions. When you're five, you're not too young."

The blurring of traditional life periods does not mean that age norms are disappearing altogether. We still have our regulations about the ages at which children enter and exit from school, when people can marry without the consent of parents, when they are eligible for Social Security benefits. And less formal norms are still operating. Someone who moves to the Sun Belt to lead a life of leisure is socially approved if he is 70, but not if he is 30. An unmarried mother meets with

> Our society is getting older but the old are getting younger.
> JACK C. HORN

greater disapproval if she is 15 than if she is 35. A couple in their 40s who decide to have another child are criticized for embarrassing their adolescent children. . . . Expectations regarding age-appropriate behavior still form an elaborate and pervasive system of norms, expectations that are woven into the cultural fabric.

Both legal and cultural age norms are mirrored in the ways people behave and the ways they think about their own lives. Today, as in the past, most people by the time they are adolescents develop a set of anticipations of the normal, expectable life cycle: expectations of what the major life events and turning points will be and when they should occur. People internalize a social clock that tells them if they are on time or not.

Although the actual timing of life events for both women and men has always been influenced by various life contingencies, the norms and the actual occurrences have been closely connected. It may be less true today, but most people still try to marry or have a child or make a job change when they think they have reached the "right" age. They can still easily report whether they were early, late or on time with regard to one life event after another.

The life events that occur on time do not usually precipitate life crises, for they have been anticipated and rehearsed. The so-called "empty nest," for instance, is not itself stressful for most middle-aged parents. Instead, it is when children do not leave home at the appropriate time that stress occurs in both the parent and the child. For most older men, if it does not occur earlier than planned, retirement is taken in stride as a normal, expectable event. Widowhood is less often a crisis if it occurs at 65 rather than at 40.

It is the events that upset the expected sequence and rhythm of the life cycle that cause problems—as when the death of a parent comes during one's adolescence rather than in middle age; when marriage is delayed too long; when the birth of a child comes too early; when occupational achievement is slowed; when the empty nest, grandparenthood, retirement, major illness or widowhood occurs "out of sync." Traditional timetables still operate.

For the many reasons suggested earlier, the traditional time schedules do not in today's society produce the regularities anticipated by adolescents or young adults. For many men and women, to be out of sync may have lost some of its importance, but for others, the social clocks have not stopped ticking. The incongruities between the traditional norms and the fluid life cycle represent new freedoms for many people; for other people, new uncertainties and strains.

There is still another reality to be reckoned with. Some timetables are losing their significance, but others are more compelling than ever. A young man may feel he is a failure if he has not "made it" in his corporation by the time he is 35. A young woman may delay marriage because of her career, but then hurry to catch up with parenthood. The same young woman may feel under pressure to marry, bear a child and establish herself in a career all within a five-year period—even though she knows she is likely to live to 85.

Sometimes both traditional and non-traditional views are in conflict in the mind of the same person. The young woman who deliberately delays marriage may be the same woman who worries that she has lost status because she is not married

> In youth we learn;
> in age we understand.
> MARIE EBNER-
> ESCHENBACH

by 25. A middle-aged man starts a second family, but feels compelled to justify himself by explaining that he expects to live to see his new children reach adulthood. Or an old person reports that because he did not expect to live so long, he is now unprepared to take on the "new ways" of some of his peers. Some people live in new ways, but continue to think in old ways.

Given such complications, shall we say that individuals are paying less or more attention to age as a prod or a brake upon their behavior? That age consciousness is decreasing or increasing? Whether or not historical change is occurring, it is fair to say that one's own age remains crucial to every individual, all the way from early childhood through advanced old age. A person uses age as a guide in accommodating to others, in giving meaning to the life course, and in contemplating the time that is past and the time that remains.

In sum, there are multiple levels of social and psychological reality based on social age, and in modern societies, on calendar age as the marker of social age. The complexities are no fewer for the individual than for society at large.

From "The Changing Meanings of Age"
by Bernice Neugarten and Dail Neugarten, May 1987, pp. 29-33.
Reprinted with permission from Psychology Today Magazine.
Copyright ©1987 (PT Partners, L.P.).

1. State the authors' thesis. Be careful to weigh all the important points to arrive at a balanced representation of their argument.

2. Provide illustrations of the "blurring of traditional life periods."

3. Investigate how different cultural norms with respect to age may influence behaviour over the family life cycle.

4. Predict how the social meanings of age may change in the future. Base your projections on current Canadian statistics. What type of statistics would be most relevant?

5. Assess the extent to which you use age as a guide to understand, judge, or anticipate events in your own life, and in the lives of others.

6. Examine all the references to retirement in this article. Do you detect any underlying biases? Explain.

7. "Only with industrialization and the appearance of a middle class and formally organized schools did childhood become a clearly definable period of life." Do you agree? Refer to Joy Parr's article on families of the past. How does our current view of age affect our vision of the past?

CHANGING FAMILY FUNCTIONS

With the following words from *Families in Canada Today*, Margrit Eichler sets the stage for a re-examination of key dimensions of family interaction: "Change . . . is everywhere evident, and most clearly experienced in the personal struggles of people who try to determine a path through an area they thought was well charted, but where suddenly the signposts have disappeared."

☐

☐ DIMENSIONS OF FAMILIAL INTERACTION

For our purposes, the most important dimensions of familial interactions are the following: the procreative dimension; the socialization dimension; the sexual dimension; the residential dimension; the economic dimension; the emotional dimension.

It must be noted that this is not an exhaustive list. One extremely important dimension which is not included is the legal dimension. The reason for ignoring it here is that it cross-cuts all other dimensions. Besides, it represents an extraneous factor, while the other dimensions are largely internal to a family system. The same applies to the time dimension. Other dimensions which are important but not dealt with here include a social dimension (interactions with friends, acquaintances, etc.) and religious and ethical dimension. This discussion is limited to those dimensions which are considered the most important ones.

Within each dimension, various degrees of interaction can be identified. In the following paragraphs, each dimension will be briefly described. . . .

Procreative dimension. Procreative interaction ranges from a couple having biological child(ren) with each other and only with each other, over one or both of them having child(ren) with other partners plus having child(ren) together, to their having child(ren) only with other partners or having none at all.

Socialization dimension. Interaction in the socialization dimension ranges from both spouses being involved in the socialization of the children, over only one of them being involved (e.g., in the case of a divorce in which only one parent has custody and the other does not even have visitation rights), to neither of them being involved (e.g., when the child has been given up for adoption or when there are no children to socialize).

Sexual dimension. Sexual interaction ranges from a marital couple having sex only with each other, over having sex together as well as with other partners, to having sex only with other persons or being celibate.

Residential dimension. Residential interaction ranges from all family members sharing the same residence day and night, to all or some of them living in completely separate residences, with a multiplicity of intermediate arrangements.

Economic dimension. Economic co-operation can refer to a wide variety of possible relationships. As far as familial interactions are concerned, the most important economic relationship regards support obligations and actual provision of support (i.e., a sociological rather than a legal definition of support) between family members. Economic co-operation in this sense, then, ranges from one family member being totally responsible for the support of all family members, to a family in which all members are totally economically independent (e.g., by purchasing their own food and shelter or by paying their share of any joint expenses). In between are various degrees of partial support responsibilities: for instance, one person being responsible for some but not all family members (e.g., when a husband-father provides for himself and his children, but his wife pays for her own expenses including her part of the shelter and food when shared), or one family member is only partially responsible for some other family members, such as when spouses pay their own expenses and share all expenses related to the support of children.

Emotional dimension. Emotional interaction ranges from all family members being positively emotionally involved with each other, to being negatively emotionally involved or not being emotionally involved at all. Emotional involvement may also be asymmetrical—one person may love a family member who is emotionally uninvolved or negative towards that person (e.g., an emotionally absent parent/spouse, an autistic child). . . .

THE MONOLITHIC VS. THE MULTIDIMENSIONAL APPROACH TO FAMILIES

Definitions of the Monolithic and Multidimensional Approaches

The monolithic approach to families is characterized by the assumption that high interaction in one dimension coincides with high interaction in all other dimensions of familial interplay. In other words, when two people are married, it is assumed that either they will eventually have children together where there are none as yet, or that any children that are present are the biological children of the marital partners. It is further assumed that both parents are involved in the socialization of children, that the marital partners have sex only with each other, that all family members live in the same residence, that either one (and occasionally two) members of the family are totally responsible for the support of all family members, and that familial relations are characterized by mutual positive emotional involvement.

By contrast, the multidimensional approach to families is characterized by the assumption that interaction in any of the dimensions identified can vary independently. For instance, a couple may be high in interaction in the procreative dimension (i.e., they have a child or children together) but they may be low on the socialization dimension (e.g., only one of them is involved in parenting the children). That is, while congruence between dimensions is *assumed* in the monolithic approach, this assumption is converted into an empirical question in the multidimensional approach.

Each generation may believe that it experienced the greatest changes. However the period from the end of World War II to the present has challenged the culture's fundamental values as profoundly as any coherent set of changes since the enlightenment.

GEROME KAGAN

Consequences of a Monolithic vs. a Multidimensional Approach to Families

Consequences of the monolithic versus the multidimensional approach can be summarized as follows: The monolithic approach makes (1) an assumption of congruence which leads to (2) a bias in the data collection process, which leads to (3) an underestimation of the incidence of non-congruence and (4) inappropriate categorizations, as well as (5) inappropriate models which, in turn, lead to (6) a misidentification of what constitutes "problem" families, and inappropriate questions.

By contrast the multidimensional approach (1) examines empirically the degree of congruence and noncongruence concerning the various dimensions, thereby (2) uncovering the prevailing bias in data collection and (3) the resulting underestimation of non-congruence. It leads further to (4) a critical examination of currently accepted categorizations and (5) of currently accepted models of the family, and an attempt to develop more appropriate ones, as well as (6) a redefinition of what constitutes a "problem" family, and the re-posing of questions.

From *Families In Canada Today: Recent Changes and Their Policy Consequences*,
"Beyond the Monolithic Bias in Family Literature" by Margrit Eichler,
Chapter 1, pp. 6-11. Copyright ©1988 Gage Educational Publishing Company.
Reproduced by permission.

1. Which approach most clearly reflects your view of family interaction, the monolithic or the multidimensional? Why?

2. In what ways might cultural background influence the types of family interaction in each dimension?

3. For each of Eichler's six "dimensions," pinpoint an area of family interaction that was once well charted but where the signposts have now disappeared. Explain the value of this reading in clarifying some of the changes that families are experiencing today.

4. Follow newspaper and magazine accounts of a current family issue. To what extent do the views and responses of policy makers reflect a monolithic approach to families? A multidimensional approach?

5. When reviewing the literature two opposing perspectives on the "state of the family" become evident. The pessimistic view sees the family as declining in importance, with some of its functions now obsolete. The optimistic view sees family as alive and well and getting better at meeting individual needs. Research and debate these perspectives.

HEALTHY FAMILY SEXUALITY

A major developmental task for families at all stages of the life cycle focuses on sexuality. Many accounts of contemporary life point only to negative, controversial, or problematic sexual behaviour in families. Yet a sexually healthy family is not only one that avoids the extremes of sexual neglect and sexual abuse. It also actively promotes the sexual well-being of all its members through unique and integrated patterns of family interaction. In this selection, James W. Maddock provides a ground-breaking overview of healthy family sexuality.

☐

In recent years, the terms "family" and "sexuality" have been publicly linked in a particularly negative way, that is, in the emerging recognition of the problem of intrafamilial sexual abuse. This has simply deepened the prevailing attitude that sex in all of its manifestations is a *problem* of families rather than an integral part of family process. It is easier to point out what has gone wrong with sexuality in families than to identify signs of health or effective functioning. Part of the dilemma is the issue of competing values in a pluralistic society, making the question of what is "normal" or "healthy" sexual behaviour a subject of considerable debate. . . .

> Sexual love is trust plus lust.
> LETTY COTTIN POGREBIN

. . . "Healthy" family sexuality can be generally defined as: *the balanced expression of sexuality in the structures and functions of the family, in ways that enhance the personal identities and sexual health of individual members and the coherence of the family as a system.* . . .

Family sexual health is characterized by:

1. A balanced interdependence among all family members based upon respect for both genders. . . .

2. A structure that defines and maintains between members suitable physical, psychological, and social boundaries which are relevant to their respective stages of the life cycle while supporting appropriate gender identity/role socialization and erotic development.

3. Effective and flexible patterns of communication and interaction to exchange nurturance and affection and to promote the capacity for intimacy, including the facilitation of erotic expression between appropriate persons in developmentally suitable ways.

4. A shared system of culturally relevant sexual values and meanings that allows for coordination of goals and purposes among family members while permitting them a reasonable amount of freedom for individual decision making and personal sexual expression.

Within the context of contemporary American culture, these criteria suggest a profile of the sexually healthy family that distinguishes it from the extremes of neglect or abuse. . . .

[In sexually healthy families] both male and female family members have the opportunity to initiate behaviour, to influence decision making and to establish appropriate personal boundaries. Both genders can exercise self-control (erotically and otherwise), as well as give up control temporarily for periods of spontaneity, play, and emotional expressiveness. Children in the family are not viewed simply as "products" of the family, but as individuals whose unique characteristics are reflected, in part, in their sexuality. There is a generational structure through which appropriate guidance, protection, and support are supplied by parents to permit the unfolding of childhood and adolescent sexuality in age-appropriate ways. The sexuality of younger members is respectfully nurtured rather than exploited to meet the needs of the older generation. The family supports the sexual differentiation of its members, allowing them as much freedom as possible in line with personal integrity and family values. Transactions in the family are designed to foster the development of a solid sense of gendered self-identity, of erotic capacity, and of rewarding sexual lifestyle.

To promote positive body/self-images in all members, the sexually healthy family utilizes positive forms of touch and physical interaction. The unique physical attributes of each family member and his/her potential for erotic expression are viewed positively. Sexual boundaries are clear and functional, though also flexible to allow for appropriate adaptations to changing developmental requirements of members. There is respect for the physical and emotional privacy of each member while allowing for supportive, positive energy and information exchange between various family members.

> The real issue isn't making love; it's feeling loved.
> WILLIAM H. MASTERS and VIRGINIA JOHNSON

The marital partners are secure in their personal sexual identities and exhibit an appropriate degree of flexibility in sexual role taking and role making. Wife and husband convey to each other and to their children respect and appreciation for the erotic aspects of their relationship. The spouses participate in erotic and affectional interaction that is regarded as mutually rewarding. Their patterns of sexual exchange reflect freedom of choice and the capacity for negotiation, along with warmth, caring, and concern for each other's welfare. Their erotic interaction is based upon a sufficient degree of shared sexual meaning and interest to be considered satisfying to each. Included in their relationship is an agreed-upon system of responsibility for the reproductive potential and possible consequences of their sexual expression. The sexually healthy family communicates effectively about sex, using language that can accurately convey sexual information, reflect feelings and attitudes of members, and facilitate decision making and problem solving regarding sexual issues. This requires a viable language system regarding sexuality and patterns of communication that are responsive to individual needs and styles.

Parents provide positive sex education for their children, combining accurate information with a specific context of family values, guided by developmental principles. Sexual attitudes and values are transmitted from one generation to the next primarily through positive interaction patterns in everyday life. However, the family also has at its disposal a body of accurate information about sexuality that can be shared between the generations and among members of the same generation, with appropriate consideration for the developmental stage of each family member. Developmentally oriented sex education is premised upon a principle of *gradualism* that neither artificially inhibits the age-appropriate erotic interests and expressions of family members nor prematurely exposes individuals to situations that they are not equipped to handle.

Members of the sexually healthy family share an overall value system that permits effective and rewarding sexual decision making, encouraging autonomy consistent with respect for individuality but balanced by concern for the integrity of the family unit. The social boundary of the sexually healthy family permits information exchange between the family and its environment so that it can remain meaningfully related to its social context. Thus the family's value system represents the uniqueness of the family while also sufficiently reflecting its community context; conversely, the family accepts the capacity of its members to appropriately represent its sexual integrity to the outside world.

There can be no single version of family sexual health, nor is there any one means to promote it. Because sexuality is a fundamental dimension of family experience, events of sexual significance often accompany individual and family life cycle transitions. In addition, shared sexual meanings and values sometimes fluctuate significantly and rapidly in a family's life cycle. For these reasons, it is a hallmark of sexual health that a family can master and adapt to new sexual circumstances both inside and outside the system and can also transform its sexual structures and functions to accommodate more fundamental alterations in its life circumstances. This is the ongoing process of balancing between stability and change within the context of an ever-shifting social (eco)system, an expression of health as survival with meaning and integrity. . . .

> The living world is a continuum in each and every one of its aspects. The sooner we learn this concerning human sexual behavior, the sooner we shall reach a sound understanding of the realities of sex.
>
> ALFRED KINSEY

From "Healthy Family Sexuality: Positive Principles for Educators and Clinicians," by James W. Maddock, *Family Relations*, Vol. 38, No. 2, April 1989, pp. 130-136. Copyrighted 1989 by the National Council on Family Relations, 3989 Central Ave. N.E., Suite #550, Minneapolis, MN 55421. Reprinted by permission.

1. Examine the four criteria for family sexual health. Explain how each employs concepts included in family systems theory.

2. In outlining the second criterion Maddock refers to "appropriate gender identity/role socialization." Distinguish between sex and gender. Identify the values or biases that could underlie the use of the term "appropriate."

3. James Maddock claims that ". . . events of sexual significance often accompany individual and family life cycle transitions." Support this claim with specific examples.

4. Explain how forces or circumstances within and outside the family may affect the achievement of healthy family sexuality at each stage of the family life cycle.

5. People who have been sexually abused as children may carry the emotional scars with them for the rest of their lives. Research Canadian sources to determine the nature and extent of sexual abuse within families.

■ SINGLEHOOD

Marriage today is no longer considered inevitable. Nor, for some, is it a "normal" expectation. Many reasons lie behind the decision to postpone marriage or remain single. In the following excerpt from Marian Engel's short story "Anita's Dance," we enter into the mind and musings of Anita as she reflects upon her solitary life.

☐

It was a morning fit to convert any pessimist, and a Sunday to boot. Anita spent part of it in the garden virtuously weeding; then she poured enough coffee to float an army into her special mug and brought it out into the garden. Instead of reading, she sat stretching her neck to the sun and thinking how lucky she was; nothing to do but please herself all day. From time to time friends lectured her about being selfish and set in her ways, an old maid. And it was true she was sometimes lonely. She had, however, no reason to feel sorry for herself when she compared her life to theirs. She had a house, a garden, a car, a piano. A good job. A greedy, bad-tempered cat. Two eyes, a nose, and ten fingers, all in good working order. What did she have to feel sorry about? And was happiness selfish?

She mused over her library book. She had never really wanted to get married, except for a brief and embarrassing episode when she was at university. A boy she was very fond of had wanted her to drop her scholarship, marry him and put him through law school. Her fondness had ceased abruptly when he argued that, being male, he had more right to an education than she had. Winning the argument had hurt a lot.

Those days were over, she thought, and if she was wrong, she had no daughter to tell her so in exemplary form. I have my house, she thought, my garden with delphiniums and daisies and poppies. My piano, on which I have taught myself to play the simplest and saddest waltzes of Chopin. I have company in the form of a bad-tempered cat. What is more, I have a date with Clive this afternoon. I feel good with Clive. The something that is between us is nothing; there is no self-conscious-

> Singleness is not a curse, not a disease, not a pathological condition to be avoided at all costs, but an option—one possible way to live.
>
> JERRY BOREN

ness. We swim towards each other as if the water were our element. All's right with the world.

She had wanted to study literature but on practical grounds had chosen economics instead. She still, however, attempted to keep up with good books and now she was reading a novel by a man in England called Berger, who was supposed to be both good and avant garde. She opened it now, and put on her sun-glasses.

It was good: his main characters were small souls, which showed a sort of left-wing point of view, but she liked the way he got into both their heads at once and managed to stay there, so she could feel both the room they were in and the beating of their rather restricted hearts.

It took place in a small employment agency; both characters, the owner and his clerk, were weighing large changes in their private lives while appearing to deal with clients. The owner, a fiftyish man who had always lived with his sister, was considering independence; marriage even.

She looked up and smiled at the sun. That was funny. She read on.

A woman came into the agency to look for a housekeeping job. A largish, comfortable, middle-aged woman. The proprietor had an instant vision of the comfort she could provide for him: a well-kept house—not too well-kept, Canadian and mowed in the lawn departments, just a sort of comfy English house, fish and chips for tea, a kettle on the hob.

"I could live with that," Anita said to herself. "What I couldn't live with, not ever, is a set-up like this plus a job, plus three children and entertaining for a junior executive now portly and senior. No wonder I'm the way I am."

She frowned at the book, closed it, and put it down. It had revealed to her a seam of domesticity she had been avoiding recognizing; it was cosy, and it was basically English working class, and basically (except for a mob of children) what she had come from.

She had never wanted her mother's life, one of flying elbows and fits of bad temper and aspirations that were a muddle of impulses. Her mother had never seemed to be able to think anything through, she was always anaemic from child-bearing and exhausted from scrubbing; crying out 'You girls . . .' Get this, fetch that, turn off the soup, scrub the sink, do the dishes, iron that. When she was an old woman they had bought her an automatic washing machine with a window in the door and found her sitting on the basement steps watching it like television. 'I was remembering the day Lanie got her hair caught in the wringer,' she said.

Anita shuddered; that dream of cosy domesticity was a male dream; she'd been living in a man's world too long. The real thing she'd lived through and it was what had made her so happy to get a scholarship to university. Never mind that she'd had to char and work in a grocery store to put herself through.

She stretched lazily. The cat was scowling at her through the kitchen window; he didn't like her to be happy. Too bad for him. She was going to enjoy this day. Clive and she weren't meeting until two and she didn't even have to change.

The world is divided into couples and so being single can feel like playing musical chairs and every time they stop the music, you're the one who's out.
MERLE SHAIN

From *The Tattooed Woman* by Marian Engel.
Copyright © The Estate of Marian Engel, 1985.
Reprinted by permission of Penguin Books Canada Limited.

1. Explain how past experience and circumstances shaped Anita's attitudes to marriage and singlehood.

2. Outline the range of emotions and attitudes Anita expresses. In what ways do these expressions reflect the varying perceptions and myths associated with singlehood? How might these myths be affected by gender, age, culture, and socio-economic status?

3. Explore some of the issues and problems faced by contemporary singles.

4. If you were doing a comprehensive survey of singles, who would you include? Compile a questionnaire that would determine both the advantages and disadvantages of singlehood.

5. Investigate differences in the male and female experience of singleness. Compare the nature and significance of their support systems.

6. What percentage of the Canadian adult population do single people represent? How has this percentage changed over the last two decades? Can any trends be discerned? If so, propose a hypothesis to account for the trend.

7. In the essay that opens this section, Claude Guldner cites an example of a woman living alone who has constructed a "family of choice." Do you agree that the people included in this network can be considered a family? Why or why not?

DEALING WITH STRESS

Stress is an inevitable and recurring element of family life in contemporary times. The tentacles of stress reach out to all family members and find their way into every stage of the family life cycle. In the earlier Mastering Transitions reading, Nancy Schlossberg suggested that the response of individuals and families to stress is related to their interpretation of the situation, their inner strengths, their external supports and options, and their coping strategies. With these factors in mind, assess how well the Downton family in this next selection is coping.

☐

Family man John Downton has problems. And worries. Big problems. Big worries.

He's among the 19,000 Bell Canada technicians and operators who've been on strike for three months. No end is in sight. Talk is the strike may go on till Christmas.

Downton, 32, a cable technician, says he'll survive. There are ways and he still has a few means. Then there's the *Asset*.

First, the problems:

He figures he's already out about $13,000 in base pay and hefty overtime. He's lost about 12 pounds he can't afford either. He's down to a skinny 110. Worrying does that. He can't get interested in more than a meal a day.

The family savings of $2,500 are long gone. He's just cashed in the RRSPs which paid $2,300 after taxes. "That's what we're living on now," he says.

The mortgage on his four-bedroom bungalow in the Brampton neighbourhood where he grew up is $676, plus $125-a-month property tax. "This is the only thing I don't want to lose over any kind of strike, no matter how long it goes: my house—or my family," he says.

There's still food to buy. The shelves in the basement larder, once piled high from bulk buying, have been reduced to a dozen cans of soup and vegetables, five boxes of Kraft Dinner and a box of spaghetti. Before the strike, the family of four spent $100 a week and more on groceries. It's about $50 now.

The hydro, natural gas, $80 a month interest on a $5,000 loan from his credit union and, of course, the telephone must be paid.

"Our social life is history," he says. No entertaining friends, no movies, no dining out or ordering in. Even Sunday drives are out. They can't afford to use precious gasoline on pleasure. Besides, there's no money for repairs on the 1981 Mustang's slipping clutch or if the 1979 Bronco goes clunk.

His everyday shoes are holed through the soles. He'll make them last on the picket line till winter if he has to. Then he'll wear his boots.

"I've given up my freedom. I'm not free to go anywhere. I won't go anywhere and spend money. The only place I go is the picket lines," he says.

The strike began June 24 after 72.5 per cent of the Communications and Electrical Workers voted 51.3 per cent to reject the company offer. A total of 83 per cent voted earlier this month on a new offer, which was rejected by 52.2 per cent.

Technicians made $714 a week before the strike. Operators made $461. The union says job security and pensions indexed against inflation are the key issues, as well as wages. Bell contends it has offered the union exactly what it asked.

Downton, a steward in Local 26, which covers an area from Toronto's High Park to Mississauga and north beyond Orangeville, says he fully supports the strike. He also sees himself as a loyal Bell employee. He misses his tools and his job of 15 years, repairing cables to restore telephone services to customers.

But despite the problems brought on by the long strike, Downton figures he's fortunate.

Mainly, he's thankful for the Asset. It's something money can't buy, but

It's a recession when your neighbour loses his job; it's a depression when you lose yours.

HARRY S. TRUMAN

priceless in any crisis. Only he doesn't call it an "asset." He just describes it as a "great" wife—plus parents and friends—behind him all the way.

Diane Downton, 29, who's become the family breadwinner, says her husband worked hard to provide for the family. "I figure I should help wherever I can. It's my turn now."

The term is supportive family. Sociologists and labour historians interviewed say this is essential to the success of any long strike.

"Absolutely crucial," agree York University sociologists Anton Turrittin and Paul Grayson.

"If you get it, it is a rhetorical question," Grayson adds.

"If you know you are able to keep food on the table, you can be more sanguine than if you can't," he says. "If the mother sees too much lost for what is gained for the family, she may withdraw support."

Labour leaders have long realized the importance of that support. Labour historian Laurel Sefton McDowell of the University of Toronto's Erindale campus recalls Mine, Mill and Smelter Workers' leader Bob Collins talking about a 1941 miners' strike in Kirkland Lake: "They understood very well that to get the support of the men, they had to get the women behind them."

Women's auxiliaries and family social events centred on the old-time union hall helped build morale and strong unions. Today, of course, women are among the country's most powerful labour leaders, reflecting their emergence in the work place.

The Downton's wanted to be a traditional family when they married 10 years ago. She'd look after the home and he'd earn the bread. When the children came, she quit her job with a games manufacturer to be a housewife and mother.

But after the strike started, she hung up her apron and went out and got her old job back to see the family through.

Besides, she added, it was to help her husband get to know their sons, Ryan, 4, and Adam, 2, better and be a break from routine for her. They didn't know the strike would drag on so long.

He became "Mister Mom," looking after the boys, the cooking and cleaning. "I've learned to appreciate the work a housewife does. I wouldn't want to do it for a living."

She says one of the hardest things about the strike is missing the children during the day, particularly not being a part of Ryan's first experiences in junior kindergarten.

But asked about the strike's major impact on them, she replies: "It's brought our family a lot closer. We have to be there for each other more. Definitely. That's a lesson many people never learn."

To the same question in another interview, her husband says, "This has brought us closer as a family. No doubt about that."

The family survives chiefly on the $196 a week she nets from her job. Strike pay is $100 a week. The family rents out a two-bedroom apartment in the basement for $450 a month. The friendly tenant pops in occasionally with hamburgers or a pizza from fast food outlets for the family.

For extra money, Downton's thinking about renting out one of the spare bedrooms upstairs.

He began looking for a temporary job to help the family through after the latest company offer was voted down. But he'd found companies wanted a commitment he'd stay on. He couldn't give it.

Other strikers say much the same thing. Only two of 10 technicians interviewed on a picket line at Trinity Square the other day said they had temporary jobs, though most have now started looking in earnest. They'd held out this long on remnants of savings.

A picket captain explained why he hadn't taken work to supplement his strike pay and savings: "Am I going back (to Bell) next week, or not? You don't want to make a commitment. . . . I don't want to leave the guy I'm working for in a lurch. I don't want to leave him with a bad impression of a Bell employee."

All but two said their families or girlfriends were helping them get through the strike in such ways as taking the lead in cost-cutting, moral support and comfort or, in the case of girlfriends, treating. Three indicated that if anything good can happen during a strike, it was more time with families.

The strike at Bell has made Downton realize what's important in life. And it isn't money. It's his family.

Under the last contract, his basic pay at $714 a week came to $36,128 a year. But his T4 last year read $52,000. The extra was in overtime. He took lots of it. He said he wanted to provide a better life for his family.

"It sounds like a lot of money," Downton says. "You work a lot of hours. It burns you out. But if there's a major cable failure, you're obligated to work. You have to fix it whether it's 7 o'clock or midnight. I'd work lots of times 24 hours."

He and his wife say he often wouldn't get home at nights till the children were ready for bed or long after they were asleep.

He realizes now how time with his family is precious. He'll remember that when the strike is over. "It won't be just mother and two kids or father and the two kids, but mother, father and two kids."

In his study, *1978-79 Strike At INCO: The Effects On Families,* former Laurentian University sociologist Henry Radecki found Sudbury's family units emerged stronger and more united. That was the major effect, greater even than the devastating economic impact from which few had recovered a year later, he says.

"The major effect was greater cohesiveness of the family. The survey found that during the course of the seven-month strike, the family became stronger, more cohesive, more resistant to adversity," said Radecki, who now lives in retirement in St. Catharines.

"Adversity seems to create a situation where families seem to draw on members for support, for reliance, for comfort," he says of that strike.

On the other side of the coin, historians and sociologists point to a 1958 strike in Sudbury by the Mine, Mill and Smelter Workers before the Steelworkers came in. The wives told the guys to get back to work. They didn't have strike pay to put food on the table. The three-month strike ended just before Christmas on terms favourable to the company.

The truth is, of course, if you once develop a resource, it becomes part of your character in such a way that you are more or less unaware of it. Throughout my whole career, I have drawn on various strengths within myself, without acknowledging where they came from. Everyone does this. It is like discovering you have a tolerance for pain. The tolerance is always there but it only shows itself when pain occurs.

TIMOTHY FINDLEY,
from THE TELLING
OF LIES

Labour historian John Lang, now secretary-treasurer of the Confederation of Canadian Unions, says the back-to-work movement started at a rally organized by the mayor and middle-class women, but miners' wives backed it and that was that.

From early on in the history of trade unionism, women standing behind their men helped change society's attitudes, leading eventually to labour reforms and collective bargaining legislation. "When the men were herded to jail the women would replace them on the picket line," says historian Craig Heron at York University.

None of that concerns Downton, of course, who has enough to worry about with today's problems.

Opening the larder's last can of Mini-Bits for his sons' lunch, he notes ironically that the strike hasn't given him much time with his wife. When she gets home, they eat and he's off to the picket lines often till 11:00 p.m.

"I want to show her how much I care. I haven't been able to do that as much as I want to," he says of his preoccupation with the strike. "But I will."

From "Surviving the Strike" by Walter Stefaniuk,
Toronto Star, September 23, 1988, pp. C1-5.
Reprinted with permission—The Toronto Star Syndicate.

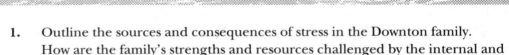

1. Outline the sources and consequences of stress in the Downton family. How are the family's strengths and resources challenged by the internal and external pressures they face? How might the impact of the strike have been different if the family were at an earlier or later stage of the family life cycle? If this were a single-parent family?

2. Describe the Downton family's coping strategies. Compare these strategies to authoritative "models" on coping with stress in the family.

3. What is the significance of the term "Mister Mom?" Analyze the relationship between gender and power that this selection presents.

4. Stress can come from negative and positive life experiences. Identify a wide range of stress-producing situations arising from circumstances and conditions within the family and from outside sources.

5. Using the structural issues outlined in the overview essay as a framework, analyze the impact of the strike on the quality of functioning in the Downton family.

6. What discoveries do families often make in response to stress?

7. Examine the current economic climate in Canada. Determine what hedges families can make against a downturn in the economy.

FAMILY VIOLENCE

Among the forms of family violence are sexual abuse of children, spousal assault, neglect of the elderly, and homicide. Family violence can range from neglect to abuse to death. Reports of family violence are invariably received with expressions of shock, disbelief, and anger. For is not the family the very embodiment of support, love and caring? In the following excerpts from a story entitled "Simple Solutions," Jan Thornhill traces the events in one couple's experience of violence.

☐

It's probably unnecessary to say that our arguments started over nothing, but they did. Just some little irritant, like a sliver of wood needling one gently through a sweater, or a piece of gravel in one's shoe. Something very small. But that was all that was needed, its tiny existence poking at whatever large resentment we both harboured at the time, poking so incessantly that one or the other of us would eventually strike out in response, abruptly and viciously, as a chained dog might do, teased beyond endurance by some idiot with a stick. And it would go on from there, gathering momentum, me ranting, eloquently I thought, him stumbling over his tongue, the two of us finally becoming so loud that the background clamour of the mice would be drowned out by our accusations: You this . . . You that . . . You . . . and names would fly. Ricocheting off the walls, the ceilings, like sharp-edged ping-pong balls.

As violent as all this sounds, and of course it was, it was also, for a long time, only verbal.

When he was really angry, furious, language would evade him. As words fell off my own tongue, beautifully ordered, more clearly expressing my thoughts than at any other time, I would watch his face, fascinated, watch what my words could do to it. First, blood would gather in the hollow below his Adam's apple, then rise from there . . . up his neck, finally turning his whole face, his ears even, a vivid, ugly red. It was then that his features would begin to contort, twisting into themselves. It was as if all the words he couldn't release were trapped under his skin, churning and rolling there like something alive desperate to get out. The way they eventually found, of course, was through his fist. . . .

We had another argument. He started it. It had something to do, I think, with the size, or uniformity of shape, or country of origin, of the vegetables I had put in the salad, or steamed, or fried. It grew from there, each of our faults multiplying in the other's eyes, self-generating like a colony of aphids sucking vital fluids from a plant; the same as always. But then something happened, something changed. He raised his fist. For a moment I was at a loss for words, hearing only his, a threat to "drive me one," an expression I'd never heard before but one I understood. It took me a moment but then I said, or more likely screamed: You do that . . . go ahead . . . Hit me . . . "Drive me one." I watched his face, so distorted it was unfamiliar, relax, and as it did he lowered his hand, slowly, as if it was just something his arm happened to be holding and not part of his body at all, letting it hang finally, limp as a glove, at his side. We both stared at it then, the way we might have stared at a dinner guest who had done something uncommonly rude, stuck his hand inside the roast chicken, for instance, or spat on our floor. I could hear the mice then, beyond the silence we were in, the silence we had made. They were in the kitchen, rifling loudly through boxes of dried goods, cracking walnut shells with hammers, opening cans.

Before bed, we set out a second trap, this time with a watermelon jelly bean balanced on a trigger, gleaming lipstick red.

The mice would often keep me awake at night. I'd lie there beside him, him sleeping, nothing resolved. Eventually, to end whatever argument we'd had, I'd falsely admit my imperfections, my inadequacies, my guilt. I'd weep. And so there I'd lie afterwards, wishing him dead, the flesh surrounding my eyes, the skin of my whole face, still swollen, stinging beneath the surface from the toxins, anger-produced, that hadn't been released, going over the argument, retracing its inception, trying to decide if he really was the one in the wrong and not myself. But at those times it was impossible to fault myself instead of him. He started it, I was the victim, it was I who'd been wronged. And while I lay there, sometimes for hours, the mice would keep me awake, tap-dancing to unheard tunes and playing horseshoes on the other side of the wall.

THE FIRST TIME

I remember being overwhelmingly flabbergasted the first time he actually hit me. It was a punch, a right hook that caught me just under my left lower jaw. My feet let go of the floor briefly and I flew backwards a couple of yards before my fall was broken by the edge of the counter meeting a vertebra of my lower spine. For a moment, the absolute awe I felt stifled any other reaction. Then came a brief fury, just long enough for me to spit out several awful words, and then came the pain, a toss-up between which was worse, my back or my jaw.

I did not weep. He did not move. For a couple of minutes we were a still photograph: a kitchen, yellowish lighting from above; linoleum floor; stove, table, fridge; unattractive tiles above the counter; oven-mitts decorated with Christmas trees; a plate of crumbs; and two people, a man and a woman, both expressionless, showing no clue of what has just occurred. The man, for instance, could have just asked the woman what was for dinner tonight, or, where were his brown pants, did she know?

I forgave him . . . .

You know how hard it is to put a cork back into a wine bottle once you've opened it and let it sit around for a while? How you can't uncook a burnt roast? Well, later . . . he gave me my first black eye. For what. Was it a disagreement over that spot there? Or was it a TV show? Was it the flavour of a toothpaste? Was it turquoise? Cobalt blue? It doesn't matter; I was given my first black eye. I know now that I should have refused it, should have said, "No thank you, those colours don't flatter me" and handed it back, but I didn't know how. . . .

I suppose it will sound peculiar if I say that I found a certain power in making him hit me, but it's true. Yes, the incredible power of the victim. It was very simple; I'll explain. As our arguments built, it was what I could say as opposed to what he couldn't that made his fury accelerate. As he lost control, I proportionately gained it. And when he was finally careening with that knowledge, because he knew as well as I did what was going on, he'd finally grab a handful of my hair and back-hand me one, or punch me. In the face. To shut me up. Later, while nursing whatever bruises were rising, I'd wallow in my moral superiority: he'd hit a woman again; he'd hit me. So there was the power of inflicting guilt too. But he wasn't stupid, he knew that was what was happening as well, which is why his remorse was always finally over-whelmed by his recognition of my manipulation so that, during the next fight, he'd use his fists again. If only to shut me up. But it was always me who called the punches, as it were.

(Oh, really? Gimme a break. You're missing something important there, I think. Sure you had control, but only so far, only for so long. Then you lost it, then you gave it up. But that's what you really wanted, isn't it?

You thinking: Good, now I'm not responsible. Thinking: Good, *he's* in control. Thinking: He can hit me . . . hell, he can kill me, but it won't be *my* fault. Thinking: Phew, what a relief.

Except that, each time, unfortunately, you were not the only one who relin-quished it—don't you remember—you made sure of that by pushing him as far as you did. So half the time, at the worst of times, *nobody* had control. That's what made it so crazy; that's what made it go on the way it did.) . . .

☐ HINDSIGHT *OR* PASSED TIME CAN BE LIKE A GOOD PAIR OF GLASSES: I SHOULD HAVE LEFT HIM LONG BEFORE I DID.

Things got worse. First he broke my jaw. He didn't believe it when I told him, jeered at me as I sipped soup for a couple of weeks, soaking bread in the broth. I will never eat bananas again.

Then it was my nose. I remember I had done something for him that I knew he hadn't wanted to do himself. I thought it had been a nice thing for me to do but apparently I'd done it in a different way than he thought it ought to have been done. So he broke my nose. I hadn't cried in front of him for months, not since before he'd first hit me, but this time there was an automatic flow of tears. I remember being infuriated about that, about that loss of control. There was also a startling amount of blood. As I mopped it up with kleenex (I have one of them still, kept as a memento. It's stiff and brown now, in a baggie in my bottom drawer), he told me not to be a martyr. . . .

FIGHTING BACK

I could tell the instant he came in the door one night, just by the way he stomped the snow off his boots, favouring his bad knee, by the way he hung up his coat, by the way fire and steam spewed from his nostrils as he breathed, that it was not going to be one of our quieter evenings.

For a change, I armed myself. I hid a hammer beside my favourite chair. I turned on the TV. I sat there. I waited.

But when the time came I didn't reach for the hammer even though I had the chance. I mean, are you kidding? What the hell did I think I was going to do with it? Spread his brains all over the living room carpet? . . .

And EVERY time, EVERY SINGLE time, I'd say to him, or to myself, or to both of us: I'm leaving. That's it. First thing in the morning, I'm gone. . . .

But the next day, there I'd be. The sky would turn Lorne's blue outside the blinds, the streetlights would fade off, the sun would rise, reflecting in through the living room window from the building next door, and there I'd be, having slept on the couch again, still not ready to make the move. Telling myself he would change, really, it wouldn't happen again. And I believed myself because I couldn't believe him. So there I'd lie, in whichever position hurt the least, listening to the mice having their wake-up showers and using their exercise machines, waiting for him to get up, for him to pretend I wasn't there. Then, at seven-thirty, I'd hear him finally in the bathroom, and I'd hear, too, drifting down from upstairs, mildly distorted but always recognizable, Barbra Streisand tunes.

FEAR

I'll be honest, I was afraid. I jumped a lot. I cringed. I didn't want to be dead, not really. But even so, I'd find myself thinking things like: He'd sure feel bad if I was dead. Then he'd be sorry, especially if he did it, if he were to blame . . . he'd be really sorry then . . . wouldn't he be?

Actually, it got to the point where I felt so threatened at home that I became almost fearless outside. I was immune, invisible. I felt isolated from the danger of dioxins accumulating in my fatty tissues, from threats of nuclear war. I jay-walked recklessly. But at home, I jumped. The smallest noise would make me jump. And there were many noises, because there were many mice. . . .

There are often simple solutions which one overlooks. For instance, it is a well-known fact in some circles that cats eat mice. It had not occurred to either of us to get a cat; neither of us had ever lived with one, so I suppose we thought their reputation as pest-controllers was an exaggeration. But then fate stepped in and a friend forced one on me. It was half-blind. The friend's other two cats harassed it, snuck up on it and slashed purposely at its unseeing, milky eye. So I accepted it, felt sorry for it and took it home.

He was furious. It's blind in one eye, he said. It can't judge distances. It can't catch mice. What a stupid thing to do. So he broke my nose again.

In the silence that ensued, as I searched for kleenex, as he looked at a magazine pretending he was on a subway train amongst strangers, I heard the cat, the half-blind cat who hadn't been in the house for more than an hour, the handicapped cat who would never catch mice. So did he. She was making strange deep-throated gravelly sounds in the kitchen. We both watched as, a moment later, she batted a mouse around the corner and into the living room. She swallowed it whole.

In the deeper silence then, as I held my head back to stem the flow of blood, as he said nothing, I could hear, quite clearly, the cat purring on the far side of the room.

For several days we did not speak. He vaguely acknowledged the cat who slithered seductively between his legs, but he wouldn't even look at me. On the fourth day he did. He tried to disguise it but I could tell, this time, he believed what the bruises said. I hoped he was pleased. On the fifth day, he bought me some carnations. They were two different colours, I remember, pink and white. He handed them to me without saying a word. Later, that same night, he made me eat them. That same trigger sprung again, by something unmemorable as always, something as insignificant as the breath of a mouse stretching towards a jelly bean. But it *was* sprung, so he knelt on the side of my head and force-fed me the carnations.

I imagine that, seen from a distance, by an unsuspecting observer, it might have made an amusing scene. I say this only because I did see it from a distance, painlessly, from a floating position just below the ceiling. What are they doing? I asked myself. What are those silly people doing? Look at them! And then I got bored and began to look around, past the comical struggle below, and saw the cat down by the kitchen, head cocked in favour of her one good eye, waiting patiently by a crack in the wall, waiting for the mice I could hear above my head, amplified by my proximity, playing their anarchic game of soccer again.

Well, I finally left. Not the next day, not the next day after that. Not until months later, but I did leave. It was the carnations, I think, the smell of them, strong whiffs I would get at different moments, that made me go. I took the cat. She's can-fed now and has learned to be amused by a tin-foil ball, but sometimes I think she must miss the mice that supplemented her diet before, and so I imagine going over there—I can put myself right in front of his door.

Instead of using my key, I ring the bell because, of course, I don't have a key anymore. And that feels strange. I listen to the muffled buzz inside, and then I sense, more than I can hear, his feet approaching, a light vibration perhaps. And when, finally, he opens the door, a bit of warm air wafts towards me from behind him and it smells of him, but it smells of carnations too, so I am strong. I find that I can look him in the eye, which pleases me, so, with unmoving voice, I ask if he can spare a mouse, to give the cat, to give *my* cat, because she misses them, I say, and because I know he's got some; they're still one of his problems, I hear.

From "Simple Solutions" by Jan Thornhill,
Fireweed, August 1988, pp. 49-56.

We have less control over others and more power over ourselves than we like to think.
STEPHEN VIZINCZEY

1. The self-esteem of battered women is often so low that they cannot find the strength to leave an abusive relationship. Describe the emotional state of the woman in Jan Thornhill's piece. What are the power dynamics in this relationship? How is the title "Simple Solutions" both poignant and ironic?

2. A number of theories or explanations for family violence have been put forth. These include violence as a by-product of alcohol, drugs, or stress; violence due to biological and psychological disorders resulting in individual pathology; violence as learned behaviour; violence as built in to the historical and cultural context of family and society. Which of these theories can you cite as a possible explanation for the violence depicted in this reading? Investigate available references for explanations for family violence.

3. Refer to the Circular Causality and Conflict reading in The Family As System unit. What parallels can you draw between these two readings?

4. Draw comparisons among the possible causes of spousal abuse, child abuse, and elder abuse in the family. Explain why solutions to these various forms of abuse are hampered by long-standing notions of gender and power. How do these same notions help to account for the phenomenon of date rape?

5. Draw up a list of strategies that would reduce family violence. Identify the many professionals who could play a role in these strategies. Outline principles that should inform all actions and initiatives carried out by social systems or agencies to eliminate violence in the family.

6. Explore your community for evidence of positive approaches to reducing the incidence of family violence.

VOLUNTARY CHILDLESSNESS

Even as we head into the 21st century, voluntarily childless couples are regarded with some degree of curiosity and suspicion. Classified by sociologist Jean Veevers as either rejectors or aficionados, these couples live out a child-free option. In the first selection, Veevers presents the typology of childlessness that grew out of her research. In the second selection,

Irena Straszak, a medical doctor studying psychiatry at the time of writing, analyzes some commonly held misconceptions about voluntary childlessness.

☐

A TYPOLOGY OF CHILDLESSNESS

Descriptions of childless couples have dichotomized them in terms of a number of variables: by whether they made their decision before ("early articulators") or after marriage ("postponers"); by whether they achieved it independently or by negotiation; by whether they have high or low levels of commitment to it; and by whether they are primarily motivated by reactive or proactive factors. Our data seems to suggest that some useful hypotheses can be formulated regarding the relationships among these four dimensions. The cornerstone of this hypothesis is the notion that there are two quite different kinds of voluntary childless persons: rejectors and aficionados.

Voluntarily childless persons whom we have designated as rejectors are those who disavow the parenthood mystique and who have actively and vehemently rejected the parenthood role. Rejectors are primarily motivated by *reaction* against the *dis*advantages of having children. Their decision is an immutable part of an idiosyncratic belief system, in that they cannot imagine any circumstances under which they would want to have children. Rejectors often tend to dislike children and to avoid being around them. A number of them flaunt their childlessness; others actively proselytize their antinatalist ideology and childfree lifestyle.

Aficionados are persons who are ardent devotees of voluntary childlessness because they appreciate the *advantages* of being childfree, rather than the disadvantages of parenthood. They are not so much against children as they are intrigued and beguiled by some other interest which does not include children. Such enticements may range from hard science to pottery, from art to mountain-climbing, from literature to horse racing. Such persons are "buffs" who find, in the pursuit of their passion, that children would be an impediment. They made their decisions about parenthood primarily in terms of the positive attractions of other interests. They tend to negotiate their decision over the course of their marriage, in the context of the development of other interests, and to be less definite in their commitment to it. Generally, they like children, or at least have a neutral attitude towards them, and on the issue of natalism, they tend to be apolitical, endorsing neither the pronatalist nor the antinatalist perspective. In terms of comparisons with the general population, one might hazard a guess that aficionados are more similar to parents than are rejectors, who tend to have more varied and unconventional backgrounds and childhood experiences. . . .

THE CONSEQUENCES OF CHILDLESSNESS

The most important finding of our research is simply stated in one observation: from our vantage point, it seems clear that at least some voluntarily childless couples do

When you ask someone if he or she has a family, you want to know if the person has children. Children are the essence of the family. Having them, committing yourself to their long-term needs and through them establishing intergenerational bonds is the heart of the family. We are in danger of losing that heart.

LYNN WHITE

achieve high levels of personal, marital, and social adjustment. Moreover, from our interviews, it seems clear to us that for many of the childless, the maintenance of sound mental health is not achieved in spite of being childless, but is predicated upon the continued avoidance of parenthood. This conclusion would perhaps seem "obvious" were it not for the fact that it contravenes a basic assumption of Canadian-American culture, namely that children are *necessary* for happiness and fulfilment. While it may well be that under many circumstances children do contribute to satisfactory life adjustment, the in-depth interviews we conducted do establish that, at least for some persons, alternative lifestyles may provide the same level of satisfaction.

The implications of this simple finding are manifold. The pronatalist premise that having children is a desirable goal for all persons must be modified to the more limited premise that it is not necessary for all and that for some persons under some circumstances childlessness may be a more desirable alternative. Presently, young couples are oriented towards a basic question: how many children do you want to have? More appropriately, we might rather orient them to the question: do you want to have any children? . . .

IMPLICATIONS FOR SOCIAL POLICY

Consciousness-raising: to parent or not to parent

An insidious aspect of traditional pronatalism is the implicit assumption that parenthood is inevitable. Consequently, although there may be a choice of *how many or when*, the choice of *to parent or not to parent* is not raised to the level of awareness. It is not known how often pronatalism is in fact "coercive," in the sense of leading couples to have children they did not especially want for the sake of social approval, rather than for other reasons. There is reason to believe, however, that it does happen (Flapan, 1969: 409; Hardin, 1971: 265), and that such circumstances are not the most auspicious for either mother or child. Social policies which make implicit pronatalism explicit would go a long way towards lessening its undesirable effects, and towards making childlessness a viable option. . . .

Debating the pros and cons: pronatalism versus antinatalism

Persons trying to debate the pros and cons of having children, and needing to come to a decision, cannot wait for social science to develop a "parent test" for guidance in their decision. In this instance, even the decision not to decide is eventually a *de facto* decision, as the biological and social reasons for having a child will pass and the couple will find their option to have children has disappeared.

In assembling and weighing relevant evidence, a couple deliberating childbearing will find the pronatalist case excessively documented. In terms of social policy, there is no need to elaborate further the already elaborate mechanisms whereby young adults are bombarded with messages advocating parenthood. While pronatalism may provide essential psychological support for some persons facing the difficult task of child-rearing, it may also create unnecessary frustrations in others. The oversell of parenthood may lessen rather than enhance later adjustment to it, in that the actual experiences cannot live up to the romanticized expectations implicit in the advance billing. Some increase in the messages concerning the disadvantages of having children would help make expectations more realistic, and would make for a more balanced and informed decision.

From *Childless by Choice* by Jean E. Veevers
(Toronto: Butterworths, 1980).

☐

There are a lot of misconceptions about people who choose not to have children—especially women.

People say, "You'll change your mind. You've still got time. Why, my mother had her last child at forty-two!" It is as if people do not believe one can be serious about not wanting children—as if having and raising children is an essential aspect of life, or a biological drive that cannot be denied. While most people do have children, a large chunk of the population is childless, some by choice and some by circumstance. Most of these people are not unhappy or unnatural in any way, and conversely, there are people who have children for all the wrong reasons and others who are neither adequate parents nor especially happy ones.

I can't believe I forgot to have children!

R. BYRNE

In our society more than ever, women have the opportunity to make choices. They make choices about whether or not to further their education, about whether or not to marry and whom to choose as a mate, and about which career to enter or whether they would prefer to stay at home and look after children. With all these options, it is not surprising that more women are having second thoughts about having children. It is an unjustified accusation to say that such women or couples are selfish. The opposite, in fact, could be argued.

It may be quite realistic to have doubts about having a child or be convinced that it is not a good idea. There are a number of prerequisites to doing a good job as a parent and enjoying it. Unless one is brave enough to become a single parent, it is important to have a strong and harmonious relationship with a mate. Apart from the fact that marriages are breaking up at an alarming rate (this may again be related to having choices), raising a child brings a major change and stress into a couple's life.

Women have had to bear the brunt of this change and stress. It is most often women, whose incomes are lower and thus more easily sacrificed, who stay at home with the children. Maternity leaves, when available, are granted only to women, not men. Nannies are an option some couples do not want and others cannot afford. Having to care for children has an obvious impact on women's lives and careers.

Many women choose not to have children because they are happy with their present lives. They would not welcome any major change that might upset the delicate balance they have achieved with their partners, job responsibilities, families, friends and other interests or involvements. Even without defining what a good parent is, it is evident that raising a child and holding a marriage together is a formidable task. Those of us who have busy and interesting lives already do not want to become superwomen like some of our mothers.

People ask me if I won't have regrets in my old age. They wonder if my parents wouldn't like grandchildren. It is kind of them to worry about this, but I see *those* as quite selfish reasons to have a child. Besides, there is no guarantee that having grown-up children will necessarily be a comfort in the twilight years. Nor is there a guarantee that any of us will make it that far.

Others say to me, "If everyone thought the way you do the human race would become extinct." I can't say I'm very concerned about that with the worldwide population explosion. However, I am certainly not advocating childlessness for everyone but only the freedom to make that choice, without the kind of personal and social pressures that exist now.

For example, because I am a doctor and work in psychiatry, people tell me, "It's people like you who ought to be having children." People with a high level of education and financial security are believed to be the best parents, but from what I have seen these circumstances do not ensure success with children. Many wealthy, well-educated parents come with family problems to child psychiatry clinics. As for deciding who *should* be parents, I can see the dangers of a Brave New World ahead if we start down that road.

Choosing to be childless does not necessarily mean having no contact with children. I can imagine myself as a contented, doting auntie to my sister's children. Many other people who are not parents—teachers, daycare workers, pediatricians— enjoy working with children every day. We must remember, though, that some people do not really like children or may feel uncomfortable around them. This may be connected to some underlying experiences in their own families and childhoods. Be that as it may, I think society should respect their preference too.

Although deciding to have a child ultimately rests with the woman (some theologians may argue with this), the wishes of her partner must be considered as well. Many men have not been given a choice and have become fathers without much of a say in the matter. Of course, the opposite can happen as well, and a man may feel quite helpless if his partner is unable or refuses to have children. Only discussion and understanding can overcome these important differences.

Parents have told me that it is hard to imagine what you're missing before you have had a child. What they say makes sense. I suppose you can say the same about life experiences in general before you live them. Nevertheless, we do have a choice about having children, and one way or the other, the decision requires a great deal of consideration and thought.

From "Women Who Choose Not To Have Children Aren't Necessarily Selfish"
by Irena Straszak, *Compass*, January, 1989, pp. 13-14.

> Longer life expectancy and lower fertility have combined to overhaul the contours of family life.
>
> DAVID LEVINE

1. That "children are necessary for happiness and fulfilment" is a common assumption. What does Veever's research reveal? Investigate other authoritative sources and research studies on the topic. Are Veever's findings confirmed?

2. Provide evidence of how couples are coerced into parenthood. Describe the types of social policies that encourage pronatalism. What social and economic policies in Canada today have the effect of discouraging women from having children?

3. Straszak asserts that "it is an unjustified accusation to say that [childless] women or couples are selfish." Compare the values of individuals who would support either side of a debate on this point. What is your own position?

4. What do demographics reveal about childlessness in Canada? Do the statistics indicate the percentage of women or couples who are childless by choice?

5. An increasing number of women today are involuntarily childless because they are physically unable to conceive or carry a fetus to term. Conduct research into the causes of infertility and the technologies that have been introduced to surmount it.

6. "Maternity leaves, when available, are granted only to women, not men." Investigate the current laws governing parental leave. Share your findings with the class.

SEPARATION, DIVORCE, REMARRIAGE

Separation, divorce, and remarriage are increasingly viewed as normative aspects of family experience. Even the language we use to describe these events is changing: "family breakdown," for example, has been replaced by "family reorganization." Still central, however, to these experiences are complex processes and transitions. Some individuals become "stuck" along the way; most individuals muster the confidence and energy to move on. Each step is marked by powerful emotional responses. In the selections that follow, watch for evidence of processes, transitions, and a range of emotions. Macon is the creation of novelist Anne Tyler; Helen Hutchinson and Hugh Webster tell their own stories.

□

After his wife left him, Macon had thought the house would seem larger. Instead, he felt more crowded. The windows shrank. The ceilings lowered. There was something insistent about the furniture, as if it were pressing in on him.

Of course, Sarah's personal belongings were gone, the little things like clothes and jewelry. But it emerged that some of the big things were more personal than he'd imagined. There was the drop-leaf desk in the living room, its pigeonholes stuffed with her clutter of torn envelopes and unanswered letters. There was the radio in the kitchen, set to play 98 Rock. (She liked to keep in touch with her students, she used to say in the old days, as she hummed and jittered her way around the breakfast table.) There was the chaise out back where she had sunbathed, planted in the only spot that got any sun at all. He looked at the flowered cushions and marvelled at how an empty space could be so full of a person—her faint scent of coconut oil that always made him wish for a piña colada; her wide, gleaming face inscrutable behind dark glasses; her compact body in the skirted swimsuit she had tearfully insisted on buying after her fortieth birthday. Threads of her exuberant hair showed up at the bottom of the sink. Her shelf in the medicine cabinet, stripped, was splashed with drops of liquid rouge in a particular plummy shade that brought her instantly to Macon's mind. He had always disapproved of her messiness but now those spills seemed touching, like colourful toys left on the floor after a child has gone to bed.

The house itself was medium-sized, unexceptional to look at, standing on a street of such houses in an older part of Baltimore. Heavy oak trees hung over it, shading it from the hot summer sun but also blocking breezes. The rooms inside were square and dim. All that remained in Sarah's closet was a brown silk sash hanging on a hook; in her bureau drawers, lint balls and empty perfume bottles. Their son's old room was neatly made up, as sleek as a room in a Holiday Inn. Some places, the walls gave off a kind of echo. Still, Macon noticed he had a tendency to hold his arms close to his body, to walk past furniture sideways as if he imagined the house could barely accommodate him. He felt too tall. His long, clumsy feet seemed unusually distant. He ducked his head in doorways.

Now was his chance to reorganize, he told himself. He was struck by an incongruous little jolt of interest. The fact was that running a house required some sort of system, and Sarah had never understood that. She was the sort of woman who stored her flatware intermingled. She thought nothing of running a dishwasher with only a handful of forks stacked inside. Macon found that distressing. He was opposed to dishwashers in general; he believed they wasted energy. Energy saving was a hobby of his, you might say.

He started keeping the kitchen sink filled at all times, adding some chlorine bleach for disinfectant. As he finished using each dish, he dropped it in. On alternate days he pulled the plug and sprayed everything with hot water. Then he stacked the rinsed dishes in the empty dishwasher—which had become, under his new system, a gigantic storage area.

When he hunkered over the sink to let the spray attachment run, he often had the feeling that Sarah was watching. He sensed that if he slid his eyes just slightly to the left, he would find her with her arms folded across her chest, her head tipped and her full, curved lips meditatively pursed. At first glance she was simply studying his procedure; at second glance (he knew) she was laughing at him. There was a secret little gleam in her eyes that he was all too familiar with. "I see," she would say,

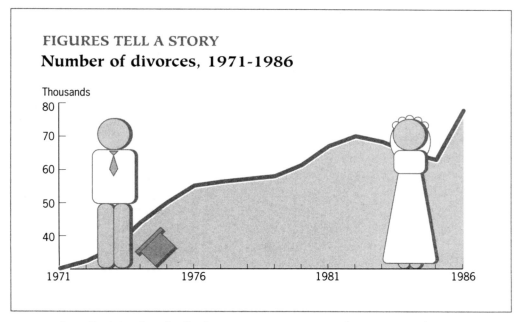

FIGURES TELL A STORY
Number of divorces, 1971-1986

Thousands

From Statistics Canada, Catalogue 84-205, Marriages and Divorces: Vital Statistics.

nodding at some lengthy explanation of his; then he'd look up and catch the gleam and the telltale tuck at one corner of her mouth.

In this vision of her—if you could call it a vision, considering that he never did glance over at her—she was wearing a bright blue dress from the early days of their marriage. He had no idea when she had given that dress up, but certainly it was years and years ago. He almost felt that Sarah was a ghost—that she was dead. In a way (he thought, turning off the faucet), she was dead, that young, vivid Sarah from their first enthusiastic apartment on Cold Spring Lane. When he tried to recall those days, any image of Sarah was altered by the fact that she had left him. When he pictured their introduction—back when they were barely out of childhood—it seemed nothing more than the beginning of their parting. When she had looked up at him that first night and rattled the ice cubes in her paper cup, they were already moving toward their last edgy, miserable year together, toward that sense of narrowly missed connections. They were like people who run to meet, holding out their arms, but their aim is wrong; they pass each other and keep running. It had all amounted to nothing, in the end. He gazed down at the sink, and the warmth from the dishes drifted gently up into his face.

Well, you have to carry on. You have to carry on. He decided to switch his shower from morning to night. This showed adaptability, he felt—some freshness of spirit. While he showered he let the water collect in the tub, and he stalked around in noisy circles, sloshing the day's dirty clothes underfoot. Later he wrung out the clothes and hung them on hangers to dry. Then he dressed in tomorrow's underwear so he wouldn't have to launder any pyjamas. In fact, his only real laundry was a load of towels and sheets once a week—just two towels, but quite a lot of sheets. This was because he had developed a system that enabled him to sleep in clean sheets every night without the trouble of bed changing. He'd been proposing the system to Sarah for years, but she was so set in her ways. What he did was strip the mattress of all linens, replacing them with a giant sort of envelope made from one of the seven sheets he had folded and stitched together on the sewing machine. He thought of this invention as a Macon Leary Body Bag. A body bag required no tucking in, was unmussable, easily changeable, and the perfect weight for summer nights. In winter he would have to devise something warmer, but he couldn't think of winter yet. He was barely making it from one day to the next as it was.

At moments—while he was skidding on the mangled clothes in the bathtub or struggling into his body bag on the naked, rust-stained mattress—he realized that he might be carrying things too far. He couldn't explain why, either. He'd always had a fondness for method, but not what you would call a mania. Thinking then of Sarah's lack of method, he wondered if that had got out of hand now too. Maybe all these years, they'd been keeping each other on a reasonable track. Separated, demagnetized somehow, they wandered wildly off course. He pictured Sarah's new apartment, which he had never seen, as chaotic to the point of madness, with sneakers in the oven and the sofa heaped with china. The mere thought of it upset him. He looked gratefully at his own surroundings. . . .

. . . He didn't eat real meals anymore. When he was hungry he drank a glass of milk, or he spooned a bit of ice cream directly from the carton. After the smallest snack, he felt overfed and heavy, but he noticed when he dressed in the mornings that he seemed to be losing weight. His shirt collar stood out around his neck. The vertical groove between his nose and mouth had deepened so that he had trouble shaving it. His hair, which Sarah used to cut for him, jutted over his forehead like a shelf. And something had caused his lower lids to droop. He used to have narrow gray slits of eyes; now they were wide and startled. Could this be a sign of malnutrition? . . .

The worries changed, grew deeper. He wondered what had gone wrong with his marriage. Sarah had been his first and only girlfriend; now he thought he should have practiced on someone else beforehand. During the twenty years of their marriage, there'd been moments—there'd been months—when he didn't feel they had really formed a unit the way couples were supposed to. No, they'd stayed two distinct people, and not always even friends. Sometimes they'd seemed more like rivals, elbowing each other, competing over who was the better style of person. Was it Sarah, haphazard, mercurial? Was it Macon, methodical and steady?

When Ethan was born, he only brought out more of their differences. Things they had learned to ignore in each other resurfaced. Sarah never got their son on any kind of schedule at all, was lax and unconcerned. And Macon (oh, he knew it, he admitted it) had been so intent on preparing him for every eventuality that he hadn't had time to enjoy him. Ethan at two, at four floated up into his vision as clearly as a colour film projected upon the bedroom ceiling. A chortling, sunny little boy, he'd been, with Macon a stooped shape above him wringing his hands. Macon had been fierce in teaching him, at age six, how to swing a bat; it would have wrenched his soul to have Ethan chosen last for any team. "Why?" Sarah had asked. "If he's chosen last, he's chosen last. Let it be, why don't you?" Let it be! Life was so full of things you couldn't do anything about; you had to avert what you could. She laughed when Macon spent one fall collecting Wacky Packs, which had these jokey stickers inside that Ethan liked to plaster his bedroom door with. He'd have more than anyone in the whole third grade, Macon vowed. Long after Ethan had lost interest, Macon was still doggedly bringing them home. He knew it was absurd, but still, there was this one last sticker they had not yet managed to get hold of . . .

> From *The Accidental Tourist* by Anne Tyler.
> Copyright ©1985 by Anne Tyler Modarressi.
> Reprinted by permission of Alfred A. Knopf, Inc.

☐

HELEN HUTCHINSON: Do you find it difficult to talk about your divorce?

HUGH WEBSTER: Well, I can talk about it all right but I'm not quite sure if I can get into the depths of it because now I can sit back, be objective and assess a lot of things that happened, but without the emotional involvement. I'm not sure how valuable that is to anyone else having problems in their own marriage. Sure, I've been through the lot; I've gone down as far as I could possibly go in that kind of a man/woman relationship. But if I were put back into the same situation again, even after what I think I've learned, I might very well do the same things all over again, I just don't know.

HH: Has being divorced affected your attitudes towards your current marriage in that you don't have to hide behind a facade any more, you don't have to hide the cracks in your marriage from other people?

HW: Not having to live behind that mask any more, not having to project the kind of marriage you thought you wanted and the idea that this is what you had, when it wasn't what you had at all, is a freeing experience, though it takes time to feel that freedom. After the split, a terrible rupture which I think is the important thing, there's a kind of spurious freedom. I didn't have to fight any more, I didn't have to protect myself any more, I didn't have to make excuses any more. Then I went through a period where I was completely aimless; if it hadn't been for my work requiring me to go on tour, to be on stage very night, places I had to be and things I had to do and audiences I had to please, I don't know what would have happened. There was just that terrible aimlessness. I never sensed a real freedom until I remarried. And my second marriage has made me realize something else. My first marriage was one of those awful, mutually destructive relationships. It was a "Who's Afraid of Virginia Woolf" thing, two people destroying each other and themselves. Being free of that for a long, long time, I found that I almost lost the dynamic of my life. I hadn't realized that all those years of being on edge like that had given me some kind of impetus to live at a pace that I now realize wasn't my real pace at all. I guess that my divorce, and my remarriage, forced me to learn quite a lot about myself.

HH: I know what you mean when you say you were forced to learn about

> Remarriage is the triumph of hope over experience.
> SAMUEL JOHNSON

yourself. I had to come to grips with my first marriage and found it was all wrong; it was a myth. I looked at it for a long time and boy, is that a painful thing to do because what it really means is looking at yourself. You ask what the heck did I do and why, and how did it go so askew, but eventually you come face to face with that ghastly creature called yourself. I realized I'd done everything for the wrong reason; I'd tried to live up to a myth that was created for me in high school and university. I'd let the residue of my Catholic upbringing tell me I wasn't supposed to be divorced, that whatever the cost, I had to hold this thing together. I was trying to live by the standards of ladies' magazines and TV commercials. It was a completely false life. I was trying to be the good woman and was also playing the role of the good woman wronged which is a dirty, rotten game because that's the tyranny of the weak. When everyone said, poor Helen, I sat down and started thinking about myself as poor Helen; it wasn't until later that I realized poor Helen was doing a lot of manipulating. I found it very hard, but in retrospect, crucial, to substitute a more truthful image of myself in my own mind.

HW: I found that out very dramatically. I was talking to a friend about lying to yourself, attempting to live up to an image you've been projecting for yourself, and he told me about an experience he had with his wife when their marriage had gone right to the edge. They were having an argument about something silly, taking out the garbage. She said, why don't you take out the garbage, at which point he said, because I'm a bastard. Just that suddenly he realized that he wasn't the knight in shining armour he had imagined himself to be, but was an honest-to-God bastard. Then he was able to begin living like a human being, to look at himself, to see his own faults, and to see what he was doing wrong. I've always remembered that story, and every now and then I say to myself, why am I doing this . . . because I'm a bastard . . . well, stop being one.

HH: Did you try to blame the other guy for what happened?

HW: The business of pinning the blame on the other person after it's over is just a pointless exercise and nearly as pointless during a break-up. But it doesn't do any good to accept all the blame yourself either because if you do, and we've both done it, you simply smooth over cracks that shortly show up all over again. You can't hold it together by yourself. You have to go at it with more introspection than just total willingness to accept all the blame. While nobody wants all the ties that are formed in a marriage, nobody wants their marriage to fall apart, no matter how rotten it's become. Nobody wants to go through a divorce and all that mess. But if you do find yourself in that situation, it becomes a very deep experience, an experience where depth can't be avoided. So you dig deep into yourself and as you say, it's horrifying what you can find there.

But that digging is a real advantage in approaching a second marriage. You face it with fewer romantic illusions of what's ahead than you could the first. And by the time I remarried, I was older; I've never known how much difference that made or how much of that maturity was found in my divorce. Legally I was old enough to get married the first time, but mentally and emotionally I was far, far too young. With my second marriage, there's just as much passionate involvement but now I can be intelligent about it. I guess I'm freer to be myself and free enough to be able to let

> Remarriage is an art. It requires more self-understanding than most relationships, as well as an insight into the past that keeps an eye on the future.
> BENJAMIN SCHLESINGER

Elizabeth be herself, something I could never do before. In my first marriage I was a worm of self-contained resentment but now I find I just don't have room in myself to hold on to the kinds of resentments I'd always bottled up before. And I know that if I found my marriage floundering now, I'd be free enough to get help from outside; I could honestly admit I was in trouble.

HH: After my divorce, I was given custody of the children; you weren't. How much difference did that make?

HW: That's probably the thing that drove me down deepest, a black, black period of my life, adjusting to not having the children any more, even though I would have them occasionally. It seems silly now, but I remember taking their Christmas presents to them when they were small. I went to the house on Christmas night, gave them their presents, then said good-bye and walked away. Suddenly, with everybody heading for parties and all the rest, I found myself walking back streets until I wound up at an all-night restaurant. In moments like that, it's just as if there's nothing left. And you tell yourself, even now, that if it hadn't been for the divorce maybe they would have been different, maybe they wouldn't have had some of the problems that they've had. And because I had the children only at intervals, it seemed as though they often arrived at a moment of crisis in their lives. Then it was hard slogging to reassert the relationship. The relationship never really works the same way again. It's one of the heartbreaks that follows anyone who's been divorced. . . .

HH: Do you think it's better for children to live in a second home, with or without a step-parent, than in a rotten, angry home?

HW: A lot of my friends told me it would be at the time I was weeping my eyes out over the loss of the kids. They kept telling me it's better for the kids to be free of all the anger, but at the same time. . . . I was raised in an angry home and vowed that it was never going to be like that in my own home, that my marriage was going to be roses and all the rest of it; but I fell into every trap my parents fell into. I didn't listen to the signals. After my first marriage was all over, I said that's it; I'm obviously no good at this sort of thing so I'd better stay out of it and lead a bachelor's existence for the rest of my life. The only part of it I wanted to have anything to do with was the kids; that was real. All I can say after that is that I fell in love again.

HH: Weren't you scared?

HW: No. Is anybody afraid when they fall in love? Besides, after a divorce, after you've had the lash, you've been through a fundamental experience that shook you to the bottom. After that you can't approach that kind of a relationship with the same naiveté you faced your first marriage with. I guess that's one of the reasons why you read second marriages are often more successful than first ones. You learn to respect yourself first, which is the most important thing, and through that you learn to respect the other person so that you've got two individuals standing up straight instead of two people leaning on each other. And you know what happens when people lean; eventually they fall over.

From "Divorce and Remarriage" by Helen Hutchinson and Hugh Webster
in *About This Country in the Morning*, Peter Gzowski (Ed.)
(Edmonton: Hurtig Publishers, 1974), pp. 216-218.

> Frequently married persons practice a consecutive spousing which is a sort of polygamy done in parts.
>
> **VIRGINIA SATIR**

1. How would you describe the emotional tone of the first piece? Assess Macon's ability to come to terms with the break-up of his marriage.

2. Research the developmental tasks associated with separation and divorce. Predict whether Macon is likely to achieve these tasks, using examples from the reading to support your position.

3. Both Helen Hutchinson and Hugh Webster have experienced divorce and remarriage. Describe the impact of their divorces on their second marriages. Devise criteria by which you might assess the impact of remarriage on their quality of life. Check your criteria against research on satisfaction with remarriage. What do statistics reveal about the success rate of remarriages?

4. Investigate authoritative sources to identify factors that increase the risk of marriage breakdown.

5. In his book *The Power of the Family,* Michael Nichols states that "the common perception that divorce implies a defect in one or both partners and that divorce means the break-up of the family only makes things worse." Describe the consequences of this perception for individual and family recovery. What parallels can you discern between Macon's experience and the recollections of Hutchinson and Webster?

6. Nichols also states that "the transition from being together to being divorced is a road without maps." Despite his statement, visualize such a map. If that map were based on family systems theory, what guidelines might it contain to ease the journey through the transitional stages from separation to divorce?

7. Which of the following statements most reflects your understanding of remarriage? Analyze why you have come to feel as you do about remarriage.

> The remarried population have in all likelihood encountered adverse economic, psychological and social situations. And if they had children, their divorce and remarriage brought additional challenges and responsibility.
>
> —John Peters

> Remarriage after divorce is often a solution to some of the financial, psychic, emotional and social losses which follow in the wake of marital failure.
>
> —Emily Nett

CHILD CUSTODY

"Natalie" is but one of the gripping case studies in Susan Crean's powerful and emotionally charged book, *In the Name of the Fathers.* Crean proposes that for the people involved custody means much more than a set of abstract legal rights. Social, cultural, political, emotional, as well as legal dimensions of child custody are all brought forward for intensive scrutiny. As you read the case that follows, several of these dimensions will become evident.

□

I met Bruce in 1970 at school and we married that same year. I noticed he was prone to extreme fits of temper, but these were not directed at me personally and I felt I could somehow influence him into changing this behaviour. Shortly after we married I became pregnant. During my pregnancy we argued frequently and more often than not, the argument would end with him hitting me or throwing me up against the wall. I told myself things would get better after the baby was born. But they only got worse. When Amy was two years old I became pregnant with Noah. Again the abuse escalated with the pregnancy. I had extreme nausea and if I refused to respond to Bruce's sexual advances, he would fly into a rage, rant and rave and throw me around the bedroom and keep me awake until I gave in from sheer exhaustion. If I did not give in he would rape me; he insisted that it was up to me to meet his sexual needs. He accused me of being frigid and repeatedly told me there was something wrong with me. After arguments during which he assaulted me, he would insist we make love to make up. Many times I thought I'd throw up when he was forcing me to have intercourse.

I threatened to leave many times during the marriage. Bruce would insist that he was sorry and was going to change. He always promised it would never happen again. I wanted to believe him, and I wanted our marriage to work. And anyway, I wondered, how would I ever manage on my own? Most of my married life was spent either pregnant or nursing a baby; there were three more after Amy and Noah—Jamie, Kate, and Jonathan. I had no friends because we moved so frequently due to Bruce's job changes. He also discouraged me from visiting my family, saying that I was always different when I returned from a visit.

The children were the only bright spot in my life. I threw myself into mothering. I nursed them all for a year even if it meant taking them to work with me at the clinic where we lived in Espanola. I took on mothering the way other people take on careers. But it became increasingly clear to me that living with Bruce was like living a life sentence. As long as I stayed with him my children and I would be abused, Jamie in particular, as Bruce singled him out and in his rages would hit him, kick him, or throw him on the floor. In May 1980, I told Bruce we would no longer live with him. He left the house in July and agreed that the children should stay with me.

> People are not interchangeable pieces in a child's life.
> AIRIE THOMPSON-GUPPY

For a year and a half (of the three years I had the five children with me) Bruce refused to support us claiming he was unemployed. When I asked him for money for the children he told me to get my boyfriend to support me.

After the separation I met Buddy, who became a friend and supporter to me and my children. We eventually began living together and in April 1983 we became parents of twins. During this period Bruce filed for divorce and custody of Amy, Noah, Jamie, Kate, and Jonathan. He then obtained a court order to have us all psychologically assessed. Dr. Harris was chosen by Bruce and his lawyer to do the assessment. I immediately assumed that Dr. Harris must be an intelligent and educated person, and that he would recognize what my children and I had been through. He came to my house and spent approximately sixteen hours interviewing me, Buddy, and the children. When I told him about my marriage and the abuse Dr. Harris acted as though he believed me, but he didn't. In his report he said that he found no evidence of violent or aggressive tendencies in Bruce's psychological testing. Still, up until the last few pages he argued for maintaining the status quo. Then he changed his argument because of new information he had become aware of. The information was (a) that I was expecting twins, and (b) that Buddy, who had been steadily employed for fifteen years, was out of work because of a plant shutdown. Dr. Harris then recommended that two of my children, Kate and Jonathan, be placed in their father's custody and sent to live with him.

The trial took place in the winter of 1984. I was still convinced that once the judge heard my story and the evidence of witnesses, he would not split the children up. I went to court expecting justice and recognition of the bond between my children and myself, expecting protection for my children and myself. Instead, lip service was paid to my parenting. I was described by the judge as an excellent mother, hard-working and resourceful. However, he concluded that I had condoned the violence in my marriage by staying for ten years and having five children, and that I had not been assaulted as badly or as often as I said I had. He said that there were probably only a few isolated incidents. I feel the abuse I have survived was dismissed with flippancy by the judge. He almost completely ignored my claims about rape and sexual abuse, and he denied my grounds for divorce, which were physical and mental cruelty.

In April 1985 I received the news that I'd lost custody of my daughter Kate, then four, and my son Jonathan, then six, to my husband. When I found out I really thought I was going to die. I didn't know how I would ever go on. The children were shocked, angry, and bewildered. They would say, "Who is this Dr. Harris? Who is this judge? They don't even know us; how can they decide things for us?" Kate and Jonathan refused to take their clothes with them when they went to live with their father in Sudbury. After access visits they would refuse to go back and would have to be carried crying to the car. They would cry almost the whole way to Sudbury from Espanola and beg me to turn the car around and take them back home. Jonathan said he wished he'd never been born, that he wanted to be back inside my tummy. Kate said she hated being a kid. And one day they asked how many days there were in five years because their father had said that after five years they could decide for themselves where they wanted to live.

Joint custody is a question of involvement, not residence.

PHILIP EPSTEIN

Buddy and I split up six months later, partly due to the stress of the loss of Jonathan and Kate. I decided to appeal the case and asked my lawyer to find the best appeal lawyer he could. However, it took eighteen months to get to court. There were always lengthy delays obtaining transcripts and my lawyer kept telling me that it took a long time to get into appeal court. Finally in October 1986 we got there—but it was too late. Three judges all agreed that the trial judge had made a serious error in principle, that he should not have split up the children. However, because almost eighteen months had elapsed, they did not want to uproot the children. They also noted that Buddy was no longer living under the same roof with us.

It is now six months since that decision. I feel my children and I have been betrayed and victimized by our so-called justice system. I feel like I have an open sore that won't heal until my children are returned to me. It is as if they had been aborted after I'd given birth to them, nurtured and cared for them. . . .

There are no lobbyists for children.

MARY VAN STOLK

From *In the Name of the Fathers* by Susan Crean
(Toronto: Amanita Enterprises, 1988), pp. 177-179.

1. Sole custody, joint custody, and shared parenting are custody options. How do they differ one from the other? Describe some of the sacrifices and compromises each entails. Suggest situations where each approach would be the most appropriate. Under what circumstances might any one approach have negative ramifications for mothers, fathers, or the children?

2. Investigate the interrelationships that exist between views of motherhood, the status of women, and custody practices over time. Make projections for the future. Provide a supporting rationale.

3. Inquire into Susan Crean's statement that "money talks in custody courts." Assemble and weigh background data from a variety of sources. To what extent do your findings confirm or reject Crean's assertion?

4. How may child custody issues be influenced by one's cultural background?

5. "For a year and a half Bruce refused to support us claiming he was unemployed." In an alarming number of cases, husbands default on their court-ordered support payments. What recourse do women have through our justice system? Research the nature and extent of this problem.

6. "[The judge] concluded that I had condoned the violence in my marriage by staying for ten years and having five children." Do you agree? Why or why not? Refer to the Family Violence reading.

SINGLE-PARENT FAMILIES

Single parents, who are most often women, fall into various categories: the separated, the deserted, the divorced, the unmarried, the single person who adopts a child, or the widowed. Each family with a lone parent is unique, yet when one individual has to play out all of the adult roles and responsibilities similar problems often result. The first reading is based on a longitudinal study of female single-parent families conducted by Carolyn Gorlick, a sociology professor from the University of Western Ontario. In the second selection, profiles of actual single parents give faces to the single-parent phenomenon.

Female single parent families in the aftermath of marital separation frequently experience a downward mobility into poverty.

Of all low income Canadians 56 percent are female, and families headed by women are 4.3 times more likely to be poor than male-led single parent families (National Council of Welfare, 1988). These trends have led to what has been called the "feminization of poverty." Although there is some debate over whether poverty continues to be "feminized" (in terms of increasing female poverty rates) there are nevertheless significant numbers of poor women who are not benefiting from upward swings in the economy, and who find themselves (with their children) applying for social assistance.

In 1987, the Sole-Support Parents Advisory Group, made up of representatives from single parent organizations across Ontario, was formed to advise the province's Social Assistance Review Committee (SARC). The Group tells us that being the head of a single parent family on social assistance means spending fifty to seventy-five cents of every dollar on shelter and living in substandard housing; becoming more dependent on food banks (undoubtedly a result of cost of living increases—1986 "real" benefits were comparable to those in 1975); facing negative societal perceptions; dealing with an inadequate child care system which reinforces the stresses of single parenting; and watching the visibility of their children as poor increase. Frequently, the anxiety and powerlessness a single mother feels affects her self-esteem and perceptions of her role as a good provider. As a single mother concerned about the impact of long term welfare dependency on her family explained to the Social Assistance Review Ontario (1987):

> Welfare teaches our sons to be glad they are not women and teaches our daughters to reinforce the myth of expecting a Prince Charming to enter their lives to help them get off the system. It also teaches our daughters to expect a continued welfare life for them and their children.

□ SOURCES OF SUPPORT

In the aftermath of separation, there are frequently changes in the social support networks of single parent families. Roles, norms and forms of interaction must be re-negotiated, with new expectations and available resources potentially enhancing or minimizing family adaptation.

It appears that low income female single parents inhabit a world in which social support comes mainly from other women and from their own children (combined total of 49 percent), followed by parents and other relatives (28 percent) and lastly by a small number and proportion of male friends (12 percent) and officials (11 percent) including counsellors, social workers, and family physicians. Furthermore, it is female friends and the parents' own children who provide the most support of all types. (From the study's data four categories of support have been identified:

- □ close—love, comfort, caring;
- □ esteem—from those, such as children, for whom the person is an important part of their lives;
- □ informational—useful suggestions, advice; and
- □ instrumental—services e.g. babysitting, or access to services.)

Contrary to the beliefs of some, male friends provide relatively little support of any kind. Neither relatives nor parents provide much either. Professionals supply significant support, but mostly informational.

There is an ominous correlation between the amount of support available to single mothers and the number of children they have. It appears that everyone except the professionals tends to avoid parents who, because they have more children, may need help the most. Thus, there may be many single parents for whom their own children and formal service providers far overshadow the support available from family and friends. For them, the information and advice they receive from professionals plays a larger role than for other single mothers. In sum, it appears that low levels of income are not only an economic but also a social deficit potentially altering the relationships developed by single parents both within and outside the immediate family.

□ HEALTH EFFECTS

Although studies have shown that poverty does not cause a specific illness, the context or environment of poverty does lead to ill health. The visibility of their children as poor and the accompanying sense of personal blame reinforces a single mother's fears of her child's ill health. As one single mother noted:

> How has living on Family Benefits affected my family? My two-year-old son is small for his age. I don't like to think about it, but deep down I know that his size is probably a result of poor nutrition (Social Assistance Review of Ontario 1988).

Single parents report higher emotional and physical disorder rates amongst their children than mothers in two-parent families. Furthermore as a female single parent's stress level increases, she will use more pediatric services and visit the family physician's office more often. Although it appears that children of female single parents are hospitalized more frequently, in part that trend might be explained by some physicians who will hospitalize children more often and for longer periods if they become aware of negative home conditions. Although the number of childhood diseases is comparable across social classes, children of low income families are more likely to suffer longer with greater illness severity than those from upper income groups.

Previous studies have noted that low income single mothers experience greater psychiatric disturbance, more frequent and severe headaches, and higher rates of tranquilizer and analgesic use compared to mothers in dual parenting situations. More recently, the view that the single parent family is pathological is being challenged. Subsequently, findings should not be seen as evidence of inherent pathogenic traits in this family.

Instead current research reveals the importance of the context in which the family lives. For example, the children of conflict-ridden two-parent families are often under greater stress and are potentially more disturbed than the children of single parent families. Perhaps familial discord prior to marital separation, accompanied by economic stressors and changes in social support in the aftermath of separation, are the reasons for the single parent family's ill health rather than absence of another parent.

Recent studies have shown that measures of psychiatric and social functioning were similar for single and two-parent families, implying that the problems of single parent families result from the stresses and strains of living in poverty and not from psychiatric disorders or inadequate social relationships. Finally, although the female single parent's ill health has frequently been associated with not-wanted or abrupt expansion of roles and responsibilities, the lack of choice and the perceived inability to access and organize resources around these new roles might also be involved.

Without significant social policy changes including:

☐   higher levels of income maintenance
☐   accessible and appropriate housing
☐   adequate child care subsidies and services, and
☐   realistic and comprehensive efforts to assist recipients when ready to engage in an "exit strategy" from welfare

the dependency of these families on social assistance will not just continue but grow.

From "Economic Stress, Social Support and Health/Well-Being of Low Income Female Single Parents" by Carolyn A. Gorlick, *Transition*, March 1989, pp. 6-7.

> . . . whether truncated by death or divorce or by the departure of grown children, we don't stop being a family. And a family doesn't need two parents to make a family.
> LETTY COTTIN POGREBIN

☐

Shirley's husband in her northern Ontario farming community was abusive and alcoholic so she left him and raised her eleven children on her own on a small farm with electricity but no running water. Most of the children are now grown, working, and raising families.

The hardest thing about single parenting, for Shirley, was disciplining her children. "They think they can run all over you. It seems to be much easier to take orders from a father than from a mother."

Apart from the lack of money she feels that growing up with only one parent had few really bad effects on her children. "They weren't ridiculed. It didn't seem to bother them."

The separation itself was a positive experience for the children, Shirley says. "To them it was a relief" for all the fighting and bad feeling to end.

"They each had their own chores to do. Their room was always their own. The girls kept dishes done up, and the boys carried in the wood and the water."

"There were two sets of neighbours I could turn to when I needed a hand. I didn't drive so I had to depend on them to take me into town once a week. When I had the chance I would go and help them back . . . even it out."

"I used to raise my own chickens and pigs, and then the neighbours would come and help slaughter. I still have a big garden and I do my own canning."

Her experiences with the welfare system and social workers were mixed. "I had one . . . that used to say 'Go back to your husband, it doesn't matter how things go, if he kills you fine, it doesn't matter, as long as the kids have a father.' "

She had that worker for two years "of her coming whenever she'd like to. . . . She'd walk in on me, always a bunch of stuff she'd heard from someone else about what a bad person I was."

"Well . . . I got so mad at her, I put her out one time, I had the steam iron. . . . I was going to clout her with it," she laughs.

Holidays have been happy times in her family. "The kids would all come home, and we'd look forward to it. . . . We were a very close-knit family, and we still are. There was a lot of love showed every which way in the ways that counted most."

"I have no regrets. They've grown up into fine adults."

Bonnie sees single parents from two sides—personal and professional. An urban mother of two (her son is 11, her daughter 13) her husband left her two years ago. She works part-time as a nurse and is in training as a family counsellor.

"Sometimes I feel really lonely. The first year was really really tough, having to deal with the kids and a low self-esteem, feeling that I had been rejected. . . ."

"Yes, there are periods of loneliness now, but there are also times when I'm really quite happy to be on my own and not have the hassles that sometimes a marital relationship does demand."

"The first year was quite traumatic in terms of our new roles, but I would say it's worked out very well." During that first year, Bonnie and her husband worked to establish a successful joint custody arrangement.

"The separation had come as quite a shock to the children. We made it clear to them it was between Dad and me, and it had nothing to do with them. I lived in the family home, and their dad moved three blocks away."

"Both my ex- and I would say that our relationships with our children are better than [when we were] a couple. . . .

Support from the community has been good. "My impression would be that they haven't felt stigmatized by it. . . . People understood, cub leaders and teachers."

"When there were parent-teacher interviews, we both went . . . It was a lot of work."

"In terms of my personal life, I suffered a lot more. I didn't have the free time he had. When the children were with me, it was free time for him, but when the children were with him, it was time for me to work and make money. . . ."

The first year she took in a boarder to help care for the children. "Now they're old enough that they take care of themselves, and that has helped a lot."

"At present, I'm working four and a half days a week in my field placement, and I'm working another two shifts a week on nights. . . . It's good for the children in that the work that I do on the weekends is nights. So in effect the children don't miss me. . . ."

"*I* miss me, and I don't get to sleep. I miss an average of one day's sleep a week. . . ."

Availability of credit has been a problem. "Financial institutions don't like single mums. I tried to buy a car last year—I was earning forty thousand dollars— and they wouldn't consider me at all. They won't look at support payments, casual earnings, a re-financed house. They wanted my ex-husband's signature."

"The interesting thing is that I had done all the banking in my family for eighteen years. I had established credit ratings. But that's just not considered." Bonnie finally found help through a women's credit union after exhausting almost all other possibilities.

"The hardest thing is having to be responsible for all the decisions. I miss free time for me. I don't take very good care of me in terms of what I need. It's OK in my mind to be away over supper hour and work an evening if I'm at work, but if a friend says, 'Can you come over for supper and maybe go out to a show?' I can't leave my kids alone—it's a real head game, with the guilt."

Dating is a question. Bonnie shies at introducing dates to her children. "I don't want them to have to evaluate every single person that comes through the door as a prospective parent."

"I think there tends to be a stigma. For example, there is still the automatic assumption that if the kids are having trouble in school or with the law, it's because they come from a broken home. That really rubs me wrong."

"It's much better that they be in a single parent home without conflict on a day-to-day basis than with two parents who are fighting constantly. Bright children from single homes are still bright and intelligent and do well at school, and they can still value family life."

Sandra, 32, is a victim of a system and a world that just don't seem to care. A childhood abuse victim, she lives in public housing on mothers' allowance with her 11-year-old daughter. She's been plagued by health problems: epilepsy, uterine cancer, a bout of prescription drug abuse, chronic back problems.

"I'm considered no good, no use for society. . . . You think I don't work and raise my daughter?" The two live on about $600 per month and it doesn't go very far. $178 for rent, $60 for the lease on her TV, $40 for hydro.

"Every cent I have goes to my daughter. Her clothes—all brand new." Sandra shops for herself at a used clothing store and smokes roll-your-own cigarettes. She doesn't mind used clothes for herself but wants to spare her daughter the indignity.

"She just can't understand why the other kids have all these things and she doesn't."

Since her mother died a month ago, Sandra has no one to turn to, friend or family. She has little reason to trust the authorities. Children's Aid workers once took her daughter directly out of school and placed her in substitute care after Sandra had a seizure. Sandra was not even informed of this move, and she was cut off mothers' allowance, having to live on welfare benefits of less than $200 per month. She says she even lived on this amount for months after her daughter came back. "I didn't eat. I lost sixty pounds in two months."

> Family is content, not form.
> GLORIA STEINEM

Things became much worse nine months ago when she received severe back injuries in a bus accident. Now she visits a doctor every few days for spinal injections. These trips carry another painful burden: a choice between taking the bus or a cab. In either case, it's money she doesn't have. The pain makes walking to the bus difficult, but a cab is too expensive.

Sandra feels that if she weren't a welfare mother, she would get better treatment and more help to deal with her injuries. "The anger has built up so much for the injustice."

It is a lonely road. "We've been alone about nine years. It's an awful long time to be alone. You don't want to go amongst people." For the past four years, Sandra has rarely left the house.

Her daughter shares her hurt. "I told her her father didn't want anything to do with her. She said 'That's alright, I've got you.' " But she says her daughter is bitter, and they often fight.

Clearly, the two share a deep bond. And there is some fun too. "There's a neighbourhood drop-in centre," says Sandra, with children coming in to play. Sandra loves to help people and enjoys the company of children, but her back injury and grieving for her mother have made it hard to feel very sociable.

"For the last month, I've been so lonesome. But I've got to go on for my daughter."

Suddenly after eighteen years of marriage, Laurie announced to Mark that she was leaving. They were back-to-the-landers living in western Québec and at the time, mid-1986, Paula was 14, Jimmy was 11, and Tom was 6. The boys stayed with Mark on the farm; Laurie and Paula moved to a nearby village.

"My situation was somewhat special in that . . . I had been full-time househusband," says Mark. "It was really important to both the boys that they stay [in the family home].

"It really upset all of them, and it still does. . . ." The most noticeable effect was on Tom, the youngest. "He couldn't deal with the anger and the fear in the way the other kids could, so he dealt with it irrationally. On weekends when the kids would go to Laurie's, he would cry going and cry coming back—I would, too. . . . He was an extreme behaviour problem at Laurie's place."

The experience was hard on Mark as well. "I was very overwhelmed, shattered," he remembers. "On a positive side, Jimmy for me was a tower of strength. Every time I would feel upset, no matter how sad he would feel, Jimmy was always there for me."

"He'd put his arms around me and comfort me . . . he was quite amazing. . . . Tom in his own way too was quite amazing, he would rally around. I don't know if I hadn't had the boys living with me whether I would still be healthy and whole."

The separation affected the children in many ways. In school, both boys had difficulties with concentration, and Tom occasionally misbehaved.

The best sources of support for Mark were friends, with whom he got together on a regular basis. A psychiatrist and a marriage counsellor also provided useful insight.

Mark cannot separate the problems of single parenting from the trauma of separation. "For me the difficulty of being a single parent had an awful lot to do with the difficulty of breaking up the relationship."

Money was a tremendous problem. After many years of working as a househusband and looking after the farm, he had no source of income other than meagre support payments. Mark is bitter that because he is a man he would have had little chance of being awarded spousal support in court. Eventually he found work as a local newspaper reporter.

"I was doing double duty, but I also didn't sleep. I was so overwrought that . . . I would go to bed at three in the morning, get up at seven. Occasionally I'd go to bed when the sun was rising. . . . This table saw the imprint of my head a number of times."

Time has passed, Mark and the boys have moved to town, and life is a little easier now. He is able to see positives in his life. A close relationship with the kids has really built up. Making the childrearing decisions on his own has been a good experience, and he finds the children have fewer behaviour problems now than when he was married.

"It's really made me a much stronger person, made me able . . . to see myself standing alone a lot more easily. You get a feeling—hey, I can do this—it takes a while to get that feeling. It's tough, but 'when the going gets tough, the tough get going.' "

From "The Good, the Bad, and the Lonely—Single Parents Talk About Their Experiences" by Ish Theilheimer, *Transition*, March 1989, pp. 9-12.

1. Summarize the initial findings of Dr. Gorlick's research on female single-parent families. Do any of the findings surprise you? Why?

2. Cite instances where these findings are borne out in the profiles of Shirley, Bonnie, and Sandra in the second selection. Account for any discrepancies.

3. Discuss the implications for single parents of the social policy changes advocated by Gorlick. What social policy changes would you have advocated? Justify your choices.

4. "The view that the single parent family is pathological is being challenged." Assess the significance of this change in outlook.

5. Investigate the support systems available for the single-parent families in your community. Consider during your investigation the changing needs of these families as they progress through the life cycle.

BLENDED FAMILIES

Increasingly, family albums tell the story. Statistics and demographics confirm impressions. A headline in the December 1989 issue of *Transition* magazine says it all: "The Blended Family Has Arrived." Previously stigmatized, the blended family is now regarded as a common family form. Yet challenges remain, both for the members of blended families themselves and for the rest of society. The first selection is written by Gae Miller, a woman who has been married, divorced, remarried, widowed, and remarried again—with a resulting brood of both step- and biological children. In the second selection entitled "The First Tango," Jocelyn Laurence recalls the shaky steps that led to her acceptance in a blended family. The steps, as she recounts them, are as intricate as the dance itself.

☐

The term blended family is a relatively new one, popularly associated with the high rates of divorce and remarriage in our own time. For those of us who have spent time in the kitchen, blending may conjure gentle images of melted chocolate losing itself in white batter, neither remaining what it was, but neither destroyed. The image may be electronic, with murderous blades whirling noisily through awkward mixtures which stick at certain stages; neither wood spoon nor human hand dare interfere until the machinery is stopped. I have often wondered which connotation is more accurate, taking into account the limitations of analogies.

The blended family is actually an ancient tradition, common to all tribes and civilizations. Whatever the society, Will Durant states, "The greatest task of morals is always sexual regulation; for the reproductive instinct creates problems not only within marriage, but before and after it, and threatens at any moment to disturb the social order with its persistence, its intensity, its scorn of law, and its perversions." In the simplest, most primitive tribes, sexual unions were easily formed and easily dissolved. The nurture of children was communal and lasted only until puberty, when the jolly cycle began again. In somewhat more sophisticated societies, there emerged clear goals for marriage, whatever form it took, and marriage was often obligatory. Death and divorce have long led to the phenomenon of remarriage. Widows among Old Testament Jews were passed on to their deceased husband's brother, or nearest living relative, and got on with the begets and begats. Happily, suttee, that old Hindu custom of burning the widow alive in her husband's funeral pyre (presumably so he didn't have to do without in the afterlife) has died out.

Many societies recognized grounds for divorce, such as adultery, stinking, nagging, impotence and so on. In the past, American Indians were said to "laugh at Europeans for having only one wife, and that for life; they consider that the Good Spirit formed them to be happy, and not to continue together unless their tempers and dispositions were congenial."

We are living through a transitional period in our own social order, in the evolution of sexual morals and the value of children. Time does not allow us here to trace the historical and religious root of the value of chastity before marriage, marriage to one partner for life, the rearing of many children. Most of us would recognize in this description of rural America the model marriage of our grandparents and perhaps parents:

"With the coming of a settled agricultural life, unions became more permanent. Under the patriarchal system the man found it uneconomical to divorce a wife, for this meant, in effect, to lose a profitable slave. As the family became the productive unit of society, tilling the soil together, it prospered—other things equal—according to its size and cohesion; it was found to some advantage that the union of the mates should continue until the last child was reared. By that time no energy remained for a new romance, and the lives of the parents had been forged into one by common work and trials."

Because we are living in a transitional time, clearly leaving the agricultural way of life behind in more ways than one, responses of the community to new, or newly acknowledged, sexual behaviour are confused, hypocritical, and sometimes corrosive.

Premarital sex is no longer a big deal unless you happen to be a young adolescent ready to roll but economically dependent and faced with a barrage of conflicting messages from peers, parents, the media, and the church, if any. We are a society in a kind of limbo when it comes to marriage. A wedding is still a big, expensive occasion, but why people do it, and what they expect from it, are vague. The allowance of premarital sex has largely eliminated the stereotype of the panting groom and blushing bride, but Romantic Love as a basis for matrimony appears to be still with us. It may be called happiness or personal fulfillment by those focussed on the importance of me, but I fear we are still governed by the vagaries of hormones. We continue to nurture "the custom of binding a man and a woman together for a moment with its lightning." Even the ancient Spartans, occasionally releasing a group of young men into a darkened room filled with young girls to copulate, conceive, and later marry, boasted a lower divorce rate than we have.

The law has caught up with reality in Canada by making divorce easier, and by recognizing that it usually takes two to fail. The key word here is fail. Any divorced person, whatever the bravado assumed, knows failure. The idea was to mate for life, produce 2.5 perfect children, and to live happily ever after; and it went bust. The White Lace and Promises Department didn't offer even a limited warranty. There wasn't an instruction book in English which remotely applied. The decision to abort likely came in the midst of an emotional crisis, and forever after one is teased in quiet moments with visions of better alternatives. The responses of extended family, community and credit managers often feel punitive to the already wounded.

Children are viewed with stunning polarity in this society confused about marriage. At the same time as some women are fighting for the right not to bear children, others are paying thousands for in-vitro fertilization. Popular magazines tote up the total cost of raising a child. My own mind used to boggle as I added up the cost of the eleven pairs of winter boots piled in my doorway. With no family business to pass on, with little in the way of meaningful work for them to do, children are reduced in some quarters to consumers. Resources decided means less for me. Who needs them? In ancient times, some people believed that they would be attended in the afterlife by their children. To the best of my knowledge, only the Mormon Church in our time preaches the eternal nature of the family, and ritualizes the sealing of parents and children to one another for all time. Predictably, this organization has a lower than average divorce rate, and treats the birth of each child as a special blessing.

The blended family is truly the phoenix of all human relationships as it rises from the ashes of old catastrophes. To begin one may be an act of profound courage or the most abject stupidity. On the whole the community offers only tentative support to the blended family, and nowhere is there a specialized agency to offer counselling at any stage.

If there is anything in our society more confused than the why's and where-fore's and how's of the first marriage, it is these aspects of the second. We begin with such high hopes that the traumas of the first mess will not be repeated that we trip and founder over hidden obstacles. We may try so hard to compensate for our own (and, we fear, others') view of ourselves as failures and losers that we leave ourselves emotionally bankrupt. I suspect that I raised eleven children and tolerated six more, taught full time, kept a reasonable house, and played supersubsequent wife to prove that my divorce was not my fault. We are threatened by the continued needs and demands of ex-spouses. If our spouse shows signs of continued feeling for an ex, we

The original plot goes like this: first comes love. Then comes marriage. Then comes Mary with a baby carriage. But now there is a sequel: John and Mary break up. John moves in with Sally and her two boys. Mary takes the baby Paul. A year later, Mary meets Jack, who is divorced with three children. They get married. Paul, barely 2 years old, now has a mother, a father, a stepmother, a stepfather, and five stepbrothers and stepsisters—as well as four sets of grandparents (biological and step) and countless aunts and uncles. And guess what? Mary's pregnant again.

BARBARA KANTROWITZ
and PAT WINGERT

are doomed. Try harder. If our children or stepchildren hate us, or if they get into trouble, it is a burden larger than most of us can bear. We are not prepared, for a bevy of adolescents we have taken on in fond hope, to turn on us as if we had set out to wreck their lives. We may not realize at the outset that time and money will be in such short supply, because there is the drain of support payments or a previously accumulated debt. Grandparents and other relatives may complicate the scene and create conflict, or they can be a marvellous help towards the harmony of the unit.

The children in blended families may need help with a myriad of difficulties. They may bear unwarranted guilt in a divorce or death. They may be victims of unspoken hostilities, which they merely feel but can't express. They may grieve deeply for a missing parent, and they may manipulate desperately to coax their natural parents back together. Often they feel ignored in the face of a new and incandescent adult relationship. Their turf may be invaded by undesirable aliens. They may lose their familiar turf altogether, and have to fight for a corner as an interloper. There are ghastly possibilities for threatening relationships kept secret in a sort of children's network. Worst of all, I believe, is the torment of a child at the hands of a parent masquerading as protector. Blessed is the child whose natural parent remarries someone who truly loves all the children.

I am not confident that a paid bureaucrat, psychiatrist, psychotherapist, or school counsellor represent adequate community response to the blended family. All of these people are limited by time, resources, and their own experience. At one stage in my life I blundered through the gamut, and emerged dazed by two offers of sexual service, one attempt at touch therapy, the invaluable suggestion that a couple of showers together a week could save the marriage, and repeated autobiographical details from someone who kept forgetting he had seen me before. It seems to me that there might be definite advantages in a self-help group willing to guide seekers to whatever the truth might be and to stay close as a variety of responses are tried. The blended family needs an accepting support network. The church community is an ideal setting were it always possible.

War in itself is not desirable, yet the community honours the courage of those who soldier on, even against insurmountable odds. It sometimes calls for that kind of courage to stand fast and make a loving home after losing to divorce or death. If not all religious groups can see fit to sanctify the blended family, I would ask you as you consider your resolutions to keep a special place in your heart for the folks who keep on trying.

From "As If Families Matter" by Gae Miller,
Journal of Ontario Family Studies-Home Economics Educators Association,
Vol 7, No. 1, July 1988, pp. 13-14.

☐

I t was shortly after moving into Gary's house almost a year ago that I decided to teach his daughters the tango. Meredith, who was 8 1/2 at the time, and Julia, who'd just turned 7, had been leaping about the living room to Rodion Shchedrin's percussive version of *Carmen*, wildly clacking homemade castanets constructed from cardboard and beer-bottle caps and string. The tango was a whim on my part, since I had no real idea of the intricacies of the dance, merely a notion (culled from dance lessons at school when, as part of a class of awkward, sweaty girls, we thundered around the gym) of the basic moves and manoeuvres. But I demonstrated what little I knew, first with Julia as a partner, then with Meredith, until they'd grasped the essentials and were off on their own, partners to each other. I sat watching them as they tangoed back and forth, one small set of arms held rigidly out like the prow of a rowboat, Meredith's other arm wrapped firmly around Julia's waist and Julia's hand clutching Meredith's shoulder. I fell in love with these tiny, determined dancers. I loved their seriousness, the way the turns made them giggle and lose their step momentarily, the way their mouths wobbled between squirming self-consciousness and a deep interest in getting it right. They were counting the beat out loud while their ponytails bounced heartily to the music. It was around then, having more fun with a couple of children than I'd have believed possible, that I thought, I can't allow myself to love them too much. They're not really mine.

I had always liked children but had never imagined they would like me. With no kids of my own, I'd seen myself as the kind of person who precipitates crying fits in perfectly behaved babies and makes small children blanch and go to their rooms. When I first met Julia and Meredith, I was so anxious that they would like me (and I them) that for the first few occasions I barely noticed them. Surrogate parents have a profound—and practical—need for acceptance. I was so braced for rejection that I'm astonished it didn't actually happen. What did happen is that the three of us, Meredith and Julia and I, began to play.

Julia started it. She has a warm and accommodating nature that comes both from her heart and from being the youngest, the one who has to run a fraction faster to be there at the same time as everyone else. She's also a very physical child who loves to hug and swing on your arm and hold your hand and just cozy up to someone she likes. She decided quite early on that someone was me, and I, grateful for her large and inclusive spirit, responded with games and stories and conversations from my own childhood that I'd thought I'd forgotten. Julia became so carried away with her small and tender devotions that for a couple of weeks she took to calling me Mummy, insisting that it was quite logical and indeed possible for her and Meredith to have two Mummies. The idea made me slightly uncomfortable (though the compliment pleased me enormously), particularly when their own (and much be-loved) mother was alive and well and occupying a large portion of their lives. I had no wish to usurp her position or cause her even peripheral pain. Besides, I wasn't sure I wanted to be Mummy to children who (I kept coming back to this) weren't actually mine.

Meredith had no such impulses, however, no urgent and obvious need for the acceptance I might provide. Intelligent and extremely self-contained, she began by being politely interested in me. She reminded me very much of myself at the same age when, as the elder child, I took a certain pride in being as adult and independent as possible. I decided to take the only action possible—none—and leave her alone to make her own decisions. It was Meredith who, a few months after my arrival, announced cheerfully that she knew why I was living at the house—I was there to help pay the rent. Parents often mention the terrible (and the implicit word here is truthful) things their children say. What they rarely talk about are the times when kids simply parrot remarks they've heard. Perhaps adults tend to avoid the topic because their children then become not intuitive geniuses but blind bearers of received wisdom. At any rate, several possible reasons and sources for this remark occurred to me, few of them Meredith's own and none of them malicious. So while Gary was calmly explaining to her that she was in fact wrong, I managed what I hoped was a reasonable facsimile of the archaic smile and reminded myself that the pain making me hold my breath for a long second had little to do with the small person who had just spoken.

I suppose, as the numb phrase has it, I must have done something right. Slowly—to me, nearly miraculously—Meredith started hanging out near my chair after dinner, draping her arm over my shoulders, sniffing out the situation. The day she first hopped casually onto my lap I felt absurdly like a loony naturalist, tempted to announce to the civilized world that I'd just won the trust of an obscure and skittish but immensely valuable animal, and terrified that the slightest movement would drive her away.

In the beginning, I deliberately spent as much time as I could with both the children. On the days and nights they were with us, I made sure I was home. I wanted, I suppose, to make them feel as secure as possible, to accustom them to my presence in the house and in their lives, to let them know that my attention and caring weren't transitory. It was in some ways an oblique confession of love. It was also such a private and peculiar emotion, particularly in the context of children, that I rarely talked about it in those terms. Instead (a dead giveaway) I became obsessed with the girls in conversation. Despite what my friends, family and even virtual strangers said about taking on a lot (despite the fact it was repeated to me so often I almost came to believe it), I felt privileged. I wasn't in Meredith's and Julia's company out of a sense of duty or obligation; I actively wanted to be around them. They were (and are) engaging and zippy and endlessly involving. It was, as I understand it, much like the process a new mother goes through with her baby.

Of course, like many new mothers I ended up skimping on the attention I gave to the kids' father. He became, for a while, just that—the kids' father, not the man I fell in love with. He, more sanguine about the parental role than I, would want to talk about books or paintings, the way we had done endlessly and effortlessly in the past. My dogged and blinkered concern, meanwhile, would be Julia's spelling or Meredith's occasional insomnia. It wasn't that he had no interest in the girls. He loved them with a single-mindedness and an intensity and generosity that I sometimes found startling. But he had had more practice than I in changing modes from parent to child-free adult. I had entered so fully and enthusiastically into being a parent, albeit part-time, that I found it hard to extricate myself.

I hadn't realized, too, what an emotional—and thus erotic—drain children can be. The cliché about being a parent is that you become too exhausted for romance and certainly for sex. That's not quite true. What you become is used up. All the emotions that go into eroticism—love, inventiveness, nurturing, adventure and security, and finally a sense of losing yourself in another human being—are channelled into caring for children. It is (and this is a difficult admission) as satisfying in many ways as love between adults, perhaps more so since children are infinitely appreciative and elastic and fulfill our culture-wide need for a simplicity that belies experience.

In fact, Gary and I had to get to know each other all over again as parents. It wasn't, I now realize, easy. We both have large egos; we both require absurdly large quantities of attention. Yet we both saw quite quickly that Meredith and Julia mattered more, in the end, than anything we could conjure for ourselves. For the first few months, though, we would have circular, tentative, sometimes quite ungentle conversations about the children when what we were actually doing was checking to see whether the other person, the individual we first knew, was still there.

This concentration on Julia and Meredith was something I was prepared for, was prepared to do. When Gary's mother thanked me for being good with the children, I replied lightly that it was easy, and meant it. What I was far less prepared for—and what is perhaps hardest to set down—were my attacks (and there is really no other word for them) of jealousy, resentment, and just plain loneliness. One night Gary and the kids were drawing at the dining-room table, crouched under the small spread of light that is perfect for dinner parties but, we discovered, less effective for family activities. I was doing the dishes in the kitchen, listening to them laugh and bicker and spill paint on the table, when I suddenly (and humiliatingly) found myself in tears, missing my brother and my mother and my father desperately, yearning for the flesh-and-bone connection Gary has with his children, wanting the reflection of shared blood in someone else's eyes. I still find that stories about the kids' births, family stories about their early childhood that even I, now, know off by heart, can set me adrift. It's uncomfortably similar to the dislocation you can feel when your lover talks about his past and you know, with a certainty bordering on pathology, that all those events are unreclaimable by you except through anecdote. Even walking down the street, if I happen to find myself behind the three of them as they swoop over the sidewalk, borne (in my overburdened imagination) by some invisible biological flood force, hand in hand to some invisible future I can never be a part of since I was never a part of their shared past, even then, in the most innocent of circumstances, I can feel so terribly isolated and so terribly sorry for myself that I'm appalled at the depth of my need for all of them.

But loneliness is a comparatively acceptable emotion. There are evenings, though, when Gary and I have just settled down to talk after the children have been planted in their beds and Meredith appears because she can't sleep and I want to tell her to *go away*, she's had her father's attention all evening and now I want an hour or two of my own. This silent tussle has, I suppose, nasty Freudian undertones, viewed from a certain perspective. Seen from another angle, however, it's merely the clash of two very strong and demanding people. Meredith can be quite sophisticated and self-mocking about her sleeplessness ("I've read all the publishers' names on all the books on my shelf"), but the grace of her intrusion can't always dilute the fact that where one moment ago there were two of us, now there are three, and it is my needs, as the adult, which must of necessity be temporarily suspended.

Adults have a tendency to dwell on what they learn from children. They usually mean that children remind them of what they've always known but would sometimes prefer to erase. Yet if Meredith and Julia unwittingly make me face my own competitiveness (and, of course, the battles long gone for my own father's attention and approbation), they have also allowed me to care for them in the total (and totally respectful) way we can only seem to manage with our children. Meredith and Julia have reminded me about pure love, the kind of self-abnegating love that is rarely possible—and probably not even advisable—among adults; a love that ends up acting as a standard against which we can measure our supposedly wiser but in fact rather tattered emotions.

And slowly I'm starting to form my own history with them. It will never make them "mine" any more than a shared history with a lover will, but it does establish connection, precedent, understanding. There was the evening that Meredith and I spent making drawings for Gary, both of us at the desk in my study discussing books and hair and how to draw feet properly. There was the winter afternoon Julia and I raced along Queen Street under a big, grey umbrella, on our way to buy earrings for her mother's birthday and late for lunch with her father, and she was worrying about how cold my hands were, chafing them in hers and finally offering me one of her minuscule mittens. Meredith ropes herself around my waist or arms all the time now; Julia has a proper and touching respect for my separateness. I'm actually very proud of all of us, to have got even this far. I haven't told them yet in words that I love them, but of course I do.

From "The First Tango" by Jocelyn Laurence,
Toronto Life, October, 1985, pp. 33-34.

1. In the opening paragraph of the first selection, Gae Miller presents two contrasting analogies for the blended family. Explain which analogy comes closest to your understanding of life in a blended family. Suggest other analogies and illustrate why they might have been equally appropriate.

2. Describe the range of needs and emotions experienced by the blended family in the "The First Tango." What challenges did family members face in reaching mutual acceptance? Discuss these challenges from a systems perspective.

3. Review the history of divorce and remarriage as outlined in Gae Miller's article and in other authoritative sources. Pinpoint the values and assumptions underlying the changing laws, attitudes, and practices over time.

4. Gae Miller states that "the blended family is truly the phoenix of all human relationships as it rises from the ashes of old catastrophes." Explain how this image may represent either hope or concern to a newly blended family.

5. Lillian Messinger, a social worker at Toronto's Clarke Institute of Psychiatry

and author of *Remarriage: A Family Affair*, has worked with and studied remarried couples for over two decades. Her research revealed that couples were "poorly prepared for the major upheaval [remarriage] caused their children." Gae Miller similarly reports that "children in blended families may need help with a myriad of difficulties." Identify what some of these difficulties may be. How would they change over the life cycle?

6.   Describe how the following concepts, as outlined in the Guldner essay, may differ in remarried and intact families: self-concept; affective needs; power; roles; alignments; communication. Search the literature to determine the accuracy of your theories.

DUAL-EARNER FAMILIES

While the dual-earner family is currently described as an "emerging lifestyle," historical evidence indicates that the dual-worker family is not a new phenomenon. Dual-earner families in contemporary times face major challenges. Joan Quilling, the author of the first selection, outlines the historically changing work roles of men and women. In the second reading, Robert Glossop encapsulates some of the issues faced by families that have chosen the dual-earner lifestyle. The final selection, by Dorothy Lipovenko, examines the controversial concept of the "Mommy Track."

☐

Family lifestyles are changing. No longer is one lifestyle considered the norm for industrialized nations. Instead, societies today consist of single-parent families, blended families (divorced and remarried spouses), teenage families, and poor families, to name a few. A recently emerging family lifestyle is that of the dual-earner family. More families are assuming such a lifestyle, yet little is known about historical trends which have brought about such an occurrence, research related to their lifestyle, nor the impact these families have upon the larger society.

☐ HISTORICAL PERSPECTIVES OF WORK

Industrialized nations are faced with a relatively new phenomenon, households in which both adults work outside the home. The typical family, consisting of a wage-earning husband with a homemaker wife and two children, now represents only about five percent of all families in the United States (*Changing Times*, 1982). In

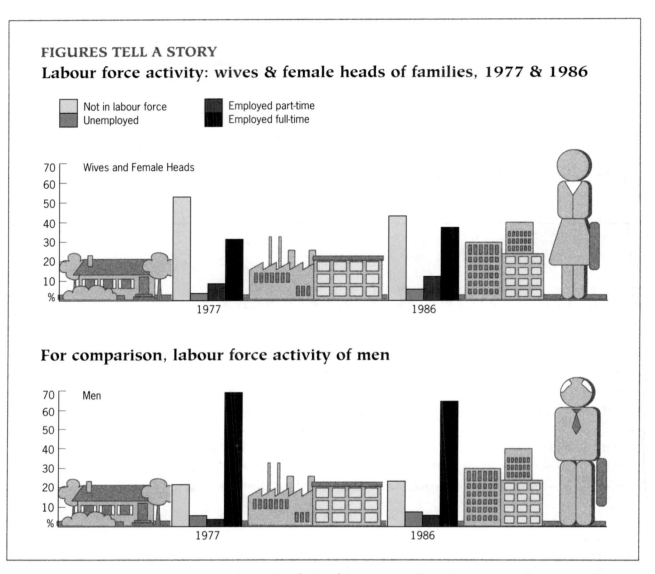

FIGURES TELL A STORY
Labour force activity: wives & female heads of families, 1977 & 1986

From Statistics Canada, Catalogues 71-001, The Labour Force, and 71-533, Family Characteristics and Labour Force Activity, Annual Averages, 1977-1984.

Canada, the number of single-parent families rose 27.6% between 1976 and 1981 (Canadian Council, 1985). These data reinforce that a changing economy coupled with an increased lifespan have fostered more diverse lifestyles. Work outside the home has become just as significant a factor in the adult female's life as it has traditionally been in the adult male's life. Is this a new phenomenon? History would tell us no. The work roles of men and women were never as divergent as they became during the industrial revolution. Until that time, work was carried out within and around the home and both partners contributed to family maintenance.

Connellan (1978) reviewed the status of work historically and summarized several work related themes. In primitive cultures, for example, work and free time were rarely distinguished. Practically all working hours were spent by both males and females tending to basic needs. The ancient Greek, Roman, and Egyptian cultures viewed work as a curse to be done only by slaves. During the sixteenth century reformation period, work was done in obedience to God. Both husband, wife, and children had a significant role to play in this effort.

The nineteenth century industrial revolution saw occupations become legitimate spheres of action. The separation of male/female work arenas became the prominent lifestyle for the middle class. By the twentieth century work as a virtue was separated from religion. During the latter half of this century, females began to enter male work spheres in significant numbers.

A review of the past reveals that over time, both males and females have played a significant role with regard to work. The industrial revolution tended to make the female's work role less visible to society since she was expected to remain in the home.

The separation of male/female work arenas held until about the 1960s when the barriers between the two worlds gradually dissolved. Today, some economists and futurists predict a return to a pre-industrial revolution work ethic. Because the nature of work is changing due to readily available technology, more work can be done in the home and transferred electronically to the work place. Should this trend become more prevalent, work contributions could be more obvious to all family members. The work done by family members would be an integral part of the family's interaction patterns. Such is not the norm today. Since work is predominantly done in an arena apart from the home and is paid for by an employer, the world of work is largely separated from the home. The interactions which occur in either area are not expected to spill over into one another. Typically, employees are terminated if their family responsibilities prevent them from performing their work roles effectively. . . .

From "Dual-Earner Family Perspectives" by Joan Quilling,
Canadian Home Economics Journal, Vol. 39, No. 2, Spring 1989, pp. 64-66.

> Daycare is just an abstract concept until you have a child. After you have a child, it is a gut-wrenching issue. And it is the issue that spills first from the lips of every working parent I talk to.
>
> WENDY DENNIS

☐

Up early in the morning in time to get kids dressed, lunches made and kids delivered to daycare or school before mother and father must arrive at their places of employment. Then proceeds a regular day of business, meetings, phone calls, assembly lines and/or memos before rushing to pick up the kids by a pre-determined time so that their caregivers do not charge us with breach of contract. Then, home to prepare a meal while T.V. babysits the kids. Once a week, we're off to the community college to take a course on Introduction to Microprocessing for the sake of career advancement and twice a week off to exercise classes in order to keep our bodies fit enough to pursue this pace. Baths and homework are supervised prior to our scheduled amount of time for interpersonal relating before we watch the National News which, thank God, now comes on at 10:00 p.m. instead of 11:00 p.m. because the Canadian Broadcasting Corporation shrewdly realized we can hardly keep our eyes open past 10:30. Weekends have assumed their own schedule, often even tighter than the weekdays as we set off to Canadian Tire to purchase the insulating materials that will occupy us on Sunday before, if we can manage it, friends arrive for dinner. . . .

More and more, our home lives, our times together have taken on the routines, orderliness and time-management techniques of the office and the factory. Family experts tell us, in all seriousness, that we must make appointments with our children, that we must arrange a meeting of family members at least once a week and that we must write each other memos so that we all know where everyone else is. And, if your fridge and bulletin board look anything like mine, you'll know that these experts have simply confirmed the habits we have come to take for granted. . . .

Only in part does this trend toward dual wage-earning families as the statistically normal pattern of economic functioning reflect an increase in the personal aspirations of individuals for a 'richer' lifestyle. For many families, two incomes have become necessary simply 'to make ends meet'. . . .

From "Family Time or Prime Time? Jobs, Leisure and Relationships
in the 1980's" by Robert Glossop, PhD, *Perspectives*,
Vanier Institute of the Family, May 11, 1986, pp. 2-7.

□

Will men on the Daddy Track please stand up? No takers? That's because there is no Daddy Track. A young man on the fast track to management would consider it career suicide if he signalled a move into the slow lane to raise a family.

But a leading U.S. business consultant, in a much publicized recent article, argues that companies should establish a Mommy Track for women who want, or need, to merge child rearing and managerial aspirations. The Mommy Track is like the overnight milk run—it gets you to your destination, but slower. Conversely, consultant Felice Schwartz argues, corporations should target women who are fiercely committed types—with no intention of motherhood or even marriage—and buy them tickets on the express train to management.

> At work you think of the children you've left at home. At home you think of the work you've left unfinished. Such a struggle is unleashed.
>
> GOLDA MEIR

While Ms Schwartz is under attack for promoting a double standard that could hurt some women, many mother/managers who want to get off the daily tightrope are grateful to their new ally for speaking up. But Ms Schwartz's *Harvard Business Review* article, which ignited the controversy, and her subsequent defence of her proposal in a recent edition of the New York Times, beg the question: why no suggestion of a Daddy Track? Why derail the careers of ambitious women, even temporarily, to accommodate the unequal division of child rearing that exists among many intelligent, two-job couples?

One could argue there would be no need for a Mommy Track if more fathers assumed equal responsibility for child care, say, making that 5 p.m. day-care pickup or taking the kids to the dentist.

Sadly, the experts agree, not much has changed despite all the rhetoric, the goodwill of shared parenting and the Lamaze classes.

"There aren't many men who are willing to share," notes sociologist Margrit Eichler, who studies the family. "And women are willing to accept men on unequal terms."

Ben Schlesinger, a professor of social work at the University of Toronto, agrees. "Despite all the changes, our attitude is that it's the women's job" to raise the children.

A case in point: a Toronto lawyer was stranded when her nanny left without warning. Until she found a replacement, the lawyer was forced to reschedule her clients so she would be home when the kids got in from school. When asked about her husband's role in all of this, she replied: "The children are my responsibility. I may not like it or want it that way, but that's how it is."

In the course of interviewing parents on the fast track, Prof. Schlesinger said, he was puzzled by women's acceptance of the status quo. "I challenge them (women) on it and they say, 'for the sake of peace in the home. If he does a little bit, I'm satisfied.' "

As long as husbands and fathers sense that women are reluctant to negotiate tougher terms and, if society persists in reinforcing the notion that daddy's work is more important than mommy's (note which working parent is called first to fetch a sick child at school or day care), change will be illusive.

"Organizations are still fairly intolerant of men who let their personal side of life interfere with their life at the office," says Prof. Ron Burke of York University's faculty of administrative studies. "A man who wants to go on a Daddy Track would be considered a wimp and get beat up for it."

But employers cannot take all the blame. Men are more comfortable in the work environment and that's where they want to stay. Studies show men report feeling more competent and successful at work, Prof. Burke says, and more in control managing a staff than looking after children.

The bottom line, says Dorothy Mikalachki, a researcher for the business school at the University of Western Ontario, is that career mobility and children do not pose the same emotional conflict for men as women.

She interviewed men and women MBA grads who had been classmates at the business school to determine the impact of a young family on their careers.

"The women went on and on with great emotion and anguish about how important their children were and how difficult it was maintaining their career. The men replied, 'oh yes, my family is more important now,' but they wouldn't elaborate."

Dr. Eichler may have the right idea. She suggests men need social support to feel confident about the Daddy Track and she has been lobbying the federal government for a national ad campaign to encourage men in this direction.

But wouldn't it be wonderful, she suggests, if men had a role model to lead the way, say the prime minister or a major corporate figure who took the Daddy Track. Indeed.

From "Pardon Me Boys, Is This the Mothers-Only Choo-choo?" by Dorothy Lipovenko, *The Globe and Mail*, March 31, 1989.

I happen to believe that if society values kids, it has to provide facilities to enhance their development, to grapple with the pressure of the cost and stress involved in getting them to and from day care, to offer affordable home care for when they are sick. Daycare is not just a facility. It is an attitude. You can't get all upset about the breakdown of the nuclear family and not provide support systems and work programs to preserve it.

DEBORAH BERNSTEIN

1. What insights does Quilling's historical overview provide about the phenomenon of the dual-earner family? Differentiate between dual-earner and dual-career families.

2. Describe the kinds of compromises that dual-earner couples are obliged to make. How do these couples rationalize the "time poverty" that results? What are the possible effects, both positive and negative, on the mother, father, and children, respectively? What is your definition of "quality family life"?

3. In an article on dual-earner families entitled "Finding Time for the Family," Wendy Dennis writes that "reclaiming our families will involve rewriting laws, altering the way public funds are spent, creating mechanisms in the work place, in our culture and our own lives." In light of Lipovenko's article on the "Mommy Track," compile a list of specific recommendations that would effect the above changes.

4. Analyze the basis for changes in power when a family becomes a dual-earner one. In what areas of family life might changes in the power base be affected? Investigate the impact on overall family satisfaction and functioning.

5. React to the statement from the final reading: "Organizations are still fairly intolerant of men who let their personal side of life interfere with their life at the office." Compare your reaction with that of someone of the opposite sex.

CHANGING GENDER ROLES

Long-standing myths about and traditional expectations of gender roles are deeply ingrained in family patterns and behaviour. However, as new social and economic realities settle in, families are gradually redefining expectations and breaking down stereotypes. In the first reading, columnist Wendy Dennis offers glimpses into many worlds: her parents', her own, a friend's, and her daughter's. The advances in female entitlement, while not yet complete, are striking. In the second reading, David Suzuki—whose early days are recounted in the Ways of Knowing About Families section of this book—describes his own experiences with role cycling.

Two little girls chat idly in the back seat of my car. Sara, my bright-eyed, lanky 5-year-old daughter. Jessie, her "big cousin," of the blonde ringlets and straightforward manner. Girl talk is in the air. Intense discussion about neon-yellow socks. Out of the blue, Jessie poses a question. It jolts me from distraction. A lot hangs on how my daughter answers this question, for me. Blithely unaware that her query raises the most murderous issue of her parents' generation, Jessie asks, "What's the difference between boys and girls?" "Boys only wear one earring," Sara replies.

I smile. A triumphant smile. Nearly two decades of feminist theory and political action and, unconsciously, my daughter hands me an icon attesting to the distances we have travelled. What would I have said at her age? That boys are bigger, smarter, stronger? Still, there has been a price. Feminism is wonderful as an ideal, but putting it into practice has been quite another matter. Sara's father and I brought her into the world fully expecting to raise her in an intact family; she grows up instead in two households.

The newspapers bleat statistics about the breakdown of the nuclear family, but let me tell you that statistics give no inkling of what it means, on a personal level, when a family breaks down. It has more to do with taking a deep breath and walking into your child's cheery yellow room, where she is drawing with magic markers at her desk, to tell her that her world is about to cave in. It involves searching the cupboards at bedtime for one of her father's ties because only by clutching this precious relic of his can she make it through the night. It means drawing her near when she sees two beaming parents with their newborn and asks, "Do you think *they* live together, mommy?"

Shortly after my husband and I separated, an uncle whom I adore called to express his regret. He has watched several marriages in our extended family come apart, so he was inured to the news when it was announced, but the words he spoke that day have haunted me. "Wendy," he said, "you know how fond I am of both of you. I'm very sad about this. If this decision will make you happier, then, I guess, it's for the best. But I don't understand you kids today. I don't understand what it is that you want."

Something better, I want to say. Something more just. It hasn't been as clear for us as it was for you. We came to marriage with a stubborn vision in our heads that our lives might include more choices than our mothers'. That we might make relationships of true equals. For a moment, I consider saying these things, but I don't. He will not understand. Sometimes I have trouble understanding them myself.

I am 6, waiting with my mother at the airport for my father's return from a business trip to New York. He travels a lot, my father; I miss him when he is gone. He comes back, not only with trinkets and pretty dresses for my two sisters and me, but also with stories, captivating stories that tell of the places he has been. I press my nose up against the glass door, anxious to spot him debarking. When he does, I break free of my mother's grasp, burst through the door and race out to the tarmac, where I leap into his arms. "Wendy," I hear my mother calling worriedly behind me.

"Be careful. Come back." But I pay no attention. Fathers have thrilling adventures; mothers wait patiently at home for them to return. It is in my father's world that I, at 6, long to be.

I am 17. Throughout high school I stand near the top of my class. The year I graduate I win the staff award for best all-round student, and an entrance scholarship to university. None of this matters to me, however, as much as the gap I feel for what I haven't been able to pull off—getting a boyfriend. I would trade all of these successes in a minute for the sweet thrill of showing off to envious girlfriends at my locker the ID bracelet of just one vaguely presentable guy. I can remember sitting at home one New Year's Eve, watching the ball drop in Times Square, thinking what a piece of shit it was to be a girl. If I were a boy, at least I might have a date tonight. Sure, I would have to risk rejection, but, for me, the *possibility* of rejection was less awful than the certain rejection that came with the powerlessness of having to wait by the phone.

I was so lousy at being a girl. I wasn't pretty in the way you had to be. I had short, frizzy hair when long, silky, iron-your-hair-on-ironing-boards hair was in. I had too many opinions and no talent at all for stifling them. The qualities that had stood me in good stead winning prizes, it seemed to me, were the very same qualities that were sabotaging my possibilities of getting a date. Occasionally, some real nerd would call to ask me out and my mother would say, "Go, dear, it's only for an evening. You might have some fun." And I'd always think, No, I can't go. It's torture. I'm going to have to pretend that he's riveting when he's boring and his jokes are dumb. But I did go, of course. One boy, any boy—a date—was better than no date at all. Finally, I gave up on being a girl and tried to be a boy instead. So I told risqué jokes in class and talked like a trucker, and wound up with a bunch of male buddies who thought I was terrific to consult when they were having problems with their girlfriends.

Then, of course, there was the whole knotty question of sex. The truth is, I wanted to do it. I know now that so did every other girl, but I didn't know that then, and it created some confusion, I can tell you. Every signpost in the culture around me indicated that I wasn't supposed to want to do it. Nice girls didn't do it. I heard boys brag about girls they had screwed in the back seats of cars, but no girl I knew ever bragged of being screwed in the back seat of a car. How to resolve these mixed messages?

At 20, I set off to hitchhike my way through Europe. I can assure you that my main goal is not to see the world's great art. Sex and drugs and rock and roll are in the air, and my interests lie in meeting some dark stranger. I wind up in Morocco with an Arab paramour and watch life go by from the rooftops of Fez. This is my sweet rebellion. At last, like my father, on big, noisy airplanes to faraway places. Free, powerful and alive.

I come home and get married, the following summer, to a nice Jewish boy. Foreign soil is one thing; at home I feel the tug of familiar rules. I keep my own name, and relinquish my aspirations. Somebody's got to do it. I have this crazy dream that I want to write; he wants to get a doctorate. There is no security in writing; we need hard cash to live. So I go into teaching, a nice vocation for a girl. No one forces me to do it. I do it myself, egged on by twenty-one years of female conditioning. The marriage doesn't last very long. It is nobody's fault. We are young. We want different things. When we part, I take with me, along with my share of the Dylan albums, a lesson learned. It is going to take more than a marriage to make me whole.

I give up on men for a while, and discover women. They had always seemed so dull to me before, so humourless, so silly. But suddenly all of these amazingly vital women appear out of nowhere, fulfilling their dreams. The books are coming off the presses fast and furiously, and I am reading them voraciously. I can remember staying up all night to finish *The Female Eunuch* and putting the book down and thinking, Oh my God. This is all so obvious. Why didn't I think of this before?

Then, all those hostile years, prowling the landscape, both guns out of the holster, poised to pick off the enemy. It's all *their* fault. *They* did this to us, the bastards. We have discovered a Truth, and it is now our job to spread the word, thus retooling the entire world, and the men who run it, by tomorrow. I am reading, around this time, Susan Brownmiller's *Against our Will*. It has such a stunning impact on me that I call the Rape Crisis Centre the day I finish it to volunteer my services. There are a lot of angry, passionately committed, poorly paid young women in that shabby College Street office, trying to mobilize their anger to move mountains. It is hard to get funds. Everybody is exhausted. At such times there is nothing to do but turn men into voodoo dolls into which we can viciously stick pins. Then I go back home and attend dinner parties, where all the women, including me, clear tables at which men are sitting, discussing life and art. If I make an issue out of this, I'm over-reacting, a hysterical female. All the other women seem to know their place. Those are the moments when I get so weary, so tempted to just give up, even though I know in my heart that giving up is not even an option any more. Inevitably I do make an issue of it though. I rise and deliver a stinging oration—Marc Antony-calibre material, I imagine—on the unfairness of it all. I fully expect the men to leap from their chairs, throw off years of conditioning, shout "I believe!" and dutifully begin carrying plates into the kitchen. Their eyes just glaze over. I want to hack them to bits with the carving knife. All of them.

I am on the cusp of 30. By this time, I have been living for a few years with a man I deeply love. I have not thought much about kids before, but, suddenly, almost overnight, it seems, I want them. By now, desperately unfulfilled teaching, I have quit to go to journalism school. In fifteen dizzying, exhilarating, exhausting months I throw myself into my courses, remarry, move into a first home, give birth to a baby and begin a demanding second career as a freelance writer. I am a woman of the '80s. I can have it all. I soon discover that there are a few bugs to be worked out trying to be a woman of the '80s.

First of all, this business of a marriage of equals. Through this period I keep reading about relationships that are supposed to be 50-50, but I look around me and do not *see* anybody living in a truly equal relationship. In most of the marriages I observe that last and work, men are being forced to make certain accommodations, but they are not dividing themselves in the same way that women are. I do not see men clustered in animated circles at parties obsessively trading the nanny stories.

> Each man, woman and child is a potentially creative artist in the invention of family roles.
> SIDNEY M. JOURARD

The stories bore them. They are not the ones living with that raw panic when support systems break down and the boss still expects you in.

A close friend of mine who by day is a corporate vice-president and by night mothers two children and who, with whatever few gasps of energy she has remaining, tries to be a wife, is so strung out when I call her one evening that she bursts into tears on the phone. She has rushed home from the office that day, leaving before any of the men, because she's got a half-hour to bake a birthday cake for her daughter's party tomorrow and her daughter, being a kid, knocks over the flour and spills sprinkles all over the floor, and my friend goes nuts and starts screaming at her because all she can think of is that she's got to get this task finished before the next one hits, and the next one.

Such strains, and others, begin to take their toll on my own marriage. We each have our own problems and pressures. Our needs begin to clash. Loss of love is not the issue here. We are just ordinary, decent people trying to live together in a world where all the rules have changed. In the only ways familiar to each of us, we try our best. Oh how we try. There is a lot at stake here. But we are speaking different languages. In the end, we cannot invent the dialogue to bridge the distances between us. I can remember watching an episode of *Hill Street Blues* in which Captain Furillo, who has just separated from his second wife, a tough, smart, ambitious public defender, is out on a dinner date with a female cop. He is in pain, trying to make sense of why his marriage has come apart, and he delivers a line that rivets right through me. It seems to crystallize a truth so many of our generation have had to face. "As my wife says," he comments sadly, "these days, just because two people love each other, it doesn't mean they're going to make each other happy."

My life now is not without its burdens and its pains. It is far from an ideal way to live. But I think it is a better way to live than the way so many of our parents did, staying together because they had to, out of financial need, or for the kids. Feminism taught me that with selfhood come choices. Some of them have been thrilling; some, tough and awful. Recently it struck me that I don't think much about being a feminist any more. I am one. I am much more comfortable being a woman than once I was, freer now to enjoy the simple, time-worn pleasures of being female, such as having some fun with fashion, baking cookies with my daughter. I live no longer by the text. The precepts are wired in. I have worked strenuously to absorb those that seemed to fit and to reject those that didn't. Nor am I obsessed any longer with remodelling men, for their own good, in my holy image. I do what I have to do. So must they. Maybe one day we'll manage it together. Maybe.

Scenes from the present. It is a sunny afternoon. I pick my daughter up at school. Her teacher greets me at the playground gate. "This has been a special day for Sara," she tells me proudly. "She went farther on the monkey bars than any of the boys." I smile. I recall winning a teacher's praise for printing inside the lines. After school, she dresses as Madonna, and comes downstairs to dance a wonderfully sensuous woman-dance in the living room. Together we sing and dance and laugh and I am thinking, How different my daughter's world is from the world I knew. There she struts, rife with the power of her femaleness, my little Eve redeemed.

Yet she inherits a world that still, by and large, belongs to men. They write the laws that she will live by. The boys she outdistances on the monkey bars now may pass her in salaries later. What will happen to her, I wonder, when she discovers that, in this world, men still hold the better cards? Unlike what I experienced, she encounters the social structures not only with a sense of female entitlement, but also cheered on by a raucous chorus of uppity women. I suspect it's going to be tricky keeping this girl down on the farm. Where men will be when she is ready to embrace them, I cannot say. All I can do is wish her the judgment to distinguish those who will meet her on fair terms from those who will not.

From "On Growing Up" by Wendy Dennis,
Toronto Life, September, 1985, pp. 37, 54-57.

□

A year ago, while I was working on a TV film in L.A., I called Tara, my wife, in Vancouver. "How did your day go?" I asked. "Well," she said, "I took the children to The Bay for a couple of hours. I got Severn a winter coat and two dresses for Sarika." "Well, that's great," I said. "But what did you *do?*"

Six months later, Tara called me from Boston, where she commutes from Toronto to teach writing at Harvard. "How did your day go?" she began. "Well, I took the kids to the Eaton Centre, and we had a great time looking at fish in the pet store. Didn't manage to buy them anything, except a stuffed bear." "Good for you," she replied wryly. "But what did you *do?*"

What a difference six months make!

Tara has been a committed feminist as long as I've known her and has taught me that it's one thing to *talk* a good line about being a liberated male, but it's a totally different thing to *live* it. Her incredible patience has helped me slowly to overcome a lifetime of conditioning as the only son with three sisters in a traditional Japanese-Canadian family.

I have tried to be as supportive of Tara as she has been of me—from her determination to keep her maiden name to her decision to go on for a Ph.D. at the University of Wisconsin to her application for a faculty job.

Tara is immensely talented and fills many roles—not only as my partner and friend. She is a wonderful daughter, daughter-in-law, stepmother and scholar. While working on her doctorate, she even managed to have two children. She earned the job at Harvard, but it has turned our lives upside down. I was coming down to the wire in a three-year television series called *A Planet for the Taking*, as well as hosting *The Nature of Things*. Severn, then age 4, was to be enrolled in a French-immersion kindergarten and Sarika, at 18 months, had become much more active. Toronto became our base of operations, instead of Vancouver.

Now, I would have to put my body where my mouth was. We had to have someone—me—to be responsible for the children, while Tara was in Cambridge, Mass., three nights a week.

Now, instead of Tara's twisting her schedule and life to fit mine, I was going to have to conform to the needs of the children and *her* career.

It hasn't been easy. For one thing, as the final shooting for *A Planet for the Taking* took place, I *had* to be at work, yet during shoots I found myself constantly worrying about Severn and Sarika instead of my lines. Life became one mad round of rushing to complete commitments, then tearing off to attend a birthday party or school skate sale. To be frank, I'm still only playing at it; we have a nanny, which lets me go to work and make short trips. And when Tara comes home, she is so delighted to be with the children that I just lie back and let her take over.

> The true liberation of women cannot take place without the liberation of men.
>
> MADAME THERESE-FORGET CASGRAIN

I loved the role of traditional father—playing with the children when I came home from work and taking the family camping. But this is different. Being a single parent is terrible! It is impossible to concentrate fully at work—there is always the dread of the emergency phone call in the middle of the day (as when Severn's school bus was hit by a car). This is familiar to every mother, but I had no idea.

But the most crushing part of the single parent role has been the dozens of little things I do every day *without acknowledgement:* dressing the children, making their beds, picking up and putting things away, doing dishes—a never-ending battle against *entropy.* No one ever says "Thanks," or "Good for you, David." That's all it would take to make me feel great.

I have two concerns about changing sex roles. First, Tara seems able to give herself to the children totally. I have to struggle to do it—I'm often juggling my schedule or a business commitment in my mind, while going through the motions of parenting.

My more serious concern is with the consequences of what Tara and I are doing as we try to define new roles. We are wracked with *guilt* about what we are or are not doing for the children and our own relationship. We love our jobs, yet feel wretched that they divert time away from the family; on the other hand, we feel we're not doing the jobs as well as we could because we try to stretch family time. Our friends tell us that our daughters are very lucky to have us as role models, that it's good for them to see their father scrubbing floors and their academic mother commuting to work. They claim that it's *quality* not *quantity* of time that matters.

But I know that we *don't* know whether our daughters are lucky. This is all very new. So we muddle along doing the best we can, hoping our life styles don't leave the children psychically scarred. But now my life is settling down, and I've already learned that a day running the house and enjoying the children is quite an achievement.

From "My Wife, My Equal" by David Suzuki,
Chatelaine, September 1985, p. 48. Reprinted with the author's permission.

1. Drawing on the Wendy Dennis selection, provide illustrations of "the distances we have travelled" in changing gender roles. To what extent and in what ways do "men still hold the better cards"? What personal and policy changes are necessary for women and men to meet "on fair terms"?

2. Describe how gender issues change over the stages of the family life cycle.

3. David Suzuki explains that he grew up as "the only son with three sisters in a traditional Japanese-Canadian family." Referring to his recollections of his early years (included in the introductory unit), comment on how his early conditioning might have contributed to Suzuki's struggles in adult life.

4. Illustrate how circumstances and personal choice may combine to produce a change in male and female roles in a family.

5. Role cycling occurs when one sex carries out a role that was thought to be a traditional role for the opposite sex. Provide illustrations of role cycling from the Suzuki selection. What factors complicate or facilitate such arrangements?

6. Summarize the costs and benefits of changing gender roles for individuals, families, and society.

7. Compare and contrast the main issues and concerns cited in these two readings. What conclusions can you draw?

THE SANDWICH GENERATION

Often characterized as "sandwiched" or "squeezed," the middle-aged generation frequently finds itself "caught" between the conflicting loyalties and demands of adolescent children and aging parents. A no-win situation, complicated by stress, guilt, resentment, desperation, love, and respect, seems inevitable. In this reading, John Fitzgerald elaborates on a problem he characterizes as "one of the most pressing social issues of the 1990s."

□

The fury of the attack was what surprised her. Helen was standing in the kitchen of her north Toronto home one morning talking on the telephone. Her children were out, her husband was at work and her 80-year-old mother—who with age had developed bouts of paranoia—suddenly became angry that not enough attention was being paid. "She grabbed a can with an open lid from the top of the bin and came at me," Helen recalls. "My own mother!"

For several long minutes, the two women were locked in a macabre slow-moving dance across the kitchen floor, the mother clinging fiercely to Helen's dress with one hand and wielding the can with the glistening serrated edge with the other. "I can't tell you what those moments were like," Helen says with sadness and disbelief. "When I finally calmed my mother down and wrestled the thing away from her, she apologized. 'I must be a sinner,' she said. She knew what she'd done. And that hurt me more than anything else. Sometimes," Helen goes on, "I could just scream. I've got the business to run. I've got a teenaged son having problems in school who needs me. And I've got my mother, whom I love a great deal, living with us. It just gets to be too much sometimes. I find myself taking a drink or two every night now just to get through it."

The woman's real name isn't Helen—"I don't want to sound like an ungrateful daughter, airing the family laundry and all," she says as she begs for the privacy of a pseudonym (given to all but the officials in this story). But her story could be told by anyone shouldering responsibility for a needy elderly relative as well as a job, a household, a young family and the everyday *Sturm und Drang* of getting by. Sociologists describe the Helens of society as "The Squeezed Generation," the mortgaged, middle-aged people sandwiched between the competing demands of their own lives, their children and their elderly parents. For now, personal accounts like theirs are footnotes in the sprawling chapters of family life. But they are also distant early-warning signals of a problem that looms ahead.

It's a problem of colliding numbers. Already the squeeze is starting to close in on baby boomers. Parents in that bulge of the population are beginning to see their own young families move inexorably into their most expensive years—the teenaged years of clothes, cars and university tuition—just as medical science is mastering the mechanics of prolonging life for the elderly. By 2001, according to the Ontario government's white paper on health and social service strategies for the province's seniors, the number of people between the ages of 65 and 74 will increase by approximately 38 per cent; in the over-85 group, those who will undoubtedly require the most extensive services, it's 110 per cent. Coincidentally, governments grappling with the upward spiral of social service costs—education and, particularly, health care—are starting to pass on an even greater share of those responsibilities to families. Sooner or later, the squeeze will be everybody's problem. And when its vise constricts the boomers, the problem of coping will become one of the most pressing social issues of the 1990s.

If the experience of today's squeezed generation is any indication, boomers are going to find it a tough challenge. "Many of the people we've seen are doing what they're doing out of a sense of love and/or duty," says Sunnybrook Medical Centre's Jassy Tracey, who is coordinating a study on the needs of those families who care for elderly parents suffering from dementia. "But many of these people are also resentful, frustrated and angry by the absence of options. They're doing their part but they know of very few adequate support systems to help them. It's already too late for some of these people. They see their lives going by. Fast." . . .

Old age doesn't have to mean a downhill slide into alienation and helplessness, of course. Many seniors not only look after themselves but provide crucial financial, logistical and emotional support for their children and grandchildren.

> Children have an irredeemable obligation toward parents. Nothing they do can ever make up for the initial parental gift of life and nurturing.
>
> HARRY J. BERMAN

Eventually, though, age, illness or a meagre income forces them to call on the younger ones for help in return. Already, families provide the bulk of care to the elderly: an estimated 75 per cent of the health care needs of Canada's 2.9 million people over 65. In part, that's because of the high cost of putting one's parents into an institution. Families of the 45,000 elderly Ontarians in nursing homes and homes for the aged pay between $700 a month for a bed in a government-subsidized home and as much as $3,000 a month for a top-of-the-line private rest home. And already such facilities are packed. According to the Metro Community Services department, in October 1986, the average length of time people waited between application and admission to a seniors' home was 104 days; by the end of 1988 it had risen to more than 250 days.

Every passing day makes the question of what to do with dependent elderly people more acute. "If we just continue on the way we've been going," says Mavis Wilson, Ontario's minister for senior citizens' affairs, "the provincial health budget in the future is going to be astronomical. The challenge for all of us is to come up with some innovative ways to deal with all the numbers." Wilson, 39, wants to deal with the impending crisis by encouraging people to stay out of institutions. "Most of the elderly want to remain as independent as they can for as long as they can," she says. "Families should be responsible for families and communities responsible for each other. The government should be there to assist the community in that job but not take it over." In many cases, that means those who do take it over will be younger members of the family with other responsibilities—the squeezed.

Of course, that's the way it's always been in other times and other cultures. But those cultures—the Chinese and Japanese, for example—exact a price of social rigidity and narrow horizons. In this society, the desire to help may be there, but the rules are muddled.

"No matter what you do, it's a lose-lose situation," sighs Mark, an electronics company executive and, at 38, himself a father with a young family. He and his wife, Kim, a junior partner with a fledgling marketing firm, bought a large house so they could take in Kim's parents. Her mother was a victim of Parkinson's disease. "Their families on both sides had been wiped out in the Holocaust," Mark recalls. "How could we not feel we had to do everything after what had happened to them? They were fine people. My father-in-law had a heart condition and we knew the burden was too much for him looking after a wife with Parkinson's. He literally had to carry her on his back from room to room."

"We felt desperate for him," he continues. "Morally, we had to take them in. But we had no freedom anymore. We had to stay with her, dress her, take her to the bathroom, do everything for her. It seems that if you don't do anything, you feel guilty, and what you do do has a price."

The young couple modified their house for the new occupants, putting in railings, an intercom, even a separate kitchen and bathroom. "It cost plenty to make the adjustments and of course we weren't reimbursed. There's no government money for this. We kept wondering what we'd do if something happened to my father-in-law. He was a great help with his wife and very self-reliant. What we'd feared happened, and he died three years ago. And for 15 months, until she was able to get

Age segregation and ageism erode family life and perpetuate ambivalence over responsibility to one's elders.
ROBERT N. BUTLER

a bed in a nursing home, my mother-in-law was here. It's hard on everyone living with a person who's sick. There was my mother-in-law's coughing fits and the accidents and the spitting up. It was like having a young child in the house again, only we were watching her deteriorate. At some point, you end up thinking this can only be happening to you."

How Mark and Kim faced their problem seems singularly heroic—and probably atypical. Boomers are the most coddled generation in history, and the one that has experimented most with family values. How many others like them would be willing to make similar sacrifices? Says University of Toronto gerontologist Blossom Wigdor, "Baby boomers are very individualistic, very competitive. They're not by nature team players. They love their parents, but they also want to get on with their own lives. They find it difficult for someone to invade their space." . . .

This generation's attitude to its obligations is different from that of its predecessors, explains Dr. Carol Cohen, a geriatric psychiatrist at Toronto's Sunnybrook Medical Centre. "In many ways, we're smarter, more fortunate. We're used to delegating, hiring services. If we're so neurotic about our kids and getting the best for their schooling . . . when it comes to our parents, we'll demand the same. . . .

For boomers with heavy mortgages and young children to raise, institutionalizing mentally or physically disabled parents may be expensive, but the alternative is even more costly. Those who turn to an agency for an attendant to provide round-the-clock care will pay as much as $10 an hour, or $240 a day. But Queen's Park says it can do little more than it is already doing to help make home-support services more affordable. Senior Citizens' Affairs Minister Wilson points out that the government is already spending $48 million on home-support programs—such as visiting homemakers and health care workers, meals on wheels, volunteer visitor programs and Alzheimer's support services. Nor can her government afford to expand its expensive pilot project, called One Stop Access, to coordinate such services. When it is formally launched early in 1989, that program will function in five Ontario regions, including East York. One phone call by a senior's family will bring a case worker to do an assessment and make appropriate arrangements. Although just about everybody, including Wilson, believes home-support programs cost the province less in the long run than institutional care, there's little chance of more public support immediately. The government knows taxpayers would object to bearing the dual burden of maintaining institutions and paying for expanded province-wide homemaker programs. Consequently, Queen's Park is also exploring other options, including encouraging home-sharing among seniors and launching small group homes. . . .

The squeezed can also find support services for themselves. Sheila Freeman conducts sessions at the Jewish Family and Child Service emphasizing communication skills to help adult children cope with their dependent elderly parents. "We have to remember that sick elderly people are not going to get young and well," says Freeman evenly. "How do we get along with that reality? Some younger people make the mistake of trying to do the whole thing by themselves." Often, we encourage our dependent parents to be passive consumers of amusements and services in the same way that we silence frolicsome children by planting them in front of the TV. Instead,

[The family] is inescapable and necessary, but not always comfortable and not always sweet, and sometimes profoundly exigent, demanding and tyrannical. But without it we cannot begin our lives, sustain our lives and we cannot grow comfortably to the end of our lives.

VIVIAN RAKOFF

says Freeman, "Caregivers should ask for help anywhere they can get it, especially from the rest of the family."

On a day-to-day level, she adds, that may mean negotiating, broadening responsibilities, enlisting children to help visit, telephone, do the shopping or run other errands for their grandparents. Equally important—and perhaps tougher—is learning to talk things out, to level with children about how much they can demand of parents who are also caring for an older generation. Freeman also urges her clients to learn to set responsible limits on their time, to read current literature about the physical and psychological effects of aging and to make themselves aware of what resources are out there to help.

For some, however, the value of such advice is diffused by cold realities. Carol is a 48-year-old divorced real estate agent with a teenaged son. Her parents, both in their 70s, live in their own apartment in Etobicoke. Her father has a history of heart trouble. "I don't know how many times my mother has called me in the middle of the night to tell me my father seems to be having shortness of breath. I'm never sure what's real and what isn't. So I race over there and try to calm them down. If the shortness of breath doesn't go away, we're off to the emergency ward. I could write a book on what it's like sitting in some emergency ward at 3 a.m. watching the clock with this sick feeling in my stomach—thinking, Is this it?—knowing I'll be a wreck at work when I meet six clients the next day.

"My ex-husband lives across the country and I find myself trying to be mother, father and friend to my son," she continues. "These are hard, questioning years for him and it's important I be around, to talk, to cheer him at a baseball game. But my mind always seems so preoccupied with my parents. I've tried to make my parents more reliant on themselves by not going every time they call. But I always end up giving in. Over time, you lose something. Maybe you care a little less. And you feel guilty about that and so you keep at it, going through the motions. There's no easy way out."

There isn't. But there is the sense that, ultimately, looking the other way is impossible, no matter how hard the slogging gets—and that what matters are still those themes parents impress upon their children: filial duty, loyalty, respect, the enduring tie of blood. "I wish I didn't have to go to the nursing home to visit," says Doris. "It's hard to see the lives of people you love turned around, to see how needy they've become. It's threatening as hell. I think, Maybe I'll become like this, dependent, cranky, unhappy with my life. And then I think, Who'll look after me? I try and realize how my parents must feel. I mean, my father gets pushed around in a wheelchair like he was a baby in a carriage. I guess the bottom line is: As tough as it gets, I'm not prepared to write them off because they're old."

When it comes to the family—to child-rearing and care of the elderly—this society is in an unprecedented flux. Until we develop new rules for our most important and demanding relationships, and more creative social-support policies, the squeezed will continue to pick a precarious way along the emotional road between clamoring, needy generations.

Sometimes very young children can look at the old, and a look passes between them, conspiratorial, sly and knowing. It's because neither are human to the middling ones.

MARGARET LAURENCE, from THE STONE ANGEL

From "The Squeezed Generation" by John Fitzgerald,
The Globe and Mail, Toronto Magazine, January 1989, pp. 36-41.

1. Illustrate how the nature and quality of family functioning for the sandwich generation, their children, and elderly parents in these case studies is affected by the "competing demands" of intergenerational households or other care-taking arrangements. Outline the "price" that each family member pays. Explore the complex range of emotions involved.

2. Drawing on this selection and other background sources, investigate the extent to which the sandwich generation currently provides instrumental (day-to-day functions), financial, and expressive (emotional) support for its elderly parents. Analyze how the provision of support could be spread across family members, acquaintances, community services, and government assistance.

3. Describe how any one of the family situations in the article illustrates either the family systems or social-exchange theory.

4. "Families should be expected to assume even more responsibility for their aging parents." Debate this proposal.

5. Edward DeBono, an internationally recognized authority on thought processes, outlines a framework for analyzing information and ideas. Comprising the framework are six different foci for thinking: facts and figures; emotions or feelings; positive aspects; negative aspects; creative ideas; and control or "orchestration" of all ideas. Analyze "The Squeezed Generation" using DeBono's framework. How does considering each of the components separately give you a more complete picture?

6. Fitzgerald writes that other cultures, "the Chinese and Japanese, for example—exact a price of social rigidity and narrow horizons" for the familial responsibility taken on by younger people. Do you think this is a fair assessment? Research these cultures and discuss your findings with the class.

7. Describe the relationship between the phenomenon of the sandwich generation and the family life spiral diagram found earlier in this book. Account for any discrepancies.

POVERTY AND FAMILIES

A 1984 national task force on poverty arrived at the unsurprising, yet still unsettling conclusion that "serious deprivation *does* exist in Canada." More significantly, the report entitled *Not Enough: The Meaning and Measurement of Poverty in Canada* documented the statistics, feelings, and multi-faceted dimensions of poverty. Material was gleaned from public meetings held across Canada and from existing documents, statistics, and written briefs. Of special interest are first-hand experiences such as those recounted below. Following these vignettes, Statistics Canada provides a capsule view of poverty as it affects children, a most vulnerable group.

From Vancouver, a woman wrote down her feelings for the task force: "You asked: What does poverty mean to me?

Well, to me poverty means not being able to buy food that is nutritional, instead of spaghetti and potatoes with the occasional two pounds of hamburg. I don't go to the food bank because I don't want to take food from someone who may need it more than me.

Not having that all-important job to go to.

Not being able to buy even the cheapest clothes to put on my back.

Doing the laundry in the bath tub because I can't afford to go to the laundromat.

Making sure that I make my phone calls before I leave home. I can't afford to give B.C. Tel. any of my precious quarters.

Not being able to buy someone you know the odd cup of coffee.

Losing people you called friends because you're now a bum and not the fit and proper working class.

Having absolutely no sense of security and worrying about what will happen if you get sick or die at home. In my case, no one would know for a week or more.

Wanting to sell some of your personal effects and knowing that if you do, they will simply deduct it off your next cheque.

Feeling like dirt, now that I'm broke.

Having the government always cut back on the poor and not on themselves. The rent, phone, hydro, food, etc., goes up continually, but my spending capital in fact goes down with each raise in expense.

Dreading every time you have to go to the welfare office, walking slow before you get there, then making a dash for the door, hoping no one sees your face as you go in to beg again. . . ."

> Poverty demoralizes.
> RALPH WALDO EMERSON

And from Alberta:

Ms. B. is a single-parent woman, 34 years of age, with two school-age children (8 and 10). Ms. B. is physically handicapped and requires prescription drugs. As of July 1, 1983, this family's shelter allowance was $505 per month. Their three-bedroom apartment in the inner city, including utilities and one parking spot, is $700 a month. The casework supervisor has authorized an additional $150 a month in excess of the shelter allowance since the oldest child is doing well in the neighbourhood elementary school and the apartment owners allow children. Their food and tobacco allowance as of July 1, 1983, is $361 a month. A single-parent family in Calgary with two school-aged children would spend approximately $350 per month in order to eat nutritiously but simply, that is, no baked goods or frozen pre-cooked foods. The family's clothing and household allowance is $129 a month. Since a "no-frills" pair of denim slacks for boys is approximately $15, the two boys wear hand-me-downs. Ms. B. does some sewing, but the machine is worn and there is no money left at the end of the month for incidentals, such as having the sewing machine fixed. An application to the Burns Memorial Fund for Children has been submitted in order to send the boys to summer camp. In summary, after necessities, that is, food, clothing and shelter, there is no discretionary income. . . .

And from Newfoundland:

An elderly couple in their 70s were living in a shed with no running water. It was heated by a wood stove for which wood had to be hauled. The gentleman was blind. Both of them were receiving old age pensions and had enough money to live on, but they were not physically or mentally capable of looking after themselves.

FIGURES TELL A STORY
Percentage distribution of families by income groups, 1981-1986

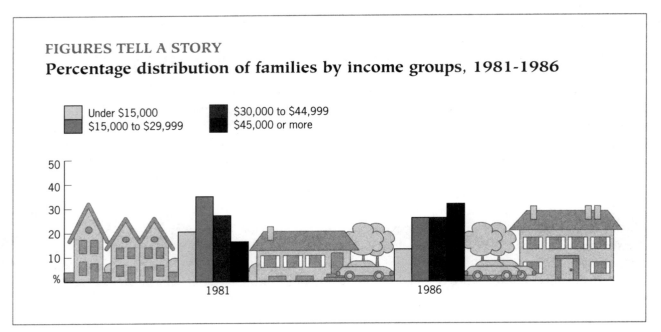

From Statistics Canada, Catalogue 13-208, Family Incomes: Census Families.

They had no bedclothes and no dishes, and they were being exploited by some of their neighbours. It took over a year of advocacy on the part of our association [Provincial Human Rights] to convince the social services people that this couple should be put in a situation where they could receive proper homemaker services and be allowed to live at a level of dignity. . . .

From *Not Enough: The Meaning and Measurement of Poverty in Canada*,
published by the Canadian Council on Social Development,
Ottawa, 1984, pp. 13-20. Reprinted with permission.

☐

One indication of whether a nation is investing enough in families with children is the poverty rate among children. In Canada, children now make up the single largest group of poor people in the country. In 1986, more than a million children were growing up in poverty—that is, about one child in six.

In 1986, despite a modest decline in the rate of poverty, there were still 120,000 more poor children in Canada than in 1980. During the same time period, the overall number of children fell by 3.7 per cent. The following table shows trends in child poverty from 1980 to 1986.

Poverty Trends for Children Under 16, 1980-1986

	Number of Poor Children	Total Number of Children	Poverty Rate (per cent)
1980	896,000	5,983,200	15
1982	1,113,000	5,865,900	19
1984	1,209,000	5,816,200	20.6
1986	1,016,000	5,759,100	17.6
Percentage Change, 1980-1986	+13.4%	-3.7%	+17.3%

From Statistics Canada, *Income Distributions by Size, 1986*,
as presented in *Poverty Profile 1988*,
National Council on Welfare.

The increase in child poverty since 1980 cannot be explained away by the recession. Childless couples had a lower poverty rate in 1986 than in 1980, while families with children ran a greater risk of being poor during the same period. A family with one or two children was twice as likely to be poor as a childless couple, while a family with three or more children was almost three times as likely to be poor.

The risk of poverty is not the same for all children living in Canada. Some children are at greater risk:

☐ Not surprisingly, most poor children live in two-parent families. However, the risk of poverty for a child in a single-parent family headed by a woman is five times greater than for a child in a two-parent family. Looked at another way, 61.8 per cent of the children of female single parents are growing up in poverty, compared with 12.2 per cent of the children of two-parent families.

☐ Most poor families are supported by a family head who is working either full- or part-time. However, the risk of poverty is much greater for families where the head of the family is unemployed. The poverty rate for families headed by persons not in the labour force is 23 per cent, compared to 9 per cent for families where the head of the family is doing paid work.

☐ The risk of poverty is greater for younger children. Twenty-one per cent of children below the age of six, and 19 per cent of those between the ages of 6 and 14 are growing up in poverty.

Finally, as the accompanying table shows, there are tremendous variations in the rates of child poverty across the country.

Child Poverty by Province, 1986

	Number of Poor Children	Percentage of Child Population
Newfoundland	44,600	26.8
Prince Edward Island	5,100	15.5
Nova Scotia	39,000	19.8
New Brunswick	33,600	20.2
Quebec	282,100	19.2
Ontario	268,700	13.4
Manitoba	58,600	24.3
Saskatchewan	64,600	25.7
Alberta	93,600	15.6
British Columbia	126,300	20.2
CANADA	1,016,000	17.6

From Statistics Canada, *Income Distributions by Size, 1986,* as presented in *Poverty Profile, 1988,* National Council on Welfare.

From *A Choice of Futures: Canada's Commitment to Its Children,* published by the Canadian Council on Social Development, 1988. Reprinted with permission.

1. Compare the various ways in which poverty is defined and measured. Explain the shortcomings and strengths of each approach. What do "definitions" and "measures" not convey about poverty? Why are these omissions highly significant for the individuals and families in these case studies?

2. The *Not Enough* report makes the following point: "Below a certain level of well-being, one can talk about the poverty of income, the poverty of spirit, and the poverty of power." Theorize about the interrelationships among these three kinds of poverty. Test your theory using evidence from the case studies in this selection and from other background sources. Explain why one must be prudent in generalizing about poverty in families.

3. A significant finding of the 1984 task force report is that poverty has become "feminized." Referring to statistics and other background sources, provide an explanation of this finding. Explore the issues and implications for women, families, and society.

4. Many working people live at or near the poverty line. Following the pattern of the preceding case studies, write your own case study of one or more of these "working poor" families. What frustrations and dilemmas do these families experience?

5. Analyze the statistics in the fact sheet on children and poverty. Identify the various societal issues that are associated with these figures. Choosing one of these issues, research current periodicals, journals, magazines, and newspapers for background information and contemporary developments. Write an essay analyzing the causes and possible remedies for this particular societal problem.

THE ENDURING FAMILY

It will not be uncommon . . . for children born in the 1980s to follow this sequence of living arrangements: *live with both parents for several years, live with their mothers after their parents divorce, then live with their mothers and stepfathers, live alone for a time when in their early twenties, live with someone of the opposite sex without marriage, get married, get divorced, live alone again, get remarried, and end up living alone once more following the death of their spouses.*

G. WILLIAM SHEEK, *A NATION FOR FAMILIES*

☐

"God placed the solitary in families," comforting words from the Bible . . . families, by blood, by obligation, by necessity, by desire . . . and sometimes, if one is very lucky, by love. It is a word that implies solidity, a rock-solid foundation, a place to go home to . . . to grow out of . . . to grow away from, and yet to remember and hang onto . . . never to be totally forgotten or left behind. The place where one begins, and hopes to end . . . the thing one works hard to build on one's own . . . the pieces like building blocks reaching high into the sky. . . . Family . . . what images that conjures . . . what memories . . . what dreams.

DANIELLE STEEL, *FAMILY ALBUM*

■
OVERVIEW ESSAY
by Emily Nett, Ph.D.
Professor, Department of Sociology
University of Manitoba

■
READINGS

THE ENDURING FAMILY

by Emily Nett

The family is a distinctly human invention. In many other species, relatively permanent mating groups are to be found, in which the adults care for the offspring until they are able to feed themselves and escape the dangers in their environments. Only humans, however, establish and perpetuate stable groups based on sets of norms, values, and beliefs that are organized around sex, reproduction, child-rearing, and other related activities. The resulting cultural elaborations on rather minimal biological functions are shared ideas about what families *ought* to be and how family members *should* behave toward each other. They constitute the family institutions which throughout millions of years of human history have comprised a central part of every society and have guided the behaviour of family members within them.

The family is believed to be one of humankind's oldest institutions. Indeed, it may have been the first that early hominids invented as they were evolving from other primate forms. Will the 21st century be the point at which this human heritage will end? Are we witnessing the death throes of the family, as critics have said, or is the report of its demise vastly premature, to paraphrase Mark Twain?

In the minds of some people there may be no question about the survival of the family institution. After all, our ancestors have come through natural disasters, wars and conquests, and revolutionary technologies and ideas—all of which have altered life drastically throughout prehistory and history. Yet human beings continue to form families, and even to draw emotional and physical sustenance from them in troubled times. The kind of caring relationships learned in families and nurtured by them is the essence of families today. It is the basis for cooperation and altruism in other important areas of social life. It makes us truly human.

But what about the recent scientific discoveries and technologies? What effects will in vitro fertilization and genetic engineering, for example, have on the family institutions of the future? And what about pollution, radiation, starvation, AIDS, political violence, and other life threats occurring on a scale not yet known on this planet? What would families look like in a world radically transformed by environmental or political disaster?

Social scientists are far from being able to answer such questions. Just posing them, however, has merit. They point to the knowledge that a given kind of family institution always functions in a particular social and physical environment. This is true whether we are discussing families of the past, present, or future. Even those entirely in the imagination take on forms that permit them to adapt to their surroundings. Science fiction and fantasy literature, like Sterling Alam's fictional "report" of family life in 2020 in this section, illustrate the point well. In their futuristic visions of unknown worlds can be found unique family arrangements, often with gender relations that are quite different from ours.

One example is Ursula Le Guin's novel *The Possessed*. This is a story about two contrasting worlds. Urras is a planet much like Earth, with its gender-differentiated families, its rich and poor, and its wars between nations. Centuries before the time in which the novel is set, a group of idealists from Urras travel to the bleak moon Annares. Here they establish a utopian civilization, characterized by genuinely equal conditions for everyone regardless of sex, age, or family origins. This is a classless and genderless society in which the character traits of egotism and competitiveness, the greatest threats to their survival, have been effectively extinguished. The story opens with Shevek, a physicist from Annares, travelling to Urras. He hopes to re-unite the two worlds that have been cut off from each other for centuries.

On Annares children are cared for by either or both parents, not just the mother, and no sex distinctions are made in their treatment, task assignment, or learning. After reaching maturity they are not required to have contact with, or feel any obligation toward, their parents or other relatives. They marry and have children, or not; they may have heterosexual or homosexual relationships, or both, as they wish. In this fictional world, friends and the various communities in which both sexes work hard to assure everyone's welfare constitute the major emotional supports, not families. This is possible because the society has dispensed with economic dependencies and property as features of family bonding. Shevek willingly returns to bleak Annares after his visit to the world of his emigrating forebears. To him Urras, despite an abundance of material comforts and lush vegetation, is socially alienating. The power ploys and gamesmanship which infiltrate all the relations of the denizens of Urras, even their marriages, confuse and repel Shevek, whose own marriage on Annares is based on mutual commitment, concern, and trust, as are his work and community ties.

In contrast to Annares, most North Americans are tied emotionally and economically to one or more families for the greater part of their lives. This is as true for the Baby Boomers (born between 1946 and 1964) as it was for their parents. Children grow up in family households where they are almost totally dependent on the emotional and financial resources of two parents, a parent and step-parent, or one parent. At the present time, three out of four households in Canada are family households. The Canadian census definition of a family is a husband and wife, with or without never-married children, or a parent with one or more children who have never married, living together in the same dwelling. Adopted children and step-children are counted as children, as are guardianship children under 21 years of age. The three forms of domestic family are all variants of a nuclear family.

It is an interesting but little known fact that over the last 60 years there have been only minor fluctuations in the proportions of families found in each of the three categories of nuclear family. At any given census-taking period approximately a third of all domestic families have consisted of only a couple; around a tenth had one parent with children; and well over half included a couple with unmarried children. The most striking change in family over the decades has been in size, which continues to decline as the result of falling birth rates. Family households have also dropped in proportion to all households. The decline is due almost entirely to more persons living alone. Very few households today contain unrelated persons.

Despite the marriage law reforms of the 1970s and 1980s, which specify similar rights and duties for both spouses, marriage in Canada entails asymmetrical dependencies for women and men. Wives are still dependent upon husbands for financial support and husbands continue to be dependent on wives for emotional well-being and household maintenance. About half of all Canadian wives work solely in the home and are totally dependent on their husband's paycheck. Even the half who also work for pay outside the home earn only one-third as much as the average husband does. As the main breadwinners, husbands rely for their gender identity and their sense of worth on being able to play the provider role successfully. Even when a marriage ends in divorce, as approximately 10 out of 1,000 in existence do now, the impetus to remarry is not the same for the sexes. Divorced women are impelled to re-marry because of their greater financial need; divorced men are more likely to remarry for social and psychological reasons. Most divorced persons do re-marry.

A recent trend in families is the increased numbers of 18-24 year olds choosing to remain living with their parents. It is a lot cheaper for them than setting up in their own place, as an earlier generation did. There is little doubt that economic conditions can alter family composition. Indeed, throughout the centuries family households in North America have been adaptable, or malleable (*malleable* refers to their ability to change size and shape under various economic and social conditions). The age distribution of the Canadian population also affects households. The current increase in persons living alone resulted mostly from larger numbers of widowed seniors. Increasingly, middle-age people are caring for an elderly relative, either in or near their homes. With the elderly population predicted to increase as the Baby Boom generation attains old age in the first quarter of the next century, there may be a doubling up in living arrangements.

The scenario of life-long involvement with family seems especially probable if resources (jobs and money) become scarcer as the result of world tensions and economic crises. In the past families have opened their hearts and doors to relatives in financial and emotional need, and the facts about the youth and the elderly today indicate they still do (Nett, 1990). The best available data make it clear that great numbers of North Americans will experience diminished economic circumstances. Already Baby Boom couples with children have felt some stress in this regard. The real income of dual wage-earner couples, compared with that of single wage-earner couples fifteen years ago, has fallen nearly ten percent (Edwards and Snyder, 1988). Furthermore, speculation has it that Canada/Quebec Pension Plan payments to future retirees may be reduced if not entirely eliminated. In an excerpt from *The Big Generation* included in this section John Kettle anticipates this probability, and describes alternate solutions to the sharing by kin that has occurred in the past.

Although futuristic fiction of movies, TV, and novels places great emphasis on new technologies, the most revolutionary changes of our times probably have been moral and ideological. *Morality* refers to notions about what is right and wrong. It consists of ideas that are shared by most members of a group or society, or those that are imposed on them by the few in power. The most powerful institutions are generally the religious and political ones. They establish and perpetuate the norms and justify them with a set of beliefs about the nature of the social world and how it should function (an *ideology*). Joy Parr points out in her article in this section that most human experiences are not "natural" and "universal," but are in fact social constructs. As such they are liable to vary with times and places. The main ideas prevalent at any given time (in her example, about "childhood") are especially amenable to change when certain groups who do not benefit from those ideas question them and try to establish their own (a *counter ideology*).

Since the "sexual revolution" of the 1960s an ideology counter to the family ideology that was strong in the preceding period has developed. This counter ideology includes the notion that *alternative lifestyles* are as valid as the conventional types of domestic family, and therefore should be treated as family. Alternative lifestyles refers to more or less permanent relationships that involve practices stigmatized under the former family ideology, such as pre-marital sex, extra-marital sex, homosexuality, singlehood for life, and out of wedlock childbearing and parenthood. With greater public tolerance these relationships have come to be spoken of as "options." Curiously, as can be noted from the statistics already cited, despite the availability of many more socially acceptable domestic arrangements, the great majority of Canadians continue to choose essentially the same kind of intimate bonds as their parents did, including marriage and children. Robert Whitehurst (1989) proposed a "mainstream hypothesis" to explain the persistence of conventional families. It assumes that when people make choices they tend not to take the risks involved in deviating too far from the mainstream norms. The cost of social disapproval is simply too great. I also suspect that there may be a strong element of social wisdom built into certain practices that endure.

As Lois Sweet's article indicates, there is a war being fought today over who has the right to define family. On one side are those who want the term to cover other groups than those comprised of persons considered to be related by blood and marriage (Nett, 1988, p. 20). They note that the idealized qualities of the modern family, such as intimacy, commitment, love, and concern, are its distinguishing features. By extension they would designate all groups that share those ideals "families." People involved in such relationships, the special interest organizations that represent them, and the helping professions that provide services to meet their particular needs are understandably concerned that the human rights of such minorities should not be violated. These rights include, for example, the right to be covered by insurance policies, to inherit property, and to be treated with dignity and respect as the partner or child of a homosexual, etc. On the other side are those who resist sweeping away the more conventional meanings of family embodied in legal, religious, and sociological constructions. For them the essence of family is in the functions it performs for societies everywhere, namely controlling and regulating sex and reproduction and socializing the offspring of any sexual unions. For a variety of reasons they see no point in legitimating different kinds of relationships, regardless of their personal merit, by redefining them as "families." The debate has entered the political arena, as Sweet says. It is safe to assume that the disagreement will continue into the future. How the struggle will be resolved is impossible to say at this point.

Meanwhile, certain family sociologists are predicting fewer changes in the next two decades than were experienced in the past. Settles (1987), for one, expects a "dampening effect" on the rate of change affecting morality. However, paradoxically, while the overall pattern of conventional domestic family life endures as the most common experience of Canadians, the average person now has a greater likelihood of being involved for at least a part of her or his life in one or more alternative lifestyles.

If the anticipated lull in the pace of change in social values materializes, will it provide a better chance for individual North Americans to create more enduring relationships? For some time now a strong interest in family well-being has been evident among family therapists, counsellors, and educators. The quest for the characteristics, dimensions, and properties of families that last, even in the face of adversity, is not surprising in view of the forecast of difficult economic and political times ahead.

Perhaps the most important factor behind this search for family strengths is that, while a majority of women and men expect to receive the greatest amount of satisfaction from their marriage and family relationships, a significant number are in fact doomed to disappointment and frustration. Many couples are faced with major problems in their marriages, which in turn have implications for their children's development. By focusing their attention on the successes, researchers and practitioners have shed much light on how all families might foster their own wellness and stability. Many family professionals today believe that it is indeed possible for people to build strengths into their individual families. They also think that society must provide the support necessary for them to be able to do so.

Early in the last decade, Curran (1983) compiled a list of fifteen family strengths. Her book, *Traits of a Healthy Family,* was based on therapists' testimonies and their responses to questionnaires. Further research on actual families by other investigators (McCubbin and McCubbin, 1988) reduced the list to ten strengths that have been linked with the ability of families to cope and endure. Good physical and emotional health habits, sound financial management, and respect for and acceptance of personality differences in family members are all traits that contribute to a family's ability to cope. Family routines, celebrations, and traditions create a quality called *family coherence.* This fosters loyalty, pride, faith, trust, respect, caring and shared values. (Rona Maynard's "Rituals" article emphasizes their role.) These qualities are important to all stages in the family life cycle. Although it seems to be just common sense, there is little doubt that many families neglect or minimize these aspects of good family life. For example, the habit of the entire family sharing meals daily has been eroded by the varied schedules of members and a greater distance between work place, school, and home. Not all families have found a good substitute for the loss of so important a routine.

Another important quality in strong families is *family hardiness*, or the confidence members have in their family's ability to meet the challenges of life. This involves the sense of being in control of events, a belief in life's meaningfulness, involvement in community activities, service to others, and a commitment to learn and to explore new and challenging experiences.

Families that have both *coherence* and *hardiness* form what McCubbin has called the "regenerative" family type. This is the strongest of the four enduring types McCubbin describes. According to him, regenerative families do more than merely survive. They are high in marital satisfaction, child development satisfaction, family physical and emotional satisfaction, and overall family well-being. Regenerative families cope well throughout the family life cycle.

Two traits involved in family strength deserve special attention: communication and support network. Both have special significance for today's family life. For modern couples expect much more out of marriage than to play the conventional roles of wife and husband. They seek love, understanding, respect, and emotional closeness in a relationship. To maintain a satisfying marriage two people must be able to listen carefully, talk openly and honestly, and signal their love, appreciation, and concern for each other. Only in this way can agreement be reached on goals and the means to achieve them.

'Til Death Do Us Part, a book by Jeannette and Robert Lauer (1986), reports on a study of people whose perseverance and work on their marriages paid off in lasting relationships. The Lauers say, "People explain their long-term, satisfying marriages mainly in terms of four keys: having a spouse who is one's best friend and whom one likes as a person; commitment to marriage and to the spouse; consensus on fundamentals; and shared humour." Each of these "keys" is tied into the use of appropriate verbal and non-verbal communication. The research of Benjamin Schlesinger and Shirley Tenhouse Gibbon, taken from their book *Lasting Marriages,* corroborates these findings for a Canadian sample.

The well-being of today's smaller-sized family is particularly dependent upon outside resources. The family therapists who answered Curran's survey commented that admitting to and seeking help with problems is an important trait of healthy families. Calling upon in-laws, relatives, and friends during crises is often critical for the safety and stability of children's lives. Neighbours and mutual self-help groups (such as single or divorced parents, families of convicts, alcoholics, etc.) can also be sources of help for families. A good support network is known to be invaluable in the prevention of child abuse, in both two-parent and solo-parent domestic groups. On a more positive note, informal support networks provide children with a wider circle of loving and accepting adults. Children develop trust and a sense of their own worth and competence in these groups. These are traits that will in turn help them to be effective parents.

The concept of family health includes not only how the family functions internally, but also its transactions with the community and the resources provided to it by the wider political and economic structures (Nelson and Banonis, 1981). The laws, the tax system, day care and welfare provisions, and services offered by social agencies and family educators are all ultimately important for the well-being of families. Careful attention must be paid to the kinds of social policies that affect our families. We must assure they are in the best interest of as many different types of families as possible. Shaping the future of families so that they will be better able to adapt and adjust to the new world ahead is a task for everyone—for society as well as for individual family members.

BIBLIOGRAPHY

Curran, Delores, *Traits of a Healthy Family.* Minneapolis, MN: Winston Press, 1983.

Edwards, Gregg, and David Pearce Snyder, *Families and the Future: Sustaining the Social Base of Our Economic Enterprise.* NCFR Report. Minneapolis, MN: National Council on Family Relations, 1988.

Lauer, Jeannette C. and Robert H. Lauer, *'Til Death Do Us Part: How Couples Stay Together.* New York: The Haworth Press, 1986.

McCubbin, Hamilton I., and Marilyn A. McCubbin, "Typologies of Resilient Families: Emerging Roles of Social Class and Ethnicity," *Family Relations* 37 (July 1988): 247-254.

Nelson, Patricia Tanner, and Barbara Banonis, "Family Concerns and Strengths Identified in Delaware's White House Conference on Families," pp. 43-59 in Nick Stinnet et al. (eds.), *Family Strengths #3: Roots of Well-Being.* Lincoln, NB: University of Nebraska Press, 1981.

Nett, Emily M., *Canadian Families Past and Present.* Toronto: Butterworths, 1988.

Nett, Emily M, "The Family and Aging," Chapter 10 in Maureen Baker (ed.), *Families: Changing Trends in Canada,* Second Edition. Toronto: McGraw-Hill Ryerson Limited, 1990.

Settles, Barbara H. "A Perspective on Tomorrow's Families," Chapter 7 in M. B. Sussman and Suzanne K. Steinmetz (eds.), *Handbook of Marriage and the Family.* New York: Plenum Press, 1987.

Whitehurst, Robert N., "Alternative Life Styles: Two Decades of Change," Chapter 13 in G. N. Ramu (ed.), *Marriage and the Family in Canada Today.* Scarborough, ON: Prentice-Hall Canada Inc, 1989.

FAMILIES OF THE PAST

What's past is prologue! Or so they say. Certainly one can hear the echoes of bygone families in present-day family life. Joy Parr, editor of the book *Childhood and Family in Canadian History,* describes the malleability of families down through the ages. What else can you learn from past echoes?

Heidi, Horatio Alger, Anne of Green Gables, Oliver Twist—a milk maid, a street vendor, a farm girl, a parish apprentice—four working children, three of them orphans, each raised in a different kind of household, expecting a different kind of adulthood, all well-known through fiction though their lives are not too fabulous to have been fact, these young people are convenient reminders that childhood and family have histories. We remember them, enjoy them, believe in them because in many senses their tales are true, even though they describe early years very different from the childhoods we ourselves experienced. Comparing our own families with our parents' and grandparents', our own childhoods with our children's and grandchildren's, makes the same point. Childhood and family change through time, not just a little but a lot. . . .

In writing the history of life in the private sphere, three especially helpful rules of thumb seem to have emerged. The first is that childhood and family are only minimally biologically determined. Even though children are physically different from adults . . . ; even though kin are biologically more similar to their families than to persons with whom they share no blood ties, and these similarities endure through generations; still it is misleading to think of childhood and family as founded in nature. Childhood and family are shaped by historical rather than biological processes; they are social rather than natural relationships; they form and are transformed by their economic and cultural context. Blood ties are almost always a bad place to begin to understand the boundaries between private and public life, the nature of the marriage bond, or tensions and sentiments between parents and children. Although these ties may turn out to be important it is best to start with the particulars of time and place, with economic needs, social priorities, and the exercise of power, because these are the environments in which childhood and family are embedded and within which they change.

The second rule of thumb is that inferences drawn from the present about family life in the past are dangerous. This is part of a venerable general rule of the historian's craft, but one especially hard to keep sight of in discussions of the private sphere. Confusions of past and present arise partly from the problems we have convincing ourselves that the experience of childhood and family has not always been the same and partly from the fact that in the past the most vigorous investigators into childhood and family have been present-oriented social scientists. The conclusions reached in the influential *Centuries of Childhood* are a case in point. Its author, Philippe Ariès, described himself as "struck by the original characteristics of the modern family" and therefore eager "to go back into a more distant past to discover the roots of modern childhood." He located those beginnings in the sixteenth century, when children possessing recognizably modern characteristics appeared to fade from the records, and concluded that before that time childhood did not exist. Distracted by his search for the familiarly modern he overlooked the youth cultures, apprenticeship bonds, childhood devotions, and law, all of which firmly divided the early years from adulthood long before the trappings of purity and innocence were required of young people. To the frustration of historians, he thus declared missing a part of the past which was plainly present, and provocative in its distinctiveness from later forms.

For a time, the emphasis scholars placed on the present lent curious qualities to historical descriptions of childhood and family. It appeared as though the past were implacably and inevitably driven to become modern, the old patriarchal order to decay, large extended families to contract, affection to replace calculation in dealings with kin. The search for modern roots edited out features of the past unlike the present, selected a straight line to right now from the wide oscillations between tradition and change in the past. For historians whose stock in trade is an untidy world of paths barred, not taken, and retraced, such linear accounts of transformations in family seemed suspiciously simple. Indeed, upon closer examination, families have not become relentlessly more nuclear. Most households in western Europe enclosed only a nuclear family, a single couple and their children, and this was the pattern long before industrialization, right back into the medieval period. The locus of authority has shifted in and out of the private sphere. Sentiment has changed through infinite convolutions and no grand design. The master plans questioned, we have returned to the particulars of time and place.

And there in the mass of detail on individual children and families emerges the third rule of thumb: what is easy to find out is not always important to know. In general, it is not easy to find out about childhood and family life. We are dealing largely with activities in the private rather than the public realm, with people who saw each other so often that they had little need to compose letters to one another, with youngsters not yet old enough to write even if they were of a class from which literacy was expected in adulthood. Some questions interested churchmen, census takers, and tax collectors before they interested historians of the family and for these relatively reliable records exist. With computer assistance we can determine who lived together, whether or not they were kin, how many were children, how many adults. Thus a large number of studies have been written which deal with childhood and family through the window of co-residence. But in many ways they leave begging the most important questions about family behaviour. "Kinship does not stop at the front door." Family members, particularly in early industrial cities, seem to have been highly dependent upon one another for material and moral support even when they did not share the same roof. Knowing who lived together does not tell us much about "the content of social relations, both within households and between them." It has become clear that families have shared characteristics in size, membership, and age distribution yet have had very different environments in which to grow. Thus to infer much that is meaningful about behaviour and attitudes among kin from the fact that they lived in structurally similar families is unwise.

We (must) treat family as a highly malleable social relation. For individual children the experience of beginning school, of entering the labour force, of marriage and death clearly varied immensely depending upon their family's class position, their own position in that family and the historical circumstances under which they made that and previous transitions. Family experience, and the experience of individual family members, clearly changes over the life cycle. Migration transforms aspects of the family and childhood, often reshaping but seldom destroying kinship networks and traditions. Family strategies and fertility respond rapidly to short-term demographic and economic crises. Shifting labour market opportunities and changes in the organization and structure of the economy redefine the age and sex of family members working outside the home. "Family size and solidarity" have gone through a "series of contractions and expansions" as "the security offered by the state waxed and waned." Thus children's lives and their experience in families are entwined in the political, social, and economic relations of which family relations are a part. The private sphere is not separate from or determined by the public sphere. The two are embedded in the same set of historical processes. In Canada the changing role of the state, the rhythms of migration, and reappraisals of the economic usefulness of children consistently have been part of the remaking of family and life cycle.

> We are tomorrow's past.
>
> MARY WEBB

New France was populated by the "poor and the dispossessed," by "soldiers, smugglers, girls from orphanages who came as individuals" bound by temporary pre-migration obligations to philanthropists, masters, or military commanders. Their geographical origins were diverse so that the settlers of the St. Lawrence were without shared experience in any one French regional culture. Because they did not bring common traditions to the new land, and the geography and political economy of the colony mitigated against the formation of villages, community life did not develop strongly along the valley, and the festivals and communal work patterns of Old France did not become entrenched. Despite the best laid plans of metropolitan officials, the priorities of state intruded little into the lives of individual colonists. Religious orders were scantily staffed and their influence small. In the countryside, family ordered community and, by the partible inheritance of the Custom of Paris, neighbours increasingly became kin. Social contacts included few who were not in some sense family. Through the troubled life of the colony, this network of kinship was a bulwark against chaos, the sole continuing institution of support in the lives of the common people.

In Old France, children often lived outside their own families as apprentices. The colonial economy did not create as many favourable positions for artisans. Hired labour was not plentiful or cheap. Thus apprenticeship was not so common a childhood experience. Rather, young people stayed and worked in their own families, their contributions and the ideal of family self-sufficiency highly valued, and good reason for parents to moderate the paternal authority established in law and to be tolerant of behaviour unacceptable among the children of France. In New France, most authority was familial, most dependence upon family; neighbourhood and community were scarcely distinguishable from family, and children in the country-side traded early work in the family interest for an ample portion of indulgence among kin.

In fur trade society, conditions were different and the strength of networks, particularly male networks, of support and responsibility outside the family were crucially important in determining behaviour among kin. Among the officers of the Hudson's Bay trade were many men from fragmented London families who were recruited through the Grey Coat charity schools. Their long uninterrupted terms of service in the fur trade country further attenuated the British ties of company clerks and labourers because few managed much contact with the outside world during their years of work in Rupert's Land. For these men, family life was extremely important. The kin groups they headed were closely knit. They pressed the company to provide schooling and work for their children and arranged for their baptisms. And by the early nineteenth century, many Hudson's Bay men leaving service in the trade took their families to settle in Red River or in the Canadas and there maintained households marked by firm solidarity and strong identification with their mixed blood kin.

By contrast, the late-eighteenth-century rivals of the Bay men, the Norwesters, left behind strong ties with Scots kin, valued friendships on both sides of the Atlantic, and broad institutional links in Montreal when annually they went up past the lakehead into the fur trade country. These competing obligations often drew them great distances away from families formed in the Northwest, made their attachments to their country wives impermanent and their sense of obligation to their native offspring slight. Thus two quite different kinds of families and experiences of parenthood emerged in the same territory at the same time and among men engaged in the same economic activity.

In nineteenth-century agricultural settlements life cycles and cycles of migration formed one another. Migrants typically moved as families and considered mobility as an element of family strategy. A contemporary conservative commentator likened the process to the transplanting of trees with soil around their roots so that they might thrive in a new place. The St. Lawrence settlers who moved up the Ottawa into western Quebec in the 1820s left behind a world in which family and neighbourhood were nearly one, and found the pace of settlement so rapid that they could not readily recreate the community network of kinship by settling their sons nearby. Later migrants who followed church and government assisted colonization compa-

For men and women are not only themselves; they are also the region in which they were born, the city apartment or farm in which they learned to walk, the games they played as children, the old wives' tales they overheard, the food they ate, the schools they attended, the sports they followed, the poems they read, and the God they believed in.

SOMERSET MAUGHAM, from THE RAZOR'S EDGE

nies to the Saguenay, Hébertville, and Lac St. Jean followed a course that more often allowed them to preserve the essentials of family life in the old rangs despite their geographical mobility. They, too, moved into scantily settled parishes and, while the children and the savings of the family were still small, saw the surrounding farms taken up by others who were not kin. But later, when their sons began to come of age, these families chose to begin again in a newly opened district nearby, placing the solidarity of the kin group over attachment to any particular piece of soil and settling, parents and children together, within hailing distance of one another. In the longer-established farming regions of Quebec, children could not stay within the neighbourhood kin net after their early working years at home and continue in agriculture unless they were daughters who married nearby inheriting sons or the one, usually younger, boy of the family chosen to take over the farm and with it the care of his parents. Most young people migrated to the cities where in the crowded precincts occupied by industrial workers they might try once again to reconstitute a family life in proximity to kin. . . .

By the twentieth century childhood and schooling had become closely identified. Most young people spent considerable time in public classrooms under state or church authority. But still in 1931 children made substantial contributions to the incomes of working-class households, homeless youngsters were more than four times as likely to live with private families as in institutions, and seventy per cent of these guardianship children had been taken in by kin, most commonly by relatives whose resources were sorely stretched as a result. As teachers offered youngsters guidance in the classroom, social workers and government officials theorized in public about the proper management of home and family. Youth employment bureaus provided help in job searches. Published manuals on child-rearing analyzed feeding, discipline, and the proper role of play. While the state sought to shore up rather than to supplant the family, child care professionals planned for a new domestic order. How unwelcome was this advice, how influential or how different from the course parents charted privately in adapting to city life is not yet clear, although rural families, among them the Dionnes, found that the values of urban "experts" diverged radically from their own.

Changes in childhood and family in Canada have been complex. They include no pattern of authority gradually passing away from the home to the sphere of church or state. The individual settlers of New France were sent there as part of an imperial design, but the families they established on the St. Lawrence were little constrained by government officials or the church. There were later times when the state placed onerous war-time demands on households, and when a conquering power destroyed the accumulated wealth of commercial families. In the nineteenth century the church guided the settlement of colonists on new lands chosen for exploitation by secular authorities. But the faithful who followed these plans were seeking to preserve traditions of family work and kin as community; these traditions were older and in some senses more dearly held than the conventions of either spiritual or temporal obedience, and in the next generation they regrouped around family again with the migration into town.

Within English-Canadian families there seems no linear central tendency to change in the compass of either sentiment or obligation. Solitary pioneer families drew kin nearby through time and then saw most relatives move far beyond the network of assistance, their services to some extent replaced by hired labour, which unlike helping kin resided within the household.

The duration of childhood has been flexible before changing perceptions of the economic usefulness of children. In seventeenth-century Montreal, young people did not enter apprenticeships until age sixteen or seventeen or go to war or west on trading trips until they were eighteen, so that only those engaged in domestic service worked outside their own families before they set up their own households in the city. Two centuries later, much younger Montreal children were on the streets at dawn on their way to work, doing jobs not substantially different from those performed by their parents save perhaps that they were paid less. From the seventeenth century, the state prescribed some boundaries on child labour, prescriptions from the public sphere with which parents sometimes agreed, which sometimes they flouted with penalty, sometimes with impunity knowing that their own power exceeded the state's. As past childhood was unlike childhood in the present, past family was unlike the family we know today. The distinctions between private and public life have been no more fixed through time than the customs differentiating youth from adulthood or stranger from kin.

There are those who perceive the pliancy of these boundaries as a recent innovation, who fear that the private sphere has lately been made vulnerable to public intrusion and that the individual's last haven from an authoritarian state thus is imperilled. Yet, high barriers defending the home from public agency or an attempt to make permanent any one set of domestic forms and values—the families of our own childhoods or of our grandparents—will not resolve the tensions within family life or the contradictory priorities of the productive and reproductive spheres. If the past has lessons they are that the connectedness of private life to social life is inescapable, that the malleability of the family is an enduring characteristic, and that the resolution to dilemmas in the private sphere must be found in a challenge to, rather than a retreat from, the prevailing consensus in the public sphere.

From *Childhood and Family in Canadian History*, by Joy Parr,
1982, pp. 7-16. Used by permission of the Canadian Publishers,
McClelland and Stewart, Toronto.

1.   How could Parr's three rules of thumb affect the writing of history of life in the private sphere? Write anecdotes from your family history to illustrate each rule of thumb.

2.   Philippe Ariès's *Centuries of Childhood* has recognized historical value. However, Parr points out that Ariès violated a "venerable general rule of the historian's craft," and by so doing arrived at an invalid conclusion.

What other examples exist of myths that have persisted because of "linear accounts of transformations in family"?

3.   A popular future forecasting technique is trend extrapolation. It has recently received sharp criticism because of its limited scope, since it does to the future exactly what Ariès work did to the past. Investigate the soundness of this criticism.

4.   On a time-line illustrate the migration patterns of families, the changing nature of childhood, and the relationships of church/state and families in Quebec from the time of New France to the present.

5.   At the 1987 national conference of the Vanier Institute Dr. Terrence Morrison said:

> Society passes back and forth, in cyclical style, between times of preoccupation in private affairs and times of preoccupation with public issues. . . . The family, unlike any other social setting, by virtue of its linkage position between the private and the public, is a focal point of both cycles.

Where in the cycle are we at present? Justify your placement decision. In what direction is our society moving?

6.   According to sociologist Susan McDaniel, when you see a modern issue as emerging for the first time in history you develop a crisis perspective. When you see a modern issue as evolving over time your perspective is one of historical continuity. Select one contemporary family issue. Locate two print sources, one written from a crisis perspective and the other from a historical continuity perspective. Describe the tone of each piece. State the conclusions reached in each. Scrutinize each to determine if the three rules of thumb, as observed by Parr, are heeded.

LASTING MARRIAGES

What qualities contribute to the endurance of marriage? In what ways is marriage both satisfying and unsatisfying? These questions were the focus of a 1981 Canadian study of lasting marriages, headed by Dr. Benjamin Schlesinger of the University of Toronto's Faculty of Social Work. The people who were surveyed had all been married at least fifteen years. Compare their responses to the questionnaires with your own. Any surprises?

This study involved 129 couples in the Metropolitan Toronto area who either were interviewed (sixty-two couples) or were mailed the two questionnaires (sixty-seven couples). The couples were contacted through an advertisement in a Toronto newspaper, and all volunteered for this study. A lasting marriage was defined as one that "had lasted at least fifteen years and contained at least one child." There were two questionnaires: a checklist, and a five-question/open-ended questionnaire. Husbands and wives responded to the same two questionnaires separately. Our interviews were completed between November 1980-March 1981. The research team included nine social work students who were completing their Masters of Social Work degree at the Faculty of Social Work.

THE COUPLES—BACKGROUND DATA

The number of years married ranged from fifteen to forty-three years, with an average length of twenty-five. The men and women ranged in age from thirty-three to seventy years. The average age was forty-eight years. The number of children in each family ranged from one to nine, with an average of three children. Forty-three per cent were Protestant, 31 per cent were Jewish, 18 per cent Catholic, 2 per cent were Other, and 6 per cent reported no religion or did not answer the question. Seventy-two per cent of the participants had had at least some university or post-secondary training, and only 12.9 per cent had had less than Grade 11. The largest group of people had graduated from university. Most of the respondents were working full-time. The largest single category of occupation for women was "Not Working Outside Home" (23 per cent). All of the couples lived in the urban area of Metropolitan Toronto. This was a middle class sample.

CHECKLIST

We asked the men and women in these lasting marriages to check from a list those factors important in helping a marriage last. The answers are listed in Table 1.

The items chosen by more than 90 per cent of the men and women included "respect for each other," "trusting each other," "loyalty," and being "comfortable with each other."

Some other items checked by more than 90 per cent of the respondents were "loving each other," "counting on each other," and "considering each other's needs."

Those items considered unimportant in making a marriage last included "primary priority is the job and not the marriage," "primary priority is children and not the marital relationship," "separate vacations," "only one partner working for pay," "emotional support of friends," and "similar financial backgrounds."

Proportionately more women than men believed that "recognizing one's own needs in the marriage," "having a positive relationship with the children," "having similar life goals," "sharing feelings and emotions," and "having a sense of humour" were extremely important factors.

It is only possible to live happily ever after one day at a time.
MARGARET BONNANO

Table 1

Items chosen by more than 75 per cent of the respondents as being factors "extremely important" in helping the marriage to last.

Category	Item	Per cent of Respondents Choosing	Ranked Importance
Qualities in the Marriage	Respect for each other	98.1	1
	Trusting each other	97.3	2
	Loyalty	94.6	3
	Willingness to make sacrifices	84.9	13
Couple Interaction	Comfortable with each other	94.6	3
	Friendship	82.6	14
Intimacy	Loving each other	92.6	4
	Fidelity	89.1	9
Emotional Aspects	Counting on each other	91.9	5
	Considering each other's needs	90.7	6
	Providing each other with emotional support	89.9	7
	Sharing sadness	85.3	12
	Sharing joys	84.9	13
Communication	Honesty in communication	89.9	7
Views	Commitment to making the marriage last	89.5	8
Values	Give-and-take in marriage	88.8	10
Individual Identity	Recognize partner's needs	87.2	11
Problem Solving	Ability to solve problems	84.9	13
	Ability to confront and work out problems	82.6	14

OPEN-ENDED QUESTIONS

The Most Important Factors in Lasting Marriages

In our open-ended questions, we did not have our subjects check any items. We left it open for them to state their own responses. The first question read: "What would you say are the most important factors that contribute to a lasting marriage?"

Table 2
Most Important Factors in Lasting Marriages, in Order of Importance by Sex
(N = 129 couples).

Order	Women	Men	Order
1	Love	Love	1
2	Mutual respect for partner	Mutual respect for partner	2
3	Trust	Trust	3
4	Communication	Communication	4
5	Commitment	Loyalty	5
6	Honesty	Honesty	6
7	Friendship/companionship	Commitment	7
8	Sense of humour	Good sexual life	8
9	Fidelity	Friendship/companionship	9
10	Caring	Fidelity	10
11	Loyalty	Sense of humour	11

It is of interest that both men and women listed the four most important factors in a lasting marriage as love, respect, trust, and communication. . . .

The second question asked, "What were your expectations of marriage at the time you were married, and how do these compare with your expectations today?" Both men and women headed "traditional expectations" at the top of the list, but this changed to more "shared responsibilities" and "independence" of expectations today. . . .

Our third question was, "In what ways has your marriage been satisfying, and in what ways has it been unsatisfying?"

Table 3
In what ways has your marriage been satisfying? Men and Women in order of importance.

Order	Men	Women
1	Friendship	Friendship/companionship
2	Personal growth	Shared interests and goals
3	Supportive partner	Building a home life
4	Children	Love
5	Secure lifestyle	Children
6	Love	Helping one to grow as an individual
7	Financial	Supportive and understanding
8	Common interests	Security and belonging
9	Sex	Sexual satisfaction
10	Communication	Contentment

There appears to be some difference in the response of men and women. For men friendship, personal growth, and a supportive partner are the most frequent replies, while for the women friendship, shared interests and goals, and building a home life are the three most frequent satisfying elements in a lasting marriage. . . .

Table 4

In what ways has your marriage been unsatisfying? Men and Women in order of importance.

Order	Men	Women
1	None	None
2	No response	Sex
3	Not sexually satisfied	Financial
4	Money problems	Husband's workload
5	Children too demanding	Husband's lack of understanding
6	Constraints on personal freedom	Children
7	Insufficient commonality of interests	Sacrificing career for marriage
8	Work too demanding	Interference from in-laws
9	Too few friends	Poor communication
10	Not enough time together	Lack of time alone as a couple

Although the men and women state that there are no unsatisfying aspects in their lasting marriages as the most frequent response, we note that money problems, children, and sexual dissatisfaction emerge as some unsatisfying aspects.

From *Lasting Marriages* by Benjamin Schlesinger and Shirley Tenhouse Giblon
(Toronto: Guidance Centre F.E.U.T. 1984), pp. 18–26.

1.   Imagine that as a newspaper journalist you interviewed Schlesinger and Giblon at the time this study was released. Write a column that would give your readers an accurate account of this study.

2.   React to the definition of "lasting marriages" used by the research team for this study.

3.   Although the focus is entirely different, compare the findings from Schlesinger's study on lasting marriages with the findings on critical family strengths outlined by Emily Nett in her essay. How are the findings alike/different?

4.   A classic study of the 1960s, conducted by psychologists John Cuber and Peggy Haroff, identified five distinctly different types of enduring marital

relationships. These were labelled as the Conflict Habituated, Devitalized, Passive Congenial, Vital, and Total. In a small group, generate a list of what you think could be characteristics of each style. Check this list with the original study findings found in various authoritative texts.

5. The 1980s saw a trend towards researching marital and family strengths. This was a refreshing change. Research during the previous decade had tended to accentuate the negative. In what direction do you see research studies moving in the coming years? Provide reasons for your perspective.

LOVE IN THE LONG TERM

The elusive, enduring nature of love changes its face at every stage of the life cycle. Perhaps the seasoned insights of Robertson Davies have captured love's most stabilizing element. What do you think?

☐

Let us understand one another at once: I have been asked to discuss the pleasures of love, not its epiphanies, its ecstasies, its disillusionments, its duties, its burdens or its martyrdom—and therefore the sexual aspect of it will get scant attention here. So if you have begun this piece in hope of fanning the flames of your lubricity, be warned in time.

Nor is it my intention to be psychological. I am heartily sick of most of the psychologizing about love that has been going on for the past six hundred years. Everybody wants to say something clever, or profound, about it, and almost everybody has done so. Only look under "Love" in any book of quotations to see how various the opinions are.

Alas, most of this comment is wide of the mark; love, like music and painting, resists analysis in words. It may be described, and some poets and novelists have described it movingly and well; but it does not yield to the theorist. Love is the personal experience of lovers. It must be felt directly.

My own opinion is that it is felt most completely in marriage, or some comparable attachment of long duration. Love takes time. What are called "love affairs" may afford a wide, and in retrospect, illuminating variety of emotions; not only fierce satisfactions and swooning delights, but the horrors of jealousy and the desperation of parting attend them; the hangover from one of these emotional toots may be long and dreadful.

But rarely have the pleasures of love an opportunity to manifest themselves in

> Love is a constructed experience built with feelings, ideas, and cultural symbols.
> ARLENE SKOLNICK

such riots of passion. Love affairs are for emotional sprinters; the pleasures of love are for the emotional marathoners.

Clearly, then, the pleasures of love are not for the very young. Romeo and Juliet are the accepted pattern of youthful passion. Our hearts go out to their furious abandonment; we are moved to pity by their early death. We do not, unless we are of a saturnine disposition, give a thought to what might have happened if they had been spared for fifty or sixty years together.

Would Juliet have become a worldly nonentity, like her mother? Or would she, egged on by that intolerable old bawd, her nurse, have planted a thicket of horns on the brow of her Romeo?

And he—well, so much would have depended on whether Mercutio had lived; quarrelsome, dashing and detrimental, Mercutio was a man destined to outlive his wit and spend his old age as the Club Bore. No, no; all that Verona crowd were much better off to die young and beautiful.

Passion, so splendid in the young, wants watching as the years wear on. Othello had it, and in middle life he married a young and beautiful girl. What happened? He believed the first scoundrel who hinted that she was unfaithful, and never once took the elementary step of asking her a direct question about the matter.

Passion is a noble thing; I have no use for a man or woman who lacks it; but if we seek the pleasures of love, passion should be occasional, and common sense continual.

Let us get away from Shakespeare. He is the wrong guide in the exploration we have begun. If we talk of the pleasures of love, the best marriage he affords is that of Macbeth and his Lady. Theirs is not the prettiest, nor the highest-hearted, nor the wittiest match in Shakespeare, but unquestionably they knew the pleasures of love.

"My dearest partner of greatness," writes the Thane of Cawdor to his spouse. That is the clue to their relationship. That explains why Macbeth's noblest and most desolate speech follows the news that his Queen is dead.

But who wants to live a modern equivalent of the life of the Macbeths— continuous scheming to reach the Executive Suite enlivened, one presumes, by an occasional Burns Nicht dinner-party, with the ghosts of discredited vice-presidents as uninvited guests.

The pleasures of love are certainly not for the very young, who find a bitter-sweet pleasure in trying to reconcile two flowering egotisms, nor yet for those who find satisfaction in "affairs." Not that I say a word against young love, or the questings of uncommitted middle-age; but these notions of love correspond to brandy, and we are concerned with something much more like wine.

The pleasures of love are for those who are hopelessly addicted to another living creature. The reasons for such addiction are so many that I suspect they are never the same in any two cases.

It includes passion but does not survive by passion; it has its whiffs of the agreeable vertigo of young love, but it is stable more often than dizzy; it is a growing, changing thing, and it is tactful enough to give the addicted parties occasional rests from strong and exhausting feeling of any kind.

Infantile love follows the principle "I love because I am loved." Mature love follows the principle "I am loved because I love." Immature love says "I love you because I need you." Mature love says "I need you because I love you."

ERICH FROMM

"Perfect love sometimes does not come until the first grandchild," says a Welsh proverb. Better far if perfect love does not come at all, but hovers just out of reach. Happy are those who never experience the all-dressed-up-and-no-place-to-go sensation of perfection in love.

What do we seek in love? From my own observation among a group of friends and acquaintances that includes a high proportion of happy marriages, most people are seeking a completion of themselves. Each party to the match has several qualities the other cherishes; the marriage as a whole is decidedly more than the sum of its parts.

Nor are these cherished qualities simply the obvious ones; the reclusive man who marries the gregarious woman, the timid woman who marries the courageous man, the idealist who marries the realist—we can all see these unions; the marriages in which tenderness meets loyalty, where generosity sweetens moroseness, where a sense of beauty eases some aridity of the spirit, are not so easy for outsiders to recognize; the parties themselves may not be fully aware of such elements in a good match.

Often, in choosing a mate, people are unconsciously wise and apprehend what they need to make them greater than they are.

Of course the original disposition of the partners to the marriage points the direction it will take. When Robert Browning married Elizabeth Barrett, the odds were strongly on the side of optimism, in spite of superficial difficulties; when Macbeth and his Lady stepped to the altar, surely some second-sighted Highlander must have shuddered.

If the parties to a marriage have chosen one another unconsciously, knowing only that they will be happier united than apart, they had better set to work as soon as possible to discover why they have married, and to nourish the feeling which has drawn them together.

I am constantly astonished by the people, otherwise intelligent, who think that anything so complex and delicate as a marriage can be left to take care of itself. One sees them fussing about all sorts of lesser concerns, apparently unaware that side by side with them—often in the same bed—a human creature is perishing from lack of affection, of emotional malnutrition.

Such people are living in sin far more truly than the loving, but unwedded, couples whose unions they sometimes scorn. What pleasures are there in these neglected marriages? What pleasure can there be in ramshackle, jerry-built, uncultivated love?

A great part of all the pleasure of love begins, continues and sometimes ends with conversation. A real, enduring love-affair, in marriage and out of it, is an extremely exclusive club of which the entire membership is two co-equal Perpetual Presidents.

In French drama there used to be a character, usually a man, who was the intimate friend of husband and wife, capable of resolving quarrels and keeping the union in repair. I do not believe in such a creature anywhere except behind the footlights. Lovers who need a third party to discuss matters with are in a bad way.

Of course there are marriages that are kept in some sort of rickety shape by a

Loving can cost a lot but not loving always costs more, and those who fear to love often find that want of love is an emptiness that robs the joy from life.

MERLE SHAIN

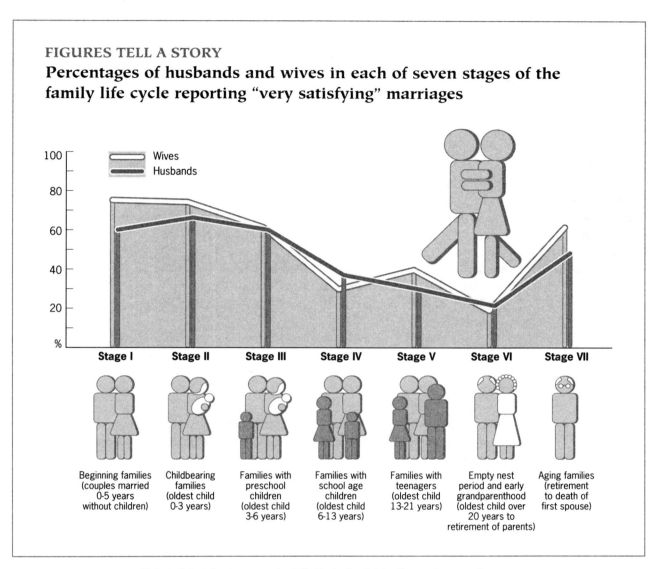

FIGURES TELL A STORY
Percentages of husbands and wives in each of seven stages of the family life cycle reporting "very satisfying" marriages

From "Marital Satisfaction over the Life Cycle Study" by Eugen Lupri and
James Frideres, University of Calgary.

psychiatrist—occasionally by two psychiatrists. But I question if pleasure of the sort I am writing about can exist in such circumstances. The club has become too big.

I do not insist on a union of chatter-boxes, but as you can see I do not believe that still waters run deep; too often I have found that still waters are foul and have mud bottoms.

People who love each other should talk to each other; they should confide their real thoughts, their honest emotions, their deepest wishes. How else are they to keep their union in repair?

How else, indeed, are they to discover that they are growing older and enjoying it, which is a very great discovery indeed? How else are they to discover that their union is stronger and richer, not simply because they have shared experience (couples who are professionally at odds, like a Prime Minister and a Leader of the Opposition also share experience, but they are not lovers) but because they are waxing in spirit?

During the last war, a cruel epigram was current that Ottawa was full of brilliant men, and the women they had married when they were very young. If the brilliant men had talked more to those women, and the women had replied, the joint impression they made in middle age might not have been so dismal. It is often asserted that sexual compatibility is the foundation of a good marriage, but this pleasure is doomed to wane, whereas a daily affectionate awareness, and a ready tongue last as long as life itself.

It always surprises me, when Prayer Book revision is discussed, that something is not put into the marriage service along these lines—"for the mutual society, help, comfort and unrestricted conversation that one ought to have of the other, both in prosperity and adversity."

Am I then advocating marriages founded on talk? I can hear the puritans, who mistrust conversation as they mistrust all subtle pleasures, tutting their disapproving tuts.

Do I assert that the pleasures of love are no more than the pleasures of conversation? Not at all: I am saying that where the talk is good and copious, love is less likely to wither, or to get out of repair, or to be outgrown, than among the uncommunicative.

For, after all, even lovers live alone much more than we are ready to admit. To keep in constant, sensitive rapport with those we love most, we must open our hearts and our minds. Do this, and the rarest, most delicate pleasures of love will reveal themselves.

Finally, it promotes longevity. Nobody quits a club where the conversation is fascinating, revealing, amusing, various and unexpected until the last possible minute. Love may be snubbed to death: talked to death, never!

> From "The Pleasures of Love," *The Enthusiasms of Robertson Davies,*
> by Judith Skeleton Grant (Ed.). Used by permission of the Canadian Publishers,
> McClelland and Stewart, Toronto.

> Every life has its basic characteristic difficulty . . . but the hardest items of all have to do with love.
>
> SAUL BELLOW,
> from MORE DIE OF HEARTBREAK

1. Choose from this reading the sentences, phrases or ideas that jump out at you; that you would like to share with your best friend or a loved one; that you would like to discuss with Robertson Davies.

2. Love, as Robertson Davies claims, does not yield to the theorist.
    However, several theories explaining how we fall in love and how we select our mate have been proposed. Investigate a number of these theories. Which one(s) do you favour? Why? How do theorists attempt to be objective about love?

3. Davies writes that, in love, "most people are seeking a completion of themselves." Do you agree with this remark? What are its implications?

4. You would think that in such an intimate relationship as marriage conversation would come easily. But according to marriage counsellors, couples talk, but few communicate. Explore the strategies intimate partners find useful in learning how to communicate.

COMMITMENT AND CHOICE

Present-day life is one of multiple choice—and so many options sometimes makes commitment problematic. In the two excerpts below, journalist and social worker Merle Shain reflects on the lessons life has taught her. Do you recognize the choice/commitment dilemma?

□

We are our choices and our choices not made. We are what we do and what we do not do as well. Just as surely as we are what is done to us, although many people talk about all that has befallen them without asking themselves how much of it was brought about by them.

The roots of love sink down deep and strike out far, and they are arteries that feed our lives, so we must see that they get the water and sun they need so they can nourish us. And when you put something good into the world, something good comes back to you.

> No partnership can be in constant fine balance. To find the right division of responsibility in your relationship calls for trial, error, humour, and flexibility.
> CAROL TAVRIS

I don't know where we got the idea that it is an either/or situation, that it's freedom or commitment, personal growth or responsibility, and that if we choose commitment it will be our loss and not our gain. Because one grows in commitment, one doesn't diminish—in fact, it is the only way to grow. And if you commit to nothing but yourself, you pour yourself into the thirsty distance, having nothing to show for it but the cancers on your soul. And you learn too late, as many people have, that man is a ladder, and each rung that takes us higher is a responsibility accepted gratefully, and that there is no personal growth without responsibility, and no such thing as freedom without commitment, nor can there ever be.

From *Hearts That We Broke Long Ago* by Merle Shain, 1983, pp. 75, 117. Used by permission of the Canadian Publishers, McClelland and Stewart, Toronto.

1. Provide personal anecdotes to illustrate: personal growth resulting from responsibility; freedom resulting from commitment; being our choices made and our choices not made.

2. Research studies on infant bonding indicate that bonding between infant and parent is a prerequisite for commitment in adulthood. Debate or write an argumentative essay on the statement: "Infants deprived of emotional bonding will be unable to establish enduring adult relationships."

3. Compare and contrast the following images of marriage: an endurance test, a life-long commitment, a love-long commitment, a personal achievement, a sacred institution, a shared experience. Select the image that appeals to you.

4. Soon after a couple's ten-year marriage dissolved, the husband reflected on the past:

    > We weren't immature kids when we got married. We were both 25 and went into marriage with our eyes wide open, or so we thought. We freely chose to love and honour and respect one another 'til death do us part; after all, that was the model we both saw in our parents' marriages. But, it just didn't work out and it's no more her fault than it is mine.

    Perhaps commitments, honestly made and seriously taken, are more difficult to keep today than they were in the past. How do you view such commitment? How does your view vary from that of your peers? Your parents? Your grandparents?

■ ESSENCE OF FAMILY

The essence of any family can be both felt and observed. Essence is defined as "an indispensable quality." Every family has such qualities that make it unique. The first selection is a daughter's tribute to her parents on the occasion of their 40th anniversary. Does she capture the essence of her family of origin? And, in the second reading, how does poet Alden Nowlan evoke the uniqueness of what he shares with his wife and son?

My first vision of you features the bumpy cardboard walls of the dining room at Islington, which the two of you were painting blue. Was it a Saturday that you were both there? Were you nervous about your change of finances? Buying a home, twenty-five year mortgage, young couple, 1952, three kids, remote location, one car: how did you shop?

In your new little house: inventing ways to pay bills, teach table manners, separate puzzle pictures, establish moral basics, fix bedtimes, impart street sense, hatch diplomacy, broaden gastronomy, identify constellations, marvel at the Press Club's Christmas magician, familiarize the alphabet, tune in Mr. Whittaker, tie shoes, explain a curtsey, contain a finger painting, sustain interest, looking forward to a grilled cheese at the Rendezvous wishing-well—not yet versed in horse-trading, regulating hallucinogenics, or making tuition payments, you set up housekeeping in your new blue dining room, with your mature marriage of seven whole years, with approximately all the change in the world ahead of you.

You were loving, interdependent, close and available. Having babies has revived my childhood memories, taught respect. Your reliability and warmth fueled me then, your foresight and support now give time depth. You taught the dignity of life, and the tenderness. Your partnership of forty years is a promise kept, a proof, cause for celebration and hope.

From "A Tribute to June Callwood" by Jesse Frayne, May 13, 1984, p. 13.

GREAT THINGS HAVE HAPPENED

We were talking about the great things
that have happened in our lifetimes;
and I said, "Oh, I suppose the moon landing
was the greatest thing that has happened
in my time." But, of course, we were all lying.
The truth is the moon landing didn't mean
one-tenth as much to me as one night in 1963
when we lived in a three-room flat in what once had been
the mansion of some Victorian merchant prince
(our kitchen had been a clothes closet, I'm sure),
on a street where by now nobody lived
who could afford to live anywhere else.
That night, the three of us, Claudine, Johnnie and me,
woke up at half-past four in the morning
and ate cinnamon toast together.

"Is that all?" I hear somebody ask.

If families are united in bonds of sympathy and understanding, if they are churches full of gratitude and dedication, if they are schools where nobility of character and a sense of service are daily living lessons, then they will be the well-springs from which go forth the streams of national greatness and the happiness and well-being of our people.
MADAME VANIER

Oh, but we were silly with sleepiness
and, under our windows, the street-cleaners
were working their machines and conversing in Italian, and
everything was strange without being threatening,
even the tea-kettle whistled differently
than in the daytime: it was like the feeling
you get sometimes in a country you've never visited
before, when the bread doesn't taste quite the same,
the butter is a small adventure, and they put
paprika on the table instead of pepper,
except that there was nobody in this country
except the three of us, half-tipsy with the wonder
of being alive, and wholly enveloped in love.

From *An Exchange of Gifts* by Alden Nowlan.
Reprinted with the permission of Stoddart Publishing Co. Limited.

1. What indispensable qualities do you detect in June Callwood's family? In Alden Nowlan's family?

2. If you could transmit one unique feature or quality from your present family to your future family, what would it be? Why did you single out this one feature?

3. In her book *Family Politics* Letty Pogrebin used metaphors to express the essence of family. Reflect on these images:

   > If the family were a container, it would be a nest, an enduring nest, loosely woven, expansive and open.

   > If the family were a fruit, it would be an orange, a circle of sections held together but separable—each segment distinct.

   > If the family were a boat, it would be a canoe that makes no progress unless everyone paddles.

   Compose some of your own metaphors.

4. Profile the essence of a family in a work of fiction or biography with which you are familiar.

FAMILY RITUALS

Families use rituals to stitch together their history. Such simple family rituals as a bedtime story, for example, might not seem very significant. But combined with their many other rituals, families may weave for themselves a rich tapestry of tradition. In the selection that follows Rona Maynard describes the depth and significance that rituals still have for today's family.

☐

Orchestrated to the last detail, our formal ceremonies are as close as helter-skelter daily life ever comes to the precision of art. They are the pictures we would paint of our attachments if we were skilled with a brush; the celebratory poems we'd write if we were masters of metaphor. Come to think of it, maybe we *are*. The wellspring of ritual's expressive power is invariably metaphor—the evocative phrase or image that stands for an elusive idea. A birthday armful of . . . tiger lilies, a Halloween pumpkin carved with panache, that homely Styrofoam Christmas ball you hang each year because one of the kids covered it with sequins back in Grade 1—there's no end to the symbols of caring that mark our rituals.

Perhaps all our rituals, by revealing deep-rooted beliefs about identity and aspirations, verge on the religious. Notes writer Jane Howard in *Families:* "Religions have endured, among other reasons, because of the scaffolding they provide from which to suspend . . . traditions. All the . . . families I care for . . . feel strongly about ceremonies that link them to the earth, to those who have trod it before them, and to one another."

In primitive tribes, religion and ritual are closely intertwined. Ancestors must be honoured, enemies magically kept at bay, vengeful gods placated or thanked as the spiritual world forever impinges on here-and-now realities. Enter ritual—any structured practice, charged with symbolic meaning and repeated over time, in which each participant plays a clearly defined role. Evidence of ceremony dates back some 60,000 years to the shells and tools discovered in Neanderthal graves. One hapless hunter, found covered with fossilized pollen, was laid to rest on a bed of brightly coloured flowers.

Anthropologists have catalogued rites for all occasions: crossing rivers, moving to a new house, welcoming strangers and cutting a baby's hair, to mention a few. Childbirth alone has inspired a panoply of practices that alert the whole community to the mother's changed status, the family's expansion and the infant's ancestral ties.

Arizona's Hopi Indians could hardly ignore a baby's arrival. As French folklorist/anthropologist Arnold van Gennep tells in *The Rites of Passage* (. . . published originally in 1909 and still viewed as a classic), the first-time mother prepared for delivery by restricting her diet and staying inside after sundown. Birth was followed, at prescribed intervals, by three ritual washings of mother and baby and a fourth involving the father and other relatives. The women of the clan then named the child and presented it to the sun (just what this intriguing gesture entailed, the terse van Gennep doesn't tell). Finally, the maternal grandmother invited everyone in the pueblo to a special feast.

Throughout human history, to live has been to ritualize—to impose the comforting order of ceremony on the inevitable tumult of conflict and change. Ritual reminds us, to quote Ecclesiastes, that "To every thing there is a season, and a time to every purpose under the heaven: a time to be born, and a time to die; a time to plant, and a time to pluck up that which is planted." Which explains the devotion of some seemingly lapsed urban Jews to the traditional harvest rite of Sukkot. To keep the custom, you build a hut in the back yard, which you then festoon with vegetables, fruits and berries. The whole family eats there for the next eight days, never mind the chill of a typical Canadian September. Writes regular celebrant Michele Landsberg in *Women & Children First:* "The rules say you have to know it is temporary, so you must see the sky through the roof. And it has to be flimsy; a reminder that we're all just passing through."

Above all, ritual embodies an image of how things ought to be while hinting that trouble will strike if we approach it lightly. Think of the elaborate bedtime rites some youngsters insist upon—the favourite book, the extra glass of water, the check for monsters under the bed, the door left ajar at just the right angle. To some weary parents, the procedure is a mere delaying tactic. To the child, it's protection from harm in the dark passage toward sleep.

We educated adults fear no lurking monsters. Nor would we worry, as superstitious tribes have done, that our children's family loyalty depends on the preservation of the placenta by the appropriate relative. But custom persists in every family's life. In the downtown high-rise and the suburban bungalow, it serves the same order-keeping purposes it has met in the Stone Age cave and the Arizona pueblo.

The ceremonies of the '80s take a dazzling variety of forms, not all of them connected with national or religious holidays. There's ritual in the characteristic way a clan greets new neighbours (with homegrown tomatoes, or a smile and a nod). There's ritual, too, in the serving of morning toast—or is it granola at your table? My own family is a touch fanatical about cinnamon-raisin bread buttered straight from the toaster and served with cottage cheese.

More than the name on the mailbox or the number on the door, details like these are the essence of home. And home remains the focus of some of our deepest, most primordial emotions. What could be more disturbing than the fear that discord or death will threaten that flawed but treasured sanctuary where everybody knows which section of the paper you read first, and how much milk you take in your coffee? Just as the ancient Hindus gave each baby two names, one for public use and the other a family secret, so we all value that obscure sense of kinship founded on the rites of daily living.

As Robert Frost summed up, "Home is the place where, when you have to go there, they have to take you in." It's also the place where customs and in-jokes welcome you back. "When I was a boy," recalls a grandfather, "you couldn't leave the house without somebody calling, 'Don't forget to walk the dog.' Visitors were puzzled because there hadn't been a dog at our place for years. I guess we just like having our own special way of doing things."

Ceremony used to revolve around places of worship—an altar or a sacred spring—and still does in some cultures. The festivities often call for a banquet of rare, costly and elaborate dishes. This pattern persists as we largely secular celebrants affirm family loyalties around the dining room table. In Laurie Colwin's novel *Family Happiness,* the aristocratic, fiercely perfectionist Solo-Miller family makes a shared cause of a Sunday breakfast spread that hasn't varied in decades. "At each place was a juice glass, a coffee cup, and one of Wendy's breakfast plates, which were decorated with pheasants and cornflowers. All juice was squeezed fresh: Henry, Sr., believed that harmful metals leached into juice from cans. . . ."

Ah, tradition. Some two-career couples now count themselves lucky to eat home-made, sit-down meals well spiced by conversation. "The evening meal is the one time of day when we're all together," observes the working mother of a 12-year-old, "so there's no reading at the table. I'll put some classical music on and Bob pours the wine. It's the only chance the three of us have to talk about our day." This family has made one concession to let-it-all-hang-out relaxation. Friday nights, they rent a classic movie for the VCR, order a pizza and eat in front of the dread TV.

"All meals are rituals, and dinnertime especially," says James Schmeiser, a University of Western Ontario religious studies professor who also teaches courses on marriage and chairs the interdenominational Canadian Liturgical Society. But some of our evening meals add up to a pretty sorry statement of shared identity. I sensed dinnertime was in trouble when a visiting 10-year-old sat down at our table still plugged into his Walkman—a standard practice in his own household, where everybody bops to a private beat. There are far more ominous portents. Would you believe that according to a University of Pennsylvania study, half of all parents who still eat with their children are munching in darkness by the TV? And that much of the time, they've grabbed the food from takeout joints?

The workaday world is too much with us. So it's perilously easy to neglect a side of life that many have struggled to preserve despite formidable odds. Survival was the issue when Anne Frank and her family hid from the Nazis in the secret annex. Yet father Otto still took pains to write the 14th birthday poem that a grateful Anne copied into her diary. As the young chronicler also noted, the Franks observed both Hanukkah and Christmas with improvised gifts. There's no suppressing the hunger for connectedness—with our culture as well as with our nearest and dearest.

The Quach family of Toronto understand that feeling. When they fled Vietnam for Canada in 1979, they faced the multiple upheavals of a new language, a bone-chilling winter and a city teeming with strangers. They had no friends and few relatives in their adopted country. To support their five sons, ages four to fourteen, Quen works in a bakery and his wife, Si, in a sock factory (she must rise at five to start her shift on time). They now have the trappings of North American affluence: a Buick Skylark, a suburban house. Most of the colour photographs on the living-room wall show the family posed at a nearby plaza, framed by gleaming store windows.

> Good families prize their rituals. Nothing welds a family more than these. Rituals are vital especially for clans without histories, because they evoke a past, imply a future and hint at continuity. . . . A clan becomes more of a clan each time it gathers to observe a fixed ritual. . . .
>
> JANE HOWARD

The Quach boys now trick-or-treat at Halloween and unwrap gifts at Christmas. But every winter, the family celebrates Chinese New Year, just as Quen's Chinese parents always did in Vietnam. Both Vietnamese and Canadian guests share a host of traditional dishes: chicken, crab, lobster, duck, noodles and shrimp wrapped in rice paper. "We work so hard every day," Quen says. "Just one day a year it's nice to relax and be happy with all our friends."

Steven Wolin, a psychiatrist at George Washington University Medical Centre's family research centre in Washington, DC, has explored the binding force of rituals carefully maintained and some shock waves of rituals gone haywire. He and his colleagues studied the ritual life of more than 100 families in which at least one parent was an alcoholic—a well-known risk factor for alcoholism in the next genera-tion. The researchers looked at a wide range of rituals: holidays, dinnertime, weekend and evening habits and the treatment of visitors. "We didn't see any families in which dinner time was absolutely unchanged," Wolin remarks of the havoc that alcoholism wreaks in any home it touches. But the researchers did observe a hopeful pattern. The harder the families tried to preserve their rituals, the less frequent the alcoholism in their adult children. Such is the power of ceremony to wrest order from chaos.

The Washington study has a heartening message for us all. As the University of Western Ontario's Schmeiser says, "If families are to survive, then ritual is one of the most powerful tools we have." For one thing, it sets aside a time and a place for what we might as well call the counting of blessings—those elusive sentiments so easily lost in the morning scramble to wrap the sandwiches, or the 7 p.m. sprint from stove to table.

Corny? On any other day, you might think so. But celebrations, like theatrical performances, entail preparation that gradually alters participants' state of mind. You have to stuff the turkey before distant relatives descend on Thanksgiving—also bake the pies and ready the hearth for a roaring fire. Wolin compares such festive nest-feathering to "putting on makeup, practising one's lines, getting into the mood for a role in a play."

What's more, ceremony presents an unparalleled opportunity for self-expres-sion. Tradition unlocks a store of ready-made symbols for love and loyalty, from chocolate hearts to anniversary roses. But one of ritual's greatest pleasures is the creation of new, personal symbols. Schmeiser urges married couples to shrug off inhibitions and explore the potential of ritual.

His advice for a romantic anniversary: dream up the perfect menu, light the candles and bring out the good crystal. Now comes the hard part: the exchange of gifts. "You can't just spend five minutes in a flower shop grabbing something," he cautions. The trick is to make or find some token that sums up what your partner means to you—and it might not be costly or rare, as long as it reflects thought. Lines from a poem will do. A more adventuresome couple made an anniversary vase of clay combining the water dear to one of them with the earth beloved by the other. To anyone else, it was just bric-a-brac. To them, it told a story that is theirs alone.

Two caveats come to mind. First, the personal symbol that says it all can only arise from genuine feeling. There's no room for fakery. Second, Schmeiser says, you can't create a sense of ceremony with a single event "any more than you can learn about art by visiting a museum once." Like choral music, custom thrives on practice, and calls for many voices.

I doubt if any of us truly understand our private stories until we attempt to tell them—through notes on a page, images in a poem or gestures in a ceremony—and let the climax catch us by surprise. Religion, art and ritual all share the power to tap emotions we don't even know we have. When our father died two winters ago, my sister and I planned a funeral with poetry readings, a flutist and a reminiscence by our mother (our parents were long divorced). This was the way the Maynards always did things. By reviving the old pattern, we recaptured the best of what our parents had always stood for together.

"A ring when it's rolling has no end," a folk lullaby says. So too with our fast-rolling family rituals, be they religious holidays or simply favourite observances: the yearly planting of the vegetable patch, the roasting of the Sunday chicken till the skin crackles.

They fly past like the ruffling calendar pages old movies used to show, alerting the audience to ever-advancing years. Practices endure while faces change. The matriarch who has hosted Christmas dinner for at least 20 years hands the festivities over to the next generation. Yesterday's bride has her wedding dress recut—the proverbial "something borrowed" for a daughter. They're not exactly art for the ages, these year-in, year-out festivities of ours, but they're the next best thing to immortality. So on with the show!

From "Rituals" by Rona Maynard, *Homemakers' Magazine*, pp. 26-40.

1. Select from this reading those points which highlight the importance of rituals to enduring families.

2. What part do ritual and ceremony play in your family life? Do you consider them important to a sense of continuity and well-being? Explain your answer.

3. Differentiate between rituals, ceremonies, traditions, celebrations, rites of passage, and symbols. Provide examples of each.

4. In their study of family rituals, Wolin and Bennett divided rituals into three areas—everyday patterned interactions, family traditions, and family celebrations. With this framework in mind examine family rituals in blended families. Devise a set of guidelines that blended families might use to honour old rituals and establish new ones.

5. Choose a specific family ritual, and identify the symbols that form a part of it. Investigate the meanings behind the symbols. What new interpretations may be brought to family rituals and symbols by subsequent generations? By incorporating a different ethnic perspective?

6.   Use these statements as the basis for discussion:

It is the unspoken message of ritual that makes it so powerful.

When transgenerational rituals are part of a major life transition, there is a heightened anxiety level within the system.

TODAY'S YOUTH— TOMORROW'S FAMILIES

Tomorrow's families are being shaped by the values and expectations of today's youth. The following profile of 2000 Canadian youths between the ages of 15-24 was compiled in 1988 by Donald Posterski and Reginald Bibby. Like most snapshots, this one reveals more than what first meets the eye.

☐

☐ "I'M COUNTING ON ME"

Young people have assigned the primary role on the stage of life to themselves. Their script for existence combines the self resources of their nurture and nature—the way they have been brought up and the characteristics they have been born with. Their age has told them to look to themselves, to use their will power, and find answers. Science has not only won their confidence, it has taught them to experiment and problem-solve. They believe what they have been taught.

☐ FAMILY IS IMPORTANT

The task of growing up and moving from dependence to independence can interject tension into the finest of families. But for the young, the family is not essentially a small group of people from which they must plan an escape. The family is valued highly, affirmed as a strong source of influence, enjoyed much of the time and always a place to come home to. The highest compliment the young have to pay to their parents is that they are planning on becoming parents themselves.

☐ RELATIONSHIPS ARE CENTRAL

The young are social creatures. Friends are a driving force in their lives. They talk on the phone a lot, help each other figure out who they are, buy each other gifts, experience what it is to be loved and accepted and sometimes—taste betrayal. In some instances, today's youth may be the first generation to be raised by their peers.

THE ECONOMY MATTERS

For the young, life is more than just relationships. Carving out a high standard of living is important too. Success and a comfortable life are not just values—they are goals that deserve to be pursued—unrelentingly. The young are aware they live in an interdependent world and that they are not strong enough to overcome the odds of economic slowdowns and extended recessions.

EDUCATION IS A GIVEN

The road to the good life demands an education. A diploma is not just an exit visa from the halls of higher learning. For most it is a passport into the workplace. The young have aspirations to levels of education that far exceed the achievements of their parents. Some will succeed. Most will have to adjust what they consider to be adequate.

RELIGION IS AN OPTION

If education is like standard equipment on a new automobile, for eight out of ten, religion is one of those optional extras. It's not that young people are mad at God or are making declarations of disbelief, it's simply that they are not planning on going to church or the synagogue unless they are intending to get married or desire a religious service for their newborn baby. They will find other reference points for their belief and behaviour.

REFLECTING THEIR WORLD

In many ways, modern youth are reflections of their modern world. For ample reasons, they do not see themselves as potential "change agents." Whether the subject is religion or capital punishment, sexuality or alcohol use—the young are walking in the footsteps of adults who have gone before them. For adults, the impact of modelling is worthy of serious reflection. Youth would do well to question their acceptance of the status quo.

> Luck is what happens when preparation meets opportunity.
> PROVERB

FEELING ENTITLED

Canada parades herself as a land of opportunity. Young people hear the promises and are living with high expectations. The expectations translate into desires for immediate security and quick significance. In their minds, education entitles them to the kind of work for which they are now qualified and a salary in keeping with the style to which they have become accustomed. On the one hand, society may be over-promising, on the other, the expectations of the young may be unrealistic.

☐ PERSONALLY FOCUSED

Personal priorities are consuming the energy of the young. There is also a growing disillusionment with the institutional and the bureaucratic in society. Consequently, whether the alternative for involvement is a political party, a religious organization or the neighbourhood community league—personal agendas are favoured over collective concerns. With only six percent placing high importance on being a leader in the community, there is an open door for those who have the drive to serve and shape society's future.

☐ SOMETIMES AFRAID

A consequence of the personal dominating this stage of life is that the social problems of the country are then perceived through personal grids. Accordingly, 15-24-year-olds are primarily concerned about personal safety (sexual assault and AIDS) and the consequences of drug and alcohol abuse. During the last few years, the threat of nuclear war has declined as a perceived problem, while pollution has increased on the social concern scale.

☐ SOMETIMES STRUGGLING

The steps from school to work and from dependence to independence are proving to be difficult for many youth today. Several segments of the youth population are especially affected. Those who have been both out of school and out of work for at least six months; the 19 percent of 20-24-year-olds who are not working; the one in five who are feeling like they are not as good as others; and those whose lives are in a holding pattern because they have few prospects of leaving home to establish their own lives—are all worthy of special attention and compassionate response. These young people need advocates more than they need critics.

☐ CONVENTIONAL

Don't compromise yourself, you are all you've got.
JANIS JOPLIN

The younger generation cannot be characterized as being radical and rebellious. In fact, they are living well within the prescribed boundaries of Canadian society. Only a few are refusing to jump through the hoops of defined cultural normalcy. In the main, they are getting educated, going to work, falling in love, committing themselves to a spouse or partner, having children, and while they pursue their personal goals—they are looking for some pleasure in the midst of coping with life's problems. Today's youth are a conventional generation.

☐ IDEALISTIC AND OPTIMISTIC

The young are also idealistic and optimistic. They see the glass of water half full rather than half empty. While in school, they are positive about finding a good job. If they are unemployed, they expect to get work. They think that working hard will assure them a promotion. When they get married they anticipate staying married. Some adults charge them with "being naive." Other members of the older generation see the young as the sun breaking through on a cloudy day.

ABLE AND ASPIRING

Canada's young people are an *able* generation. They are bright and competent. They are not limping around with inferiority complexes. They are informed. They are not lazy. Certainly they lack experience. But where they are not equipped, they are ready to be trained and educated. They deserve access into the adult world.

Canada's young people are an *aspiring* generation. They have hopes and goals. They are attracted to the fine things in life. They are intending to achieve. They are ready to pay the price that excellence demands. Young people are more than potential for tomorrow. They deserve to be believed in—today.

From "A Snapshot of Canadian Youth" by Donald Posterski,
Transitions, Vol. 19 (3), September 1989, pp. 12-13.

1. Slot yourself into the survey findings. Where do you feel most comfortable/ least comfortable? Discuss those feelings with your classmates.

2. Critically examine the effect of gender and age on the selected value goals. Comment on the significance of gender socialization on the value goals.

3. "On the one hand, society may be over-promising, on the other, the expectations of the young may be unrealistic." As you see it, what systems in our society tend to over-promise? Which ones tend to create unrealistic expectations in the young? Which systems provide you with a balanced view of life? Justify your answers.

4. Several comments made by the authors beg discussion. Express your views on these statements.

> The young are walking in the footsteps of adults who have gone before them. . . . Youth would do well to question their acceptance of the status quo.

> Young people are more than potential for tomorrow. They deserve to be believed in—today.

■ FUTURE IMAGES OF FAMILY

In *The Wizard of Oz* the crystal ball owned by the Wicked Witch of the West gave her a distinct advantage over Dorothy. While it may be reassuring to turn uncertainty into certainty, can you imagine life without wishes, hopes, dreams, and fantasies? The first reading is not so much a future image of family as it is a call for us to take up battle positions. According to columnist Lois Sweet, whoever wins the right to define "family" will shape its future. Next is the scenario John Kettle uses to introduce readers to his book, *The Big Generation*. It outlines one possible future for the Baby Boom cohort. The final selection was written by sociologist Sterling Alam as though he were a world citizen at the beginning of the third decade of the 21st century. The future holds a rich diversity of possibilities. In what forms do you think the family will endure?

☐

I harbour no fantasies about what the family will be like in the year 2001. I'd like to, but I can't because I believe a war is being waged over the family today.

I think the kinds of families we'll have in the future depend on who wins the war.

This war is being fought over who has the right to define "family." The winner will then be able to use public money to support that definition.

Right now, there's a lot of confusion over "the family"—confusion largely created by what is known as the New Right. U.S. President Ronald Reagan is one of its most persuasive proponents.

Reagan the actor paints fluffy verbal images of a happy, healthy (implicitly white) nuclear family—Mom in the kitchen, Dad bringing home the bacon and the two kids playing with the kittens.

In Canada, unfortunately, we have a contingent of Conservative MPs who mouth the same rhetoric.

You don't have to like these people to feel warm inside when they talk about family. You feel this way because it isn't your intellect that's responding—it's your emotions.

After all, family is a very evocative concept. It conjures up images of security, acceptance, innocence and love. These images bring out the child in all of us.

But our desires can blind us to reality. In real life the New Right does little to support real families.

Since coming into office, Reagan's public policies actually deprive many children of food and the resources to protect them from abuse.

When a 1983 U.S. statistic pointed out that 22 per cent of children in that country lived below the poverty line—as opposed to 14 per cent 10 years earlier—one senator noted wryly that Reagan seems to believe that "life begins at conception and ends at birth."

A similar battle is being fought here.

Prime Minister Brian Mulroney has already de-indexed the family allowance, and in so doing has served notice that even the family is not sacrosanct.

At the same time, Canadians aren't embracing, encouraging or supporting the many different kinds of families that exist today. Instead, we're fighting over what constitutes a legitimate family.

In the process we ignore other, viable "families"—single parents, couples living without a marriage certificate, homosexuals—people who are committed to sharing their lives and caring for each other out of choice, not necessity.

We argue back and forth about what is needed to keep the family afloat. The thinking behind our questions is all wrong. So are the answers:

Will universally accessible day care contribute to family breakup? (Yes. It will encourage women to leave their homes.)

Should we provide a living income to single parents on welfare? (No. They'll get the impression we support their life style.)

Should we give working women fully paid maternity leave? (No. Instead of working, they'll choose to breed.)

One positive aspect of the questions, however, is that they indicate the degree to which "family" has come out of the closet and into the public domain. That is as it should be.

As a society, we are finally recognizing that what goes on in a family is not distinct from, and unimportant to, the rest of society.

We now see a contradiction exists when laws against beatings or sexual abuse—in the work place and on the street—are enforced but such crimes are tolerated in the home. The government has had to step in, however inadequate its intervention may be.

> There is more to life than increasing its speed.
> **MAHATMA GANDHI**

But this has happened largely because groups opposed to the objectives of the New Right have raised moral questions about the family.

Feminists exposed wife battery, sexual abuse of children and the undemocratic and non-egalitarian nature of the patriarchal family. They knew that if relationships in the family changed, the impact on society would be nothing short of revolutionary.

The New Right knows that too and so do fledgling groups like Canada's own R.E.A.L. women.

That's why they're so opposed to sexual equality. They would rather punish children with inadequate day care and poverty than tolerate diversity in families.

Perhaps, by the year 2001, the battle will be over. Maybe by then, people fed up with politicians who play with their basic needs will have summoned the courage necessary to resist candy-coated images in favour of meeting genuine human needs.

From "Today's Battle Over Family Will Forge Its Future Form"
by Lois Sweet, *Toronto Star*, September 26, 1986.
Reprinted with permission—The Toronto Star Syndicate.

☐

☐ 1975

It is eleven o'clock on a mid-September morning in Vancouver and Eric Hobson is still asleep. As he was yesterday at this time, and the day before.

Eric, who is sixteen, got a job cleaning up at a hamburger restaurant in the spring term and worked there through most of the summer vacation. The manager said he would be trained as a cook at the next opening. That was when Eric decided to drop out of school. But for one reason or another—a fight in the washroom over his girl friend, showing up late a couple of times, a hot exchange with the manager about a missing cap—he was fired. It was the week before school opened. It was also the week his father announced he had met a woman, fallen in love, and was going to set up house with her. And proceeded to do so.

Eric cannot stand his mother's crying and angry outbursts and drinking bouts. He comes down from his room in the quiet small hours of the morning, makes endless sandwiches, drinks milk, eats up all the cookies, goes back to his room and his radio, and smokes. He takes meals at home only when he is out of money. . . .

As soon as he gets up, usually around noon, he leaves the house. But at this hour he is still in bed.

At the other end of the country, in Montreal, Maggie Kadar is running down the hall to her history class. It is not a subject she does well at, though she finds the Canadian history fitfully interesting. Chemistry is where she shines, and although she hasn't yet made a firm decision, it is the field she will make her career in.

Maggie—Magda to her family—was born in 1961, five years after her parents made a panicky exit from Hungary. They met in the Hungarian community that sprang up in Montreal after the revolution, married, worked, and bought a small house. Magda grew up speaking Magyar at home, English at school. After each election, the Kadars are less sure they like living in Quebec, and their daughters have become reconciled to the prospect of moving west, though given their choice, they would pick Montreal over anywhere they know.

☐ 1985

Maggie and Eric have been married for six years, and she is wondering how much longer she will be able to bear it. Eric did go back to school and then on to regional college for a cooking course, which he quit in the middle of the second year. He moved to Calgary at the beginning of 1979, starting a succession of greasy-spoon café and restaurant jobs. The Kadars left Montreal in 1979, convinced that Quebec was going to separate. Maggie's father found a job with the provincial government in Edmonton, and Maggie enrolled in biochemistry at the University of Calgary. Her freshman year was the first she had spent away from home; she was married before the spring. Her parents did not hear about it until the summer vacation, when she at last told them she would not be returning home.

Eric works in a steak house, much patronized by wealthy Japanese and Korean oilmen and eastern Canadian tourists. Maggie is tutoring some first- and second-year students and doing research during the summer vacation for an American pharmaceutical company that has opened a Canadian branch based in Calgary.

They have less and less to talk about. He is a cable freak, with a videotaper, a library of blue movies, and a growing passion for the new murderball games and the annual sudden-death Lougheed Cup finals. She plays the lute with a small group—plucked strings and bowed strings—and is currently reading through all of George Orwell, after the success of the 1984-85 man-and-his-works series on cable. They have no children, entertain little—his friends and hers don't mix—and, after one unsuccessful vacation in New York, now take short breaks in the Central American package resorts.

1990

Maggie Hobson, now Maggie Kadar again, holds a research job at Tomson-Laws Biologicals, the company she worked for as a summer student. She rents a farmhouse near Lethbridge with Marc Thibodeau, a thirty-three-year-old lawyer, and Vincent Narayan, a twenty-eight-year-old out-of-work actor. Maggie spends most of her week at home, using the terminal in the work room. When she has physical experiments to do she takes the one-hour magtrain ride into Calgary or works with a colleague on the spot over the videolink.

Marc uses the terminal and videolink for some of his work, but spends more time travelling and with clients than Maggie cares to. He has become a real estate expert specializing in international franchising. He hops about the west in the small carpter, uses the transPacific hypersonic when his clients are paying, tries to stop in Singapore for a weekend if there is time, and has a secret passion for kinky Asian gadgets, the more chrome and lasers the better.

Vince has not been offered a part in two and a half years. He is a natural sybarite, soft-spoken, elegant in homemade clothes, a man who can take a morning to make lunch, a sweet-voiced singer. Maggie sometimes thinks she loves him even more than she loves Marc.

2000

After Marc's suicide in 1998, Maggie and Vincent could not bear to go on living on the farm. They moved with two other couples into a house that had been on the outskirts of Lethbridge when it was built in 1929 but is now half lost in a jumble of 1970s shopping malls, 1980s office and service complexes, and 1990s apartment buildings. One couple, the homosexuals Pat and Peter, are in their mid-thirties and have been together for only two years. They run a second-hand video store. The other couple, Frank and Marie-Anne, are both in their forties. They married in their later twenties when they lived in Toronto, have a teenage daughter Elise, and like backpacking, bicycling, and skiing, but are becoming a little less hearty about it. Frank is one of the far too many doctors in town. He works four mornings a week at the clinic and alternate Sundays at the neurasthenic hospital.

The house has two large bathrooms and one large room—made by knocking out the wall between the kitchen and dining room—where most of the cooking and eating goes on. Vince, Marie-Anne, and Pat share the cooking unless one of the others is inspired. The three couples contribute equally to the rent and the groceries; transportation units are fetched from the rent-all as needed. Clothing and books move around as freely as smoke or as Elise; but people regard musical instruments more personally and look after their own.

The economy's gradual slide from recession into depression not only pushed more families and households into city commune-homes, it stirred up a buzz of political activity. It was William Marcus, born in 1946 at the leading edge of the baby boom after the Second World War, who first succeeded in mobilizing his generation's political potential. With terminals and videolinks in every home and workplace, canvassing was no longer a matter of trudging from door to door. Marcus ingeniously matched the household telelogs on commercial cable shows, which any advertiser could buy, with the voting patterns on the cable referendums, which could not be analyzed below electoral district level. This allowed him to pump a very well-aimed message straight through the cable into three million videolinks. As subsequent history proved, he was close to ninety per cent on target. Within a year, Marcus's new party, Class Action, was swinging more than half the referendums.

Today, many people expect William Marcus to be the country's chief executive within five years. He has survived three attempts to electrocute him, but carries the livid scar of a severe laser burn across his right temple.

2015

Maggie and Marie-Anne and Pat and Peter all think Calgary is getting dirtier, noisier, more decadent. The black market is the highest priced in the west, and since the San Andreas refugees moved across the Rockies, the quality of nearly everything has been watered down. On a trip back east for her father's funeral, Marie-Anne found a certain charm in sleepy, old-world Toronto that promised a pleasanter life. The four of them are discussing a move. What holds them back is that Maggie, fifty-four, now research vice-president of Mitsubishi-Tomson Biologicals, is the only one with a job; and the life of people trying to survive on government support alone is grim.

Before Frank walked out on them, he and Maggie had had one of those rare inspired conversations when insights and what-ifs and recollections of old research click into place. Within a year Tomson-Laws had a patent on what proved to be a highly effective preventive for strokes. The money to develop it for mass production came from a Japanese merger. Other biochemists and companies were working the same territory, and today it is as rare to hear of someone dying of cardiovascular disease as it is to hear of death from smallpox, cholera, typhoid, diphtheria, polio or malaria plagues that once wracked whole populations.

Pat and Peter have opened a pot'n'trot with a frankly nostalgic 1980s decor, but it is taking time to catch on.

2025

Maggie ran into gentle, idle Vincent Narayan on the Yonge Street Mall last year, after she and Peter moved to Toronto; the three of them now live in the Eaton Centre, which was converted from a shopping centre a few years back. What is left of its open space retains something of the building's original character; it is now the city's central bartamart.

It is spring, and New Class Action is making a last effort to influence the retirement referendum. Even the Grand Old Man of the original party, William Marcus, now in his seventies, has been persuaded to give up a week of sailing in the Caribbean to campaign. All the citilites have been reserved for months and political plugs flood the links. The generation of the post-Second-World-War baby boom is the core of this last-ditch move to restore retirement pensions, but now for the first time they are fighting a younger portion of the electorate that is almost as numerous as they are and much brighter and better organized—a population that most definitely does not want to support the millions who could lay claim to a pension.

> With intelligence and a modicum of luck, the emergent civilization can be made more sane, sensible, and sustainable, more decent and more democratic than any we have ever seen.
> **ALVIN TOFFLER**

2050

Vincent Narayan died this morning, April 26. He would have been eighty-eight next month. In a day or two Maggie will pull herself together and move into a seniorary. These are the government's only support program for the aged.

2060

"Would I have been happier if we had had a child? Perhaps even a grandchild? M-M—What was his name?—Marc sometimes said he wanted a child. Eric didn't. Vince certainly didn't. I don't think I did. I did want to do well. Well, research manager wasn't bad; and in a big Korean transnational company. It's hard now, though. There aren't many of us left. You can't even talk to the people running things now. Funny accents—phony ark-sents. Words you never heard. No soul. No love. Perhaps I would have hated a grandchild. Could I have been happier . . . ?"

> From *The Big Generation* by John Kettle, pp. 11-16. Used by permission of the Canadian Publishers, McClelland and Stewart, Toronto.

☐

The changes in family life discussed in previous chapters of this book are also consistent with and even essential to longer life. When we are able to live several hundred years we will need a much slower rate of population replacement, otherwise we will have a population problem far more serious than that feared in the last century. Francoeur and Kirkendall point out that we now have the technology for reproductive regulation and an ethic that no longer requires everyone to reproduce. In the future we will only need enough children to replace those who die in accidents. The care and training of these children will be the responsibility of the entire society rather than the exclusive domain of parental couples. The few children we will have will be valued by everyone.

We are already well on the way to a child-caring system appropriate to the future. The most important features of our child-caring system are the child-care communities and the concept of voluntarism in parenthood. The child-caring communities encompass much more than the antiquated day nurseries. They are communities of adults who share responsibility not only for the physical care of children, but for their total education and socialization. Because groups of adults volunteer, no one needs to devote twenty-four hours a day to child care. Each individual child will spend much time in a group setting, but some of it will be spent with a primary care person.

The exact mix of group and primary care will vary for each child depending upon need and the preference of the parents and the care person. Some mothers and fathers will choose to spend a number of hours as a group care person as well as in the primary parent role. Others will be content with less personal involvement. The maturing child will be able to choose which adult to relate to most intimately. No child will ever be deprived of the security and intimacy of a primary relationship because child care is seen as a community responsibility. The needs of each child for both social experience and interpersonal intimacy will be met. Parents will not be held totally responsible for their children past the time that the children can give their voluntary consent. Children are not "owned" by their parents, to be molded to fit the latter's image, or to be abused at will. We are considerably more lenient than were previous generations regarding a number of family forms and sexual practices. At the same time, we are intensely intolerant of ineptitude or exploitation when the welfare of children is at stake.

We now have an open and flexible family system as Kirkendall points out. This, too, is for those who live a long life. "Till death do us part" was no easy vow even when the average life span was fifty years. The rule-burdened marital traditions of the twentieth century were too brittle to survive the rapid social changes in the twenty-first century. With prolonged life and the demise of these traditions came a plethora of family forms and patterns of relating. The traditional patterns were rendered obsolete by the social and ethical decisions that came with the profound biological changes arising from *in vitro* fertilization, the use of sperm and ovum banks, the ability to render youth temporarily infertile as they entered puberty, gestation in artificial wombs, gender selection at the time of conception and genetic engineering. We are using these biotechnologies, but are still trying to sort out their consequences, and to establish a vital resiliency for assessing the worth of interpersonal relationships.

The flexibility of our twenty-first-century family system provides a good foundation for the future. Even now we have no set age for marriage, parenthood, or an "empty nest." Many people never pass through these "stages"; those who do choose their own time and sequence. In 1984 divorce was so common that "serial monogamy" was an acceptable form of fidelity. Even then some people were experimenting with so-called alternative family forms, such as communes, group marriages, open marriages, intimate networks, and cohabitation. Today we move quite freely in and

In the excitement of the trip, the last thing in the world that would occur to you is that the strangest glimpses you may have of any creature in the distant lands will be those you catch of yourself.
MARGARET LAURENCE,
from THE PROPHET'S
CAMEL BELL

out of all of these variations and many others besides. None are viewed as "alternatives"; all are accepted. Intimate personal relationships are valued highly, and are experienced in a variety of forms. The ideal relationship is seen as ongoing, not necessarily permanent, but intimate and mutually supportive. This flexible "family" definition is consistent with the other characteristics of our society such as longevity, humanism, multiple careers, non-hierarchical administration, and high mobility. It is also essential in such a world to have one relatively stable source of individual alliance and emotional support.

We have come close to achieving complete androgyny (sex role equality) in our society; a condition which I feel sure we will achieve in the not too distant future. Even now both sexes are taught to develop warm, emotionally supportive personalities. Both men and women should be treated equally as citizens of the universe. Our concern is that when persons enter an intimate relationship, it should enhance the life of each partner. Such a relationship does not require either gender to be subservient to the other, nor is there any implied loss of identity. No names are changed, nor is the new status symbolized by rings or distinctive clothing. The need for legal or religious control over such relationships is being renounced. As the years go by, fewer and fewer children receive inheritances. This is because the basic needs of both children and adults are provided by society. What little property is needed is held by the individual rather than by the family, and upon death what remains reverts to society. Sex is seen as a pleasure appropriate to a variety of occasions both inside and outside of a primary emotional relationship.

The formal tie called marriage has been largely dispensed with. People move freely between different kinds of relationships. Most spend a portion of their lives in a group relationship, but the major share is spent with single primary partners. The attraction of a committed, intimate relationship is most powerful. There seems to be no substitute for the security and satisfaction of having a reciprocal caring relationship with one primary individual. Even with all of the flexibility available and essential in a space-age society, the most common form of intimate relationship remains monogamy. We expect this trend to continue well beyond 2020.

1. What do you consider to be the critical issues raised by Lois Sweet?

2. The future of the family will depend, to a great extent, on which of the two contending visions of family gains political and judicial acceptance. Will it be the right-wing ideology of family or a model based on reality? With the first selection in mind, investigate the pros and cons of each perspective.

3. The most compelling future scenarios are often those that contain elements of plausibility. Evaluate the accuracy of Kettle's projections thus far. Referring back to Lorna Marsden's article on the Baby Boomers, speculate on the plausibility of Kettle's future projections.

4. Your generation will go through life in the wake of the Baby Boom cohort. Think of the implications of this phenomenon. In what ways could this affect your life? Devise a future scenario for your age cohort.

5. Flip through this book. What traces of Alam's 2020 vision can you recognize in the readings? What assumptions are made by Alam as he describes life in the future?

6. Select five of what you consider to be Alam's most interesting developments. State the plausibility of each development. Share your selection with other students. Through discussion, compile a list of the major gains and possible losses for the individual and the family if such developments did occur.

7. Fantasy and science fiction allow us to abandon our existing reality and enter into a brave new world. This type of fiction often explores the created family, consisting of "social relatives" who share a common situation, need, or goal. Canadian authors Margaret Atwood in *The Handmaid's Tale*, Margaret Laurence in *A Queen in Thebes*, and Judith Merril in *Survival Ship* created unique families. Examine these or other works of fantasy or science fiction for the variety of family images conjured up. Which ones appeal to you? Why?

INDEX

A

Abortion, Victorian, 22
Adolescence, 130-33, 161
Affective needs, 157
Age
   of marriage, Victorian, 20-21
   new perspectives on, 160-65
Age norms, blurring of, 163, 164
Alignments in families, 156
Alternative lifestyles, 243
Apprenticeship, 249-50, 252
Ariès, Philippe, 248, 252, 253
Arranged marriages, 102-107

B

Baby Boomers, impact of, 14-16
Bibby, Reginald, 132
Blended families, 207-14
Boundaries, 156
Buss, David, 99, 100, 101

C

Causality, circular, and conflict,
   52-55
Change
   first and second order, 88
   slowing rate of, 244
   transitions as, 97

Child care, 15, 127, 155, 200, 202,
   217-219, 277
Child custody, 197-99
Childhood
   as adulthood, 163
   shaping forces, 247
   as stage of life, 161
Childlessness
   aficionados vs. rejectors, 185
   consciousness-raising, 186
   consequences of, 185-86
   pronatalism vs. antinatalism, 186-87
   social policy implications, 186-87
   typology of, 185
   voluntary, 184-88
Children
   poverty rate among, 235-36
   schooling of, 251
   sexual abuse of, 30, 34
   socializing, 128-29, 163
   Victorian attitude to, 22
Cluttered nest, 136-37, 242
Coalitions, in family, 48-51
Cohabitation, 108-110
   age of, 109
   dissolution of, 109
   frequency of, 108-109
   geographical distribution of,
    109-110
   institutionalization of, 108
   as prelude to marriage, 109
   reasons for, 109
Commitment vs. choice, 263

Support network
   and family health, 245
   in New France, 250
System, defined, 28

T

Transitions, 95-98
   four S's, 97-98
   types of, 96
Triangles, in family, 48-51

V

Violence, 179-83

W

Widowhood, Victorian, 21

Women
   mating preferences, 100
   and power, 64, 65
   role in Victorian marriage, 21
Work, historical perspectives of,
   215-17

Y

Young adults
   factors for leaving/remaining in
     home, 135-36
   failure to leave home, 135
Young-old, 161
Youth, 161
   Canadian, profile of, 272-75

Z

Zigler, Edward, 75